AMOR DEI

AMOR DEI

A STUDY OF THE RELIGION OF ST. AUGUSTINE

THE HULSEAN LECTURES FOR 1938

BY

JOHN BURNABY

FELLOW OF TRINITY COLLEGE, CAMBRIDGE

Wipf & Stock
PUBLISHERS
Eugene, Oregon

Wipf and Stock Publishers
199 W 8th Ave, Suite 3
Eugene, OR 97401

Amor Dei
A Study of the Religion of St. Augustine
By Burnaby, John
Copyright©1938 by Burnaby, John
ISBN 13: 978-1-55635-501-1
ISBN 10: 1-55635-501-7
Publication date 5/22/2007
Previously published by Canterbury Press, 1938

Foreword to the 2007 Edition

IN THE seventy years since John Burnaby launched *Amor Dei,* and even in the sixteen since I had the satisfaction of waving from the quay as it set out on a second voyage, a great deal has changed in the navigation of Augustinian waters. Remarkably, there are more authentic Augustinian texts in circulation than John Burnaby could have known: whole collections of Sermons recovered from sources where they lay unsuspected, and a remarkable collection of letters. Considerable strides have been made in the historiography of the late Roman Empire. A classic biography has appeared, reappeared, held the field for a generation, and now been caught up by rivals. The chronology of the Augustinian writings, which in Burnaby's day had not advanced far beyond what Augustine himself told us in the *Retractations,* has been extensively filled in. There are first-rate critical editions of works that in the thirties could only be read in the seventeenth century recensions of the Maurists. And what is one to say of the new discussions? There have been critiques from all approved points of view, feminist, postmodernist and whatever; there have been constant arguments about the significance of his political thought; there have been reappraisals of aspects of his doctrine which had been supposed uninteresting. Most strikingly, Augustine figures strongly in discussions of an untheological, even anti-theological nature. One thinks of recent works of moral philosophy and of political theory that have devoted chapters to evaluating his legacy. In this most eclectic and diverse generation, where virtually nothing is left that everybody can be thought to have read, there remain very few popular refrains. But "Augustine began it all!" is certainly one of them.

The reader seeking an a more or less up-to-date account of major themes and topics in Augustinian scholarship is likely to turn first to the Encyclopedia, *Augustine through the Ages,* edited by Allen Fitzgerald (Grand Rapids, Eerdmans, 2001). But one of the few weaknesses of that work is a lack of interest in scholars who made Augustine accessible to earlier generations, and I can find no mention of John Burnaby in its pages. Yet I run into his name fairly frequently elsewhere, in a widely eclectic range of writings. Scholars and thinkers are still turning to *Amor Dei* when it matters to them to find an authoritative exposition of the central core of Augustine's reflection on the relations of God and man. In what John Burnaby set out to accomplish in his Hulsean Lectures, he has not been superseded.

Oliver O'Donovan
New College, Edinburgh

FOREWORD TO THE 1991 EDITION

by the Regius Professor of Moral and Pastoral Theology

JOHN Burnaby's *Amor Dei* can be read in two ways. On the one hand it is part of an important and exciting debate about the nature of Christian love which was sparked off in the thirties with the publication of *Agape and Eros* by the Swedish thinker Anders Nygren. It might better have been called 'Agape *or* Eros'. As Burnaby wrote: 'Against the Both-And of the Catholic Protestantism . . . sets with obtuse insistence its Either-Or' (p. 4). There is nothing like a sharp antithesis to stimulate a sharp debate, and this one proved sharp enough to keep going for forty years or more. Among the many traces of it in mid-century thological literature, the general reader will perhaps remember one of the most popular contributions, C. S. Lewis's *The Four Loves*, which, without mentioning Nygren by name, opens with some sly remarks on how easy the author thought his task would be when he first approached it intending to write . . . *Agape and Eros*!

Of those who responded to Nygren's Either-Or, Burnaby alone saw the importance of contesting his interpretation of Augustine. This was the more remarkable as Nygren's second volume, which contains his account of Augustine, appeared in German only the year before Burnaby's Hulsean Lectures. Nygren's view that Augustine formed a 'synthesis' of agape and eros thus supervened rather late upon Burnaby's maturing thoughts. But few readers will have felt any discomfort as a result, since Burnaby makes Nygren seem quite inevitable. He was, in fact, Burnaby's great opportunity. He provided the prism through which Augustine's thought could be focussed on the questions of contemporary Christian theology in the wake of the anti-idealist reaction. The introductory chapter to *Amor*

Dei is an impressively taut evocation of the theological situation, sketching in the main postures with judicious economy of line. And there in the centre of it all we find Nygren, ready to enter the lists as a champion of the present age against the Christianity of the greatest doctor of the Western church. How, we wonder, could the book have been conceived without him?

The other way of reading *Amor Dei* is against the background of a scholarly discussion of St Augustine's religious ideas. The "eudaemonist" features of Augustine's theory of love had been the subject of debate for a decade or more before Nygren wrote. Adolf Harnack and Karl Holl had published a weighty exchange on their bearing on Augustine's conversion, and this had excited wide interest in Germany. Heidegger and Jaspers both had views on the subject, and when, in 1929, a gifted young philosophy student called Hannah Arendt wished to clarify her position in relation to these two teachers, she did so by means of a thesis called *Der Liebesbegriff bei Augustin*, surely one of the most fascinating curiosities of twentieth century scholarship! At the same time as Burnaby was publishing *Amor Dei*, another Swedish theologian, Gunnar Hultgren, was publishing a work on the same subject in French. But of all this literature only Burnaby's book has left a lasting impression. It is easy to see the qualities that gave it its influence. Notwithstanding his concern for the systematic questions, Burnaby had the rare capacity, won through intellectual self-discipline, for self-effacement. Where other works superimpose their own interpretative schemas upon Augustine, here the cool sympathy of the true exegete allows the master's voice to sound with its own note. Burnaby quickly earned the trust of readers who wanted to know what Augustine really thought, and how he came to think it.

It heightens the interest of this book that it is the one major legacy of a scholarly career which was not, by our present standards of mass-production, over-prolific. When John Burnaby gave the Hulsean Lectures in 1938, he was a layman in his mid-forties, a classics Fellow of his Cambridge college, hitherto unpublished. *Amor Dei* and the war between them changed the direction of his career. He was ordained to take responsibility for his college chapel during the war years; and when they ended he joined the Divinity Faculty, becoming Regius Professor of Divinity from 1952 until he retired six years later. The fruit of his teaching labours can be seen in three books intended to introduce students to different aspects of theological study, *Is the Bible Inspired?*, *Christian Words and Christian Meanings* and *The Belief of Christendom*. They fulfil the pedagogic task that they set themselves with the same sensitive Christian judgement that is evident in *Amor Dei*. But the inner eye of the scholar remained fixed where it had always been, and Burnaby returned to the study of Augustine whenever the duties of routine teaching permitted. He translated and edited a volume of selections from the *De Trinitate*, and he contributed a brief but penetrating discussion of the *Retractationes* to the international Augustine congress of 1954. When I had the pleasure of meeting him, near the end of his life, he was thinking again about the questions first raised in the Hulsean Lectures, and these were the subject of his last article, published at the age of seventy nine. It was his contribution to a volume of essays in honour of Nygren, a gracious tribute of gratitude to one about whom he could say that 'the adversary's questioning has been the occasion of learning'. He was, I would judge, neither afraid nor ashamed to end where he began, for he had found in Augustine of Hippo a Christian whose thought was large enough for a modern believer to devote a lifetime to. A new generation of Burnaby's readers will sense something of that largeness, and will, I hope, also appreciate the largeness of the sympathy that could communicate it so well.

OLIVER O'DONOVAN
Christ Church
Oxford

PREFACE

THE Hulsean Lectureship has generally been held by theologians of distinction ; and in appointing me to deliver these Lectures, the University conferred upon me an honour which I had done nothing to deserve. I can make no claim to be regarded either as a scholar or as a theologian, and the subject with which I have attempted to deal is one that calls for a wide learning and a profound theological capacity. This must be my excuse for having contributed but little towards a critical treatment of Augustine's doctrine of the love of God. I have confined myself almost entirely to exposition ; and I am aware that the day may be held to be past when mere exposition of Augustinian religion could serve any useful purpose.

I do not share that opinion : else these lectures would not have been written. I think that our English theology of the last half-century, in seeking fresh inspiration from the Christian humanism of Alexandria, the Logos-doctrine, and the Greek tradition generally, has been too much disposed to dismiss Augustine, with a regretful admiration for the author of the *Confessions,* as the fatal genius whose example has led the Christian Church into the diverging by-ways of Papal ecclesiasticism and Calvinist betrayal of the God of love. It matters little that English theologians should continue to father upon Augustine such particular extravagances as the identification of the visible Church on earth with the Kingdom of God—an identification which he actually called *insania,* or the belief that sexual intercourse was a consequence of the Fall—a belief which in his last and most illiberal work he repeatedly denied. It matters much that in a time when so eminent a Christian thinker as Ernst Troeltsch could regard ' the blend of Neo-Platonism and New Testament Christianity' as the ' only possible solution' of present-day problems in religious philosophy, we should have ceased to listen to the greatest disciple and the profoundest critic of Plotinus.

Augustine's Platonism is manifested in the centrality for his religion of *amor Dei*—the love of God which appears in men as the pursuit of eternal values and the delight in whatsoever things are lovely. His Platonism is Christian because he finds the Supreme Value and the most compelling loveliness in the love which is God's own Being ; and because he believes that *amor Dei* is God's gift of Himself to His children—a gift which, offered in the divine humility of Christ's Incarnation and Death, and sealed by the continuing presence of the Spirit of Holiness, brings God and man, without confusion, into a most intimate and most real unity.

Each of the great controversies in which Augustine was engaged made its contribution to the development of his thought. But it is not in the literature of controversy that the peace which passes all understanding finds free and full expression. If all the works of Augustine were lost but his *Expositions of the Psalms* and his *Homilies on St. John*, we should still possess all we needed for a reconstruction of his personal religion ; and upon these and his *Sermons,* as will be seen, I have drawn most largely. I have made my own translations, except in the passages from Plotinus, where I have to thank Sir Ernest Debenham for permission to use the fine English of Stephen Mackenna, and in those from François de Sales, of whose inimitable French the version by Dom Mackey is easier to criticise than to improve on. I have used the Benedictine text, correcting it by the Vienna Corpus so far as the latter has extended, except for the *Confessions* in which I have followed the Teubner text of M. Skutella (1934). I have given scarcely any references to the enormous literature, but I have added in an appendix a list of those books to which I am principally indebted. The eight lectures delivered have been expanded and rearranged as ten chapters.

The years in which this book has been written have been a time in which pride, hatred, and violence have seemed the rulers of this world, and the meditation of an ancient ideal has been too easily oppressed by a sense of futility. St. Augustine stands for the faith that an advancing knowledge and an increasing love of the Eternal God is the only foundation upon which frail men can build the love of one another and learn to live together in peace. *Sero te amavi, pulchritudo tam nova, tam antiqua.* It may be that at long last a broken world will come back to the love of that Beauty which is old, but ever new.

CAMBRIDGE, *June,* 1938.

INSPIRA DOMINE MEVS DEVS MEVS

INSPIRA SERVIS TVIS FRATRIBVS MEIS

VT QVOTQVOT HAEC LEGERINT

MEMINERINT AD ALTARE TVVM

AVGVSTINI FAMVLI TVI

CONTENTS

xiii

I

Introductory : The Embarrassment of the Anti-Mystic

Despréaux s'échauffe, et criant comme un fou : Quoi ! mon Père, direz-vous qu'un des vôtres n'ait pas fait imprimer dans un de ses livres, qu'un chrétien n'est pas obligé d'aimer Dieu ? Osez-vous dire que cela est faux ?— Monsieur, dit le Père en fureur, il faut distinguer.

—Distinguer, dit Despréaux, distinguer, morbleu, distinguer, distinguer si nous sommes obligés d'aimer Dieu !

Madame de Sévigné.

I

Martha, Martha, thou art careful and troubled about many things ; but one thing is needful. For Mary hath chosen the good part, which shall not be taken away from her.

BURKITT once said that ' the greatest service the textual criticism of the Gospels has done for Christian philosophy has been to get rid of the false simplification expressed in " *One* thing is necessary ".' [1] St. Luke's latest commentator is not so sure as Burkitt that the reading of the great uncials—' Few things are necessary, or one '—preserves the original text ; and many will agree with Professor Creed that this reading ' does not appear to yield a tolerable sense '.[2] But the confusion of the manuscripts is evidence that the gravity and difficulty of the religious question involved was felt by ' Christian philosophy ' at a very early point in its development. *Unum necessarium* has been a text of Christian mysticism throughout its history. Even Meister Eckhart's paradoxical exaltation of the active Martha above the contemplative Mary does not really oppose the mystical tradition, but only rejects its perennial misrepresentation. For what Eckhart meant, as Otto well says, is that ' Martha with her never-wearied doing and acting proves that she has already found what Mary still desires and seeks : the deep unmoved repose at the centre, in unshakable unity and security '.[3]

When von Hügel wrote what a high authority has called ' the best book on mysticism in the English language ',[4] he took his stand deliberately on the side of Burkitt. He held the mystical to be no more than an ' element ' in religion—a necessary

[1] F. C. Burkitt, *Jesus Christ,* p. 48 n.
[2] J. M. Creed, *The Gospel according to St. Luke,* p. 154.
[3] R. Otto, *Mysticism East and West* (E.T.), p. 176. Cf. W. R. Inge, *Christian Mysticism* (3rd edit.), p. 161.
[4] E. Underhill, *Mysticism* (12th edit.), p. 498.

3

element indeed, but *not* the one thing needful. Von Hügel's typically Catholic approach refuses even to claim for religion as a whole any monopoly of human life : it is ' the deepest, the central life ', but not the only one which man has to live. And similarly ' the mystical element in religion ' is but one, albeit the most vital, of the spiritual ' forces and functions ' which lead men to God. [1]

Against the ' Both—And ' of the Catholic, Protestantism here as everywhere sets with obtuse insistence its ' Either—Or '. There was enough of the Catholic spirit in Archbishop Söderblom to prevent his drawing from the distinction of ' religions of culture ' and the ' religion of revelation ' the inference that all ' mysticism of infinity ' is illusion. He still believed that the longing for the infinite and the longing for righteousness are both alike ' portals of revelation ', that they are ' the two eyes through which humanity views the divine '.[2] But, with all the respect due, it must be submitted that he set a false sign-post upon cross-roads of Christian inquiry, when he opposed to the ' mysticism of infinity ' a ' mysticism of personality ' as the peculiar property of the religion of revelation, and found the goal of the first to be the absorption and extinction of the human in the divine, the goal of the second to be the fellowship of man and God.[3] Söderblom's ' mysticism of personality ' is mystical only in the sense in which all religion is mystical ; and the truth is rather that the recognised ' mystics ' have saved Christendom from forgetting that fellowship with God is the true end of religion. The confusion of this life of fellowship with the Eastern ideal of absorption or extinction has in the great Christian mystics, it is true, been a recurrent danger ; but that the injury resulting has been rather to the adequate intellectual expression of their Christianity than to their Christianity itself is proved by the constant warnings which they have given against the pursuit or over-valuation of the ecstatic experience.

[1] Fr. von Hügel, *The Mystical Element of Religion*, esp. vol. II, pp. 387 ff.
[2] N. Söderblom, *The Nature of Revelation*, pp. 123 ff.
[3] *Ib.* p. 100.

The road along which Söderblom's analysis pointed has been eagerly followed. What von Hügel's accommodating hyphens had enabled him to house within a single one of his three ' elements of religion ', is cloven through by the ruthless dichotomies of Friedrich Heiler in his great book on prayer. Mysticism is there defined as ' that form of intercourse with God in which the world and self are absolutely denied, in which human personality is dissolved, disappears, and is absorbed in the infinite unity of the Godhead '.[1] The goal is ecstasy, for which all moral activity serves but as the means of purification. Opposed to the mystical, both in principle and in almost every feature of practical expression, is the prophetic religion, based on the dynamic assertion of life, proclaiming God's self-revelation in the world's history, and finding communion with Him in the doing of His will and in that alone. Since Heiler was to draw most of his examples of both mystical and prophetic prayer from Christian sources, it was necessary for him to warn us that within Christianity the mystical type of religion is rarely observable in its purity. But it was, to say the least, unfortunate that he should have chosen to differentiate mystical from prophetic religion by a characteristic which in many of the examples to be quoted is not merely obscured by borrowings from the type opposed to it but entirely absent. Our confidence in a definition of mysticism as the denial of human personality is not increased when we find that Heiler is obliged to speak of mysticism in its Christian form as ' personal mysticism '. From here it is an easy step to the position of Dr. Oman, that ' in the strict sense there is no such thing as a Christian mystic, because in so far as there is use of a historical revelation and of a Church with its cult, fellowship and active service of others, the religion is not mystical '.[2] Did Buddha's religion, then, cease to be mystical in the moment when he chose the ' active service of others ' and the founding of a Church rather than Nirvana for himself ?

[1] F. Heiler, *Prayer* (E.T.), p. 136.
[2] J. Oman, *The Natural and the Supernatural*, p. 420.

We are not brought nearer to the understanding of a phenomenon by the denial of its existence.

Heiler's own conclusion was more moderate. No one will dispute his statement that mysticism is not a peculiarity of the Christian religion. He is on ground less certain when he says that it penetrated into Christianity from the outside, and that Augustine and Pseudo-Denys were the ' gates by which it entered '.[1] The gate stands open in the New Testament : Christian mysticism would have been impossible without St. Paul and St. John. But Heiler does stop short of treating the mystical as the irreconcilable foe of the prophetic religion. He finds that these two tendencies attract as well as repel one another, though he offers no explanation of the fact.[2] None the less, it has been the natural result of his work to encourage the belief that the mystical element is not only an alien but a mischievous intruder into the Christian religion.

Our present concern is not with the general question of the mystic's title to existence within Christianity. Our subject is the form which the religious motive assumed in the thought and life of the man who was both the greatest figure of the patristic age and incomparably the most powerful influence upon the history of Western religion during the thousand years which followed his death. We may be excused, then, from either selecting one of the innumerable extant definitions of mysticism or constructing a new one of our own. It is not our thesis that *amor Dei*, as Augustine understood it, is the essence of mysticism. The love of God, in one sense or another, is the ultimate motive for the religious life not only of all who profess and call themselves Christians but of many who do not. But it will readily be allowed that while no mystic feels any need to explain what he means by the love of God, the non-mystic constantly betrays a more or less embarrassed consciousness that the words cannot for him retain their natural significance. When we are bidden to love God, what is really *meant* is that we should . . . do or

[1] *Prayer*, p. 170.   [2] *Ib.* p. 171.

be this or that which to the simple mind would seem to be by no means the same thing. To the non-mystic, and still more to the anti-mystic, Christ's summary of the Law presents a *difficulty*. The first great commandment cannot mean just what it says : it needs explanation, and when we have begun to explain it we do not find it easy to stop at explaining it away.

This embarrassment of the anti-mystic can be observed at the present time in two very different regions of Christian thought. The first is that of the ' social Gospel ' in its various forms in England and America. The vitality and the attractive power of this movement are derived from its profound sense of shame at the moral collapse of civilisation, and its honourable refusal to acquiesce in the disaster which seems imminent. We know, indeed, that Christ if He came to-day would find little faith on the earth, that His disciples are but a small fraction of mankind. But the faithful few may not take the easy way of repudiating their responsibility for the world's sin. For if the mystery of the Kingdom is really theirs, whose fault is it that they are still so few ? The answer which forces itself upon them is that a Christianity which has become irrelevant must have been perverted : the talent hidden in the earth must tarnish. It must be rubbed clean before the money-changers of the world will accept it for circulation.

No one has rubbed harder than Professor John Macmurray ; and we choose his work as an example of the process, not so much because the example is extreme, as because it can best be studied and has probably had the widest influence in a book published by the Student Christian Movement.[1] There is a pathetic naïveté, perhaps something of the heretic's age-long deficiency in sense of humour, about Macmurray's ideal of an ' empirically-minded ' religion, ' leading the progressive movement with science as its technical adviser ', and his pessimistic prediction that in default of so complete a transformation ' religion can no longer perform any positive function in society ',

[1] J. Macmurray, *Creative Society*.

7

and must ' fade away '.[1]   The only movement that religion can ever lead is a movement of return, upon which science is neither competent nor willing to give technical advice.   The greatest of the prophets have been condemned as reactionaries by their own generation ;   and *Repent ye, for the Kingdom of Heaven is at hand* is not ' a demand for a revolution in mental outlook, in view of the fulfilment of a process of social development ' ; [2] it is the recall of rebels from a hopeless enterprise.   Macmurray himself, because his aim is religious, would call his fellow-Christians back —back from their self-inflicted exile in a far country where they are feeding upon the husks of idealism, to the one real world of experience.

His reason for preferring the Christian to the Communist view of life is just that Communism places its Kingdom of Heaven at the end of the temporal process as its goal, whereas Jesus says *The Kingdom of Heaven is within you,* and so sets the temporal process itself in the frame of an eternal reality. But this reality is ' a reality of the temporal in the temporal ' : it consists in the life-experience of individual men and women, in birth and death, work and love, the aspects of life which are ' eternal ' inasmuch as they are unchanging—substantially un- affected by whatever variation may take place in their outward conditions.   The ' core of the eternal aspect of human life ' is to be found in men's mutual need of one another ;   and since co-operation in work has no more than the ' utility-value ' of a means, while the values of love are intrinsic, it is on the mutuality of love as personal communion that religion is ultimately based. Religion is belief in the centrality for life of personal relationship, and its task is to realise communion.[3]   It is transcendent only in the sense that it *intends* and has the power to create a fellowship which surpasses what is real at any given moment.   Its ' spiritual world ' is the natural world transformable and awaiting trans- formation by the creative activity of love.[4]   Its method is simply

---

[1] J. Macmurray, *The Structure of Religious Experience,* p. 11.
[2] *Creative Society,* p. 62.
[3] *C.S.* pp. 91 ff.   Cf. *S.R.E.* pp. 25-47.   [4] *S.R.E.* pp. 106 ff.

the overcoming of love's one enemy—fear. All fear is centred and symbolised in the selfish fear of death, which sets the individual in defensive isolation from his fellows ; and death is therefore, in a sense, the last enemy to be destroyed. But death is a fact, and triumph over its power cannot be won by denying its reality, but only by accepting both the fact of death and the fact of our dependence upon one another as elements in the consciousness of eternal life. Belief in God is primarily reconciliation to the world, capacity to live as part of a whole which is in God's hands.[1]

That is Macmurray's religion. He does not limit it to the kind of activity which we call practical. He recognises the functions not only of public worship as the expression and the strengthening of community, but of religious reflection (in which he would presumably include prayer) as a necessary phase in the process of development, in which intention is directed to the widening and deepening of community.[2] He believes, in company with von Hügel and the classical mystics, that there must be a ' polar rhythm ' of withdrawal into solitary contemplation and of return into the common life.[3] But in the necessity of withdrawal he finds the danger of religious falsification. A true religious idea must be related in intention to the real life of co-operation and fellowship, and this intentional reference, together with the return to reality which it requires, can be and often is avoided by referring the idea to ' another ' world which is imagined and not experienced. When this happens, the results for religion are a false dualism of the material and the spiritual, the natural and the supernatural, and a false individualism of private piety, which paralyse its energies ; and Macmurray thinks that the Christian's most urgent duty is to denounce and combat the ' pseudo-religion ' of other-worldliness.[4]

We need not dwell on the more conspicuous points of hiatus between this version of Christianity and that of the New Testament. Its author has succeeded in convincing himself, by the

[1] *C.S.* pp. 36-51.   [2] *S.R.E.* pp. 65 ff.   [3] *Ib.* p. 88.
[4] *Ib.* pp. 99 ff.   Cf. *C.S.* pp. 53 f., 168.

usual method of disregarding or distorting evidence to the contrary, that Jesus was a social revolutionary—not merely preaching a religion which must have the effect of turning the world upside down, but championing an oppressed class against economic injustice ; that the kingdom He sought *was* a kingdom of this world ;[1] that His message of forgiveness was to restore men's confidence in themselves and not to shatter all confidence save the assurance of faith.[2] The problem of suffering absorbs itself for Macmurray in the problem of death ; his complaint against ' pseudo-religion ', that it attempts to deny the ' reality ' of death, presumes a belief in the natural immortality of the soul instead of the very different Christian belief in a promised resurrection of soul and body from the dead ; and he overlooks[3] the destructive significance, for any this-worldly eschatology, of Christ's saying that in the resurrection there is neither marrying nor giving in marriage.

It is impossible, if we believe in a God who really exists, not to believe in ' another ' world ; for that other world is posited with belief in God.   If God exists, He constitutes another world. Karl Heim[4] has analysed the relations of transcendence which have validity for the known world of human experience, and has drawn a sharp distinction between them and the ' wholly other ' kind of transcendence which belief in God implies.   And if, from the scarcely-veiled Stoicism of Macmurray's theory, that the last enemy to be destroyed is not death but the fear of death, we turn to Karl Barth's exposition of the First Epistle to the Corinthians, in which the Resurrection of the Dead becomes nothing less than a ' paraphrase for God ', a truth which bursts all the boundaries of our human thinking, it is not difficult to make up our minds which of the two has come the nearer to authentic Christianity.   Most certainly there is a false otherworldliness ; but it arises not from the confession of another world, but from misunderstanding of the true relation of that

---

[1] *C.S.* pp. 63, 76-89.   [2] *Ib.* pp. 111 ff.

[3] As R. Niebuhr does not (cf. *An Interpretation of Christian Ethics*, p. 42).

[4] See his book *God Transcendent* (E.T.).

other world to this. The other world is not a substitute for this world, a better cosmos destined one day to replace the bad one in which we live. It is simply the eternal world of God, into which it is His will that we pass through and by means of our life in space and time.

But we have referred to Macmurray in order to illustrate the embarrassment of a certain type of professedly Christian thought in regard to the possibility of the love of God. Macmurray himself underlines the necessity of distinguishing between the belief in a God who really exists, and who would still exist though all the world denied Him, and the belief in an idea of God which is held by every idolater. He rightly refuses to lend himself to the propagation of belief in God as a 'serviceable idea', in disregard of the all-important question whether the God so conceived exists or no.[1] He thinks that a nominally atheist Communism, in its fearless and confident self-surrender to a so-called 'process of history', which uses alike the recalcitrance and the willing service of men in its infallible working, has in fact recovered 'the core of a real belief in God' which many Christians have lost.[2] But as a Christian he is not satisfied with the idea which is the objective counterpart of this attitude of faith. His own idea of God's nature is reached by the reflection upon mutual relationship, which universalises the experience of community. The God into whose hands we may and must commit ourselves is the 'universal Other' or 'infinite person' in whom our finite relationships are grounded.[3] But the environing world with which man has to be integrated is wider than the world of his fellowmen ; and that is why the idea of Man cannot be substituted for the idea of God. Humanism is not enough.[4]

Now Macmurray accepts the classification of values which goes back to St. Augustine. There are values for use and values for enjoyment or intrinsic values. Science (which for Macmurray is not the search for truth but the acquisition of mastery over the

[1] *C.S.* p. 17. [2] *Ib.* pp. 23 f.
[3] *S.R.E.* pp. 79 f. [4] *C.S.* p. 95.

external world) deals with utility-values, art with intrinsic values ; and religion unifies the divergent or dissociated attitudes of science and art, by making mutual service the basis of human co-operation, and fellowship its aim. So love pre-supposes service but is not identified with it ; on the contrary, love is the end, service the means. But interest in utility-value concentrates attention upon general knowledge of the properties which objects possess in common, interest in intrinsic value always upon the unique individuality of the object to be enjoyed.[1] If then God is to be considered as the universalisation of concrete experiences, we ought to conclude that His being falls within the sphere of use, not of enjoyment ; for love is essentially an attitude of interest in the concrete particular. But then we shall be committing just what for Augustine was the radical error of the *Civitas Terrena* in its pagan cults : [2] we shall be using God that we may enjoy the world, instead of using the world that we may enjoy God. God will be really reduced to a ' serviceable idea '. The helplessness of Macmurray's position in face of this dilemma is well shown when he comes to define the intention of religion as comprehending the universal co-operation of men for the satisfaction of needs, and the universal ' appreciation ' of all men by all men.[3] We can conceive of a state of society in which universal co-operation was real ; but the notion of universal appreciation of every human being by every other is in the conditions of the world we know a manifest absurdity. So long as we are confined to this world, to speak of God as the ' infinite Person ' can bring us no nearer to the possibility of personal contact with Him ; for within this world God is nowhere realised. His being consists in the ' intention of mutuality '— which may be a ' serviceable idea ', but is certainly a poor substitute for the Father of Jesus Christ.

[1] *S.R.E.* pp. 25 ff.

[2] *De Civ.* xv. 7 : Boni ad hoc utuntur mundo ut fruantur Deo ; mali autem contra, ut fruantur mundo, uti volunt Deo : qui tamen eum vel esse vel res humanas curare iam credunt. Sunt enim multo deteriores, qui ne hoc quidem credunt.

[3] *S.R.E.* p. 86.

Introductory : *The Embarrassment of the Anti-Mystic*

Between the ' social Gospel ' and the ' theology of crisis ', the distinctive ' heresies ' of English-speaking and German-speaking Christianity at the present time, there is at first sight extremely little in common. On this side we find a markédly anthropocentric immanentism, on the other a theocentrism which at least is continually on its defence against the charge of a too exclusive emphasis upon the transcendence of God. If it is true that ' one-world ' religion is prevented by the insecurity of its grasp on the divine personality from accepting the first great commandment without reservations and interpretations, there must be a different reason for the same hesitancy when it appears in a theology built upon the prophetic *Thus saith the Lord*. For the ' Word of God ' in this theology is not a body of revealed truths ; it is *Dei loquentis persona,* God Himself coming into touch with us in the only possible way, God ' over against us ', His ' I ' speaking to our ' Thou '.[1]

Barth himself is too Pauline in spirit, and too deeply acquainted with the *cor inquietum,* the heart's restlessness which possessed Augustine, not to have something of the mystic in him. But the anti-mysticism of Brunner is uncompromising.[2] He insists that ' renunciation of the world and of all contact with the life of man is always *logically* connected with mysticism ', because it is a form of religion ' which tries to *create* a relation between God and the soul of man ', making union with God ' a state which has yet to be attained ', and therefore requiring a ' division between God and the world as the object of our action '.[3] Brunner therefore must put his own *interpretation* on the words *the second is like unto it*. The second commandment is ' like ' the first only as the fruits are ' like ' the tree, as the actions of a man are ' like ' himself. The first commandment is fulfilled, *not* by the love which (verbally) it commands, but by something else—namely, faith.[4] Or rather, ' the love which God commands

[1] Cf. H. R. Mackintosh, *Types of Modern Theology,* p. 292.
[2] His *Die Mystik und das Wort* I have not seen ; but any of his books make his position plain enough.
[3] E. Brunner, *The Divine Imperative* (E.T.), p. 310 (italics mine).
[4] *Ib.* p. 309.

is the love which He Himself is, and which He gives. To love Him truly *means* to let oneself be loved by Him';[1] and that is faith. And if in the act of faith we are laid hold upon by God's will, identify ourselves with it and affirm it, and if God's will is none other than the gift of Himself to sinful men in the condescension of the Cross, then 'in the very act of faith we turn ourselves to our neighbour'.[2] The two commandments become one.

The 'theology of crisis' is professedly a revival of the Reformers' doctrine of justification by faith.[3] All natural ethic, says Brunner, aims at the realisation *by* man of that which is good *for* man, and this self-confidence is necessarily doomed to lie prostrate under the 'curse of the Law', where 'I ought' means 'I cannot'. And the same is true—so we are asked to believe —of all natural religion. The whole amazing history of men's search for the Unknown God, *if haply they might feel after Him and find Him*, came in principle to a full stop on Calvary. For the Cross is placarded in letters of Hebrew, Greek, and Latin, with the words No Road. From man to God there is no way. In the drama of salvation there is only one character that moves. The living God is from first to last the Subject, never the Object, of religion. And the man to whom God has drawn near in Christ, who in faith has accepted the divine act of forgiveness, is justified, set right with God, in the same moment that he is convinced of sin. Justification is not the end, but the beginning of everything, for it marks that 'inversion of existence' by which life begins to be lived, in Brunner's favourite phrase, '*from* God' instead of '*towards* God'. Taken up into the purpose of God, accepting his life as God's gift, the believer is free—free from the anxious moralism which makes self the centre of all activity, free 'from the world for the world', free to seek only what God seeks, the extension of His Kingdom of fellowship. In justification the divine Imperative has become the divine Indicative, yet

[1] *The Divine Imperative*, p. 133 (italics mine).
[2] E. Brunner, *God and Man*, pp. 119 f.
[3] See esp. *The Divine Imperative*, pp. 68-81.

without ceasing to be a claim and a command. The New Birth which is God's act must be realised from the human point of view as conversion. There remains the paradox that we have to become what we are ; and it is fair to ask a dialectical theologian why the Christian life may not be *both* ' from God ' *and* ' towards God ', why, if we are risen with Christ, we may not, must not, seek those things that are above. In fact it is difficult to distinguish the ' inverted existence ' described by Brunner from the ' unitive life ' which the great mystics have exemplified rather than described, except by the position which they occupy —here the goal, there the starting-point. But the anti-mystic can call no life Christian which is the goal of effort, without compromising the rigour of justification by faith. Because the mystic has sought union with God, it is *ex hypothesi* impossible for him to attain it—unless he renounce the search.

It follows that between the love of God commanded in the Gospel, and the desire for God which through the ages has inspired the struggle of minds and wills, within as well as without the Church of Christ, there is something more than a difference of nature—there is a real and irreducible contrariety. That is the theme of the Swedish theologian Dr. Anders Nygren, in his study of ' the Christian Idea of Love ' : a work of which the plan and premises were announced some years ago in the short volume translated into English under the title *Agape and Eros*, and which has recently been completed by a substantial treatise upon the history of the two ' motives ' in Christian thought—their rivalries in the early Church, the synthesis accomplished by Augustine and accepted by the middle ages, and its breaking-up by Luther.

Nygren's work suffers from its unnecessary and quite unjustified claim to historical objectivity. He professes to be concerned with facts not values. But apart from a theological background such as we have been describing, his method must appear arbitrary in the extreme. From the fact that the world into which Christianity brought the Gospel of divine Agape, of God's self-giving love to men, already knew that thirst for the

Divine which Platonism called Eros, it did naturally result that when Christians spoke of love they did not always mean the same thing. It does not follow that Eros and Agape are ' by nature completely antithetic ',[1] that they are ' two opposite attitudes to life ',[2] or that an enquiry which seeks to define ' the essential difference between Eros and Agape ' is ' compelled to view them primarily as rivals or enemies '.[3] On the contrary, one who believes that God's providence has never ceased to guide and govern the world He created would naturally draw the inference that if God has given Himself to men in Christ, it is because men need Him, and that consciousness of the need, so far from being an obstacle to acceptance of the gift, is its necessary condition. Nygren thinks that this is to obscure the real issue. Where others see a *praeparatio evangelica,* he is more disposed to find a *praeparatio daemonica ;* for he is interested in Eros not as the simple expression of a need but as the spirit of a religion which has its own way of meeting the need, and therefore must be in rivalry to the Gospel.[4] Eros-religion is anti-Christian at bottom because it is a religion of works, because it assumes that man not only desires to find his way to God but can find it by the practice of self-perfection. And he holds this false assumption to be rooted in a false theory of man's relation to God, a false understanding of the need which is to be met, in the last resort in a false conception of the divine nature itself, the God whom men ' need '. All Eros-religion is *egocentric,* since Eros is determined by an existing value in its object and therefore seeks satisfaction in the possession of what has value for the self : its desire for God is desire for an object supremely valuable, for the *Summum Bonum.*[5] Agape is *theocentric,* not because it is more ' occupied ' with God than Eros—the reverse is true—but because God is its Subject not its Object ; and it is related not to value but to the absence of value. Divine Agape is not only unmerited, but, in Nygren's phrase, ' uncaused ', wholly spontaneous and unaccountable. God loves, not righteousness nor the righteous

---

[1] A. Nygren, *Agape and Eros* (E.T.), p. 23. [2] *Ib.* p. 25.
[3] *Ib.* p. 120. [4] *Ib.* pp. 118 f. [5] *Ib.* pp. 133 ff., 165.

on the ground of their righteousness, but sinners.[1] The ' infinite value of the human soul ' is a dogma not of Christianity but of Eros-religion,[2] which inherits from the Orphic-Platonic tradition the belief in man's essential divinity, the belief that man is dear to God because he is by nature a child of God, that like is known by like and loved by like, and that what prevents such communion is the defilement of sin—a barrier which is *not* insuperable, but which Eros itself can remove through the cleansing process of asceticism. So deeply was the Christian faith corrupted by this doctrine of a fellowship with God attainable ' on God's level ', ' on the ground of righteousness ', that it needed the ' Copernican revolution ' achieved by Luther to recover the Gospel truth that God in Christ has come down to the human level, and gives men fellowship with Himself ' on the ground of sin '.[3] Of course Nygren does not mean that God loves the sinner because of his sin, any more than He loves the righteous because of his righteousness. But he maintains that Agape is the reversal of a position axiomatic for Judaism and Hellenism alike—namely, that ' the Divine can have converse only with the pure '.[4] And if we ask what then becomes of Christ's own version of *Be ye holy, for I am holy*, the answer is that the perfection of the Father in heaven, which His children are to imitate, consists just in that ' uncaused ' love which makes the sun to rise on the evil and on the good. It is indeed the *métier* of Agape to forgive.

Nygren is not to be disturbed by criticism of his analysis on psychological or ethical grounds. He knows that his Eros and Agape are artificial isolates : that regarded as moral qualities, as capacities of the human spirit, neither is self-sacrificing devotion a discovery of Christianity, nor is the pursuit of beauty and truth the monopoly of Platonism. He is not concerned, it must be repeated, with human morality but with the specifically religious motive, with that which makes a religion vital and

[1] *Agape and Eros*, pp. 52 ff., 165.
[2] *Ib.* pp. 55, 174.
[3] See *Eros und Agape II* (G.T.), pp. 507 ff.
[4] *Agape and Eros*, p. 162, quoting K. Holl.

urgent—in colloquial terms, its ' drive ' (in the religion of Agape), its ' pull ' (in the religion of Eros). And he would deny that love is rightly regarded as a natural compound in which Eros and Agape are elements : if they come together, the result is an artificial mixture. But there is a third element, whose part in the nature of love is more difficult to disavow, and the neglect of which constitutes a serious, perhaps a fatal defect in his whole construction. Eros and Agape are not the only Greek words for love. The Philia in which Aristotle discovered the richest endowment of human personality is strange neither to the Old Testament nor to the New. It differs both from Eros and from Agape in being a mutual relation, a bond which links two centres of consciousness in one ; and the Bible knows it not only as a human relationship, like that which binds together a David and a Jonathan. Behind the Law of Moses stands the Covenant which makes Israel God's people and Jehovah their God ; beyond the Body broken on the Cross is the love wherewith the Father loved the Son before the foundation of the world, the unity into which all the friends of the Crucified are to be made perfect : *that they may be one, even as we are one . . . that the love where-with thou lovedst me may be in them, and I in them.* There, surely, is the Holy of Holies of the New Testament ; and Nygren, with a candour which we may admire, owns that he can make nothing of it. The Johannine teaching is not in his view the culmination of the Gospel, but the beginning of its contamination. St. John's ' metaphysic of Agape ', ' in the very act of finding the supreme expression for the spontaneity and eternality of God's love, begins to miss something of that spontaneity and to weaken it down '.[1] For the Son cannot be other than a wholly worthy object of the Father's love ; and the characteristically Johannine ' love of the brethren ' is not the open, ' uncaused ' Agape which embraces in its divine indifference the sinner and the saint. Both Agape and Eros are ' one-way ' relations, and that makes it impossible to understand both the great commandments in terms of either. That man should have Agape towards God is

---

[1] *Agape and Eros,* p. 113.

as impossible as that God should have Eros towards man, upon Nygren's definitions. If man's love for God is to contain nothing of Eros, if it is not to be because in God he finds the satisfaction of all his needs, he can love God only *in the sense* of an absolute surrender of his own will in gratitude, ' because God's uncaused love has overpowered him and constrained him, so that he can do nothing else but love God '.[1] But this as Nygren knows is not Agape. Similarly, if the love of neighbour is to have no motive in Eros, if I am to love my neighbour neither because of the Divine which is or may be in him, nor because to love him confers merit upon myself and can become for me a ' stepping-stone ' to God, this love cannot be accounted for by anything in my relation to him as of one man to another : it will be the direct product of the surrender of my will to God's, ' really not a human love at all, but God's own Agape operating in man '.[2] For it belongs to the nature of Agape never to be evoked in response to a present value, but to create value in the person upon whom it is freely bestowed. And this is the point at which Nygren's whole scheme is left hanging in the air. There is no doubt how he would answer the question, ' What is the value which Agape creates ? ' Agape is self-giving and creates nothing but itself : love generates love, a son consubstantial with the father. Nygren may speak constantly of the ' new way of fellowship with God ' which the Gospel opens. But he is forbidden by his premises to find in this fellowship itself any value which man may rightly desire. That would be to unbar the door again to the Eros which he has excluded.

We have spoken of two strongly-contrasted types of contemporary Christianity, both which, for different reasons, appear to give no place to the love of God known to St. Augustine and to every great Christian mystic. For the first, Christian love is Philia—a mutual relationship between persons, served and expressed by co-operation for the satisfying of other needs, but

[1] *Agape and Eros*, p. 168.   [2] *Ib.* p. 169.

constituting in itself the highest of intrinsic values. Belief in God is grounded upon the conviction that for those who love community all things work together for good ; and a true idea of God is reached, primarily if not exclusively, through the reflective universalising of those mutual relationships in which community is experienced. But it is only in loving one another that we can realise the value of personality. We can indeed both desire and enjoy the realisation of Philia ; but we cannot have Philia for Philia. Its only real object is the concrete human individual with whom and for whom we live and work.

For the second, Christian love is Agape—a one-way relation of which the subject is God and the object man. Self-giving, it is self-creative : we can apply to it the Dionysian formula of St. Thomas—*bonum est diffusivum sui et communicativum ;* we may if we will call it the *Summum Bonum,* so long as we remember that this ' Good ' is not a value in the ordinary sense of the word. We may desire to receive it ; to possess and enjoy it, never. The divine gift of Agape, once accepted, makes men the channels of its outward and onward flow ; but the substance of the stream (as Berdyaev would say) is ' monophysite '—' really not a human love at all '. It cannot return upon itself : we cannot have Agape for the source of Agape. Its only object is the created world of men. And though its result is a fellowship of men with God and with one another not otherwise attainable, to think of this fellowship as the ultimate value, the end which Agape seeks, is to de-nature and de-throne the *Summum Bonum.*

It is not the purpose of our present study to claim that in neither of these two vital and sincere attempts to preach the Gospel to a generation in desperate need of it, is there to be found any deeper apprehension of the unsearchable riches of Christ than was or could be reached by a Platonist Bishop of Roman Africa at the beginning of the fifth century. *Deum et animam scire cupio,* said Augustine on the eve of his baptism.[1] *In multiloquio non effugies peccatum* was the text of *Proverbs* upon which, thirty years afterwards, he laid down his pen at the

[1] *Solil.* I. 7.

end of his most heroic effort to win nearer to the knowledge he desired.[1] He never counted himself to have apprehended ; and in these days we are more likely to belittle than to exaggerate his achievement, to reproach him for the errors which his authority made calamitous, rather than to honour him for the measure of truth which he was found worthy to attain. Both of God and of man's soul something has been learnt in fifteen hundred years. Yet we may still hold with Augustine that ' many things pertaining to the Catholic faith, and become matter of contest through the impatient zeal of heretics, call from their defenders for a more careful consideration, a clearer comprehension, and a more instant preaching : the adversary's question becomes the opportunity of learning '.[2]

The concept of *amor Dei* in Augustine is a psychological and theological complex, in which there is, as Nygren rightly observes, a synthesis of religious ideas distinct in origin. But we shall try to show that Nygren is mistaken in making the synthesis conform to the Hegelian pattern, with Eros for its thesis and Agape for its antithesis ; or rather, that neither of these two ' motives ' were known to Augustine in the ' purity ' which Nygren attributes to them. Neither Eros, nor Agape, nor the two together, will account for *caritas* without remainder : Augustine is not a compound of Plotinus and Luther, but a Father of the Catholic Church. In the Body of Christ, *caritas* is what it is in the mystery of the divine Being—the Holy Spirit of unity.

[1] *De Trin.* xv. 51.   [2] *De Civ.* xvi. 2.

II

The Platonist's Christianity

Passing away, saith the World, passing away :
Chances, beauty, and youth, sapped day by day :
Thy life never continueth in one stay.
Is the eye waxen dim, is the dark hair changing to grey
That hath won neither laurel nor bay ?
I shall clothe myself in Spring and bud in May :
Thou, root-stricken, shalt not rebuild thy decay
On my bosom for aye.
Then I answered : Yea.

Passing away, saith my Soul, passing away :
With its burden of fear and hope, of labour and play,
Hearken what the past doth witness and say :
Rust in thy gold, a moth is in thine array,
A canker is in thy bud, thy leaf must decay.
At midnight, at cockcrow, at morning, one certain day
Lo the Bridegroom shall come and shall not delay ;
Watch thou and pray.
Then I answered : Yea.

Passing away, saith my God, passing away :
Winter passeth after the long delay :
New grapes on the vine, new figs on the tender spray,
Turtle calleth turtle in Heaven's May.
Though I tarry, wait for Me, trust Me, watch and pray :
Arise, come away, night is past and lo it is day,
My love, My sister, My spouse, thou shalt hear me say.
Then I answered : Yea.

CHRISTINA ROSSETTI.

II

WE must begin, however, where Augustine began. No understanding of his religion is possible without regard to the Platonist foundation upon which all his thinking is built. His earliest considered definition of Christianity occurs in the treatise *On the True Religion*, written before his ordination to the priesthood at Hippo. The introduction to this book is occupied with a lively contrast of the weakness of pagan philosophy, its divergence from popular religion and its impotence to influence the common people, and the imposing success of Christianity in bringing philosophy and religion together, in winning the world of the unlearned to an acceptance of the truths which Plato and his successors had never ventured to preach to them. 'To turn away from earthly things towards the one true God . . . to despise this world of sense and to submit the soul to God to be cleansed by virtue . . . to run in response to the call from the desire of temporal and passing goods to the hope of eternal life and to the good things of the spiritual world ' . . . —*haec sunt*, the philosophers themselves would say, *quae nos persuadere populis non ausi sumus;* and that is the significance of the *Sursum corda* which goes up daily from humanity ' almost with one voice ' over all the world.[1] The message of Christ is the message of Plato ; and the power of Christ to convince would have extorted from Plato himself the confession of His divinity.[2]

But evidently the Catholic Church does more than exhort men to transfer their affections from earth to heaven, from sense to spirit, from time to eternity. The Church teaches a doctrine of salvation through Christ, and Augustine proceeds to define the function of this doctrine. ' Christianity begins with the prediction and accomplishment of an historic order of divine providence, for the salvation of the human race, which needs to

[1] *De Ver. Relig.* 5, 6.   [2] *Ib.* 3.

be formed anew and restored to eternal life. Upon faith in this order, the soul will be cleansed by a life fashioned into harmony with the divine commands, and will become fit for the apprehension of that spiritual Reality which is not past nor future, but ever abides the same, exposed to no possibility of change—namely, one God, Father, Son, and Holy Spirit.[1] . . . Cleaving to the eternal Creator we ourselves must needs be imbued with eternity. But since the soul, overwhelmed and entangled in sin, could not by itself see and hold fast this truth, were the comprehension of the Divine offered no foothold in things human, on which man could tread upwards from the life of earth to the likeness of God ; by God's unspeakable mercy is given the help of an historic order, whereby, through a Creature subject to change but obedient to the eternal laws, both for each and every man and for the whole human race there is a recalling of our original and perfect nature. *That is the Christian religion.*'[2] So Plotinus wrote that the way of redemption for the fallen soul is double : it must both be convinced of the valuelessness of the things to which it now attaches value, and must have its own origin and worth *recalled* to it.[3] To despise the world of sense is the way, to be ' imbued with eternity by cleaving to the eternal Creator' is the goal ; and Jesus Christ is our example. He ' reminds' us of our divine sonship, and he shows us how to scorn the flesh, its pains and its allurements.

Nearly thirty years later, Augustine is expounding St. John v. 40 : *ye will not come to me that ye may have life.* ' The meaning is ', he says, ' that the human soul and the rational spirit which is in man and not in beast, is quickened, beatified, illumined, only by the very substance of God. . . . Because of the kind of alliance which links soul and body in this life, the soul takes pleasure from what soothes the bodily senses, and pain from what offends them ; but that happiness or beatitude which is proper to the soul itself comes only by participation in the ever-living life of the immutable and eternal substance which is God.

---

[1] *De Ver. Relig.* 13.   [2] *Ib.* 19.
[3] Plotinus, *Enneads,* v. i. 1.

As the soul which is inferior to God is the cause of life to that which is inferior to itself, namely the body, so the cause of happy life to this same soul is not to be found save in that which is superior to the soul itself. . . . It must serve its Master, lest it be trodden down by its own servant. . . . *This is the Christian religion.* . . . And the whole Gospel given through Christ is this, brethren, and nothing else : the resurrection—resurrection not only of soul but of body. Both were dead, the body from infirmity, the soul from iniquity. . . . The soul can rise again only in virtue of Christ's Godhead : the body only in virtue of His manhood.' [1]

The differences between this definition of Augustine's maturity and the earlier statement of the *De Vera Religione* are indeed sufficiently striking. Platonism had led from the Delphic maxim ' Know Thyself' to the Orphic conclusion ' Embodiment is Entombment'. A deeper Christian Socratism shows man his place in the universal order, not as a ' divine something' imprisoned in alien matter, but as a ' reasonable soul' whose relation to the body it quickens and directs depends upon its relation to the God from whom its own being is derived. The concrete human person is body as well as soul, and soul's relation to body is to be mastery, not contempt. And therefore, while for Plotinus ' the true awakening' had meant ' resurrection from the body, not with the body ', [2] Augustine is now assured that the whole man has an eternal value and destiny. But he has also realised the full gravity of human need, not merely for a clearer comprehension of divine things, but for life itself. ' Both were dead, the body from infirmity, the soul from iniquity ' ; and the resurrection of soul and body demands more than the example of a good man. It demands an act of God.

Yet these differences, profound as they are, do not disguise the essential continuity of thought. Man's true end is a ' participation in the ever-living life of the immutable and eternal reality which is God '. ' Cleaving to the eternal Creator, we

---

[1] *In Jo. Ev. Tr.* 23. 5 f.   [2] *Enn.* III. vi. 6.

ourselves must needs be imbued with eternity.' That 'we too must needs have a share in eternity', [1] is for Plotinus a fact proved by our capacity for contact with the eternal; and the aim of his religion is for the soul ' to be with its own kin' [2]— the self-realisation and enfranchisement of the divine element in humanity rather than the submission of man as man to the rule of God.[3] But it was Plotinus who taught Augustine his characteristic conception of soul as the intermediary between spirit and sense, quickening because quickened.[4] For all the corrections of Neo-Platonism which his Christianity made necessary, it remained for him what he had recognised in it from the first, a *vera philosophia*.

' Popular Catholicism' it never was; and to those who gathered to hear that Homily on the Gospel, the Bishop's definition of their religion will have sounded strangely. They were well accustomed to hear him speak in another language, the language of traditional Christian exhortation, with its two essential categories—the category of *time*, of an evil present and a better future, and the category of *merit*, of man's fate in the future as determined by his conduct in the present. ' Brethren, this has always been our warning to you, we have never desisted from it, never been silent upon it. The life eternal is to be loved, the present life is to be despised. Live well now, and hope that it shall be well with you hereafter '.[5] ' I have not dwelt on the rule that all you do be done for hope of the future. For I know that the thoughts of all Christians are

---

[1] *Enn.* III. vii. 7 : δεῖ καὶ ἡμῖν μετεῖναι τοῦ αἰῶνος.

[2] *Enn.* I. ii. 4 : τὸ ἀγαθὸν αὐτῆς τὸ συνεῖναι τῷ συγγενεῖ . . . σύνεσται δὲ ἐπιστραφεῖσα.

[3] Contrast the Christian Hellenism of Irenaeus : *Adv. Haer.* IV. lxiii. 2 (Harvey) : ὑποταγὴ Θεοῦ, ἀφθαρσία.

[4] Cf. e.g. *Enn.* IV. viii. 6, 7 : μεσὴν τάξιν ἐν τοῖς οὖσιν ἔχουσαν.

[5] *Serm.* 302. 9. Cf. *De Civ.* II. 28 : populi confluunt ad ecclesiam . . . ubi audiant quam bene hic ad tempus vivere debeant, ut post hanc vitam beate semperque vivere mereantur. Morin, *Sermones post Maurinos reperti*, Denis xxiv. 1 : Christianorum fides . . . haec est, quia nos dicimus esse aliam vitam post istam vitam, et esse a mortuis resurrectionem, et esse post transactum saeculum in fine iudicium.

bent on the world to come. He who thinks not of the world to come, he who is a Christian for any other reason than that he may receive that which God promises in the end, is not yet a Christian.'[1] Both the lover and the despiser of this world may be called Christians and may receive the Church's sacraments; but one is a sharer in God's kingdom and an heir of eternal life, the other is not.[2]

No Christian Father is more uncompromising in his other-worldliness than is Augustine. But his other-worldliness is not a piece of traditional homiletic : it can only be appreciated in its intimate connection with his Platonist metaphysic.

The Seventh Book of the *Confessions* contains Augustine's account of that crucial year in his life when as a young ' don ' at Milan he first read the ' books of the Platonists '. It is in any case more important for us to know how the Bishop of Hippo understood his own intellectual and religious development, than to be sure whether his understanding exactly corresponded to the facts. But let it be said in parenthesis that the vigorous attempts which have been made to impugn the historical accuracy of the *Confessions* appear to have ended in a ' Not proven '.[3] With certain obvious reservations, we may take the tenacious and conscientious memory of Augustine in his forties as good authority for what happened in his early thirties : he is still his own best interpreter.

What he tells us is this—that, under God, he owed to Plotinus nothing less than the discovery of God as a spiritual reality. He had abandoned Manichaean dualism because its picture of the

[1] *Serm.* 9. 4. Cf. *Serm.* 108. 1 : ad hanc exspectationem et propter hanc spem christiani facti sumus. *En. in Ps.* xci. 1 : Christiani non sumus nisi propter futurum saeculum. *De Civ.* VI. 9 : vita aeterna . . . propter quam unam proprie nos christiani sumus.

[2] *Ep.* 127. 7. Cf. *In Jo. Ev. Tr.* 32. 9 : nihil aliud in hac vitae nostrae peregrinatione meditemur, nisi quia . . . hic non semper erimus.

[3] Here the judicial conclusion of Nörregaard holds the field : the ' gap ' between the early Dialogues and the *Confessions* is ' not so impassable as it has become usual to assume ' (*Augustins Bekehrung*, p. 242).

divine principle, the Good, the Light, in the ebb and flow of battle with a substantial Evil of Darkness, could not be reconciled with a conviction which (as he puts it) he ' felt in his very bones ' : ' I *saw* with complete certainty, not knowing whence or how such certainty came '—let us note these words—' that what is corruptible is inferior to what is incorruptible : what cannot be violated, is immediately to be preferred to what is subject to violation : what suffers no change, is better than what can be changed '.[1] He evidently means the three terms to be taken as synonymous. Immutability here means immunity from loss of good, and the axiom states that this immunity is itself a good whose possession must increase the total good of its possessor. Thus, in a passage of the *De Doctrina Christiana* written at about the same time, Augustine claims as self-evident the proposition that a life possessed of immutable wisdom is better than a life whose wisdom is mutable.[2] Clearly the axiom is valid without qualification only if the good assumed to be changeless is in its own kind the highest possible good. But when we call God the Supreme Good, we mean not merely that He is better than all besides, but that we cannot form the idea of a being better than His.[3] The Being of God must therefore be incorruptible, inviolable, immutable.

Now the Manichaean theology professed to maintain this belief ; [4] but the profession appeared to Augustine manifestly inconsistent with an anthropology which regarded the human soul as a part of the divine substance, entangled and ' corrupted ' by the substantial principle of evil.[5] He had accordingly rejected the dualism which was more ready to allow that God can suffer harm than that man can do it.[6] But he remained a materialist, able to attribute real being only to what is extended in time and space ; and the problem of evil demanded a solution more urgently than ever.

The metaphysic of Plotinus enabled him to solve the problem

[1] *Conf.* VII. I.   [2] *De Doctr. Christ.* I. 8.
[3] *Conf.* VII. 6.   [4] Cf. *C. Fort. Man.* 3, 11.
[5] *Conf.* VII. 3.   [6] *Ib.* 5.

of evil by enabling him to conceive the being of God as pure Spirit. ' I should have sought Thee *in the place where I saw* that the incorruptible must be preferred to the corruptible. Thence I should have perceived where evil arises, in perceiving whence comes corruption itself.' [1] Plotinus taught him where to look. He was to ' return into himself', and in the discovery that his own inmost being was spiritual to learn that the Source of all truth must be spiritual also. ' I entered into my inner self . . . and saw with such vision as the soul possesses, above the seeing soul, above the reasoning spirit (*mens*), the changeless Light '— not the ' Light' of the Manichaeans, a subtle luminous matter, but the Light of eternal truth, transcending the enlightened reason not as the greater the less, the universal the particular, but as the Maker transcends the thing made.' [2]

The vision came as the climax of an intellectual process, the well-known Neo-Platonic ' ascent' from lower to higher, from outer to inner. All judgements of value imply a standard of judgement. The reasoning faculty, which is not itself absolute, changeless, yet unhesitatingly places a higher value upon animate than upon inanimate, upon rational than upon irrational, upon immutable than upon mutable. It must then somehow be in touch with the ' immutable ' which it prefers to the ' mutable ' and which supplies its absolute standard of value. The argument, which occurs in Plotinus [3] and is often repeated by Augustine, resembles that of Descartes in the Third Meditation ; and the conclusion, whether valid or invalid, was one that Augustine could and did set down and register as a truth sufficiently established by reasoning. But Augustine believed himself not merely to have demonstrated a proposition, namely, that the mind must be in touch with an immutable reality, but to have felt the touch itself, in a momentary experience, describable only in the pluperfect tense.[4] He knew that he ' *had found* the changeless eternity of truth, above his changeable mind.' The changeless Light had manifested its absolutely sovereign, absolutely

[1] *Conf.* VII. 6.   [2] *Ib.* 16.   [3] E.g. *Enn.* v. i. II.
[4] See J. Nörregaard, *Augustins Bekehrung*, p. 65.

immaterial reality : ' in the flash of a trembling glance,' he had ' attained to that which Is '—and then it was gone, leaving only a ' loving remembrance, a yearning desire ', behind.[1]

' The knower of that changeless Light is the knower of the truth ; the knower of it is the knower of eternity ; the knower of it is love. O eternal Truth, true Love, beloved Eternity, thou art my God ! ' [2] That is the ' confession ', the sacrifice o praise and thanksgiving, into which the recollection of things past lifts up the heart of Augustine as he tells his story. But that the facts of the story told in these chapters of the *Confessions* have not been distorted in the telling is placed beyond doubt by the letter written to Nebridius from Cassiciacum in the following year. There Augustine reminds Nebridius of ' our favourite argument ' (*illa tibi notissima ratiuncula*) from the superior value of the spiritual to its superior reality ; and he says that ' sometimes, refreshed by this reasoning ', he has been led, through an act of prayer and contemplation, to so complete a conviction of ' the things that abide ' that all reasoning seems superfluous : the truth has the immediacy of self-consciousness.[3] And it was an experience of exactly the same kind which came to him a little later, when he leant from the window at Ostia with his mother a week before she died.[4] There is no ground for the claim that the intervening ' purgation ' and reception into the Church gave to the so-called ecstasy at Ostia a ' Christian ' quality lacking to the earlier experience.[5] It was recognised indeed as a foretaste of the life to come ; but it was reached by the same process of intellectual ascent, and its climax was the same momentary intuition of the eternal. The Spirit breatheth where it listeth. Before and after Christian baptism, the method of a pagan philosopher brought to Augustine a moment's immediate sense of the living and changeless God.

[1] *Conf.* VII. 23.   [2] *Ib.* 16.

[3] *Ep.* 4. 2 : tanta insunt praesentia quanta sibi quisque est praesens. Cf. *Conf.* VII. 16 : facilius dubitarem vivere me quam non esse veritatem quae per ea quae facta sunt intellecta conspicitur.

[4] *Conf.* IX. 23 ff.

[5] So K. E. Kirk, *The Vision of God*, pp. 321 ff.

The Platonist's Christianity

If Augustine is to be called a mystic, that and no other was the character of his mystical experience—a reflective ascent through the ordered values of the created world, inexplicably transformed into an instantaneous apprehension not of any particular truth, but of *the* Truth, the Light that lighteneth every man. *Invisibilia Dei per ea quae facta sunt intellecta conspiciuntur.*[1] The frequency and the uniformity of language with which throughout his writings the same flash of momentary intuition is described, make it reasonable to infer that the experience itself was neither isolated nor infrequent.[2] Vision it certainly was, but

[1] Among the ' things that are made ', the chief for Augustine is the human soul itself. This needs always to be remembered when he quotes the text, as e.g. in *Conf.* VII. 16 and 23. See *De Civ.* XI. 26.

[2] E.g. *De Mor. Eccl.* 11 : [ratio] ubi ad divina perventum est, avertit sese ; intueri non potest, palpitat, aestuat, inhiat amore, reverberatur luce veritatis, et ad familiaritatem tenebrarum suarum non electione sed fatigatione convertitur.

De Cons. Evang. IV. 20 : [anima] si quando adiuta excedit . . . hanc carnalem caliginem . . . tamquam rapida coruscatione perstringitur, et in suam infirmitatem redit, vivente desiderio quo rursus erigatur, nec sufficiente munditia qua figatur.

En. in Ps. XLI. 10 : utcumque nebulis diffugatis . . . ad hunc sonum pervenerimus interdum ut aliquid de illa domo Dei nitendo capiamus ; onere tamen quodam infirmitatis nostrae ad consueta recidimus. . . . Ecce acie mentis aliquid incommutabile, etsi perstrictim et raptim, perspicere potuimus.

Ib. CXLV. 5 : [anima] legit ibi quiddam tremendum, laudandum, amandum, desiderandum et appetendum ; nondum tenet, nondum capit : coruscatione quadam perstringitur, non est tam valida ut maneat ibi.

De Trin. VIII. 3 : ecce vide, si potes : Deus veritas est . . . ecce in ipso primo ictu quo velut coruscatione perstringeris, cum dicitur, Veritas, mane si potes ; sed non potes : relaberis in ista solita et terrena.

Ib. XII. 23 : ad quas [intelligibiles rationes] mentis acie pervenire paucorum est ; et cum pervenitur, quantum fieri potest, non in eis manet ipse perventor, sed veluti acie ipsa reverberata repellitur, et fit rei non transitoriae transitoria cogitatio.

In Jo. Ev. Tr. 18. 11 : si utcumque erexistis cor vestrum ad videndum Verbum, et ipsius luce reverberati ad solita recidistis. . . . Non mihi antea credebas quia est quod videas ; duce quadam ratione adductus es ; propinquasti, intendisti, palpitasti, refugisti. Scis certe esse quod videas, sed idoneum non te esse qui videas.

This insistence upon the dazzlingness of the light and the consequent transiency of the vision recalls, of course, Plato's allegory of the Cave in *Republic* 514 A ff. But it is not characteristic of Plotinus ; though we may

the word 'ecstasy' is misleading. Augustine's vision differs both from the Plotinian ecstasy of union with the Supreme and from the analogous experience of later Christian mystics in the crucial point, that it does not blur the distinction of subject and object but accentuates it.[1] The *lux incommutabilis* that now for

compare *Enn.* I. vi. 9 : 'if the eye that adventures the vision be dimmed by vice, impure, or weak, and unable in its cowardly blenching to see the uttermost brightness (ἀνανδρίᾳ οὐ δυνάμενος τὰ πάνυ λαμπρὰ βλέπειν), then it sees nothing even though another point to what lies plain to sight before it' (tr. Mackenna). And *Enn.* VI. ix. 4 : 'Struck perhaps by that authentic light, all the soul lit by the nearness gained, we have gone weighted from beneath ; the vision is frustrate' (ἔτι ὀπισθοβαρὴς ὑπάρχων ἃ ἐμποδία ἦν τῇ θέᾳ) (tr. Mackenna).

[1] Perhaps the closest parallel in Plotinus is to be found in *Enn.* V. vii. 36 : 'Knowledge of The Good or contact with it (ἐπαφή) is the all-important : this —we read—is the grand learning, the learning we are to understand, not of looking towards it but attaining, first, some knowledge of it. We come to this learning by analogies, by abstractions, by our understanding of its subsequents, of all that is derived from The Good, by the upward steps towards it (ἀναβασμοί τινες). Purification has The Good for goal ; so the virtues, all right ordering, ascent within the Intellectual, settlement therein (τοῦ νοητοῦ ἐπιβάσεις καὶ ἐπ' αὐτοῦ ἱδρύσεις), banqueting upon the divine—by these methods one becomes, to self and to all else, at once seen and seer ; identical with Being and Intellectual-Principle and the entire living all, we no longer see the Supreme as an external ; we are near now, the next is That and it is close at hand, radiant above the Intellectual. *Here, we put aside all the learning ;* disciplined to this pitch, established in beauty, the quester holds knowledge still of the ground he rests on, but, *suddenly,* swept beyond it all by the very crest of the wave of Intellect surging beneath, he is lifted and sees, never knowing how ; the vision floods the eyes with light, but it is not a light showing some other object, *the light is itself the vision.* No longer is there thing seen and light to show it, no longer Intellect and object of Intellection ; this is *the very radiance that brought both Intellect and Intellectual object into being* for the later use and allowed them to occupy the quester's mind. With This he himself becomes identical.' (tr. Mackenna : my italics).

Cf. *Enn.* V. iii. 17 : 'All our effort may well skim over every truth, and through all the verities in which we have part, and yet the reality escape us when we hope to affirm, to understand : for the understanding, in order to its affirmation, must possess itself of item after item ; only so does it traverse all the field : but how can there be any such peregrination of that in which there is no variety ? All the need is met by a contact (ἐφάψασθαι) purely intellective. At the moment of touch there is no power whatever to make any affirmation ; there is no leisure ; reasoning upon the vision is for afterwards. We may know we have had the vision *when the Soul has suddenly taken light.*

34

the first time but not the last shone before the eye of Augustine's spirit may or may not be comparable with the 'fire' in which Pascal's soul was drowned 'from about half-past ten in the evening to about half an hour after midnight' on November 23rd, 1654. But the effect upon Augustine was no less momentous : it was the turning-point in his life, in which he came to grips at the same time with God and his own soul. The revelation of God was for him as for the Hebrew prophet in the year that King Uzziah died a condemning revelation of self. Doubt was impossible : intellectual certainty was achieved and unshakable. But the touch, the vision, was gone in the moment of its coming. The excess of light was blinding, and in his blindness Augustine saw his sin. The reality of the spiritual is apprehended because and when the spiritual is *preferred* to the material : it is the greater reality because and when it is accepted as the higher value. *Caritas novit eam lucem.* The vision of God is the love of God ; and Augustine knew that he loved the flesh more than the spirit. 'I marvelled,' he says, 'that it was now Thyself and no idol of my own imagining that I was called to love, yet could I not stand fast in the fruition of Thee, but was first drawn up to Thee by Thy loveliness and then dragged down by my own weight . . . the weight of a carnal life.'[1] That is the link that binds his discovery of God through the 'books of the Platonists' with the struggle that ended with *Tolle, lege* in the Milan garden. The victory then gained was real, but the hopes that sprang from it were doomed to disappointment ; for Augustine's belief that nothing but *consuetudo carnalis* stood between the 'flash of his trembling glance' and an assured and

This light is from the Supreme and is the Supreme ; we may believe in the Presence when, like that other God on the call of a certain man, He comes bringing light ; the light is the proof of the advent. Thus, the soul unlit remains without that vision ; lit, it possesses what it sought. And this is the true end set before the Soul, to take that light, *to see the Supreme by the Supreme*, and not by the light of any other principle—to see the Supreme which is also the means to the vision ; for that which illumines the Soul is that which it is to see just as it is by the sun's own light that we see the sun.—But how is this to be accomplished ?—Cut away everything' (tr. Mackenna : my italics).

[1] *Conf.* VII. 23.

permanent fruition of the eternal, was illusory. Therein lies the pathos of that period of sanguine intellectualism which is recorded in the early treatises, and on which we may hear Augustine's own comment in words written not long after the *Confessions*: ' Whoever thinks that in this mortal life a man may so disperse the mists of bodily and carnal imaginings as to possess the unclouded light of changeless Truth, and cleave to it with the unswerving constancy of a spirit wholly estranged from the common ways of this life,—he understands neither what he seeks nor what he is that seeks it.'[1] Yet to the end of his life Augustine remained convinced that what condemns all intuitive experience to transiency, what prevents us from ' standing fast in the fruition of God ', is no mere necessity of our temporal existence but the infirmity and impurity of our love.[2]

The moment of vision passes, and in its passing convinces of sin ; but its intellectual fruit may be solid and permanent. The discovery that God is a Spirit was the discovery of evil in Augustine's own heart, but it gave him his solution of the general problem of evil which had tormented his mind. The unity of this double revelation is strikingly conveyed by the language of the *Confessions*.[3] *Et cum te primum cognovi, tu assumpsisti me ut viderem esse quod viderem et nondum me esse qui viderem.* The words do not mean simply, ' I saw that there was something for me to see, but that I was not yet fit to see it '. *Esse* has its pregnant sense in both cases : the supreme reality of the vision displayed by contrast (*longe me esse a te in regione dissimilitudinis*), the lack of true being in him whom the vision blinded. *Cibus sum grandium : cresce et manducabis me.* The knowledge of God is the food of grown men—but a food which like the Eucharist changes those who feed upon it into its own unchanging substance. Because change in the Creator is impossible, in the creature it is

[1] *De Cons. Evang.* IV. 20.
[2] See e.g. *De Trin.* VIII. 3 : quo tandem pondere, quaeso, relaberis, nisi sordium contractarum cupiditatis visco et peregrinationis erroribus ?
[3] *Conf.* VII. 16.

necessary. All things that are have being because they are from God ; but it is not perfect being because they ' are not that which God is '. The only true being is the Changeless, in which man participates in the measure in which he holds fast to God. From now onwards, *esse* and *non esse* for Augustine are both terms of degree. In God, Being is identical with changeless goodness. In man, ' to be or not to be ' signifies the measure in which he is approaching God's goodness or falling away from it. Evil is a ' defect of being ', but its existence is never independent of the existence of good : so long as man is capable of evil, he must also be capable of good. The possibility of corruption implies a still existing goodness in the being which is corruptible. All things are *bona in quantum sunt*.

It is commonly held that Augustine's ontology, in which evil is treated as a privation, a non-entity, does no more than evade the problem which it professed to solve ; and that his deeply Christian sense of the reality of moral evil caused him to relapse into Manichaeanism with his doctrine of original sin, in which the Not-Being, the Nothing out of which man was created is transformed into a Something with fatal power. In fact the originality of Augustine appears just in his steady refusal to hypostatise evil. It is Plotinus who identifies evil with ' Matter '—not indeed with material existence, but with the potentiality in which material existence originates. For Augustine, creation *de nihilo* is simply creation, and creatureliness means a being which is not God's and therefore not unchangeable.[1] His whole conception of moral good and evil is dynamic : man's soul is in the making and cannot stand still. Righteousness is its movement towards integration, sin its movement towards disintegration—a verging *ad nihilum*, an ' unmaking '. Change is the rule of temporal existence, changelessness is the quality of the eternal, the limit towards which the creature may approximate.

[1] Cf. esp. *C. Jul. op. imp.* v. 44 : cum dicimus . . . quia de nihilo factum est, non de Deo, *non nihilo damus ullam naturam*, sed naturam factoris a natura eorum quae sunt facta discernimus.

It has however been suggested that the ancient tendency to 'exalt immutability into the highest attribute of Deity' is a relic of the ancient materialism which finds inertia to require explanation less than movement; and that since activity no less than permanence is characteristic of the soul, the preference for the changeless is really 'a preference of the quasi-material to the unequivocally spiritual'.[1] We might not unfairly ask whether the modern thinker's attitude towards changelessness is wholly unaffected by the modern conception of matter in terms of restless energy rather than of enduring substance. But we have seen that in fact Augustine's intuitive preference of the changeless went back to his materialist period of thought, and that its formulation bears the marks of its origin. The 'corruptible' and 'violable' represented the Manichaean element of Light, a subtle material substance. Yet it was reflection on the idea of immutability that showed Augustine the way of escape from materialism. The changeless Light is the eternity of the True, the impregnable assurance of the Good.

It is said that the only conception of God which can claim to be reasonably derived from the 'empirical approach to theism' is that of the 'world-ground', in the sense of the world's Designer and therefore Creator, intelligent because purposeful, and ethically good because the development of moral personality appears to be at least included in His purpose. But 'immutability cannot subsist together with ethical excellence, which involves doing and willing'.[2] Now for Augustine too the Being of God is Intelligence and Will. Changelessness is not so much the 'highest attribute of Deity' as the *differentia* whereby God's Knowing and Willing are distinguished from the same or similar activities in men. As Being, it can never be said of God, as it must be said of men, that He was not or will not be what He is; as Intelligence and Will, it can never be said of God, as it must be said of men, that His apprehension or

[1] F. R. Tennant, *Philosophical Theology*, vol. ii, p. 62.
[2] *Ib.* p. 145.

His purpose may be directed to the same object at one time in a positive sense and at another in a negative. The empirical theologian has in the end to admit [1] that ' God's moral nature is largely incomparable with ours ' ; that for His Being, ' it is gratuitous and incongruous to suggest development from lower to higher . . ., struggle and attainment, in a word, imperfection '; and that there is ' no ground for supposing the possibility of variableness in respect of His world purpose as a whole '. That ' variation of *activity* upon or within the world is involved in realisation of the invariable purpose,' Augustine would insist no less strongly : God's providence consists in His ' use ' of man's activity, evil as well as good, for His own ends. But Augustine would not accept the inference that the ' divine immutability can only be self-identity and self-consistency through change ', if the change here meant be a change in God.

Change necessarily implies time ; changelessness does not necessarily exclude it, though there could be no perception of a time in which nothing changed. The word ' eternal ' may bear several different meanings ; but when God is conceived as changeless, though the nature of His eternity is not thereby defined, an intelligible clue is provided for the distinction of His Being from the temporal existence which we know.[2] When Augustine comes to seek for a logical grounding of his intuition —a search very different from the one described in the *Confessions* —when he comes to ask *why* we must call God immutable, the theory which he formulates, and which will be taken over and worked out in all its applications by St. Thomas, is again suggested to him by Neo-Platonism. It is that the divine immutability is a consequence of the divine ' simplicity '.[3] God alone is not a ' composite ' : He alone ' is what He has '. Wisdom and

---

[1] *Philosophical Theology*, vol. ii, pp. 148 f.

[2] Cf. *De Civ.* XI. 6 : Si enim recte discernuntur aeternitas et tempus, quod tempus sine aliqua mobili mutabilitate non est, in aeternitate autem nulla mutatio est ; quis non videat quod tempora non fuissent, nisi creatura fieret, quae aliquid aliqua motione mutaret ?

[3] *De Civ.* VIII. 6 ; XI. 10. *De Trin.* VI. 8 ; VII. 2, etc.

Goodness are in Him alone inseparable from Being. God therefore cannot ' lose ' His wisdom or His goodness without ceasing to be God, whereas all created things, including the soul, can cease to be what they were before without ceasing to be themselves. As the Schoolmen will put it, in God there is ' identity of essence and existence '. The scholastic formulation aimed at excluding anthropomorphic conceptions of Deity. We are not to think of God as of a person with a certain character, a subject of whom universal attributes are predicable.[1] He is not a member of the class denoted by the term ' loving ' : He is Love. But essence and existence are identical in God only ; and in Augustine's terminology it must be admitted that ambiguities and inconsistencies occur. He often speaks as though there were no difference anywhere between *esse* and *bonum esse,* as though being and value were everywhere identical. But this would mean the destruction of his theology. The existence of the creature is a good, because it is the gift of a good Creator, and in that sense things are and remain *bona in quantum sunt.* But Augustine is not careful to keep this sense distinct from the other, in which he asserts that the true goodness of things is their true being. Existence is a natural goodness which is unalterable ; the ethical goodness which brings men near to God is a quality that can be lost or gained. As it is gained or lost, increased or diminished, men come to share more or less fully in the Being of God. Sharing, participation, was the logical thought-form in which Plato had expressed the immanence of the changeless Reality in the changing world ; when he wanted to safeguard the transcendence of the One over against the Many, he had to speak the language of art : the Idea is the pattern or exemplar, the Particular its copy or similitude. St. Thomas did not abandon the Platonism of Augustine, but he replaced Augustine's ' degrees of existence ', the varying participations

---

[1] Cf. Plotinus, *Enn.* VI. vii. 38 : λέγομεν δὲ τἀγαθὸν περὶ αὐτοῦ λέγοντες οὐκ αὐτὸ οὐδὲ κατηγοροῦντες, ὅτι αὐτῷ ὑπάρχει, ἀλλ' ὅτι αὐτό. VI. viii. 13 : αἱ δὲ ἐνέργειαι ἡ οἷον οὐσία αὐτοῦ, ἡ βούλησις αὐτοῦ καὶ ἡ οὐσία ταὐτὸν ἔσται.

in true Being, by the *analogia entis,* in which man's being is neither part nor equivalent of God's, but a created likeness of it.

When the modern theologian insists that being must be 'univocal', that Creator and creature alike and in the same sense 'are', he does so for the good reason that the empirical approach cannot discover a God who does not depend upon the world as much as the world upon Him. If 'God' *means* the world-ground, then God without a world is not God.[1] Now this is precisely what Augustine and Thomas find incompatible with the very idea of creation. If creation is to be taken seriously, the Being of the Creator must have a necessity which separates it altogether from the contingent being not merely of the individual creature but of the whole created universe. This 'necessity' of the divine Being Augustine, following Plotinus, expresses by the conception of the divine self-sufficiency : God 'needs' nothing outside Himself to make Him what He is. His perfection excludes all indigence, because the Supremely Existent is the Supreme Good. But Plotinus, though he will not deduce God from the world, does deduce the world from God : he regards the existence of the world as a necessary consequence of the existence of God. Augustine holds, on the contrary, that there can be no 'necessity' of creation, which is the absolutely free act of love.

Id vere est quod incommutabiliter manet. Mihi autem inhaerere Deo bonum est,[2] *quia si non manebo in illo, nec in me potero. Ille autem in se manens innovat omnia.*[3] *Et Dominus Deus meus es, quoniam bonorum meorum non eges.*[4] In these three texts of Scripture Augustine sums up his Christian Platonism.[5] The changeless God who is the only absolute Being is the source

---

[1] *Philosophical Theology,* vol. ii, p. 156.
[2] *Psalm* lxxii. 20.   [3] *Wisdom* vii. 27.
[4] *Psalm* xv. 2.   [5] *Conf.* vii. 17.

and stay of a changing world, called into existence for its own perfecting and not for His.

> *Rerum Deus tenax vigor*
> *Immotus in te permanens.* . . .

We have first to see how this Platonic principle of the superiority of the changeless to all changeable good shaped and determined that quest for the happy life which for Augustine was the natural basis of religion.

III

Beata Vita

Man does not strive for happiness at all. . . .
He strives for concrete values and goods. . . .
' Happiness ' is the emptiest and most meaningless
of human words.

NICHOLAS BERDYAEV.

But as the Heathen made them several gods,
Of all God's Benefits, and all His Rods. . . .
And as by changing that whole precious Gold
To such small Copper coins, they lost the old,
And lost their only God, who ever must
Be sought alone, and not in such a thrust ;
So much mankind true happiness mistakes ;
No joy enjoys that man, that many makes.

JOHN DONNE.

And the LORD spake unto Moses, saying, Speak unto Aaron and unto his
sons, saying, On this wise ye shall bless the children of Israel ; ye shall say
unto them :

The LORD bless thee, and keep thee :
The LORD make his face to shine upon thee,
and be gracious unto thee :
The LORD lift up his countenance upon thee,
and give thee peace.

THE BOOK OF NUMBERS.

III

THE metaphysic of Plotinus is a solitary phenomenon in a world which had long lost interest in the search for truth except as a guide or apology for conduct. Apart from Neo-Platonism, philosophy in the Roman Empire meant ethics, and its common ethical assumptions were those of Aristotle. Happiness, *Eudaimonia,* is taken to be the acknowledged ' good for man ', the agreed object of all ethical activity, because it appears to be the one and only aim which no rational being can disown : dispute can only arise when it is sought to define or give content to the idea of *Eudaimonia.* Ancient ethics are therefore properly described as eudaemonistic, and so distinguished from all theories of conduct which base themselves on ' deontology ' or the sense of obligation. The only convenient translation of *Eudaimonia* is ' Happiness ' ; but it is necessary to insist that the word must be understood without its ordinary limitation, in modern usage, to the sphere of feeling. It is to mean ' the perfect life ', in so far as perfection is attainable by mankind. The Stoic who finds happiness in the subjection of all feeling to rational will is no less eudaemonist than the Epicurean who finds it in the enjoyment of pleasure ; and when Augustine sets against these the Christian assertion that it is ' the gift of God ',[1] he does no more (at first sight) than restore to the words εὐδαίμων and *beatus* the religious colour which is native to them, the stamp with which they were first minted. In the letter to Dioscorus he reminds his correspondent, who had asked him for an exposition of the systems of pagan philosophy, that the only thing we need to know is the answer to the question ' How can man be happy ? '[2] But he is well aware that in this respect the Christian religion is not distinguished from the philosophical schools of paganism. ' All philosophers in common,' he says in a sermon,

---

[1] *Serm.* 150. 8.   [2] *Ep.* 118. 13.

' in their studies, their questionings, their arguments, their lives, have sought to apprehend the happy life. This was the one cause of philosophising ; but in this matter, I think, we Christians are at one with the philosophers. If I were to ask you why you have believed in Christ, why you have become Christians, every man will answer truly, " For the sake of happiness ".' [1]

The preacher, as we know, was speaking for himself. For the young Augustine and the group of friends who had followed him to Milan, ' the ardent search for truth and wisdom ', which was their common interest, was centred on the question of the happy life ; [2] and the question, so far from being merely academic, was a burning practical problem. ' Away with all else ; let us abandon all these futilities, and devote ourselves to the search for truth alone. . . . Why do we hesitate to give up all worldly ambition and devote ourselves wholly to the search for God and the happy life ? ' [3] The first difficulty—money, and the professional career for money's sake—seemed in a way to be removed, when the wealthy Romanianus urged the formation of a community of like-minded intimates ; but the pathetic little scheme collapsed against the second difficulty—women and the claims of matrimony. [4] We see that the friends had already got so far as to be convinced, in theory, that the happy life is the *vita contemplativa,* for which the reading of Cicero's *Hortensius* had stirred Augustine's undergraduate enthusiasm eleven years before. Yet when the decisive step had been taken, and Augustine found himself, at Cassiciacum, driven into the ' haven of philosophy ' by the ' storm ' which had freed him at the same time from the world and the flesh, there was still a journey before him in which he sought direction : the ' Land of Happiness ' was still unmapped. He writes his treatise *On the Happy Life*—the first of the Cassiciacine Dialogues to be completed ; and he dedicates it, with an appropriateness which he does not fail to mark, to Manlius Theodorus : if anything deserves to be called the ' gift of God ', it is happiness. [5]

[1] *Serm.* 150. 4. [2] *Conf.* VI. 17 ff. [3] *Ib.* 19.
[4] *Ib.* 24. [5] *De Beat. Vit.* 5.

It is more than a piece of literary urbanity ; for the argument of the treatise, derivative and immature as it is, shows clearly enough the point at which Christian and pagan ethics part company. It was the favourite Stoic maxim [1] that all failure to achieve happiness comes from failure to limit our desires to that which is ' within our power,' to that of which no tyrant can rob us, which no adversity can disturb. Here, and in many later discussions of the subject, Augustine adopts a like criterion. Happiness has not been achieved so long as it can be taken from us ' against our will '. But the inference is not that it must be ' within our power ', as a condition of the self-directed will ; for the soul and its ' virtue ' are no less mutable than the body and its pleasures. It must consist in a relation of the soul to that which is ' eternal and abiding ' ; and in the *De Beata Vita* such a relation is boldly identified with the ' possession of God '.[2] Because he has read into Plotinus the Christian doctrine of Christ as the divine Wisdom, Augustine is able to accept in its Neo-Platonist form the Stoic claim that happiness belongs to the *sapiens*, the Sage. But he is already aware that the Christian can agree neither with Seneca that greatness of soul must ' shine with no good but its own ',[3] nor with Plotinus that the good for any man is ' he himself to himself through that which he possesses ', and nothing ' brought in from without ', ' no foreign substance imported from a foreign realm '.[4]

In the *De Moribus Ecclesiae* we find him struggling for a clearer expression of this divergence from Neo-Platonist doctrine. There he argues that if, as the Stoics say, virtue is the perfection of man's higher nature, the very quest for a virtue unachieved implies that the soul is looking to some real perfection ' outside itself', the pursuit of which may engender virtue in the soul ; and this real perfection must have the changelessness which belongs to no human *sapiens*, but to God, ' whose following

---

[1] Epictetus IV. 4 *et passim*.

[2] *De Beat. Vit.* II. Cf. *En. in Ps.* XXXII. ii. 18 : ergo inde beati erimus, Deum possidendo.

[3] Seneca, *ad Lucil.* 41. 6. [4] *Enn.* I. iv. 3, 4.

makes our life good, whose attainment makes it happy '.[1]
Clearer still is the statement in the much later letter to Dioscorus.
Neither the *beatificum bonum,* the ' good which gives happiness ',
nor any part of it, can be ' in the soul ' ; if the soul were happy
' through a good of its own ', why should it ever be miserable ?
The perception of our own mutability, shown in the fact of
progress towards wisdom, should lead us to recognise, ' above
our own nature ', the transcendent, changeless Wisdom, ' in
whose participation and enlightenment there is a richer and surer
joy than in ourselves '.[2]

What then must be the soul's relation to the *beatificum
bonum ?* Augustine seeks to answer this question in a passage of
closely-packed dialectic which occupies four of the ' Collected
Essays ' written before he became Bishop.[3] He begins with an
analysis of the fear which makes happiness impossible. Freedom
from the fear of losing or failing to gain what we value is
essential to happiness but not sufficient for it : it demands the
satisfaction of intellect and affection which make man what he is.
Now the only affection which is wholly desirable is the love of
that which cannot fail the lover ; and the only object conforming
to this rule is a spiritual possession, ' that which we have when we
know it '. But perfect knowledge of what is good necessarily
implies the love of it, else we should not be knowing it *as* good.
Happiness then is the possession through knowledge and love
of an eternal object ; and such an object sheds the quality of its
eternity upon its lover. *Thou shalt love the Lord thy God with all
thy heart,* and *This is life eternal, to know Thee.*[4]

We are close now to Augustine's most famous and most
characteristic definition of the happy life. In the Tenth Book of
the *Confessions,* in a prolonged ' elevation ' or intellectual ascent
towards God, on the familiar Neo-Platonist pattern, he has

---

[1] *De Mor. Eccl.* 9 f.   [2] *Ep.* 118. 15.

[3] *De Div. Quaest. LXXXIII.* 33-36.

[4] Cf. Morin, *Sermones post Maurinos reperti,* Guelferb. xxx. 1 : Quid
prodest ista non contemnere, quae amando non potes detinere ? Fugit te
dies amatus, accedit deus desideratus. Hoc ama, quo amando pervenias.

advanced from contemplation of the external world of creation to the depths of his own conscious and unconscious self—the ' abyss ' which he calls memory. He turns suddenly with the recollection that ' the search for God is the search for happiness ', to ask how it is that all men desire the happy life of which their memory can provide no experience.[1] His answer is that happiness is *gaudium de veritate,* ' joy in the truth ' or rather ' truth-given joy '.[2] Experience of joy is universal, and so is the desire to know, the unwillingness to be deceived. But the love of truth itself makes us persuade ourselves that truth belongs to the less worthy objects of our love. We shun the light of the Truth, because it is judgement, because we cannot face it without standing condemned.[3] So ends the search, with the passionate cry of the converted soul—' At long last I have loved Thee, O Beauty of all beauties oldest and newest ! '[4]—and the humble prayer of the penitent —' Give what Thou commandest, and command what Thou wilt '.[5]

The happiness which is the aim of human endeavour consists, therefore, according to Augustine, in a relation of knowledge and love which binds the soul to the one immutable Reality. The soul that sees the Truth must at the same time see its own distance from the Truth—in Christian terms, its own sinfulness : the soul that loves the Truth must at the same time desire its own amendment. Thus the whole scheme is moralised and christened. Knowledge and love will re-direct the soul's movement towards God : its changing life will become an advance, an approach, instead of a falling away ; and the measure of its progress will be the measure of its transmutation into the eternity of that which it knows and loves.

But in his first essays at a Christian philosophy, Augustine, as he notes in the *Retractations,*[6] was writing under the influence of the too sanguine belief, derived from the Platonists, in the possibility of an adequate intellectual apprehension of God here

[1] *Conf.* x. 29.   [2] *Ib.* 33.   [3] *Ib.* 34.
[4] *Ib.* 38.   [5] *Ib.* 40.   [6] *Retr.* I. 2, 4, 7, 14, 19.

and now.[1] He had thought, at Cassiciacum, that to refuse men
the hope of attaining real wisdom in this life must discourage its
pursuit no less than to assure them that a real wisdom is attainable but that only the sceptic can possess it.[2] He had his own
precious experiences of the mystic vision, and it seemed to him,
as it had seemed even to the prosaic Aristotle, that the life of
contemplation could itself enable this mortal to put on a kind
of immortality. For two or three years, indeed, he lived such
a life in the little religious community gathered in his African
home. But—*Deo aliter visum.* Even in the *De Vera Religione,*
the last work of this period, the admission has already been
made that here we know only in part.[3] And the tears of
Augustine, when the people of Hippo would have him and no
other for their priest, are of historic significance. His ordination
meant the abandonment of an ideal. Naturally enough, the
consequences of the break are not to be traced immediately or
in all that he wrote from that time forward. But the eventual
effect upon his whole outlook on religion was certain.

If there is a happiness attainable in this life, it is not enough for
the soul to be joined to the Changeless ; it must itself be lifted
somehow above the realm of change. In all the writings of
Augustine's maturity, he acknowledges that this is impossible.
Happiness in this life can only mean the happiness of hope. The
argument is set out at length in the Thirteenth Book of the
De Trinitate, where the problem is posed in the same way as in
the *Confessions :* What definition of happiness will allow us to
maintain that its nature is universally known as well as universally
desired ? and the definition offered is none other than that which
Monica had given at Cassiciacum and her son had hailed as
coming from the ' citadel of philosophy '.[4] For perfect happiness
two factors must be present : the happy man must ' have all that
he wants, and want nothing wrongly '. It is the ' crookedness

---

[1] Justin Martyr tells the same story of his own initiation into Platonism :
ὀλίγου ἐντὸς χρόνου ῷμην σοφὸς γεγονέναι, καὶ ὑπὸ βλακείας ἤλπιζον
αὐτίκα κατόψεσθαι τὸν Θεόν (*Dial. c. Tryph.* 2).
[2] *C. Acad.* III. 20.   [3] *De Ver. Relig.* 103.   [4] *De Beat. Vit.* 10.

of mankind' that makes men choose, when they have to choose, the factor which in isolation leads away from happiness, instead of that which brings them nearer to it. We should choose the good will even without the possession of its objects ; for ' he is the nearer to happiness whose will is good and is directed to that which when attained will make him happy'. He who makes the good choice, with faith in God from whom all good comes, will be enabled hereafter to that which in this troublous life is impossible, namely, to live as he would. There, ' all that will be loved will be at hand ; nothing absent will be desired ; all there will be good, God above all the Supreme Good, present to be enjoyed by them that love Him ; and—highest happiness of all—security that so it will be for ever'. Here Augustine has shown the limits within which he can accept the Stoic thesis that happiness is a matter of the will. The Terentian maxim, ' Since what you want you cannot have, best wish for what you can ' is but ' counsel to the wretched to avoid worse wretchedness'. To the ideally happy man you *cannot* say ' What you wish is impossible', for he does not wish for what cannot be ; and the conclusion is that immortality is an absolute condition of perfect happiness. For we cannot at the same time wish for *beata vita* and acquiesce in its inevitable loss : we cannot be indifferent to the persistence of that which we desire and love. The question of course remains whether human nature is ' capable of immortality' and therefore of beatitude, and to that question Augustine's only answer is the revelation in Christ. The greater miracle, the sharing of our mortal, mutable nature by God Himself, is a pledge of the lesser, our being made partakers in the immortality of Him who is the changeless Good.[1]

Christ's message was that the Kingdom of Heaven is at hand ; but His Church has never been sure what this meant. The

[1] *De Trin.* XIII. 7-12. And cf. *En. in Ps.* CXLVIII. 8 : Plus est iam quod fecit quam quod promisit. . . . Incredibilius est quod mortuus est aeternus, quam ut in aeternum vivat mortalis.

Church that brought the Synoptic Gospels into being expected a divine event in the immediate future, and some transmutation of its eschatology was necessary for its continued existence. Transmutation or re-interpretation has never been carried further than in the New Testament itself. St. Paul and the Fourth Evangelist shifted the vital centre of Christianity from the earnest expectation of the Parousia to the present gift of the Spirit. *The Kingdom of Heaven is within you.* In the Church of the second and third centuries, the experience of persecution and the awareness of its own imperfect spirituality once more projected faith into hope. The Kingdom was not yet come : perhaps it was not even at hand.

Of this historic development Augustine's was a kind of re-flection. Neo-Platonism had established him in his preference of the changeless to the changing, but it had also encouraged him to hope that by a ' stripping-off' of what was mutable in himself he might attain here and now to the Immutable. The Catholic orthodoxy of the time, so far from conflicting with this hope, offered him its confirmation in the monastic ideal. When he wrote the *De Quantitate Animae,* he saw no reason why the soul, having attained the ' tranquillity' of complete purification through the practice of virtue, should not advance from the ' beginnings' (*ingressio*) of momentary intuition of the divine to a secure ' abiding' (*mansio*) of contemplative fruition, of full and unshakable apprehension of the truth of God.[1] Even in the *De Moribus Ecclesiae,* in which love is already challenging the primacy of knowledge, the ' Two Lives' still present themselves as earthly alternatives, between which the Christian chooses according to the intensity of his religion. But the *De Civitate* is eschatological through and through. It is the ' destined ends' of the Two Cities that govern the whole perspective. And so, in the last Homily on St. John's Gospel, the Two Lives appear in all the sharpness of contrast between this world and the world to come : ' the one in faith, the other in

---

[1] *De Quant. An.* 76.

evidence (*specie*) ; the one in the time of pilgrimage, the other in eternity of abiding ; the one in labour, the other in rest . . . the one in the work of activity, the other in the reward of contemplation . . . the one fights against the enemy, the other reigns unresisted . . . the one curbs the desires of the flesh, the other gives itself freely to the delights of the spirit . . . the one helps the needy, the other is where none are in need . . . the one is disciplined with evils, lest it be over-exalted by the good, the other is delivered from all evil in such fullness of grace that it holds fast to the Supreme Good, unassailed by pride. . . . Thus the one is good, but still in woe ; the other is better and is happy.' [1]

Bene vivendum est, bonum sperandum est. The *bene* of this life, and the *bonum* of the life eternal, are two different qualities. Virtue and happiness, the moral life and the ἀνθρώπινὸν ἀγαθόν or integral good of man, must have a common source. [2] But they cannot be identified, since morality is essentially a process of transformation from the worse to the better, whereas happiness demands the transcendence of change. We may conveniently reduce the endless antitheses in which Augustine's indefatigable rhetoric paints the contrast of the Here and the Hereafter, to an interconnected series of three pairs of opposed terms : Conflict and Peace, Action and Contemplation, Faith and Sight.

1. *Conflict and Peace*

Reading the sermons of the Bishop of Hippo in these war-stricken years, we catch the thrill of poignant longing which the very word *pax*, as he spoke it, would always stir in his hearers. It was enough for him to pronounce the text, *He maketh peace in thy borders*, and one great sigh would burst from the standing crowds beneath him. [3] ' *That in me ye might have peace.* Our Lord gives as the cause of His words that for which the whole

---

[1] *In Jo. Ev. Tr.* 124. 5.
[2] *Ep.* 130. 3 : Inde necesse est fiat homo beatus, unde fit bonus.
[3] *En. in Ps.* CXLVII. 15 : versum pronuntiavi, et exclamastis.

business of our Christianity is carried on. This peace will have no end in time, but will itself be the end of all our religious intention and activity. For this peace we are initiated in His sacraments, we are instructed by His marvellous works and words, we have received the earnest of His Spirit, we believe and hope in Him, and are kindled by His love in the measure in which He gives it to us. By this peace we are consoled in and delivered from all troubles, for this peace we bear all tribulation bravely, that in this peace, free from all tribulation, we may blissfully reign.'[1]

The Nineteenth Book of the *De Civitate* has made familiar to many who do not read much Augustine,[2] his great conception of the peace of society. His picture of the world as the 'broad sea', full of fishes devouring one another,[3] is drawn from life and not from theory. But the *Pax Romana*, though crumbling, was not yet in ruins while he lived ; and the Earthly City at its best (he could still say)[4] aims at and achieves an earthly peace which is a real good, in so far as it can be *used* by the citizens of the Heavenly City.[5] Yet both this 'peace of Babylon' and the 'proper peace' which the Christian has already here by faith, are no more than a 'solace of misery'.[6] The true 'peace of heaven', that 'perfectly ordered union of hearts in the enjoyment of God and of one another in God',[7] is the realisation of the City of God itself, 'peace in eternal life, or eternal life in peace'.[8] The Earthly City believes that peace can be procured by war,[9] because its aim is not a genuine community, but domination, the imposition of one will upon others.[10] The principle of the *pax caelestis* is 'not the desire of a personal, private will,

[1] *In Jo. Ev. Tr.* 104. 1.
[2] It is one of the books 'prescribed for study' for the Cambridge History Tripos.
[3] *De Civ.* XIX. 5-9. Cf. *En. in Ps.* LXIV. 9.
[4] *De Civ.* XV. 4 : quando est et ipsa in suo humano genere melior.
[5] *Ib.* XIX. 17, 26.   [6] *Ib.* 27.
[7] *Ib.* 17 : ordinatissima et concordissima societas fruendi Deo et invicem in Deo.
[8] *Ib.* 11.   [9] *Ib.* XV. 4.   [10] *Ib.* XIX. 12.

but the obedience of love delighting in that Good which is common to all and unchanging, making one heart out of many, the perfect concord '.[1] It is the character of goodness and peace to be increased instead of diminished by the multiplication of their possessors ; indeed ' he who will not have that possession in common, will not have it at all '.[2]

Much, no doubt, of the passion with which Augustine longed for peace, came from the weariness of spirit which the Donatist controversy must have caused him. ' We shall be as it were in a city—brethren, when I speak of it, I would fain speak on for ever, especially when offences multiply. Who would not long for that city, whence no friend goes out, where no enemy enters, where there is no tempter, no stirrer of faction, no divider of the people of God, no harasser of the Church in the devil's service ? . . . There will be peace in purity among the children of God, all full of love to one another, beholding one another full of God, when God will be all in all. All alike shall we have God for our beholding, all alike have God for our possession, all alike God for our peace.'[3]

Yet Augustine does not forget that peace within is the condition of peace without, and that it is more difficult to come by. ' Brethren, it is hard for us to be without quarrelling here. To concord we are called, we are bidden to have peace with one another ; and we must strive for it with all our strength, that one day we may come into the perfection of peace. But now we are often at odds with those whose welfare is our concern. This man is in error, you would lead him into the way, he resists you, and you are at odds. The pagan resists you, and you must dispute against the deceits of idols and devils ; the heretic, and you must dispute against other devils' teaching ; the bad Catholic will not lead a good life, and you must rebuke a brother within your own fold . . . sorely troubled how to rebuke so that you may render a good account of him to the Lord of you both. . . . Often a man says to himself in weariness :

---

[1] *De Civ.* xv. 3. [2] *Ib.* 5. Cf. *Serm.* 357, ' De Laude Pacis '.
[3] *En. in Ps.* lxxxiv. 10.

" Why should I suffer those who speak against me, who render evil for good ? I would help them, but they are bent on perdition : I waste my life in being at odds, I have no peace . . . let me return to myself and be alone with myself and call upon my God ". Return to yourself, and you will find quarrels there : if you have begun the following of God, you will find quarrels there.' [1]

There is no more impressive example of Augustine's eloquence than the three chapters in the last Book of the *De Civitate,* in which he preludes his final description of the blessedness to come.[2] It is an anticipation of Pascal's ' grandeur et misère de l'homme '. First he lays bare the appalling facts of sin and suffering ; then he deals with the moral struggle from which the best of Christians can hope for no release in this world ; [3] and then he launches into the superb panegyric of nature which both serves to show that only ' sin exceeding great ' can have caused the fall of a creature so magnificently endowed, and is at the same time ground for the conviction that *the sufferings of this present time are not worthy to be compared with the glory which shall be revealed.*

[1] *In Jo. Ev. Tr.* 34. 10.   [2] *De Civ.* XXII. 22-24.

[3] The account of the Christian warfare in c. 23 is so important for the light it throws on Augustine's moral ideals, and so valuable as a corrective to the impression of scrupulosity which is easily got from the Tenth Book of the *Confessions,* that it is worth quoting in full.—In the unending struggle of spirit against flesh, ' we must be continually on our guard, lest probable opinion deceive us or clever talk delude us, lest the darkness of any error spread over our mind, lest we believe good to be evil or evil to be good ; lest fear hold us back from what ought to be done or desire plunge us into what ought not ; lest the sun go down upon our wrath, lest enmities provoke us to return evil for evil ; lest unseemly or unrestrained grief absorb us ; lest ingratitude cause sluggishness in acts of kindness ; lest our good conscience be harassed by malicious rumours, lest rash suspicion against another lead us astray or the false suspicion of others against ourselves shake our resolution ; lest sin reign in our mortal body that we should obey the lusts thereof, lest our members be made weapons of unrighteousness unto sin, lest the eye follow after covetousness, lest the desire of avenging overcome us ; lest sight or thought dwell on that which gives wrongful pleasure, lest the ear give welcome to a naughty or unseemly word, lest an unlawful act be done even if desired ; lest in this warfare, so full of toils and dangers, our own strength be the source from which victory unachieved be expected, or the cause to which its achievement be attributed.'

But this life itself is nothing less than a ' hell '.¹ The two great causes of its miseries are the ' profundity of ignorance ' and the ' love of things vain and noxious ', and those very measures of education and prevention by which human nature attempts to meet them, involve us in ' labours and pains '. ' Why is it that we remember with labour, and forget without it ; that we learn with labour and without it are ignorant ; that activity involves labour and inactivity does not ? Does not this show the tendency of our spoilt nature to sink as it were by its own weight, and its great need of help to be freed from this condition ? Slackness, sloth, idleness, negligence, are indeed vices by which labour is avoided ; and yet labour itself, even useful labour, is a punishment.' ² *Labor* here, as generally in Augustine, does not mean ' work ', which he never disparages,—there was work in Paradise ! ³—but ' toil ' which is for him indisputably one of the world's evils.

And that is true of the moral struggle itself. ' Better is war with the hope of eternal peace, than captivity without any thought of deliverance. We desire indeed to be without that war, and we burn with the fire of divine love to reach the peace of perfect order where lower is subdued to higher in fixed security ; but if there were no hope of so great a good (which God forbid !), we ought to prefer remaining in the pains of this struggle rather than by abandoning resistance to allow our vices to lord it over us.' ⁴ This is the saying upon which Fénélon seized for his sorely-needed evidence that Augustine taught no inseparable connection between self-interest and the love of God. It is in fact quite irrelevant to his problem. Here it is no ' pure love ' in Fénélon's sense which is claimed to be independent of hope. Slavery to the lower nature is pronounced the greater evil, worse even than an unending conflict. What Augustine

¹ Christ saves us ' ab huius tam miserae quasi quibusdam inferis vitae ' (*De Civ.* XXII. 22).
² *Ib.* 22.
³ *De Gen. ad litt.* VIII. 15 ff. And cf. esp. the *De Opere Monachorum*.
⁴ *De Civ.* XXI. 15.

57

insists upon is that the Christian conflict, ' this conflict of ours in which we are in jeopardy and from which we long for final victory to deliver us, it too belongs to the evils of this life '.[1] And there is no respite on earth. ' So long as we live here, brethren, thus it is with us : thus we too, veterans in this life of warfare, may have lesser enemies, but enemies we have.' [2] ' We must always be fighting ; for the concupiscence with which we were born cannot be done away so long as we live. Each day it may be lessened, done away it cannot be.' [3] In his younger days Augustine had taken the seventh chapter of the Epistle to the Romans to refer to man as he is ' under the law ' ; later he was convinced that even ' under grace ' the fight of spirit against flesh must be carried on.[4]

This sense of the moral struggle's reality and urgency, as of a warfare that ends only with death, is what marks the Christian character of Augustine's ethical dualism, and distinguishes him from Manichaean, Neo-Platonist and Pelagian alike. Against Manichaean evasion of personal responsibility, attributing all moral failure to an alien principle of evil within us, he asserts the indivisible unity of the self : ' It was I that willed and I that willed not—the self-same I '.[5] In Plotinus the absence of any real sense of sin is notorious : his conception of moral progress was one rather of detachment and emancipation than of struggle and victory ; [6] and Augustine did not need the Epistle to the Romans to discover the shortcomings of his master in philosophy as an ethical teacher.

Among his Pelagian adversaries there were two very different points of view. Pelagius and Caelestius were rigorist monks who believed that despair of perfection makes the best excuse for laxity, and that the moral fibre of the average Christian can only be kept sound if he is assured of his freedom to avoid

---

[1] *De Civ.* xxii. 23.   [2] *Serm.* 128. 11.
[3] *Ib.* 151. 5.   [4] *Retr.* i. 23.
[5] *Conf.* viii. 22. Cf. *ib.* v. 18 : excusare me amabam et accusare nescio quid aliud, quod mecum esset et ego non essem.
[6] Cf. *Enn.* i. viii. 8 : ἀλλὰ κρατεῖν ἔδει, ἄλλος ἂν εἴποι · ἀλλ' οὐ καθαρὸν τὸ δυνάμενον κρατεῖν, εἰ μὴ φύγοι.

sin 'if he will'. To them Augustine replied that if despair is Scylla, presumption is Charybdis, and that the only way to escape both is to recognise that we are not born free but have to achieve freedom : the only safe rule is ' Make neither of your own righteousness a safe-conduct to heaven, nor of God's mercy a safe-conduct to sin '.[1] ' So long as we live, our perfection is humility.' [2] Augustine was convinced that our state of moral imperfection serves the purposes of God as a constant warning against pride. The worst danger that besets man, placed as he is but a little lower than the angels, is the worship of himself; and there can be no safeguard from this danger but the daily need to pray *Forgive us our trespasses*.[3]

This was the answer to Pelagianism in its original and characteristic form, as an excessive confidence not so much in man's natural goodness as in the natural supremacy of his reason over his appetite. Stranger to Augustine and more interesting to us was the attitude of Julian of Eclanum, that singular champion of rationalist enlightenment, who seems to have been born fourteen centuries out of due time. Julian, seeing in Augustine's doctrine nothing but a vilification of the nature which God made good, asserts the moral indifference of concupiscence, understood as man's natural tendency to seek satisfaction for his animal desires, and the wholesomeness of the contest through which he is enabled to confine their satisfaction within due bounds. As usual, much of a tedious controversy could have been avoided if the disputants had defined their terms. The words *concupiscentia* and *libido* as used by Julian meant the desire regarded in itself, a natural good because implanted by the Creator, but no more than the raw material of morality ; to Augustine the same words signified a desire already disorderly and perverted, the flesh already in revolt against the spirit. Julian had the best of the formal argument, for Augustine ought to have admitted a distinction between the desire itself and the disorder in the soul which makes the desire unruly. But where Augustine saw

[1] *En. in Ps.* xxxi. ii. 1.   [2] *Ib.* cxxx. 14.
[3] *C. Jul. Pel.* iv. 28 f.

anarchy, Julian saw merely the possibility of excess : in his view
the moral life is a sort of boxing match, a fight between friends
to be fought without passion or rancour ; and to Augustine the
perversity of such an attitude was as manifest as its sanity has
become to many minds to-day. For him, it turned the Christian
warfare into a sham, and took all the seriousness out of our
earthly existence. Victory is no real good unless it has been
won over what is really evil ; that the warfare is necessary is
itself an evil, and this evil he could only understand as the penalty
of sin. Julian denied both original sin and the penal character
of the moral conflict ; and if he did not assert in so many words
the goodness of the conflict as such, the practical basis of his
ethics is the ancient Heracleitean paradox that ' War is the
Father and King of all '—man's inveterate inclination to make a
philosophy out of his own instinct of pugnacity.[1] Augustine
held that the war in our members is as evil a thing as the warring
of man against man which is its outcome ; that all real fighting
is for the sake of peace and not for the sake of exercising the
fighter's muscles or courage ; and that, as a fact of experience,
fighting lasts till death : the peace which is the ' perfect soundness
of perfect love ' is unattainable on earth.

2. *Action and Contemplation*

In the early commentary upon the Sermon on the Mount,
Augustine had fitted his exegesis of the Beatitudes to correspond
to Isaiah's seven gifts of the Spirit. ' Wisdom ', he wrote, ' is
proper to the peacemakers, in whom all has been brought to
order, and there is no movement of rebellion against reason, but
all is subject to the spirit of man, man himself being subject to
God.' [2] For ' those are peacemakers in themselves, who, com-
posing and subjecting to reason . . . all the motions of their
soul, and having their carnal desires tamed, become the Kingdom
of God. . . . And that is the peace which is given on earth to

---

[1] And here Julian might have quoted Plotinus. Cf. *Enn.* III. ii. 16.
[2] *De Serm. Dom. in Mont.* I. 11.

men of good will : that is the life of the consummate and perfect man of wisdom.'[1] The peacemakers' reward is to be called the children of God, because God's likeness is conferred on ' those who have attained perfect wisdom, and are conformed to His image by the renewal of regeneration '. What is more, ' all this can be fulfilled in this present life, as we believe it was fulfilled in the Apostles '.[2]

In the *Retractations*[3] Augustine frankly admits the difficulty of justifying such language. That there should be *no* law in the members resisting the law of the mind, is a consummation granted to no one in this life. But the passage well indicates the link between our first antithesis—Conflict and Peace, and our second—Action and Contemplation. For this wisdom, which ' sets the whole man at peace ', is there expressly identified with the ' contemplation of the truth '.[4] The peace which is the end of conflict is no mere negation : it is both condition and effect of the soul's highest activity ; and this is the first point to be emphasised in considering the use which Augustine makes of the traditional opposition of Active and Contemplative Lives. Neither Latin nor English have any convenient equivalent for Aristotle's distinction between the ἐνέργεια which is the performance of function by an organism and the πρᾶξις which may form part of the ἐνέργεια but itself denotes the outward and visible engagement of a person in his environment. But there can be no doubt that the starting-point of Augustine's doctrine is the Platonic-Aristotelian principle that *theoria* or contemplation is the true specific function of the reasonable being. In Plotinus, *Nous* is that self-contemplation of the One from which all the manifold world of existence flows. Augustine had seen immediately the appropriateness of this theology as an expression of the Christian faith in Christ—the Wisdom which is the Word or perfect Image of the Father, and at the same time the principle of creation ; and once seized, he never abandoned it.

The entire structure of the later books of the *De Trinitate* is

[1] *De Serm. Dom. in Mont.* I. 9. [2] *Ib.* 12.
[3] *Retr.* I. 19. [4] *De Serm. Dom. in Mont.* I. 10.

governed by the thought that if God's image, as Scripture teaches, is to be found in man, it must be in man as capable of sharing in the Wisdom which is Christ. In Book XII he seeks to determine the region of man's being to which this capacity is to be assigned. It can only be in that faculty which differentiates him from the brute, his reason. But the reason's function is two-fold, 'active' and 'contemplative'. 'When we live according to God, it is clear that our mind, intent upon the invisible things of Him, should be progressively conformed to the pattern of His eternity, truth, and love ; but that a part of the reasonable power of this same mind of ours must be applied to the use of things mutable and corporeal, without which this life cannot be lived. Not that we should be conformed to this world, placing our end in such goods and diverting towards them our impulse to happiness ; but that all the reasonable actions which we perform in the use of things temporal, be done in contemplation of things eternal to be gained, so that we pass through the first and cleave to the second.' [1] So is introduced the grand theme of the next two Books—*Scientia* and *Sapientia*, Knowledge and Wisdom, their spheres, functions and relations. Knowledge is of the temporal, Wisdom of the eternal ; and the temporal is the field of action, the eternal of contemplation.[2]

Sympathy is the first requirement for the understanding of any great religious genius ; and Augustine's Catholic interpreters are certainly our best guides in the study of his spirituality. But

---

[1] *De Trin.* XII. 21.

[2] Professor Gilson seems to be mistaken (*Introduction à l'Étude de Saint Augustin*, pp. 144 ff.) in thinking that Augustine represents *Scientia* as not only inferior in dignity to *Sapientia*, but naturally inclined to the degradation of egoism, the use of the whole for the sake of the part. The 'Active Reason', like Eve, is the first to suffer the corruption of sin ; but its natural and proper function is still to direct our practical life. Cf. *De Trin.* XII. 17 : cum ergo huic intentioni mentis quae in rebus temporalibus et corporalibus propter actionis officium ratiocinandi vivacitate versatur, carnalis ille sensus vel animalis ingruit quamdam illecebram fruendi se, id est, tamquam bono quodam privato et proprio, non tamquam publico atque communi quod est incommutabile bonum, *tunc* velut serpens alloquitur feminam.

they are generally more concerned to trace in the father of Christian mysticism as much as possible of that wealth of doctrine of which he is the chief source, than to distinguish what is individual in his personal religion.[1] The *De Quantitate Animae,* for example, has no doubt had an immense influence upon later thought and experience ; but in Augustine's religious development it represents an immaturity soon outgrown, and it ought not to be quoted in illustration of the characteristically Augustinian positions. The silence of the *Retractations* is not good evidence against serious changes of view. We have already observed that Augustine had begun his Christian life with the ideal of the *vita contemplativa.* His ordination to the priesthood in 391 forced a re-orientation upon his thought, and he came by degrees to regard the Two Lives as to be lived by all Christians successively rather than by different Christians simultaneously.

The first extended discussion of Action and Contemplation occurs in the *Contra Faustum,*[2] written about 400. The two wives of Jacob signify the two lives—' the one temporal in which we labour, the other eternal in which we shall contemplate the fair beauty of God '. The change of tense from present to future is deliberate, and the immediate purport is that none may hope for the vision which is Rachel till they have bent themselves to the labour which is Leah. But in the sequel a phrase is dropped [3] which makes it clear that Augustine is still thinking of an attainment of wisdom and understanding in this life ; though all who seek it must be warned that here it will bring no exemption from the ' toil of righteousness ' which is its condition.

A little later, in the *De Consensu Evangelistarum,*[4] the Synoptist and Johannine Gospels are compared to the ' two virtues offered to man's soul, the one active, the other contemplative ; the one by which we journey, the other which brings us to journey's

---

[1] Or, conversely (*cf.* E. Hendrikx, *Augustins Verhältnis zur Mystik*), a strict application of the orthodox distinction between ' acquired ' and ' infused ' contemplation may lead to the denial that Augustine was a ' mystic ' at all.

[2] *C. Faust. Man.* XXII. 52 ff.

[3] *Ib.* 53 : simul habebitur in hoc saeculo.

[4] *De Cons. Evang.* I. 5.

end ; the one whereby we labour, to purify the heart for the vision of God, the other which makes labour cease and God be seen ; the one in precepts for the living of this temporal life, the other in the teaching of that life which is eternal '. So far we might suppose that the ' two virtues ' correspond simply to the exercise of morality and religion respectively, both equally needed here and now. But Augustine proceeds : ' Therefore the one is at work, the other at rest ; for the one is in the cleansing of sins, the other in the light which lightens them that are cleansed. Therefore in this mortal life the one is in the use of a good conversation, the other is rather in faith, and only for a very few, in a glass darkly and in part, in a certain vision of changeless Truth.' A precious straw, this last hesitating sentence, to show where the wind is blowing. If indeed the ' contemplative virtue ' attains its object in this world only for a privileged few, and for them only in obscure and broken glimpses, what of the many ? Is their religion to be morality and nothing more ? The answer is that they too have their contemplation, but that it is a contemplation in the form of faith. We shall see the significance of this when we come to deal with the last of our three antitheses. Meanwhile we may note that in so far as Augustine in his maturity allows a place for contemplation in the ordinary life of Christians, it is for a contemplation shorn of the intellectualist pretensions of the *De Quantitate Animae* and claiming none of the special favours of illuminative exaltation which had meant so much to him in his youth. When he wrote the Twelfth Book of his commentary on Genesis, and speculated on the third heaven and the Paradise to which St. Paul had been rapt away, he might well have made the Apostle's words his own : he too knew a man in Christ above fourteen years ago, of whom he might glory ; but of himself he had found it better to glory in the things which concerned his infirmities.

Perhaps the real Augustine is seen most clearly in the Johannine Homily from which we have already quoted. The Two Lives are figured in Peter and John, the loving and the beloved disciples.

Peter is called loving rather than beloved; for we know our present trouble and so must needs love the Saviour who delivers us from it, whereas the Lord's love for us is less manifest in our trouble than in our joy. John is beloved rather than loving; because we as yet know not and possess not that contemplation of truth wherein true joy is given to us. Christ's last words to Peter mean: 'Let perfect action follow me, formed on the example of my passion; but let contemplation in its beginnings tarry till I come, to be made perfect when I come'.[1]

The form of this 'inchoate contemplation' is that very 'search' for God of which so many of Augustine's writings, and above all the second parts of the *Confessions* and the *De Trinitate*, provide examples. The method has been well described by the Augustinian Father Fulbert Cayré. It is, 'through an intellectual discipline, mystical in tendency, to lift up the reader, little by little, to that spiritual state which is the indispensable condition of the fuller enlightenment'.[2] The aim is not to demonstrate theological propositions, but to *show* God, to bring Him into the heart so that He may be 'felt'. So much Augustine did believe to be possible, and possible for all: the *Confessions*, at least, he did not write for an intellectual élite. And such separate acts of 'contemplative meditation', such liftings-up of the heart to God, are to be the pattern for the gradual day-by-day renewal or restoration of the divine image in the soul, grace working for the perfection of nature.

Augustine's favourite allegory of Action and Contemplation, especially in his *Sermons*,[3] is the pair of sisters, Martha and Mary. He could tell his congregations that by their presence in Church they are taking Mary's part:[4] the joy with which they welcome a true word spoken by the preacher is of the same kind as her joy, a delight incommensurable with any of the world's pleasures.[5] But the point on which he always dwells is that Mary's part

---

[1] *In Jo. Ev. Tr.* 124. 5 f.
[2] F. Cayré, *La Contemplation Augustinienne*, p. 240.
[3] E.g. *Serm.* 104, 169, 179, 255.
[4] *Ib.* 104. 4.   [5] *Ib.* 179. 6.

shall not be taken away from her. 'Assuredly there will be a " taking away" from every man who ministers to the bodily necessities of the saints. . . . To what does he minister but to infirmity, to the hungry and thirsty ? All these things will be no more when this corruptible shall have put on incorruption. For when the need itself has passed, there will be no more ministering to need : the labour will be taken away, and the reward given. . . . So the part of Martha passes, but the reward given for it passes not. . . . That which Mary chose, increased and did not pass.'[1] So congenial to his mind was this turn of the allegory that we find him following it unconsciously in expounding the 84th Psalm. The 'mother of all human actions' is 'necessity' or need : 'all the good works which are enjoined upon us are the product of need, caused by the frailty of our flesh'. The journey of the saints *from strength to strength* (*ab virtutibus in virtutem*) means that the many ' virtues ', necessary to be practised here, will disappear when the need for them passes, and there will remain the single ' virtue ' which consists in the contemplation of God.[2] Action is related to contemplation as means to end, as service to reward. The *man-child* with whom the Church is in travail is the ' fruit of contemplation ' to which ' all the offices of action are referred '. As the end sought for its own sake, contemplation alone is free ; action is its servant.[3]

These phrases are very near Plotinus. But in Plotinus, all action, whether the outcome of need or freedom, is by its very nature an 'effort towards vision'. Like ' duller children, inapt to study and speculation ', who ' take to crafts and manual labour ', men who are ' spiritually feeble ' ' find in action their trace of vision ' : they ' act from the desire of seeing their action ', they ' desire a certain thing to come about not in order to be unaware of it, but to know it, to see it present before the mind '. Action is just the ' round-about path ' to contemplation.[4] If in Augustine the relation of action to contemplation is different, it

---

[1] *Serm.* 179. 4 ff.   [2] *En. in Ps.* LXXXIII. 8, 11.
[3] *In Jo. Ev. Tr.* 101. 5.   [4] *Enn.* III. viii. 1, 4, 6 (tr. Mackenna).

is because his thought was never purely Hellenic : he could never envisage the means as no more than a kind of blurred shadow of the end. ' Martha's part is where we are ; Mary's, what we hope for. Let us do the first well, that we may possess the second fully.'[1] ' Of the good work which shall pass, the reward is a rest which shall endure. In that contemplation God will be all in all, for nothing else will be sought from Him : to be transfused by His light, to enjoy His presence, will alone suffice.'[2]

For adherence to the Platonist teaching that man's highest good is the vision of God, to which the whole moral life is subordinate, Augustine might claim the warrant of Scripture and tradition. But in what sense was this subordination to be understood ? Scripture and tradition spoke in terms of obedience, merit, and reward. Platonism, with a conception of the divine holiness which was physical rather than ethical, based on the opposition of spirit and matter rather than on that of righteousness and sin, insisted upon the need for purification. For like is known by like. Platonist and Christian were agreed that only the pure in heart may see God ; and when Plotinus said that the purifying of the soul means ὁμοίωσις θεῷ, being made like to God, he was putting forward an ideal which at first sight was in complete harmony with Christianity. ' The gist of religion is the imitation of what is worshipped '[3]—there might be a worse summary of the Sermon on the Mount. But in the Neo-Platonist scheme, the soul achieves true likeness to God only in the measure in which its activity becomes the activity of pure *Nous* or Spirit, and its purification is therefore a cleansing from the defilement of alien matter, a process of release from encumbrance, an escape. This is the ' greater virtue ' ; the ' civic virtues ' of the older Platonic tradition have their function, but it is the inferior one of bringing order and form into the chaos of

---

[1] *Serm.* 104. 4. [2] *De Trin.* I. 20.
[3] *De Civ.* VIII. 17. Cf. *ib.* IX. 17, where Augustine gives a conflate quotation of *Enn.* I. vi. 8 and ii. 3, and adds that for the Christian ὁμοίωσις Θεῷ demands the Incarnate Mediator : true divinity is not ' defiled by the flesh '.

the life of passion.[1] It has been observed that there is little stress
on asceticism in Plotinus—less than in Clement of Alexandria,
for example. But we must remember the peculiar tranquillity
of temperament of which the *Enneads* themselves are as good
evidence as Porphyry's *Life*. What is remarkable is that asceticism
is not more prominent in Augustine.

We do indeed find in his early works a theory of purification
almost identical with that of Plotinus. To see the face of God,
we must turn to Him ' from the mire and defilement of the body,
and from the darkness of error '.[2] For the sight of any object
we need both sound eyes and a right direction of them. The
sound eye is the ' mind pure of all bodily stain ', ' remote and
cleansed from the desires of things mortal '.[3] Moral purification
thus has the negative aspect of escape from the material, deliverance from the sway of bodily passions. Positively, purification
is intellectual, being the training of the mind to apply itself to
spiritual truth. But the dominant impulse is at least as much
aesthetic as intellectual. ' The face of God is that Truth unto
which love makes us yield ourselves in purity and beauty ' ; [4]
and what makes the soul unclean is ' love of the inferior beauty '
of the material world.[5] In all this Augustine is but reproducing
the famous tractate of Plotinus *On the Beautiful*.[6] Yet from the
first we can see that the Christian leaven is at work. The meaning of ὁμοίωσις Θεῷ must naturally depend upon the character
assigned to God ; and though, as we have seen, there was a
sense in which Augustine could accept the principle that ' there
is no virtue in the Supreme ' [7]—in so far as he regarded moral
activity as dependent upon need—yet the metaphysic of Plotinus
could not undo the effects of the teaching of Monica. Even at
Cassiciacum, Augustine prayed to the God and Father of Jesus
Christ, and the spirit of his devotion did not fail to reflect itself
in the Dialogues. ' Vision ', he says at the end of the *De Ordine*,
' will be given to him who lives well, prays well, and studies

[1] *Enn.* I. ii. 2.   [2] *De Ord.* I. 23.   [3] *Solil.* I. 12.
[4] *De Ord.* I. 23 : cui nos amatae mundos pulchrosque reddimus.
[5] *De Mus.* VI. 46, 50.   [6] *Enn.* I. vi.   [7] *Ib.* I. ii. 6.

well '; for God will hear the prayer of the good liver.[1] More-over, in his account of the good life itself, the moral discipline elaborated in detail in the same dialogue, though abstinence from the pleasures of sense receives first place, the stress is laid upon the social virtues of kindliness, charitableness and goodwill; [2] and in the *De Musica* the ' divinely-enjoined action ' whereby the defiled and burdened soul may be purified and set at rest, is obedience to the Gospel command to love God with all our heart and our neighbour as ourself.[3]

The apparent approval of Porphyry's maxim—' Flee from all that is bodily '—is one of the errors in the Dialogues which are noted in the *Retractations*.[4] The Neo-Platonist attitude to the body became untenable for Augustine, when he discovered that the Catholic faith in the Word made flesh was more than the acceptance of a divinely-authorised teaching and example. It was his firmer theology of the Incarnation that made it possible for the author of the *Confessions* and the antagonist of Julian to maintain a Christian ethic less defective than that which the ' sunny-souled ' Alexandrian had preached in his *Paedagogus* and embodied in his ' Gnostic '. It is to be remarked that even as early as in the *De Sermone Domini in Monte* Augustine avoids, in dealing with the Beatitude on the pure in heart, any suggestion of either asceticism or intellectualism. Purity of heart is the ' preparation of a good conscience ' for the vision ; and the ' simplicity ' in which he finds it to consist is not aloofness from things corporeal, but singleness of religious motive.[5]

Augustine never ceased to believe that through the life of moral activity men become fit for the contemplation of God. Especially in his *Expositions of the Psalms* we find passages of great beauty in which the purification of the heart is treated in the spirit and often in the phraseology of Plotinus.[6] In the full

---

[1] *De Ord.* II. 51 f. [2] *Ib.* 25. [3] *De Mus.* VI. 43.
[4] *Retr.* I. 4. [5] *De Serm. Dom. in Mont.* I. 10 ; II. 1 ff.
[6] E.g. *En. in Ps.* XXXIII. ii. 8 : Cum ergo intras cubiculum tuum, intras cor tuum. . . . Ut possis libens redire ad cor tuum, munda illud. . . . Aufer inde cupiditatum sordes, aufer labem avaritiae, aufer tabem superstitionum, aufer sacrilegia et malas cogitationes, odia, non dico adversus amicum, sed etiam

maturity of the Johannine Homilies he will speak of the ' precepts of righteousness '—' Lie not, perjure not, do not commit adultery, theft, or fraud '—as the ' stinging eye-salves ' which the divine Physician will apply to those who have ' lifted up their heart to behold the Word, and, dazzled by His light, have fallen back to common things '.[1] In a sermon on the same passage—the healing of the man born blind—the sphere of purgation is drawn wider. ' Our whole business in this life is to heal the heart's eye by which God is seen. For this the holy mysteries are celebrated, for this the word of God is preached ; this end is served by the Church's moral exhortations, touching the correction of conduct, the amendment of carnal desires, the renouncing of this world not with our lips only but by a changed life ; this end is served by all Holy Scripture : that the inner man may be purged from that which hinders us from looking upon God.' [2]

But already when he wrote his *Confessions,* Augustine had put his finger on the point where Plotinus not only fell short of the Gospel but gravely obstructed its understanding.[3] The specifically Christian ethic, as he came to see, must be an ethic based on the Incarnation, and that means an ethic divided by a great gulf from the Neo-Platonist. ' There are some ', he says, ' who think that they can be purified for the contemplation of God and for union with Him by their own virtue—whose pride is itself the deepest stain upon them ; for there is no fault to which the law of God is more contrary.' [4] The pride of Platonism is based, he admits, on a real measure of spiritual apprehension granted to such rare souls as Plotinus himself. But he claims that Porphyry's own words—' granted to a few '—should have compelled him

---

adversus inimicum : aufer ista omnia ; intra in cor tuum, et gaudebis ibi. Cum ibi coeperis gaudere, ipsa munditia cordis tui delectabit te, et faciet orare : quomodo si venias ad aliquem locum, silentium est ibi, forte quies est ibi, mundus est locus ; Oremus hic, dicis ; et delectat te compositio loci, et credis quod ibi te exaudiat Deus. Si ergo loci visibilis te delectat munditia, quare te non offendit immunditia cordis tui ? Cf. *Enn.* I. vi. 9 (quoted below, p. 90) and the ruthless ἄφελε πάντα at the end of *Enn.* v. iii (above p. 35).

[1] *In Jo. Ev. Tr.* 18. 11.   [2] *Serm.* 88. 5.
[3] *Conf.* VII. 13, 26 f.   [4] *De Trin.* IV. 20.

to acknowledge that this apprehension was a gift and not an achievement.[1] The sin which is the only barrier between man and God can be purged only by an act of God, not by an act of man : ' not by our virtue but by the divine compassion '.[2] The one purgation for iniquity and pride is in ' the blood of the Righteous and the humility of God '.[3] The soul's cleansing is a journey—in the phrase of Plotinus a ' voyage to the fatherland ' —but it is a journey which we could not make, had not the Way itself come down to us.[4] Stoic and Epicurean mistook the goal ; the Platonist sees it rightly, but the failure of his philosophy is as complete as that of the others ; ' for they all lacked the pattern of divine humility '.[5] ' Build for yourself no other road for the attainment and possession of the truth, than that which has been built by Him who saw as God the weakness of our walking. And that is, first, humility, second, humility, third, humility. . . . Not that there are no other commandments to be named ; but unless humility precedes, accompanies, and follows all our good actions, unless humility be set before us for our beholding, beside us for our adherence, over us for our restraint, then all the good of our joy in any right action is wrested from us by pride.' [6] By the ' meek and lowly hyssop ' we are purged and made clean ; and the sign of the Cross is

---

[1] *De Civ.* x. 29.   [2] *Ib.* 22.
[3] *De Trin.* IV. 4.   [4] *De Doctr. Christ.* I. 10 f.
[5] *Ep.* 118. 17. Cf. *Serm.* 141. 1 : Veritatem et vitam omnis homo cupit : sed viam non omnis homo invenit. Deum esse quamdam vitam aeternam, immutabilem . . . nonnulli etiam huius saeculi philosophi viderunt. Veritatem fixam, stabilem, indeclinabilem, ubi sunt omnes rationes rerum omnium creatarum viderunt quidem, sed de longinquo ; viderunt, sed in errore positi ; et idcirco ad eam tam magnam et ineffabilem et beatificam possessionem, qua via perveniretur, non invenerunt. *En. in Ps.* XXXI. ii. 18 : Haec aqua confessionis peccatorum, haec aqua humiliationis cordis . . . abicientis se, nihil de se praesumentis, nihil suae potentiae superbe tribuentis—haec aqua in nullis alienigenarum libris est, non in epicureis, non in stoicis, non in manichaeis, non in platonicis. Ubicumque etiam inveniuntur optima praecepta morum et disciplinae, humilitas tamen ista non invenitur. Via humilitatis huius aliunde manat : a Christo venit. Haec via ab illo est, qui cum esset altus, humilis venit.
[6] *Ep.* 118. 22.

the measure of all Christian activity which can so purify the heart that it may know the love of Christ which passeth knowledge.[1]

In the Seventh Book of the *Confessions,* after describing the momentary illumination which had followed his study of Plotinus, Augustine tells us that he found no way of gaining spiritual strength for the fruition of God, till he 'embraced the Mediator of God and men, the man Christ Jesus'. 'Not yet had I hold of my master Jesus, a hold in lowliness of the Lowly one.'[2] And in the Tenth Book, at the end of the long self-examination in which he has sought to lay bare the imperfections which still kept him from the peace of union with God, he speaks once more of those rare moments, strangely sweet, that are like anticipations of another life.[3] But the moments are fleeting as ever : 'from such communion' he passes 'into the old solitary nothingness '—but not, ike Caponsacchi's 'drudging student', 'content'. *Resorbeor solitis, et teneor, et multum fleo, sed multum teneor. I am cast out from the sight of thine eyes.* And again the only comfort is the Mediator, sent to men that from His example they might learn humility, the Victor and the Victim, *ideo victor quia victima.* 'We might have thought that Thy Word was far removed from union with man, and so despaired of ourselves, had He not been made flesh and dwelt among us. Fearful because of my sins, weighed down with wretchedness, I had it in my heart to make my escape into solitude. But Thou didst prevent me and strengthen me, saying, "Therefore Christ died for all, that those who live should no longer live unto themselves, but unto Him

---

[1] *De Doctr. Christ.* II. 62.

[2] *Conf.* VII. 24 : Skutella prefers the reading ' deum ' for ' dominum ', but I have kept ' dominum ' as better suiting the words which follow : ' nec cuius rei *magistra* esset eius infirmitas noveram.'

[3] *Ib.* X. 65 : et aliquando intromittis me in affectum multum inusitatum introrsus ad nescio quam dulcedinem, quae si perficiatur in me, nescio quid erit, quod vita ista non erit.—Clearly the same experience as that of the Ostia vision. Cf. *Ib.* IX. 25 : Si continuetur hoc et subtrahantur aliae visiones longe imparis generis, et haec una rapiat et absorbeat et recondat in interiora gaudia spectatorem suum, ut talis sit sempiterna vita, quale fuit hoc momentum intelligentiae cui suspiravimus, etc.

who died for them ".'[1] The voice of the people of Hippo—
Augustinus presbyter !—was indeed the voice of God. Only when
the mistake has been made of seeing in Augustine's moments of
contemplative exaltation his ideal of Christian life in this world,
is it possible to charge him with an ultimate indifference to the
Person of the Incarnate Christ.[2]

3. Faith and Sight

Augustinian humility is not a purely moral characteristic
which may belong to any man without regard to his religion.
It has nothing to do with self-depreciation. It is the humility
of the believer as such, the manward aspect of faith in God
as the source of all good, the necessary implication of
acceptance of the doctrine of grace. ' There is humility in
faith ' ;[3] ' faith belongs to the humble, not to the proud '.[4]
We find accordingly that as grace assumes the central place in
his theology, Augustine begins habitually to set the words of
Peter's speech at the Apostolic Council—*purifying their hearts by
faith* [5]—beside the Beatitude on the pure in heart, and to speak
of faith itself as the means of purification.

It is true that from the first he had insisted on the need of

---

[1] *Conf.* x. 69 f.

[2] The mistake is made e.g. by R. Newton Flew in his *Idea of Perfection in
Christian Theology*, pp. 214 ff., following Herrmann and others. Both Dr
Flew's citations are misleading : (a) in *De Doctr. Christ.* I. 38 Augustine nowhere
says that thoughts of ' Christ the Man ' ' belong to the *things behind* ' (Phil.
iii. 13) which must be forgotten ; (b) the 98th Homily on St. John is not fairly
summarised by the statement that ' even thoughts of the example of Christ and
of His sufferings are described as milk for babes ! ' Dr Flew can hardly have
read c. 6 : ' proinde nec sic parvuli sunt lactandi, ut semper non intelligant
Deum Christum ; *nec sic ablactandi, ut deserant hominem Christum.* . . . In hoc
quippe non convenit huic rei similitudo materni lactis et solidi cibi, sed potius
fundamenti ; quia et puer quando ablactatur, ut ab alimentis infantiae iam
recedat, inter solidos cibos non repetit ubera quae sugebat ; *Christus* autem
crucifixus et lac sugentibus et cibus est proficientibus. Fundamenti vero ideo est
aptior similitudo, quia ut perficiatur quod struitur, additur aedificium, non
subtrahitur fundamentum.'

[3] *In Jo. Ev. Tr.* 40. 8.   [4] *Serm.* 115. 2.   [5] *Acts* xv. 9.

faith for the cleansing of the soul. But its function had been
that of a necessary preliminary to or condition of moral effort.
No one will take the trouble to mend his eyesight till he believes
that there is something to see worth the seeing.[1] ' Sinners are
bidden to believe, in order that through believing they may
be cleansed from their sin. For they know not what vision
they are to gain by a life of righteousness ; and therefore,
since they cannot have the vision unless they live aright, nor
have they strength to live aright unless they believe, it is
evident that faith must be the starting-point.'[2] Here faith
is still no more than assent to the proposition that what
purifies the soul and enables it to ' see ' is obedience to the
' commandments '.

At this stage, the meaning of faith is determined by the
contrast between Reason and Authority which is dominant in
the works of Augustine's anti-Manichaean period. Authority
demands faith, reason leads to understanding.[3] But it is to be
noted that Authority's concern is rather with ethics than with
dogma : the faith which it demands is an acceptance not so
much of the Church's creed as of the Church's values and the
Church's rule of life.[4] On the other hand, whereas at Cassiciacum
Reason had promised to make God as visible to the eye of
Augustine's mind as the sun to his bodily eye,[5] her claims grew
more and more modest as the years advanced, and in the developed
theory of faith's relation to understanding, expressed in the
famous *Crede ut intelligas,* the understanding which faith makes
possible always remains in this life something less than vision :
it is but the progressive deepening of apprehension in spiritual
things, a finding which provokes search. ' The certitude of
faith is a kind of beginning of knowledge ; the certainty of

[1] *Solil.* I. 12 f. [2] *De Div. Quaest. LXXXIII.* 68. 3.
[3] *De Ver. Relig.* 45.
[4] See *De Ord.* II. 26. *De Util. Cred.* 33 ff. It is to the question ' Quomodo homini sit vivendum ' that an answer is sought both from Reason and Authority in the *De Moribus Ecclesiae.*
[5] *Solil.* I. 12.

knowledge will not be perfected save after this life when we shall see face to face.'[1]

So, as contemplation recedes into the life to come, faith enlightened by understanding according to the measure of the believer's capacity takes its place in this world. And the faith whose primary significance had been the submission to an authoritative ethic comes to denote the necessary intellectual attitude of fallen man, the children's milk, the nourishment of ' those who are not yet capable of the knowledge of things spiritual and eternal ',[2] ' whose mind cannot look upon the inner light of truth '.[3] There is no opposition between faith and understanding : the highest gifts of understanding do not make faith superfluous. But faith and vision are contraries which exclude one another. To believe is always ' to believe what as yet you do not see ' ; [4] and we naturally ask how an act of intellectual apprehension, the admitted inadequacy of which has been caused by the moral disqualification of sin, can serve to remove that disqualification.

Augustine answered the question by applying the Platonic metaphysic itself to the Christian doctrine of the historic Incarnation, the doctrine which he knew was to the Greeks foolishness.

---

[1] *De Trin.* IX. I.   Cf. *En. in Ps.* cxviii. xviii. 3 : quamvis enim, nisi aliquid intelligat, nemo possit credere in Deum ; tamen ipsa fide qua credit, sanatur, ut intelligat ampliora. . . . Proficit ergo noster intellectus ad intelligenda quae credat, et fides proficit ad credenda quae intelligat ; et eadem ipsa ut magis magisque intelligantur, in ipso intellectu proficit mens.—In the *De Utilitate Credendi* (of 391) Augustine had divided ' personae in religione laudabiles ' into those who ' have found ' and are therefore ' beatissimi ', and those who still diligently and worthily seek.   In the *Retractations* (I. 13), while not denying that some measure of real finding, a ' mental vision ' which is more than faith, is possible in this life, he insists that such ' knowledge in part ' can never come near the ' possession of beatitude '.

[2] *En. in Ps.* VIII. 5.

[3] *Ib.* X. 3.   And cf. *De Civ.* XI. 2 : quia ipsa mens, cui ratio et intelligentia naturaliter inest, vitiis quibusdam tenebrosis et veteribus invalida est non solum ad inhaerendum fruendo, verum etiam ad perferendum incommutabile lumen, donec de die in diem renovata atque sanata fiat tantae felicitatis capax, fide primum fuerat imbuenda atque purganda.

[4] E.g. *Serm.* 43. I.   *In Jo. Ev. Tr.* 40. 9 ; 79. I.   *Encheirid.* 2.

Plato himself had said that belief is to truth as Becoming is to Being.[1] Augustine quotes the saying—which was intended of course to disparage 'belief'—and his comment is that it is 'assuredly true'. For 'as the proper act of the rational mind, after it is purified, is contemplation of the eternal; so while it still needs purification, its proper act is faith directed to the temporal.'[2] The argument, which in the *De Trinitate* does but resume and develop a much earlier statement in the *De Vera Religione*,[3] is that the sin which has caused our incapacity for the vision of God itself arises from excessive 'love of things temporal' in which we are immersed. It follows that purgation must be *per temporalia*, inasmuch as contact with the eternal can only be re-established through the medium of the temporal atmosphere which we breathe. The faith which cleanses us is directed to 'the things done in time on our behalf' which formed the historic 'mission of the Son of God'.[4] It is the faith in the fact and purpose of the Incarnation.

There was nothing new in this statement of the sacramental principle. It had been the common property of the Greek theological tradition, held by Irenaeus,[5] by Origen,[6] by

---

[1] *Timaeus* 29 c.   [2] *De Trin.* IV. 24.

[3] *De Ver. Relig.* 45 : in quem locum quisque deciderit, ibi debet incumbere ut surgat. Ergo ipsis carnalibus formis, quibus detinemur, nitendum est, ad eas cognoscendas quas caro non nuntiat.

[4] *De Trin.* IV. 25.

[5] *Adv. Haer.* IV. 62 (Harvey) : ' Our Lord came to us, not as He had power to come, but as we had power to behold Him. . . . He, the perfect Bread of the Father, gave Himself to us as milk to children in His coming as a man ; that nourished as it were at the breast of His flesh, and by means of such children's food made accustomed to eat and drink the word of God, we might receive power to hold in ourselves the Bread of immortality which is the Spirit of the Father.'

[6] *C. Celsum*, VI. 68 : ' For the sake of men who were fast bound to the flesh and of the nature of flesh, He was made flesh, that He might be received by those who could not behold Him in His nature as the Word who was with God and was God. A word embodied, proclaimed as flesh, He calls those that are flesh unto Himself, making them first to be formed after the Word made flesh, and thereafter lifting them up to see Him as He was before He was made flesh.'

Athanasius.[1] But it was Augustine who used it to establish the nature and necessity of faith. It inspires one of his finest pieces of allegorical interpretation, in the remarkable sermon on the healing of the blind men by the wayside. To the request of Philip, *Lord, show us the Father,* Christ answers *He that hath seen me hath seen the Father;* but because He knew that Philip's eyes as yet could not see, He added *Believest thou not that I am in the Father and the Father in me ?* [2] ' Let him who cannot yet see what the Lord will show, not seek first to see what he is to believe ; but let him first believe, that the eye may be healed wherewith he is to see. . . . There was lacking the power for the vision of God, but not the power for the vision of a man. Therefore He who was God was made man, in order that what was seen might heal what could not see.' So the blind men sit by the wayside, and Jesus passes by. Christ's ' passing' is His incarnate life : His birth, His miracles, His death, are ' transitory works', ' temporal sacraments'. The cry of the blind men is faith active in good works. But the Lord must ' stand still' before sight can be restored to the sightless eyes. ' As through faith we perceive (*sentimus*) the passing of Christ through the temporal dispensation, so are we to comprehend (*intelligamus*) His standing in unchangeable eternity. For the eye is healed when the divinity of Christ is comprehended . . . the divinity stands, the humanity passes.' [3] The cleansing power of faith is derived

---

[1] *De Incarnatione* 16 : ' Because the mind of men lay fallen in the world of sense, the Word submitted Himself to a bodily appearing, that He might convert men unto Himself as man, directing unto Himself their human senses ; and thereafter bring them, seeing Him as a man, and through the works He wrought, to believe that He was not a man only, but God, Word and Wisdom of the very God '.

[2] *Serm.* 88. 4. Cf. *In Jo. Ev. Tr.* 79. 1 : ex rebus quae videntur, agitur in nobis ut ea credantur quae non videntur.

[3] *Serm.* 88. 9-14. Cf. *En. in. Ps.* cxxiii. 1 : Ipse rex patriae factus est via. Rex patriae nostrae, Dominus Jesus Christus ; et ibi veritas, hic autem via. Quo imus ? Ad veritatem. Qua imus ? Per fidem. Quo imus ? Ad Christum. Qua imus ? Per Christum. . . . Veritas illud Verbum est de quo dicitur, *In principio erat Verbum, et Verbum erat apud Deum, et Deus erat Verbum.* Et quis hoc videt, nisi corde mundato ? Unde mundantur corda ? *Et Verbum caro factum est, et habitavit in nobis.*

from its object : faith in the temporal manifestation of the
Eternal Word 'contempers' the believer with eternity.[1]

It has been alleged that Augustine's teaching on faith is confused, and that he fails to make any connection between this
fides historica and the 'evangelical' faith of trusting personal relationship to God in Christ, which was as real a part of his religion as
it was of St. Paul's.[2] On the one hand we find, as in the *De
Trinitate,* faith treated as a function of the 'lower' part of our
reasonable soul, the 'active reason' which applies itself to things
temporal. The whole scheme of redemption, the Incarnation,
Passion and Resurrection of Christ, forms a 'temporal sacrament'
which is therefore the object of faith ;[3] and such faith is not yet
the highest activity of the soul, in which the true image of God
is to be traced. On the other hand, Augustine will insist that
the only faith which purifies is the faith that works through love :[4]
that the faith which is *counted for righteousness* must be faith *in
Him who justifies the ungodly,* and that to believe *in* Christ is to
love Him and to enter the fellowship of His Body.[5]

It cannot be denied that faith, in Augustine's general usage of
the term, has the predominantly intellectual connotation of the
definition which he gave at the end of his life—'to believe
means simply to affirm in thought' (*cum assensione cogitare*).[6]
The opposition of faith to sight, faith as our present mode of
religious knowledge, sight as the contemplation of God which
is reserved for the life to come, tended to confirm this usage.
But the apparent cleavages and inconsistencies in Augustine's
doctrines which critics have been at such pains to lay bare, will

---

[1] *De Trin.* IV. 24. Cf. *ib.* VII. 5 : Nitentes imitamur manentem, et sequimur
stantem, et in ipso ambulantes tendimus ad ipsum. . . . Quia enim homo ad
beatitudinem sequi non debebat nisi Deum, et sentire non poterat Deum,
sequendo Deum hominem factum, sequeretur simul et quem sentire poterat,
et quem sequi debebat.

[2] So Dorner, *Augustinus,* 183 ff.

[3] *De Trin.* XIII. esp. 24.   [4] *Serm.* 53. 11.

[5] *In. Jo. Ev. Tr.* 53. 10 ; 29. 6.   *Serm.* 144. 2.   *En. in Ps.* CXXX. 1.
In the last three passages, as often, the faith of love is contrasted with the belief
of devils.

[6] *De Praedest. Sanct.* 5.

often disappear if we are careful not to divide what he never thought of dividing, and still more if we remember the character of his thought—digressive and radiating rather than synthetic or linear—as Professor Gilson finely describes it.[1] ' The Augustinian faith in its essence ', says Gilson, ' is at the same time adherence of the mind to supernatural truth and humble surrender of the whole man to the grace of Christ : the mind's adherence to the authority of God implies humility, but humility in its turn implies a trust in God which is itself an act of love and charity.'[2]

Grace, humility, love : these are the keys to which most doors in the study of Augustine will open. The word of the *Lex Fidei* is ' Give what Thou commandest '.[3] To believe *in* God is to believe that without Him we can do nothing : it is ' to be joined to God as a believer in order to share in the righteous work of Him who works all righteousness '.[4] *If thou dost confess with thy mouth that Jesus is the Lord, and believest in thy heart that God hath raised Him from the dead, thou shalt be saved.* ' If saved ', comments Augustine, ' then justified, made righteous. For with this same faith we believe that God raises us from the dead—first in the spirit, that in the newness of His grace we may live temperately, justly, and religiously in this world ; afterward in the resurrection of our flesh to immortality.'[5] Faith alone makes possible the love of God without which we can never see Him ; for it gives that measure of knowledge which is necessary for love. ' We believe that God was made man for us, for an example of humility and to show His love towards us ', and the faith that the humility of Christ in His Incarnation and Passion is the unfailing medicine for our pride, is a faith that is ' good for us '.[6] Augustine is far from the Socratic intellectualism : to know what is good is not to do it. But he is sure that no man can have a genuine belief in the Incarnation without at least the

[1] E. Gilson, *Introduction a l'Étude de St Augustin,* pp. 294 f.

[2] *Ib.* p. 36. [3] *De Spir. et Litt.* 22.

[4] *En. in Ps.* LXXVII. 8 : credendo adhaerere ad bene cò-operandum bona operanti Deo.

[5] *De Spir. et Litt.* 51. [6] *De Trin.* VIII. 6 f.

beginnings of that humble trust in God which St. Paul meant by faith.

He loved to draw the lesson of faith from the story of the sleeping Christ upon the storm-tossed boat.[1] The wind and the waves are trials and temptations, formidable to us only because faith is asleep in the vessel of our heart. To awaken our faith is to remember Him on whom we have believed, His unfailing promises and the power of His Resurrection. For Christ dwells in our hearts through faith. ' Let no man be downcast, because He is gone up into heaven, as though leaving us alone. He is with us, if we but believe : His dwelling within us is a better thing than His outward presence even before our eyes. If you believe, He is within. Were you to welcome Christ into your chamber, He would be with you ; is He not with you when you welcome Him into your heart ? ' [2]

We have tried to summarise Augustine's ideal of man's true end in the form of three antitheses in which the ' good ' life of this changing world and the ' happy ' life of a changeless eternity are distinguished and contrasted. The first of the three—Conflict and Peace—was occupied with feeling and willing ; the last—Faith and Sight—with seeing and knowing ; and first and last were linked by the middle antithesis of Action and Contemplation, in which will and knowledge were related to one another. The conclusion which seems to emerge is that all else is subordinate to the vision of God, the activity of contemplation in which man finds his peace.[3] That is the conclusion which will be drawn by St. Thomas, in the confidence that this ' primacy of intellect ' would have been disputed no more by his Christian than by his pagan master. It has been maintained on the contrary

[1] *En. in Ps.* XXV. ii. 4 ; XXXIV. i. 3 ; XC. ii. 11 ; CXX. 7 ; CXLVII. 3. *Serm.* 38. 10; 63; 361. 7. *In Jo. Ev. Tr.* XLIX. 19.

[2] Morin, *Sermones post Maurinos reperti*, Morin ix. 2.

[3] *De Trin.* I. 31 : Visio illa Dei qua contemplabimur incommutabilem atque humanis oculis invisibilem Dei substantiam . . . propter quam solam fide corda mundamus . . . sola est summum bonum nostrum, cuius adipiscendi causa praecipimur agere quidquid recte agimus.

that in Augustine's doctrine the real primacy belongs to the will. The formula *gaudium de veritate* might be interpreted in either sense ; but the truth is that a primacy either of will or intellect would contradict the most fundamental principles of Augustine's theology. In Augustine, as in Plotinus, ethics and religion are the consistent expression of metaphysics or theology. Just as in Plotinus, because the One stands above *Nous*, and *Nous* above Soul, it follows that willing is subordinate to knowing and knowing to union ; so Augustine's absolutely co-equal Trinity imposes upon him a refusal of all ' subordinationism ' in dealing with the spirit of man and its destiny.

We know that we shall be like Him ; for we shall see Him as He is. ὁμοίωσις Θεῷ remains the condition for the vision of God ; and as Plotinus too might have said, we shall see God not only ' in the measure of our likeness to Him ' (*in quantum similes*) but ' through the medium of our likeness ' (*unde similes*).[1] We shall not indeed see Him with the eyes of the body ; yet that *apex mentis* or ' point of the spirit ', in which His likeness can here and now be born and grow, is a different thing from the Neo-Platonic *Nous*. ' See how God will have us approach Him, making us first like Him that we may approach Him. The Lord says *Be as your Father which is in heaven, who maketh His sun to rise on the evil and on the good, and sendeth rain on the just and on the unjust.* As charity grows in you, working upon you and recalling you to the likeness of God, it extends even to enemies. . . . The measure of your growth in charity is the measure of your approach to the likeness ; and in that measure you begin to be conscious of God (*incipis sentire Deum*).'[2] ' There is a vision belonging to

[1] *Ep.* 92. 3.

[2] *En. in Ps.* xcix. 5 : Augustine goes on to speak of this ' consciousness of God ' as a revealing experience which discloses the inadequacy of the conceptual thinking that preceded it. *Ib.* 6 : et cum accedere coeperis similis, et persentiscere Deum, quantum in te caritas crescit (quia et caritas Deus est), senties quiddam quod dicebas et non dicebas. Ante enim quam sentires, dicere te putabas Deum ; *incipis sentire, et ibi sentis dici non posse quod sentis.*— That Augustine could so link the mystic experience of the ineffable with the Agape that forgives—even in a single isolated passage—is a fact which deserves the attention of Dr. Nygren.

our time here. . . . If we believe, we see ; if we love, we see.
. . . He who has love needs not to be sent upon a long journey
to see God. . . . He who would see God upon His throne in
heaven: let him have love, and God dwells in him even as in
heaven.'[1]

Love—this is what Augustine means—is the confounder of
all antitheses. It breaks the line between the here and the hereafter, between change and the changeless, time and eternity. It
is peace in conflict, contemplation in the midst of action, sight
piercing through faith. For in love the divine meets the
human : heaven comes to earth when Christ is born, and man
rejoices in the Truth.

[1] *En. in Ps.* CXLIX. 4.

IV

The Meaning of Love

Consider what it is that makes us hold to the distinction between desire and love, and oppose attempts to identify them. It is because we conceive desire as we feel it in consciousness, as this forward-straining, restless activity, never satisfied until it has attained its goal ; whereas love, however much it may have this at times, has also a repose in it, and a satisfaction, so that we hope to find in it our happiness, which we can never do in desire ; and with this repose it has the great contemplative emotions, joy, admiration, and wonder . . . without the straining after the future and repugnance to the present which belongs to desire. . . .

Now, what is the conclusion ? It is that desire as felt in consciousness is as clearly different from the sentiment [of love] as emotion is different from it ; that the system of a particular desire is also different from the sentiment, for this system comes to an end with its fulfilment ; but that the system of a desire that in becoming abstract persists through a number of particulars, may not be different, for it may expand so as to include all that the sentiment includes and become identical with it. If, then, we are to maintain the distinction between them, we must draw it at the point where the contemplative emotions enter—joy, admiration, wonder, and sorrow apart from its desire. . . . We must say that so far as these contemplative emotions become added to desire and harmonised with it, it ceases to be merely desire and becomes love.

ALEXANDER SHAND.

1. *De Moribus Ecclesiae Catholicae*

In the year after his baptism, Augustine was for some months at Rome. Here, within a week after the 'ecstasy' at Ostia, his mother fell ill and died ; and here, where he had once been intimate with Manichaean 'Elect', he planned and wrote, with the aim of confuting the peculiar Manichaean asceticism, a work in two parts of which the first bore the title *On the Ethics of the Catholic Church*.

As a concession to his adversaries, he begins his exposition of the Christian moral ideal, not with the precepts delivered by Authority, but with the arguments of natural Reason.[1] Reason shows that happiness, which is our acknowledged goal, requires both the love and the secure possession of the best that man's nature is capable of achieving ; that this must be the perfection of his higher, spiritual nature, a perfection to which the imperfect soul can only advance if it has a pattern to follow, a real objective to pursue ; and, lastly, that this perfection, for its security, must be based upon an eternal pattern or objective, such as can exist only in God.[2]

If unaided Reason attempt to go further than this, to gaze directly upon the divine Pattern, its eye is dazzled : it falls back into the darkness from which it came, acquiescing in its own weakness. But here the 'kindly shade' of Authority comes to our relief, with three great texts of Scripture. The first is Christ's command, *Thou shalt love the Lord thy God with all thy heart, with all thy soul, and with all thy mind;* and it imposes an absolute obligation. To our love for God there can be no limit, as there must be with it no competitor. The second is St. Paul's word, *We know that all things go forward unto good for them that love God;*[3] which promises a complete satisfaction. God is not only

---

[1] *De Mor. Eccl.* 3.   [2] *Ib.* 4-10.
[3] Augustine has *procedunt* for the Vulgate *co-operantur*.

our ' Supreme Good '—He is the ' sum of all our good things '. The third is again St. Paul's, *Who shall separate us from the love of Christ ?* and this gives us our security for the permanence of the promised beatitude. Death has no terror for the loving soul, which lives so long as it loves : the spirit joined to God is set high above all powers of this world. So are confirmed the findings of Reason : the imperative of divine Authority sanctions the natural craving of the heart. The quest of happiness is the following after God, and we follow God by loving Him ; happiness itself is the attainment of God, an attainment which is no apotheosis or absorption of the human in the divine, but illumination and sanctification of the created personality by the intimacy of God's immediate presence.[1]

Yet even now we have in the revelation of the Tri-Une Godhead a beginning of the enlightenment for which we look. The Apostle who tells us that the love of God is in Christ Jesus our Lord, preaches the same Christ as the Power and Wisdom of God, to whom we are conformed through the love which the divine Spirit sheds abroad in our hearts. For it is love that asks and will receive, love that seeks and will find : to love's knocking it will be opened. Through love and through love alone is possible the union with God in which Reason and Authority alike find man's highest happiness realisable.[2]

If this love is in Christ, and Christ is the Power (*Virtus*) of God, we can now see in what sense the philosophers are right in claiming that virtue is the way to happiness. Virtue proves to be nothing but the perfection of love to God (*summus amor Dei*). Temperance is ' love preserving itself for God in purity and wholeness ', putting off the old man and his earthly desires, using the material world to minister to life's necessities, but pursuing nothing in it as an end. Courage is ' love enduring for God's sake all pain and hardship ', resisting especially the fear of death which is innate in the embodied soul, and increased by ignorance of the body's true nature and destiny. Justice is

---

[2] *De Mor. Eccl.* 11-21.　　　　[3] *Ib.* 22-34.

love serving God only, and in the strength of that service ruling over all that is properly in subjection to the soul. Prudence is love alert and watchful to discern between what promotes our journey to God, and what hinders it.[1] The life of virtue is the life of love, and eternal life is its reward. But the life eternal, as Christ has said, is nothing but the knowledge of the true God. It is vain then to offer as a means for the attainment of perfection that knowledge of God which is perfection's reward. Love precedes and merits knowledge, as obedience to the rule of Authority precedes the enlightenment of Reason. We must follow the path to which the Church points us, and learn first to love the God whom we seek to know.[2]

But to his first great commandment Christ added a second. Love between man and man is the surest stepping-stone to the love of man for God. Yet, if the love of God is the pursuit of our Supreme Good, only he who loves God can be said truly to love himself; and if we are bidden to love our neighbour as ourselves, that can mean only our seeking to increase the love of God in him. It may be that love of God in its beginning comes before the love of neighbour, while the love of neighbour reaches perfection sooner than the love of God. But it is certain that no man who thinks little of his neighbour can ever attain to God. The first rule for love of neighbour is to 'work no ill' to him; the second, to lose no occasion for doing him good. Neither of these things is easy. To good will must be added a wisdom in action which only God Himself can furnish. If we love our neighbour, we shall neglect neither his body nor his soul. Bodily needs call for works of mercy which the Christian cannot withhold; the soul's needs are greater, and less easily met. In the schooling or 'discipline' which is the Church's medicine for the soul, there is place for compulsion as well as instruction: the Old Testament must inculcate the fear of God, the New will lead on to the love of Him.[3]

---

[1] *De Mor. Eccl.* 35-46 : compare and contrast Plotinus's translation of the cardinal virtues into terms not of love but of *Nous* (*Enn.* I. ii. 6 f.).
[2] *De Mor. Eccl.* 47.   [3] *Ib.* 48-62.

The Church will have love to be the salt and the sweetener of all human relationships, in the family, the household, the state, and the world of mankind. In some of the Church's children we see it grow to be a consuming fire. We may hesitate to acknowledge that the hermit, whom love itself drives into a life of solitude and prayer, has not thereby deserted the service of his fellows. We cannot but admire the flowering of love in the life of common poverty, chastity, and obedience, whether in the great foundations of Egypt and the East, or in the smaller, less strictly ordered communities lately springing up in the West. No less admirable are the examples of devotion shown by the Church's secular priesthood, whose place is in the tumult of the world, among men who still need the physician, who have yet to learn the life that is life indeed.[1] And so, with the praise of Catholic sainthood, the treatise ends.

The *De Moribus Ecclesiae* is a work as remarkable for its contents as for its omissions. Augustine must have been working at it and at the *De Quantitate Animae* at nearly the same time, and it was the time when his Christianity was at the height of its Platonising. Naturally its scope is limited by its subject—the Way rather than the Goal. We expect therefore to find the Christian element, the voice of Authority which points out the Way, vindicating for itself against the Platonist Reason a larger room than in the *De Quantitate Animae* or in the Dialogues. In fact, it is in the use of Scripture that the *De Moribus* most unmistakably and most astonishingly anticipates the future Augustine. He has already made his own many of those texts which will be the pivots of his Christianity, and already uses them pivotally. Of grace, needless to say, the idea is absent, or present in scarcely more than verbal form. Sin is mentioned once, and then in what appears to be a vague reference, suggestive of Origen's theory, to a pre-mundane fall of the soul.[2] The moral struggle

[1] *De Mor. Eccl.* 63-80.
[2] *Ib.* 40 : corpus homini gravissimum vinculum est, iustissimis Dei legibus, propter antiquum peccatum.—Augustine is probably thinking of the Platonic πτεροῤῥύησις. Cf. 41 : volitabit pennis pulcherrimis et integerrimis.

receives incidental and perfunctory notice in the course of the translation of the cardinal virtues into terms of love. The love of God itself is almost pure Eros. The *caritas Dei* from which nothing can separate us is our love for God : ' in Jesus Christ ', it is Christ's love for God,[1] in which the Spirit makes us participators. That God is capable of love for us is barely suggested : it is to His ' goodness and kindness ' that we owe all we are ; [2] if He may be called ' compassionate ' (*misericors*), it is only in a special sense.[3]

But it was not possible to make an honest attempt to set forth an ethic based on the two great commandments, without introducing confusion into the Neo-Platonist pattern. The command to love has as little meaning for Plotinus as it has for the modern eroticist or romantic, though for different reasons. In Plotinus, Eros is universal in the sense that ' all that exists aspires towards the Supreme by a compulsion of nature ' : [4] it is part of the necessary constitution of the universe, equivalent to the movement by which potency on every rung of the ladder of existence tends to actuality. It is ' law ' in the scientific, not the normative sense ; and it can therefore have no strictly ethical interest. Something of this, it is true, Augustine has retained in his conception of the universal desire for happiness, to which he might easily apply Plotinus's definition of Eros— ' the act of a soul in quest of good '.[5] But when Authority not only confirms the finding of Reason, that a good which can satisfy the soul's desire must be divine, but imposes the acceptance of this truth and the consequent direction of desire as an absolute obligation, then Eros is being moralised and therefore takes on a wholly new significance. It now includes explicit recognition of the Source of happiness as a Power claiming allegiance. For allegiance is the only possible relation of creature to Creator : only in loving *subjection* to God can the created soul achieve that likeness to its Creator which is possible for it, and in virtue of

---

[1] The νοῦς ἐρῶν of Plotinus (*Enn.* VI. vii. 35).   [2] *De Mor. Eccl.* 56.
[3] *Ib.* 54. Cf. the Stoic depreciation of compassion in Plotinus (*Enn.* I. iv. 8).
[4] *Enn.* V. v. 12.   [5] *Ib.* III. v. 4.

that likeness draw near to Him.[1] In a famous passage of his treatise *On the Beautiful*, Plotinus describes the soul's ascent to the Ideal Beauty in Homeric phrase, as ' the flight to our beloved fatherland ', ' whence we came, and where our Father is '. The flight is ' no journey for the feet ', no voyage by land or sea : it is a vision. ' Withdraw into yourself and look. And if you do not find yourself beautiful yet, act as does the creator of a statue that is to be made beautiful . . . cut away all that is excessive, straighten all that is crooked . . . never cease chiselling your statue, until there shall shine out on you from it the godlike splendour of virtue.' [2] Augustine quotes the passage in the *De Civitate*,[3] and the phrase ' no journey for the feet ' is a favourite with him. But he prefers to describe the journey in different terms. *Imus non ambulando, sed amando* [4]—' We follow by loving.' [5]

If it is difficult to make Eros subject of the first commandment without altering its character, it can be made subject of the second only by an equivocation or a subterfuge. ' It cannot be ', Augustine says, ' that he who loves God loves not himself ; rather he alone knows how to love himself who loves God. Self-love can do no more than seek earnestly to enjoy the supreme and true Good. . . . Wholesome self-love is to love God more than self. . . . Again, we are not to think that men

---

[1] *De Mor. Eccl.* 20.

[2] *Enn.* I. vi. 8 f. (tr. Mackenna). Cf. *De Doctr. Christ.* I. 10 : quam purgationem quasi ambulationem quamdam, et quasi navigationem ad patriam esse arbitremur. Non enim ad eum qui ubique praesens est, locis movemur, sed bono studio bonisque moribus.—For the spiritual vision and the ' sculptor ' simile, cf. *De Ver. Relig.* 64 : O animae pervicaces, date mihi qui *videat* sine ulla imaginatione visorum carnalium. Date mihi qui videat omnis unius principium non esse nisi Unum solum a quo sit omne unum (*Enn.* VI. ix. 1, etc.). . . . Qui videat date . . . qui resistat sensibus carnis . . . qui compungatur in cubili suo, qui resculpat spiritum suum. Closely as the Christian follows the Neo-Platonist, we see how Augustine has eliminated the offensive odour of Narcissism which comes from Plotinus's deification of the pure essence of the human soul.

[3] *De Civ.* IX. 17.   [4] *Ep.* 155. 4.

[5] *De Mor. Eccl.* 18. Cf. *En. in Ps.* XCIV. 1 : Pedes nostri in hoc itinere, affectus nostri sunt. Prout quisque affectum habuerit, prout quisque amorem habuerit, ita accedit vel recedit a Deo.

themselves should be united by no bond of love. Rather we should believe that the love (*caritas*) of man towards man is the surest stepping-stone (*gradus*) to the love of God.' [1] As soon as Augustine begins to describe the working of the love of neighbour, he wants the idea and the word ' benevolence '. He either does not see or sees no need to remark that if love of self and love of neighbour mean wishing well to self and neighbour, the word ' love ' is being used in a sense different to that which he has given it in the first commandment. When the love of man is called the ' stepping-stone ' to the love of God, we seem to be back again in Platonism : [2] we think of Diotima's speech in the *Symposium* or its echoes in Plotinus : ' passing on the upward way ' the lesser beauties of body and soul, we are to rise to the contemplation of Beauty itself.[3] But the relapse, if it is one, is momentary ; for in the chapters which follow, the love of man for man is expressed simply as active benevolence, and the suggestion is made that it follows rather than precedes the love of God. In making the care for men's bodily needs a necessary part of benevolent activity, Augustine is of course following a tradition of the Church so primitive and so persistent that it could not be disregarded. But he does not forget the definition already given—that to love my neighbour as myself means ' to strive to bring him to that same Good which is my own goal ', to help him to learn the perfect love of God.[4] He says that ' the care of the body is to be *referred* to the soul's health ' [5]—a phrase which like so many others in the treatise foreshadows a principle which will later become fundamental.

But perhaps nothing in the *De Moribus* is more noteworthy than the extent to which in its last chapters Augustine has for his portraying of the Christian life absorbed the spirit of St. Paul. He would not admire the hermit if he were obliged to admit that the hermit was a ' deserter from humanity '. The monastery

---

[1] *De Mor. Eccl.* 48 f.

[2] But cf. *C. Adim. Man.* 6, where the same phrase is expounded in the sense of the *ordo amoris :* every love has its proper *gradus*.

[3] *Enn.* I. vi. 7.   [4] *De Mor. Eccl.* 49.   [5] *Ib.* 56.

itself is admirable only as a living organisation of charity : the rule of charity must be supreme over any rule of abstinence or continence. Here Augustine is of course in reaction against Manichaean externalism ; but the result is a penetration of his own ideals by the ethic of the New Testament.

2. *Will, affection, desire*

Study of Augustine's doctrine of the love of God and man must take the *De Moribus Ecclesiae* for its starting-point. Nowhere else is the tension between Platonism and the Gospel more evident. Was this tension resolvable, and if so, in what degree and by what means was Augustine successful in resolving it ? These are the questions which have to be answered.

The answer given by Nygren is that the Augustinian *caritas* is an attempted synthesis of two factors which blend no more easily than 'fire and water'. Love, so far as it is human, is Eros, a desire which always and necessarily seeks its own satisfaction, whether in heaven or on earth. But it is met by grace, the 'uncaused' Agape of God ; and in the acceptance of grace Eros is cured of the pride which condemned its quest to failure.[1]

Nygren insists that *caritas* is a complex conception. But his analysis does less than justice to its real complexity. It is true that *caritas* and *amor Dei* are synonyms, and that the pilgrim soul must know *amor Dei* as *desiderium*. But if the Eros of Neo-platonism is the soul's striving after the Good, its restless pursuit of the One, the *caritas* of Augustine is not only the desire for rest in union with God : it is also the rest attained, the union realised ; and it is also the bond of unity which makes out of the many pilgrims a mighty army, a living body. Nygren's account is defective, because it makes no attempt to assimilate those human elements in the complex which resist resolution into Eros. He sees and states with admirable clarity the logical connection between Augustine's psychology and his metaphysic. For Augustine, as he says, ' there is nothing depreciatory in the

[1] *Eros und Agape II.* (G.T.), pp. 279 ff.

admission that desire occupies so dominating a place in our life. It is at bottom only an expression of the fact that we have life from God, and not like God in ourselves and from ourselves. Desire is the stamp of all that is made : it is founded in God's own will and the order of creation. . . . Human life has not its "good" in itself : its being is relative, wholly dependent upon something external to it. It does not already possess its good, but must begin by seeking it ; and that is done just through love, which is desire directed to the attainment of this good. In desire, therefore, there is nothing at all reprehensible or evil ; on the contrary, it is in the highest degree good and praiseworthy, in so far as it gives expression to the actual condition of man as a created being. If he ceased to desire, that would mean that he believed himself to possess his "good" in himself, and no longer needed to seek it anywhere else : it would be an attempt on his part to appropriate to himself something of the divine independence and self-sufficiency.' [1]

All this is true. But when Nygren describes this 'hallmark of human life' as 'a craving centred in the self and its interests', he is unjustifiably contracting the sense which 'desire' must bear if it is to correspond to the Augustinian *amor*. This is immediately apparent in the relation which he proceeds to note between 'desiring love' and the form of temporal existence. The self-sufficiency of God is a consequence of His eternity. For man, the present is never secure : the future constantly threatens to annihilate it. And 'the desiring love which seeks its good stretches out from the present and its shortcomings to the future from which it promises itself satisfaction'.[2] But the significance of temporal existence for Augustine is certainly wider than this. It lies in our consciousness of a certain power in ourselves to initiate change, to make the future different from the present, for better or for worse—in a word, in the efficacy of will.

Imus non ambulando, sed amando. When Augustine speaks of

---

[1] *Eros und Agape II.* (G.T.), p. 288.   [2] *Ib.* pp. 289 f.

love as the 'soul's movement' (*motus animi*), he is thinking not
of an 'emotion' but of the directive energy of the will in its
most general aspect.[1] 'Every love', he says, 'has a force of its
own. Love cannot be inactive in a lover, it cannot but lead
him in some direction. If you would know the character of a
man's love, see whither it is leading.'[2] Often the motive force
of love is regarded as a kind of physical gravitation in the Aristotelian sense. 'Bodies move by their weight towards their
own place : fire upwards, stone downwards. Our " place " is
where we come to rest. . . . My weight is my love : by it I am
carried whithersoever it may be.'[3] In this context Augustine is
expounding the second verse of Genesis. *Cupiditas* is the weight
which drags down to the abyss, *caritas* the upward lifting to the
Spirit's region : both are alike 'affections', 'loves'. So in a
letter he speaks of the process of Christian perfection as the
'transference of weight' from *cupiditas* to *caritas*.[4] We naturally
think of the Newtonian metaphor of 'change in the centre of
gravity'. But in Aristotle's world a 'transference of weight' is
of course an impossibility : there is no alchemy that can turn
stone into fire. Plotinus himself is a good Aristotelian. When
he interprets the myth of Eros, he sees in the Earthly Love not a
rival to the Heavenly, but its groping, ineffective imitator. All
Eros pulls one way and one way only.[5] Augustine, even in
adopting the physical analogy for human love, has introduced
into the structure of Greek thought a dualist dynamic which is
alien to it. He too may say that *cupiditas* 'imitates' *caritas;*[6]
but it is a 'perverse', a diabolic imitation, contrary and not
similar in tendency.

We remember the central theme of the *De Civitate*—the
Two Loves which have been the makers of the Two Cities.[6]
Citizens of the Earthly City live 'according to the flesh',

---

[1] Cf. *De Trin.* xv. 38 : quid est aliud caritas, quam voluntas ? *Ib.* 41 :
voluntatem nostram, vel amorem seu dilectionem quae valentior est voluntas.

[2] *En. in Ps.* cxxi. 1.

[3] *Conf.* xiii. 10. Cf. *Ep.* 55. 18 ; *De Civ.* xi. 28.

[4] *Ep.* 157. 9.   [5] See *Enn.* iii. v. 1, 7.   [6] *De Civ.* xiv. 28.

citizens of the Heavenly 'according to the spirit'.[1] We must beware, says Augustine, of understanding this in the 'Platonic sense': the body is not the cause of the soul's maladies, nor are the passions of desire and fear, gladness and sorrow, the product of the soul's embodiment, or in themselves evil, as Virgil and the Stoics would have us believe.[2] These so-called passions are nothing but the will itself in positive or negative activity: if the will is right, they are good; if it is perverted, they are evil.[3] *Amor*, as the usage of Scripture proves, is a neutral term. It is not opposed to *caritas* or *dilectio* as evil to good:[4] right will is good love, perverted will is evil love, and the passions can be expressed in terms of love as in terms of will. 'Love eager to possess its object is desire; possessing and enjoying it, is gladness; shrinking from what opposes it, is fear; aware of effective opposition, is sorrow.'[5] The true life of the Heavenly City is life 'according to God', and to live 'according to the flesh' means rather 'according to man'. In this world the 'life according to God' will know all the passions in which love takes effect. *Apatheia*, passionlessness, is not even our goal in the life to come; for though in heaven there will be no more fear or sorrow, love and joy (*amor* and *gaudium*) will abide.[6]

It is instructive to note how at the close of this psychological discussion which leads up in the *De Civitate* to the account of man's Fall, love, which at first was equated with will as the determining principle of all affective movements of the soul, has fallen back into the restricted sense of a single specific affection.

[1] *De Civ.* XIV. 1 ff.   [2] *Ib.* 3 (quoting *Aen.* VI. 730-4).
[3] *Ib.* 6. Cf. *In Jo. Ev. Tr.* 60. 3 : the Stoics 'stuporem deputant sanitatem'.
[4] Augustine can use *amor* and *amare* without scruple of God's love for men : e.g. *En. in Ps.* XXXIV. i. 12 : amat me Deus ; amat te Deus.
[5] *De Civ.* XIV. 7. Compare the modern psychologist : ' In all love there is an organisation of the lesser systems of many emotions,—as those of fear, anger, joy, and sorrow, besides others. In the presence of anything we love we are disposed to feel joy, and in prolonged absence from it, sorrow, and at the suggestion of danger to feel the fear of losing it, and when it is attacked to feel anger against the assailant.'—(A. F. Shand, *Foundations of Character*, (2nd edit.), p. 35).
[6] *Ib.* 9.

But the love which will remain in heaven is not desire but the
' unchanging love of a good attained ' ; [1] as in Paradise before
the Fall there was ' love to God undisturbed, and mutual love in
the loyal and pure fellowship of marriage ; and of this love
great delight, in that love's object was ever present to be enjoyed '. [2]
This ambiguity of denotation is characteristic of Augustine's use
of the words *amor* and *amare*. He can define love as ' seeking
after a thing for its own sake ', and speak in the same context of
the presence or absence of love for something already possessed. [3]
In the *De Trinitate* the soul's ' love of itself ' is identical with its
' willing itself ' ; and here the requirements of the theological
argument compel Augustine to distinguish appetition from
fruition. He observes in one place that it is need (*indigentia*)
which betrays the presence of love, and that when the loved
object is always at hand there is the less consciousness of love. [4]
But elsewhere he defines the love which forms the link in the
soul's Trinity as ' nothing else but the will, seeking after *or
holding in possession* an object of enjoyment ' ; [5] and in his final
comparison and differentiation of the divine Trinity and its
human image, he says that the act of will which ' proceeds ' from
the self finds its consummation in the act of self-knowledge, so
that ' what had been the quest (*appetitus*) of the will as seeking
becomes the love of the will as enjoying (*amor fruentis*) '. [6] The
raison d'être of all human love is that realised union of lover and
beloved in which desire gives place to pure delight, because need
has been met by the good appropriate to it.

It may well have been the writing of the *De Trinitate* which
led Augustine to realise something of the psychological complexity of love, and prevented him from reducing its scope to
that of any single emotion. But there can be no question of
what is dominant in his conception of Christian love. It is
desiderium—the unsatisfied longing of the homesick heart. Here
it should be enough to point to the meaning which he regularly

[1] *De Civ.* xiv. 9.
[2] *Ib.* 10.
[3] *De Div. Quaest. LXXXIII.* 35.
[4] *De Trin.* x. 19.
[5] *Ib.* xiv. 8.
[6] *Ib.* xv. 47 and cf. *Solil.* i. 14.

gives to Charity in the ' theological ' triad. It is the same in the *Soliloquies* and the early treatises, as in the Sermons, the later Letters, and the *De Trinitate* itself. ' God's right hand, stretched down to us in our Lord Jesus Christ, is to be grasped by us with firm faith, expected with sure hope, longed for with ardent love (*ardenti caritate desideremus*).' [1] ' The man in whom is the faith that works through love must hope for that which God promises. Hope therefore is faith's companion . . . and with them is the love with which we long (*desideramus*), with which we strive to attain, with which we are inflamed, with which we hunger and thirst.' [2] ' What is the worship of God but the love of Him, whereby now we long to see Him (*desideramus eum videre*), and believe and hope that we shall see Him.' [3] *Desiderium* is the constant theme of Augustine's preaching. ' The whole life of the good Christian is a holy longing. What you long for, as yet you do not see . . . by withholding of the vision God extends the longing, through longing He extends the soul, by extending it He makes room in it. . . . So, brethren, let us long, because we are to be filled. . . . That is our life, to be exercised by longing.' [4] ' Longing is the heart's treasury (*desiderium sinus cordis est*) ; we shall receive, if we extend our longing as wide as we can. That for us is the purport of the divine Scripture, of the congregation of the peoples, of the celebration of the sacraments, of holy baptism, of the songs of God's praise, of my discourse at this moment, that this longing may

[1] *De Lib. Arb.* II. 54. Cf. *Solil.* I. 13 : fides . . . spes . . . caritas, qua videre perfruique desiderat, but contrast *Solil.* I. 3 *Deus . . . sui caritas inxit.*

[2] *Serm.* 53. 11. Cf. *Serm.* 4. 1 : sperans quod nondum tenet, credens quod nondum videt, amans cui nondum haeret. *Serm.* 361. 2 : spes . . . fides . . . caritas, quam praedicatio rerum quae nondum videntur inflammat et accendit desiderio.

[3] *De Trin.* XII. 22. Cf. *Ep.* 120. 8 : sic homo fidelis debet credere quod nondum videt, ut visionem et speret et amet. *Ep.* 199. 15 : ille diligit adventum Domini . . . qui eum . . . sinceritate fidei, firmitate spei, ardore caritatis expectat. *De Perf. Just.* 19 : curramus credendo, sperando, desiderando.

[4] *In Ep. Jo. Tr.* 4. 6. Cf. *En. in Ps.* LXXXIII. 3 : Desiderium differtur, ut crescat ; crescit, ut capiat . . . quod semper habiturus es, diu desidera. *Ib.* XCI. 1 : caritas non novit nisi crescere magis magisque. . . . Desiderium ergo nostrum crescat.

not only be sown and germinate, but increase to the measure of
such capacity that it may be fit to take in what eye hath not
seen nor hath gone up into the heart of men.' [1] And, in an
exposition of the text, *No man cometh unto Me except the Father
draw him* : ' Give me a lover, he will feel that of which I speak :
give me one who longs, who hungers, who is a thirsty pilgrim
in this wilderness, sighing for the springs of his eternal home-
land : give me such a man, he will know what I mean '.[2] ' If
you would pray without ceasing, do not cease to long. Your
ceaseless longing is your ceaseless voice. You will be silent, if
you stop loving . . . the chilling of charity is the heart's silence :
the burning of charity is the heart's clamour.' [3]

It is clear that this predominance of the character of *desiderium*,
of unsatisfied longing, in Augustine's descriptions of the Christian
motive, corresponds to his whole view of the relation of this
world to the next, of the Christian life as a pilgrimage, and of
happiness as something impossible of realisation in this life. As
we have seen, his ' otherworldliness' is not merely his common
Christian heritage ; it springs from the root of his personal
religion. *Fecisti nos ad te, et inquietum est cor nostrum donec
requiescat in te.* The suggestion that the *Confessions* should be
read as the thankful devotions of a heart that has already found
rest,[4] involves a misreading of Augustine's spiritual history.
The seventy-sixth chapter of the *De Quantitate Animae* is proof
that he had once hoped to satisfy his soul, here and now, with the
vision of God. But in the school of experience he learnt that
in a world of change there can be no satisfaction of a desire for
the Changeless. In the measured and deliberate language of the
De Civitate : ' The happiness which our spiritual nature rightly
desires is to be found, as none can fail to see, in the conjunction
of two things : the enjoyment without any interference of the

---

[1] *In Jo. Ev. Tr.* 40. 10.   [2] *Ib.* 26. 4.
[3] *En. in Ps.* XXXVII. 14. Cf. *Serm.* 56. 4 : the Lord's Prayer is the ' forma
desideriorum ' : ideo voluit ut ores, ut desideranti det . . . quia et ipsum
desiderium ipse insinuavit.
[4] F. Cayré, *La Contemplation Augustinienne,* pp. 79 ff.

immutable Good which is God, and the certain conviction, exempt alike from doubt and from error, of remaining in that enjoyment for ever '.[1]

We are prepared to find that when Augustine speaks of the love of God (for which he uses the phrases *amor Dei* and *caritas Dei* indifferently), the genitive is always objective in default of a note to the contrary : [2] he means our love for God and not God's love for us. The words of *Romans* v. 5—*the love of God is shed abroad in our hearts through the Holy Spirit which is given to us*—are not only his chief Scriptural argument against Pelagianism ; this text and that of the seventy-third Psalm—*It is good for me to hold fast to God*—are together the hinges of his whole scheme of religion. But he understands the ' love of God ' in *Romans* v. 5, not of the ' love wherewith God loves us, but that by which He makes us His lovers '.[3] What is more astonishing, he always puts the same interpretation upon the genitive in the *Quis nos separabit a caritate Christi ?* of *Romans* viii.[4] The context of both passages in the Epistle of course makes it certain that this exegesis is mistaken : [5] St. Paul's genitives may not be purely possessive —they probably denote rather the source from which the love springs ; but they certainly are not purely objective, and that Augustine never wavers in so understanding them is a fact of the greatest importance for the appreciation of his own doctrine. As we shall see, the love of God which is shed abroad in our hearts is no mere human affection : in the last analysis, in the deepest sense, it *is* God's own love which is ours by His gift. But its object remains to the end God not man—or rather, man only as ' in God '.

Preaching on the text, *Iucundabitur iustus in Domino,* Augustine asks how it is possible for us here on earth to ' delight in the

[1] *De Civ.* XI. 13.

[2] Usually in the form of an insertion of the words *erga nos* : e.g. *Ep.* 127. 1 ; *Serm.* 215. 5.

[3] *De Spir. et Litt.* 56. Cf. *In Jo. Ev. Tr.* 26. 1 *et saepe.*

[4] *De Mor. Eccl.* 18 ff. *Ep.* 145. 6. *En. in Ps.* VII. 14. *Serm.* 335, etc.

[5] Julian here, as not seldom, was a better exegete than Augustine. Cf. *C. Jul. op. imp.* II. 167.

Lord' who is so far above us. He answers that it is our own act that makes Him near or far. 'Love, and He will draw near : love, and He will dwell in you.' For it is written, *Deus est caritas*. Thought and imagination are powerless to apprehend God's nature ; but a savour, a foretaste of Him, is offered to us in St. John's great text. And if the further question be put : what is charity itself ?—the answer is easy. 'Charity is that whereby we love—and love what ? The Good that words cannot utter, the Good that does good, the Good Creator of all good things '.[1] A passage like this is intensely characteristic of Augustine. He seems deliberately to refuse the admission of any object but God Himself for the love in which God's own nature and its immanence in the hearts of men is to be recognised. *O amor qui semper ardes et nunquam exstingueris ! Caritas, Deus meus, accende me !* [2] The 'love of eternity and truth '[3] was the root of Augustine's religion before he read Plotinus. Platonism was the rain which helped the roots to strike deeper into a naturally fertile soil.

3. *Vis unitiva*

The life of the tree is in the stock ; the quality of the fruit is determined by the graft. The graft which determined the character of Augustine's Christianity was the doctrine which is the peculiar treasure of Catholicism—the doctrine of the unity of Christ and His Church.

The best part of Augustine's episcopal career was tormented by what is called the Donatist controversy. As controversy, it forced him to expend much of his literary energy upon wearisome discussion and re-discussion of past ecclesiastical scandals which he would rather have seen buried. But as schism, it nearly killed Christianity in Africa ; and it drove Augustine himself to betray his own most Christian principle of toleration, and to justify the use of force against the schismatic by that fatal interpretation of the *Compelle intrare* of the parable which became a

---

[1] *Serm.* 21. 1.   [2] *Conf.* x. 40.
[3] *Ep.* 155. 1 : caritas aeternitatis et veritatis.

chief authority for the religious persecution of later ages.[1] The origin and the obstinacy of Donatism, as he truly said, lay in nothing but hatred, the hatred of brothers.[2] Its expression was a campaign of slander and lawless violence, not far short of civil war. It brought division not only into every city of the province, but into innumerable Christian families.[3] Where in Tertullian's time the love of Christians for one another had been the marvel of the unbeliever, Augustine found a fratricidal conflict which was a standing denial of Christ. When we read his dogmatic assertions that the only safeguard of Christian charity is in the unity of the Church,[4] that faith and sacraments can avail nothing where the love of unity (*caritas unitatis*) is lacking,[5] that it is folly to pretend that he who has not charity can belong to the Church's unity,[6] that the health of the Church's Body depends on charity and that schism inflicts upon it a mortal wound,[7]—we need to remember the naked facts which are the background of all this. *Origo et pertinacia schismatis nulla alia, nisi odium fratris.* 'Our life is love ; and if life is love, hatred is death.' [8]

Augustine might have developed his ideal of Church unity, had there been no Donatist schism. But in his prolonged meditations upon the Psalms and St. John, the torn and bleeding Body of Christ in Africa is never far from his mind. He bases his exposition of the entire Psalter on one constantly reiterated principle—that the voice of the Psalmist is the voice that cried to Saul on the Damascus road, *Why persecutest thou Me ?*—that the whole Christ (*totus Christus*) is not the Head alone but the Head and the members, and that Christ and His Church are therefore not two but One Man (*unus homo*).[9] In the sufferings of His

---

[1] *Ep.* 185, ' De Correctione Donatistarum. ' Augustine even appealed to the *example* of Christ in the ' violent ' conversion of St. Paul.

[2] *De Bapt. c. Don.* I. 16.   [3] *Ep.* 33. 5 ; 108. 17.

[4] *C. Litt. Petil.* II. 172.   [5] *C. Ep. Parmen.* II. 28.

[6] *C. Cresc. Donat.* I. 34.   [7] *De Bapt. c. Donat.* I. 11.

[8] *En. in Ps.* LIV. 7.

[9] See E. Mersch, *Le Corps Mystique du Christ*, vol. ii. cc. 2-4, where the mass of references fully justifies Harnack's note that on this matter references are superfluous.

members it is the Christ who is afflicted ; in their prayers it is the Christ who speaks to the Father ; in their sacrifice it is Christ's Body that is offered. ' *For their sake, He said, I sanctify Myself, that they also may be sanctified in the truth*—that is, in Myself I sanctify them as Myself, because in Me they too are I Myself (*quoniam in me etiam ipsi sunt ego*).'[1] In thankful adoration we are to realise the marvel of God's grace, namely, that ' we have been made not Christians only, but Christ '.[2] So it is literally true that no Christian can call his soul his own : all who believe have one heart and one soul or life, the single life of Christ (*anima unica Christi*).[3]

Augustine does not shrink from the extremest consequences of the realism which Greek theology had applied to the doctrine of Christ's mystical Body. What distinguishes him from the Greeks is the energy and insistence with which he maintains that this real unity of Christians with Christ and with one another is a unity of which love is the foundation and the bond. So far from this being, in his view, to moralise or rationalise the mystery, to leave a unity which is ' only moral ', it is the guarantee of its reality. For the love which is here active, the love of God in Christ spread abroad in our hearts by the Holy Spirit, is at once the supremest reality and the profoundest mystery.[4] Christ has loved us ' that we may love one another : the effect of His love for us is so to bind us to one another in mutual love that we become the Body of which He is the Head, His members linked together in that lovely bondage '.[5] The health of that Body is the unity of its members, compacted by love.[6] Dissension alone can sever the compact : in love the unity has its source and its safeguard.[7] The sin of schism is to break up what Christ came to gather into one.[8] He who loves his brother must needs ' endure all things ' for unity's sake :[9] intolerance

---

[1] *In Jo. Ev. Tr.* 108. 5. [2] *Ib.* 21. 8. [3] *Ep.* 243. 4.

[4] Augustine knows no more fitting analogy for the Unity in Trinity of the Godhead than the unity realised by the same Spirit of love in the Body of Christ. Cf. *In Jo. Ev. Tr.* 14. 9 ; 18. 4. *De Trin.* IV. 12.

[5] *In Jo. Ev. Tr.* 65. 2. [6] *Serm.* 137. 1. [7] *En.* 2 *in Ps.* XXX. ii. 1.
[8] *In Ep. Jo. Tr.* 6. 13. [9] *Ib.* 1. 12.

kills love and dismembers the Body. There can be no separation between love for the Head and love for the members : love for the sons of God is what gives the individual his membership, fastens him indissolubly in the Body whose destiny is to be ' the one Christ loving Himself '.[1]

It is thus that *caritas Christi* comes to mediate in the language of Augustine between *caritas Dei* and *fraterna dilectio*. Fellowship in the love of God is still what enables us to extend our love to the whole Church throughout the world and not to limit it to the brother at hand : like the two eyes in the body that cannot see one another but look the same way, all who love God share a common ' intention ', ' their heart's eye fixed in the light of Truth '.[2] But the love of Christ not only demands but actually includes the personal relationship of charity between brethren—*forbearing one another in love, striving to keep the unity of the Spirit in the bond of peace*—a text to which Augustine was always returning in his appeals to the Donatists. ' Through the love of Christ ', he writes to his colleague Theodorus, ' we want to win them for God. . . . Could we but stop talking of men's naughtiness, and pay honour to the good gifts of God in men, we might regain our brotherly concord and the peace we long for, the devil's promptings being overcome in men's hearts by the love of Christ.'[3] In these very noble words, worthy of a great bishop, Christian charity has risen to its full height—a height which the leaders of the African Church reached no more easily than have Church leaders of any other time or place. Augustine had to give urgent warnings to his own flock against being encouraged by high example to abuse and contempt of the schismatic.[4] Love is law in the City of God, for it is a city which is constituted by the love of its citizens for one another and for the God who is present in it through love.[5]

---

[1] *In Ep. Jo. Tr.* 10. 3 : diligendo fit et ipse membrum, et fit per dilectionem in compage corporis Christi ; et erit unus Christus amans se ipsum. Cum enim se invicem amant membra, corpus se amat.

[2] *Ib.* 6. 10.   [3] *Ep.* 61. 1.

[4] *En. in Ps.* LXV. 5 : qualiscumque episcopi vox sonuit vobis, rogamus vos ut caveatis.   [5] *Ib.* XCVIII. 4.

4. *Means and Ends*

The love of God which is the desire for union with Him, and the love of men which is the sense of unity with all those who are capable of sharing the love of God, are indeed bound up most intimately with one another. But before Augustine had learnt the full meaning of membership in Christ's Body, he had sought other ways of bringing these two loves, apparently incommensurable, on to one plane of reference ; and this led him first to the disjunctive conception of ' use ' and ' enjoyment ', in which all else is regarded as instrumental to the love of God, and secondly to the comprehensive conception of an ' order of love ', a hierarchy of values in which the lower are subordinate to the higher.

While the young convert whom the Bishop of Milan had lately baptised was attempting in the *De Moribus Ecclesiae* to ground Catholic morals upon Platonism, Ambrose himself may already have been engaged in his adaptation of the diluted Stoicism of Cicero's *De Officiis* to the needs of a handbook of Christian ethics for the clergy. Cicero, following the plan of his Stoic original Panaetius, had produced a curious combination of idealist and utilitarian morality, treating conduct first as determined by the intuitive sense of what is morally fitting (*honestum*), and secondly as affecting the external welfare of the agent (*utile*). Ambrose avows that the Christian must find his measure of moral good in the ' future ' not the ' present ', and that nothing can be called useful but that which procures eternal life : worldly wealth is more often a hindrance than a help.[1] Yet he retains the Ciceronian scheme which his principles have clearly deprived of all justification or relevance, and thereby condemns his own work to inextricable confusion. We cannot be sure whether Augustine, when he wrote the thirtieth of his ' Collected Essays ', had before him the *De Officiis* of Ambrose ; but certainly he is there making use of Cicero's terminology, which he adapts by a Platonist *tour de force* to an ethical system

---

[1] Ambrose, *De Off. Min.* I. 9.

almost as different from that of Ambrose as from that of Cicero. The good is ' what is to be sought for its own sake ' : the useful is that which is ' referred ' to something other than itself. By goodness (*honestas*) we understand the uncreated ' spiritual Beauty ' which alone is to be ' enjoyed ' ; the category of the ' useful ' covers the whole sphere of God's creative providence. The whole of morality can be summed up as the direction of our faculties of ' use ' and ' enjoyment ' to their appropriate objects. Not only all external things, but even virtue itself is subject to the judgment of reason as a means to the fruition of God.[1] That man's end is the *fruitio Dei* had been Augustine's principal contention in all his writings from the *De Beata Vita* onwards.[2] The originality and importance of this essay is indicated in its title : ' Whether all things have been created for the use of man '. In the *De Moribus Ecclesiae*, Augustine had written : ' God alone is to be loved (*amandus*) : all this world, that is to say, the whole world of sense, is to be despised—to be used only for this life's necessities '.[3] But a world that is to be used not for this life's necessities but for attaining the fruition of God, can no longer be despised. ' Things sensible ' are no longer merely an obstacle to the spirit : they can and ought to be the means of its advancement.

The conception of ' use ' and ' enjoyment ', outlined in this little article of a few hundred words, is what justifies Troeltsch's estimate of Augustine as the great *Kultur-Ethiker* of ancient Christendom.[4] A year or two later it was elaborated in the first book of the *De Doctrina Christiana,* which through the Master of the Sentences became regulative of mediaeval thought. And here we find the definition of *frui* and *uti* which brings the terms into relation with the idea of love. ' To enjoy is to cleave in love to something for its own sake (*amore alicui rei inhaerere*

---

[1] *De Div. Quaest. LXXXIII.* 30.
[2] E.g. *De Beat. Vit.* 34. *De Quant. An.* 76. *De Ver. Relig.* 24 ff. *De Lib. Arb.* II. 35.
[3] *De Mor. Eccl.* 37.
[4] Troeltsch, *Augustin, die christliche Antike und das Mittelalter.*

propter se ipsam) ; to use is to refer the object of use to the obtaining of what is loved.'[1] In this definition, we must note again the ambiguity of the word love : in fruition, the quest of desire becomes the delight of union. Only that is rightly to be enjoyed which is able to give happiness ; and that is God, the Trinity in Unity. We rightly use all that is meant to help us in our pilgrimage to happiness, to God ; our temptation is to 'break the journey' and enjoy what we should use. But if God alone is to be enjoyed, the command of Christ is enough to prove that God is *not* alone to be loved ;[2] and Augustine finds himself obliged to question his usual definition of love as the seeking after a thing 'for its own sake'.[3] Either we must love our neighbour 'for his own sake', and then he becomes an object of enjoyment ; or there must be a love proper to objects of use.

Augustine finds a solution of the dilemma in a conception of great potential fruitfulness—that of relative ends. A means which can be loved is not *only* a means. The keyword is *referre ad Deum,* 'relation to God', and the distinction of *uti* and *frui* is merged in the 'order of love'. Love is rightly due, not only to all those spiritual beings, angels or men, with whom we are linked in a common relation to God, but even to the body which depends on God through us for its well-being.[4] The *utilia* which at the beginning of the discussion had been compared to the 'vehicle' in which the pilgrim makes his journey, in a later chapter take their place in a genuine scale of values. 'That man's life', we read, 'is righteous and holy, whose values are sound (*rerum integer aestimator*). It is he who possesses an ordered love, neither bestowed on what is not lovable nor withheld from what is ; bestowed neither more fully on what is less lovable, nor equally on what is less or more, nor less or more on what is equally to be loved.' Origen had used language very like this in his comment on the text of the *Song of Songs—ordinate in me*

[1] *De Doctr. Christ.* 1. 4.   [2] *Conf.* x. 61.
[3] *De Div. Quaest. LXXXIII.* 35 : nihil aliud est amare, quam propter se ipsam rem aliquam appetere. Cf. *Solil.* 1. 22 : quod non propter se amatur, non amatur.   [4] *De Doctr. Christ.* 1. 22.

caritatem ;[1] and this same text gives Augustine his scriptural authority. But the thought which he develops from it is much wider and deeper than Origen's. ' What God has made for you ', he says in a sermon, ' is good ; but some goods are great, others small : there are goods terrestrial, goods spiritual, goods temporal ; yet all are good, because the good God made them good. Therefore it is said in Scripture : *Order in me love.*'[2] And again, in a comment on the fall of the sons of God in *Genesis* vi. : ' The beauty of the body, a good, made indeed by God, but temporal, carnal, good in the lowest degree, is wrongly loved if it is preferred to God, the eternal, inward, everlasting Good. . . . So is it with every creature : good though it be, it can be loved rightly and wrongly—rightly, when the order is observed, wrongly when the order is confounded. . . . Whence, as I think, a short and true definition of virtue is " the order of love " ; and so in the holy Song of Songs the Bride of Christ, the City of God, sings : *Order in me love.*'[3]

What Augustine consistently maintains is that however many be the things possessing value, their values are never to be regarded as independent. ' The object of our love is the good ', he says at the beginning of his ethical argument for theism in the *De Trinitate,* and he goes on to enumerate the varied goods of nature, art and morality. ' Good is this and good is that ; take away this and that and see, if you can, the good itself ; so will you see God, good not through any other good thing, but the good of every good.'[4] The good of every individual thing is

---

[1] Origen *in Cant.* III. (on *Cant.* II. 4). Origen limits himself to observing that to the love of God there should be no ' measure ', while our neighbour is to be loved ' as ourselves ', yet with distinction according to the desert of the individual.   [2] *Serm.* 21. 3.   [3] *De Civ.* XV. 22.

[4] *De Trin.* VIII. 4. Cf. *En. in Ps.* XXVI. ii. 8 : Omnis boni bonum, unde omne bonum, bonum cui non additur quid sit ipsum bonum. Dicitur enim bonus homo, et bonus ager, et bona domus . . . *adiunxisti,* quoties dixisti, Bonum. Est bonum simplex, ipsum bonum quo cuncta sunt bona, ipsum bonum ex quo cuncta sunt bona. Augustine's God is the *bonum omnis boni ;* the God of Plotinus is the ' Beyond-Good ' ($\acute{v}\pi\epsilon\rho\acute{a}\gamma a\theta o\nu$), ' not to be identified with the good of which it is the source ', but ' good in the unique mode of being the Good above all that is good ' (*Enn.* VI. ix. 6, tr. Mackenna).

as dependent and derived as its existence ; dependence and de-
rivation imply subordination ; and the category of subordination
is only distinguishable from the category of ' use ' in so far as
use may and does extend to things evil in themselves. ' It is
not that the creature may not be loved : if that love be referred
to the Creator, it ceases to be cupidity and becomes charity.' [1]
How far Augustine was, even in his old age, from rejecting all
love of the creature, is strikingly shown by a comment which
he makes in the *Retractations* on a phrase which he had used in
the *De Trinitate*. Speaking of perception as a product of
sense and material object, he had remarked that love of the
corporeal is an " alienation " of the spirit.[2] His note is : ' This
means loving a thing in such a way that the lover counts his
happiness to be in the enjoyment of that which he loves. There
is no " alienation " in loving a bodily form to the praise of the
Creator, so that the enjoyment of the Creator Himself be what
makes every man truly happy.' [3]

Augustine in fact seldom speaks of loving God ' in ' His
creatures ; and when he does, it is always to draw the lesson of
the *ordo amoris,* of the infinite inferiority of the beauty that is
made to the glorious Beauty of its Maker. ' He who made all
things is better than all things ; He who made them fair is
fairer than them all, He who made them strong, is stronger,
He who made them great, is greater : He shall be for you whatever you have loved. Learn then to love the Creator in the
creature, the Maker in the thing made, lest you be held by that
which has been made by Him, and lose Him by whom you also
were made.' [4] Again, and more characteristically : ' Why do
you love these things, but because they are beautiful ? Can
they be so beautiful as He who made them ? You admire them
because you do not see Him. But through those things which
you admire, you should love Him whom you do not see.

Augustine does not share the reluctance of Plotinus to make even goodness
predicable of the Supreme ; but he means the same thing, that good is good
because it comes from God.   [1] *De Trin.* IX. 13.
   [2] *Ib.* XI. 9.   [3] *Retr.* II. 15.   [4] *En. in Ps.* XXXIX. 8.

Enquire of the creature ; if it is of itself, you may rest in it ; if it is from Him, it is harmful to its lover only as it is preferred to its Creator.' [1]   He prefers to say that all else is to be loved ' for the sake of God ', or ' in God ' ; and for him *propter Deum* means *in Deo*, because in the Supreme Good all lesser values are included.   So he is enabled, as we shall see, even to relax the strictness of his principle that God alone is to be enjoyed.

Evidently Augustine was conscious that the formula of use and fruition, struck to designate the attitude of will towards things terrestrial and temporal on the one hand and things celestial and eternal on the other, was ill adapted to express the *ordo amoris*.   But it is a question whether his formula is not exposed to graver objections from the point of view of theo-centric religion ; whether it does not emphasise the real weakness of all eudaemonist ethics, by fixing the self in apparently un-disputed possession of the centre of things ; whether the Ego as user and enjoyer does not face the world as a claimant, regarding it in all its aspects as so much matter for his use and his enjoyment.   According to Nygren, the formula by which Augustine intended to provide for a relative love of the creature, while reserving absolute love for God, in fact makes *all* love, even the love of God, relative to the self and its enjoyment. But this conclusion is merely the consequence of Nygren's false restriction of *amor* to desire.   It is a complete misunderstanding of Augustine's definition of *frui*—*amore alicui rei inhaerere propter se ipsam*—to say that it makes love ' a means to an end '.   To ' enjoy ' is to cleave to something *in* the love which is enjoyment, not *by means* of the love which is desire.   And Augustine is no less seriously misrepresented when Nygren alleges that he makes happiness consist ' not in a *caritas* directed towards God but in the *fruitio Dei*, which *caritas* procures for us ', and that ' in principle the complete fruition of God means the cessation of love '.[2]

---

[1] *En. in Ps.* LXXIX. 14.

[2] *Eros und Agape II.* pp. 323 f. Nygren admits that Augustine himself thinks quite otherwise. Cf. e.g. *De Fide et Symb.* 19 : Frui autem sapientia Dei, nihil est aliud quam ei dilectione cohaerere ; neque quisquam in eo quod percipit *permanet,* nisi dilectione.

Whether Augustine's religion is in the last resort theocentric or egocentric cannot be fairly judged until we have done our best to understand exactly what he means by his ultimate end —the fruition of God. We shall approach this question by ascending the *ordo amoris* from below, beginning with the external goods which are for Augustine most unambiguously the proper objects of use, and which yet may be in a certain sense the objects of an ' ordered love '.

V

The Order of Love

The order of the two great commandments must not be inverted. God is to be loved wholly and above all, and this can be only when we become the recipients of His Love, one with His Life, by participating in which we become His sons, and love one another in the order of God. God does not dwell in us because we love, we love because He dwelleth in us, and become perfected in love by loving all that He loves. . . . God does not love Himself *and* things, but loves all things in Himself, in their original, never completely lost dignity, goodness, and beauty, nor loves Himself less in loving all things as they exist both within Him as ideas and outside Him in created form. . . . Because the Word made Flesh loved His Eternal Father above all with the whole choice and fervour of both His divine and human will, so it was that never son loved his mother as did He, never was there a greater love of friends, of country, of all men, righteous and sinners, rich and poor alike, no poet or artist ever surpassed His intense, joyous love for the vine-yards and olive groves, the cedar-covered hills, the waters of Galilee, the empty space of the desert lands, no one more loved the work given Him to do among busy crowds, no less than the quiet peace of Nazareth and Bethany.

BEDE FROST.

V

1. External Goods

The oldest of all objections to belief in God's providence is founded on the indiscriminate distribution of the good things of this world. Augustine refuses the Stoic answer, that the wise man will not attribute value to such things at all. The fruit of the forbidden tree was assuredly good, and the sin of Adam was not the desire for what was evil in itself, but the abandonment of what was better.[1] In the Old Testament, in its preoccupation with outward prosperity and adversity, Augustine finds the lesson that the sensual life is the life from which we all have to begin.[2] For all our bodily senses there are delights which are lawful,[3] and to profess contempt for res humanae, for all the interests of the natural man, is an act of contumely against the Creator.[4] That God's promises are for heaven does not mean that He 'deserts us on earth'; [5] and He will have us first to learn that the temporal felicity which we naturally desire is His gift. We do right to pray for a sufficiency of worldly goods, for health of body and mind, for the comforts of friendship.[6]

In all this we can see clearly enough the genuineness and permanence of Augustine's reaction against Manichaean asceticism. But it is true that God gives outward prosperity without regard

---

[1] De Nat. Boni 34.   [2] Ep. 140. 3 ff.

[3] Serm. 159. 2, where 'lawful delights' are exemplified by 'spectacula ista magna naturae . . . psalmus sacer suaviter cantatus . . . flores et aromata . . . cibus non prohibitus . . . coniugales amplexus'. To the man who once had said 'nihil mihi tam fugiendum quam concubitum esse decrevi' (Solil. I. 17), the addition of these last words cannot have been easy.

[4] Ep. 258. 2.   [5] En. in Ps. XL. 3.

[6] Ep. 130. 12 f., where health and friends are even allowed to be sought 'for their own sake'. Cf. Morin, Sermones post Maurinos reperti, Denis xvi. 1 : necessaria sunt in hoc mundo duo ista, salus et amicus : ista sunt quae magni pendere, quae non debemus contemnere. Fecit Deus hominem ut esset et viveret : salus est ; sed ne solus esset, amicitia quaesita est.

to merit, alike to the evil and the good ; and the argument which runs through the first part of the *De Civitate* is that this is precisely in order that we may learn not to over-value it.[1] These gifts which God lavishes on the unthankful and on the evil are indeed a proof of His transcendent goodness.[2] But their purpose is to be a test. ' God has given to men certain goods appropriate to this life . . . on the most just condition that he who rightly uses such goods shall receive greater and better . . . he who uses them wrongly shall neither receive the greater nor retain the less.'[3] All these things are good, but ' they ask for good men '.[4] They form the material and not the cause of moral goodness.[5] And rich and poor alike need constantly to be reminded that a man can be made happy only by that which makes him good (*inde necesse est fiat homo beatus, unde fit bonus*).[6]

Augustine has a stock phrase for the confusion of secular and spiritual motive. It is ' the left hand knowing what the right hand does '. Purity of heart means, not the avoidance of the ' left-hand felicity ' of worldly success and the praise of men, but the steady refusal to set it on the right hand.[7] The letter to Macedonius condemns the false philanthropy which directs itself merely to the end ' that men may suffer no unjust pains according to the flesh ' : Macedonius is not to think it ' no business of his ' to what end the secular tranquillity which he

---

[1] *De Civ.* I. 8. Cf. *Serm.* 50. 5 : si solis malis in potestatem daretur aurum et argentum, recte putaretur malum ; si solis bonis, recte putaretur magnum aliquod bonum.

[2] The theme of the great chapter *De Civ.* XXII. 24, summarised in *Ep.* 210. I : quantum diligat credentes et sperantes in se et illum atque invicem diligentes, et quid eis in posterum servet, hinc maxime ostendit, cum infidelibus et desperatis et perversis, quibus in mala voluntate usque in finem perseverantibus ignem cum diabolo aeternum minatur, in hoc tamen saeculo bona tanta largitur.

[3] *De Civ.* XIX. 13.   [4] *Serm.* 311. 11.

[5] *Serm.* 48. 8 ; 61. 3 : there are ' bona quae faciunt bonum,' and ' bona unde facias bonum.'

[6] *Ep.* 130. 3.

[7] *De Serm. Dom. in Mont.* II. 8 ff. Cf. *En. in Ps.* CXX. 10 ; CXLIII. 18.

strives to establish is 'referred' by those who enjoy it; else all his labour will avail him nothing.[1] That Augustine, for himself, had a profound distrust of all natural pleasures which he was little concerned to disguise, does but increase the significance of the more liberal view which as a Christian teacher he felt bound to maintain. It is summed up in his beautiful figure of the betrothal ring. 'Let not Satan steal a way into your heart, saying as he is wont, "Enjoy God's creature : why did He make it but for your enjoyment?" . . . God forbids not the love of these things (*amare*), but only the finding of our happiness in the love of them (*diligere ad beatitudinem*) : we are to make the love of their Creator the end of our esteem for them. Suppose, brethren, a man should make a ring for his betrothed, and she should love (*diligeret*) the ring given her more than her betrothed who made it for her, would not her heart be convicted of infidelity in respect of the very gift of her betrothed, though what she loved were what he gave? Certainly let her love (*amaret*) his gift; but if she should say "The ring is enough, I do not wish to see his face again," what should we say of her? . . . The pledge is given by the betrothed just that in his pledge he himself may be loved. God, then, has given you all these things ; love Him who made them.'[2]

In this passage, Augustine does for once imply a distinction between *amare* and *diligere,* but it is not the distinction between self-centred desire and 'disinterested', personal love. *Amor,* as always, is the neutral term, *dilectio* is the love of conscious preference. In the *ordo amoris* is included the whole range of the will's direction, from what is 'beneath us', through what is 'on our level', to what is 'above us'.[3] The attitude of mastery or domination is thus as essential to a rightly ordered love of *inferiora* as it is destructive of a right love of *aequalia.* If the principle of equality governs Augustine's whole treatment of the love of neighbour, it is simply because he takes seriously the command to love our neighbour 'as ourself'.

[2] *Ep.* 155. 10.   [2] *In. Ep. Jo. Tr.* 2. 11.
[3] *De Doctr. Christ.* I. 22.

2. *Self*

When Christ set beside the first great commandment, familiar to every Jew from his daily recitation of the *Shema*, a verse from Leviticus which was already prominent in Rabbinical teaching, He called this second commandment ' like unto ' the first, simply because the action enjoined in both was ἀγαπήσεις— ' Thou shalt love '. If St. Luke's ' lawyer ' had asked for a definition of ' love ' as well as of ' neighbour ', the answer might have been in terms of the Golden Rule, which in the Sermon on the Mount is given as a summary of ' the law and the prophets '. Whether it is right for us to love ourselves, whether it is right for us to wish that others should do good to us, are questions neither raised nor answered. It is simply taken for granted that men are not indifferent to their own welfare. Augustine's inference, that we needed no commandment to love ourselves, and Calvin's, that the commandment is directed against our natural tendency to love ourselves best, are equally justified. But the assertion of Luther, that *all* self-love is a *vitiosus amor,* is no more an implication of the commandment than is the scholastic rule against which both he and Calvin protested, that in the *ordo amoris* love of self rightly comes before love of neighbour.

Augustine would certainly have rejected the scholastic appeal to his authority in support of such a rule. ' Love God, love your neighbour : God as God, your neighbour as yourself. There is no other equal to God, so that you might be bidden to love God as you love that other. But for your neighbour, you are shown a rule, since you yourself are shown as your neighbour's equal. . . . May I now entrust to you your neighbour to be loved as yourself ? I should wish it, but I am still afraid to do it. . . . I need still to probe the manner of your love for yourself.' [1] A right self-love is the condition for a right love of neighbour ; for until we know how to love ourselves, in loving our neighbour we shall ' deceive him as we deceive ourselves '.[2]

[1] *De Disciplina Christiana* 3.   [2] *Serm.* 128. 5.

' Every man loves his neighbour as himself, *if he loves God;* for if he does not love God, he does not love himself.' [1] There is the theme, the constant subject of varied development.

Nygren has made much of the ' complications ' in Augustine's treatment of self-love.[2] He notes that *amor sui* appears on the one hand, especially in the *De Civitate,* as the root of sin, the irreconcilable opposite of *amor Dei;* and on the other as at once belonging to man's created nature—the image of God must love itself as God loves Himself—and defining his highest duty. Nygren explains the apparent contradiction in accordance with his view that love in Augustine is always *generically* the desire of a good to be possessed. *Caritas* as much as *cupiditas* seeks its own good, though seeking this good in God and not in the self. Both the right and the wrong *amor sui* are egocentric in kind; but while true self-love is desire of an object above the self which constitutes the self's true good, false self-love is desire to be as God, sufficient to oneself. Hence the paradoxical form in which Augustine will express the opposition and the coincidence of self-love and the love of God. ' In a manner that is inexplicable, whosoever loves himself and not God, does not love himself; and whosoever loves God and not himself, loves himself. For man cannot live of himself, and therefore by loving himself he must die; and the love of self which is against the life of the self cannot be true self-love. But when He is loved on whom life depends, the man who loves not himself for love of Him from whom he has life, loves himself the more in not loving himself.' [3]

If we have been right in rejecting Nygren's exclusive definition of *amor* as desire of a good to be possessed, it is not likely that this definition will help us to understand either *amor sui* or *amor Dei.* In fact, the desire of private possession is just what Augustine regards as the perversion of self-love and the destruction of all love to God. And we must first recognise, what Nygren has not made clear, that Augustine has *three* meanings of the term

---

[1] *In Jo. Ev. Tr.* 87. 1.   [2] *Eros und Agape II.* pp. 347 ff.
[3] *In Jo. Ev. Tr.* 123. 5. In the last sentence the verb changes from *amare* to *diligere.*

self-love : the first natural and morally neutral, the second morally wrong and the third morally right. A man is said to love himself, in the second sense, because he falsely supposes that he is pursuing his own advantage ; in the third sense, because he wins his own advantage through not pursuing it.

(*a*) When Augustine says that we needed no special commandment to love ourselves, that self-love is planted in us by nature, he is generally thinking of the instinct of self-preservation which man shares with the animals.[1] As the Stoics said, the *prima vox naturae* is *ut homo concilietur sibi* : man is ' so far his own friend, that his strongest impulse is to exist as an animal, to live in this conjunction of body and soul '.[2] In this instinctive self-love there is nothing evil. On the contrary, it is the primitive expression of the principle of individuality, the reflection in the creature of the absolute unity of God upon whom the being of the individual is dependent.[3]

In the rational soul of man, natural self-love is more than *amor suae incolumitatis* : man desires not bare existence but existence of a certain kind. He desires to be happy,[4] and because his nature is rational he will always seek a happiness which is more than the satisfaction of the body's needs. This is not yet Butler's ' cool self-love ', the calculating prudence which already thinks it knows what will and what will not contribute to happiness. It is the undetermined direction of the will to the well-being of the self, however that well-being may be conceived—a pure egoism which for Augustine is a fact of human nature, neither laudable nor reprehensible.

(*b*) The well-being of the self must consist in a certain kind of spiritual activity. It was ' man's primal perdition ', says

---

[1] *De Doctr. Christ.* I. 27.

[2] *De Civ.* XIX. 4. Cf. *De Trin.* XIV. 18 : the self-love ' naturaliter inditum ', by which ' omne animal sibi natura conciliatum sit ut se custodiat quantum potest '.

[3] *Conf.* I. 31. Cf. *En. in Ps.* XCIX. 5 : nescio quid invisibile . . . inesse omnibus animantibus . . . ad conservandam incolumitatem suam vestigium quoddam unitatis.

[4] *De Civ.* X. 3 : non enim qui se diligit aliud vult esse quam beatus.

Augustine, when he looked for his happiness in ' doing his own will ',[1] when *amor sui* became *amor suae potestatis,* the craving for independence, the soul's attempt to escape from the rule of God and to be its own master.[2] Plotinus describes the fall of the soul, in well-known passages, as an act of ' audacity ' or ' self-will ', as the ' desire for standing apart ', for ' self-ownership '. It is his semi-mythical explanation of the descent of spirit into matter, of the soul's embodiment ; and for that reason he can represent the act of self-assertion as leading inevitably to loss of the true self.[3] Augustine often uses very similar language ; but what he is concerned to explain is not the existence of the material world but the existence of spiritual evil, of sin itself ; and this gives a turn to his thought which we do not find in Plotinus. ' God is in need of no good : He is Himself the highest good, and from Him is all good. We need God that we may be good : God does not need us for His goodness. . . . If a man applies his will to the perverse imitation of God . . . willing to be in his own power, living like God without another to form or rule him—what can await him but by withdrawal from God's warmth to grow numb, by withdrawal from the truth to become void, by withdrawal from that which supremely and unchangeably Is, to lose reality in the change to evil ? '[4] The ' perverse imitation of God ' is the sin of pride, in which the individual soul constitutes itself its own end, seeks ' to become and to be the principle of its own existence ',[5] putting itself in the place of God ; and this results, by the necessary operation of the divine law, in the

---

[1] *Serm.* 96. 2 : Prima hominis perditio fuit amor sui. Si enim se non amaret, et Deum sibi praeponeret, Deo esse semper subditus vellet ; non autem converteretur ad negligendam voluntatem illius et faciendam voluntatem suam. *Hoc est enim amare se, velle facere voluntatem suam.*

[2] *Ep.* 118. 15 : primum peccatum, hoc est primum voluntarium defectum, esse gaudere ad propriam potestatem ; ad minus enim gaudet, quam si ad Dei potestatem gaudeat, quae utique maior est.

[3] *Enn.* IV. viii. 4 f. ; v. i. 1. Yet Plotinus holds that this ' original sin ' is in accord with a ' law of nature '. ' In abandoning its Superior ', the soul ' runs out to serve the needs of another ' (i.e. the world of sense), and that is why we can still say that it is ' sent down by God ' (*Enn.* IV. viii. 5, tr. Mackenna).

[4] *En. in Ps.* LXX. ii. 6.   [5] *De Civ.* XIV. 13.

subjection and enslavement of the soul which has rebelled against
its own Master, to the external and material nature which is
properly its servant. For no man can ever make himself sufficient
to himself. The love of self which is both self-satisfaction and
desire for ' self-ownership ' is vanity, and the inevitable attempt
to fill the void by possession of the world's goods is vexation of
spirit. ' Whoever lets God go and loves himself, letting God go
in loving himself, remains not even in himself but goes out of
himself too. He is exiled from his own heart through contempt
of the inward and love for the outward.' ¹ So Augustine rejoins
Plotinus, but with a difference. The impersonal Absolute of
Neo-Platonism has been clothed with the majesty and dominion
of the ' jealous ' God ; and the shadowy outlines of the pre-
mundane fall are replaced by the tragic reality of human self-
deception. Pride begets avarice, and an avarice which defeats
itself ; for the impossible attempt to obtain something ' more '
than the universal Good can only result in a shrinkage of the self,
' thrust down ' by its own act ' into the care of the private and
the partial ' which can never satisfy.²

In an important chapter of his commentary on Genesis,³
Augustine sketches the plan of the *De Civitate* which was already
in his mind, perhaps already begun. He has just ascribed the
fall of Satan and therefore ' the beginning of all sin ', to pride,
the ' love of personal pre-eminence ' (*amor excellentiae propriae*),
upon which envy always attends. True, Scripture says elsewhere that avarice is the root of all evil ; but this means not
simply ' love of money ' but that ' general avarice ' which makes
a man seek for ' something more than is fitting ', ' for the sake
of his own pre-eminence and through a kind of love of possession
(*quemdam propriae rei amorem*) '. Such love is well called
' private ', for ' all privation is a minishing ' : it reduces, not
enlarges the self. *Charity seeketh not her own*—that is, has no
delight in personal pre-eminence ; and these two loves, ' the one

---

¹ *Serm.* 330. 3 ; 96. 2. The ' lover of self' becomes a ' lover of money '
(2 *Tim.* iii. 2).
² *De Trin.* XII. 14.   ³ *De Gen. ad litt.* XI. 18 ff.

social, the other private, the one looking to the common advantage for a supernal fellowship, the other seeking to bring even what belongs to the community into its own power for the sake of an arrogant domination, the one submissive to God, the other God's rival', are the spirits of the Two Cities which are to be the theme of another work, ' if the Lord will '.

It is abundantly clear that the *amor sui usque ad contemptum Dei* of the *De Civitate* is self-assertion rather than self-love, the desire of a possession which is necessarily exclusive, the enjoyment of which actually consists in the exclusion of others. Nature makes us egoists when she sets each of us upon the satisfaction of his own desires ; individuality makes us egocentrists, because no man can jump out of his own skin or see the world with any eyes but his own. But the love of self that runs to the contempt of God is neither egoism nor egocentrism, but ' egotheism '— not selfishness but blasphemous rebellion.[1]

(c) It is Augustine's constant doctrine, from the *De Moribus Ecclesiae* onwards, that the only love of self which deserves to be so called is the love of God the Supreme Good. ' The love wherewith a man truly loves himself is none other than the love of God. For he who loves himself in any other way is rather to be said to hate himself; since he becomes evil and loses the light of righteousness, when he turns aside from the higher and more excellent good to himself—a conversion which must needs bring him to what is lower and poorer.' [2]

The contention of Nygren is that if God be conceived as the *Summum Bonum* it is impossible to avoid giving the real priority to the love of self; and that this is shown when Augustine lets slip, as he occasionally does, a phrase which appears formally to ground the love of God in the love of self.[3] Such phrases if

---

[1] Mr. Philip Leon's recent book *The Ethics of Power* is a remarkable exposition in modern form of the two kinds of *amor sui*, natural and perverted, which he calls ' egoism ' and ' egotism '. Mr. Leon's Augustinianism is all the more striking because it is (apparently) unconscious.

[2] *Ep.* 155. 15.

[3] *Eros und Agape II.* p. 357. Nygren quotes *De Civ.* x. 3 : ut homo se diligere nosset, constitutus est ei finis, etc. *Serm.* 90. 6 : Diligite Dominum,

taken at their face value would directly contradict the rule that the self is to be *used* for the fruition of God, not God for the fruition of the self ' as a private good for our own possession '.[1] *My soul,* says the Psalmist, *shall live to Him.* 'To Him', runs the comment, ' and not to itself, like the souls of the proud who rejoice in their private good, recoiling in vain exaltation from the common good of all which is God.'[2] 'The less we love what is our own (*proprium*), the more closely are we joined to God.' 'The more we love God, the more we love ourselves.'[3] These two sentences from the *De Trinitate* conflict with one another only if intention is confused with effect, act with consequence. To him who loves God, the private interest of the self *cannot* be the end sought. Augustine knows as well as Bishop Butler that to love God *in order that* our love of self may be satisfied is impossible. The self-love which is native to the human soul will become injurious to the self, will turn in effect to self-hatred, unless the image of God is restored by the transformation of this self-love into the love of Him in whose image the soul was made.[4] But the lover of God no more intends a private good for himself than is the lover of iniquity consciously moved by hatred of his own soul.

It is true that the God in whom all good is immutably realised can demand nothing of us that does not tend to our own advantage : ' when you love Him ', it is you that are the gainer : ' you will be where your being is secure (*ibi eris, ubi non peris*)'.[5] But there is never for Augustine any question, such as Nygren seems to assume, of 'harmonising' self-love with the love of God, as though they were two separate intentions

et ibi discite diligere vos. *In Jo. Ev. Tr.* 83. 3 : Qui se propter habendum Deum diligunt, ipsi se diligunt : ergo ut se diligant, Deum diligunt. It would have been fairer to have added to this last quotation the words which follow : Non est haec dilectio in omnibus hominibus : pauci *se propterea diligunt, ut sit Deus omnia in omnibus.*

[1] *De Trin.* XII. 17. *De Doctr. Christ.* I. 21 : nec seipso quisquam frui debet . . . quia nec se ipsum debet propter se ipsum diligere, sed propter illum quo fruendum est.

[2] *Ep.* 140. 68.   [3] *De Trin.* XII. 16 ; VIII. 12.   [4] *Ib.* XIV. 18.

[5] *Serm.* 34. 8. Cf. *De Doctr. Christ.* I. 30 ; *En. in Ps.* XXXVI. ii. 13 ; CXLIX. 4.

with distinct objects. No ; ' the true and highest interest of the self is served when God is loved more than the self, so that a man chooses to be God's rather than his own (*ut malit homo eius esse quam suus*) '.[1] In a passage like this, the Christian roots of Augustine's eudaemonism are fairly exposed. The self-denial for which Christ calls is a denial of the individual, personal, ' private ' will, in so far as it falls short of the will of God. I must will to belong to God rather than to myself. Only so, *ibi ero ubi non pereo.*

And Augustine knows, too, that the love of God in which the self's true good consists implies nothing less than a surrender of the self. *Sell all that thou hast, and give to the poor; and come, follow Me.* When you have given all you have, the final gift remains : *tu addendus es.*[2] Yet the form in which the Bishop of Hippo found it natural to enforce the need for such surrender upon his congregations was the metaphor of purchase. There are two remarkable passages in the 34th and 127th Sermons. In one of these he appeals to his hearers' knowledge of the efforts and sacrifices which any man will make to prolong his earthly life. If God's promise were only of an eternal life free from all that makes this life wretched, what would they not give to gain it ? ' Yet it is for sale : buy it if you will. . . . Ask not what you *have* to give for it, but what you *are*. The thing is worth—you. . . . Give yourself, and it will be yours. . . . You will say, " I am evil, and maybe God will not accept me ". By giving yourself to Him, you will be made good. To give yourself over to this faith and to the promise of God—that is to be good.'[3] If purchase, we say, then no gift : the love that is a

---

[1] *De Div. Quaest. LXXXIII.* 36.

[2] *Serm.* 345. 6. Cf. Morin, *Sermones post Maurinos reperti*, Frang. iii. 6.

[3] *Serm.* 127. 3. Cf. Luther, *De Libertate Christiana* : Anima dum firmiter credit promittenti Deo, veracem et iustum eum habet, qua opinione nihil potest Deo praestantius tribuere. . . . Ubi autem Deus videt veritatem sibi tribui et fide cordis nostri se honorari tanto honore quo ipse dignus est, rursus et ipse nos honorat tribuens et nobis veritatem et iustitiam propter hanc fidem. Fides enim facit veritatem et iustitiam, reddens Deo suum. . . . Verum est enim et iustum Deum esse veracem et iustum, et hoc ei tribuere et confiteri, hoc est esse veracem et iustum. (*Werke* VII. 54, Weimar ed.)

transaction is not love : egocentrism is not transcended. And in the other sermon, we are indeed taken a step further. For there the treasure to be purchased is charity itself. The preacher plays on the word. Nothing can be ' dearer ' than charity, then nothing more precious. ' The price of charity is yourself. . . . Why fear to give yourself, lest you be spent ? Nay, if you give not yourself, you lose yourself.' And Charity itself in Wisdom's words says, *My son, give me thy heart.—Totum exigit te, qui fecit te.*[1]

' Self-sacrifice ' is a modern phrase, so effectively profaned by common usage as to have lost the only meaning it could have borne for Augustine—the sanctification of the self in devotion to God. His definition of Christian sacrifice, based upon the famous texts of Micah and Hosea,[2] is ' every work done to the end of our union with God in holy fellowship ' ; the Christian himself, ' consecrated in God's name and devoted to God, is a sacrifice in virtue of his dying to the world that he may live to God ' ; and ' the whole redeemed community, the congregation and fellowship of the saints, is the universal sacrifice offered to God through the great High Priest who offered Himself in His suffering for us, that we might be the Body of so great a Head '. ' That is the sacrifice of Christians : the many made one body in Christ.' The Eucharist is there to keep the Church in mind of her sacrificial character : ' it is made manifest to her that in that which she offers she is offered herself '.[3] ' If you are the Body of Christ and His members, it is the sacrament of your-selves (*mysterium vestrum*) that is set upon the Lord's table, the

---

[1] *Serm.* 34. 7.

[2] *Micah* vi. 6-8 and *Hosea* vi. 6 are quoted in *De Civ.* x. 5, together with *Hebrews* xiii. 16, and the conclusion is drawn that ' quaecumque in ministerio tabernaculi sive templi multis modis de sacrificiis leguntur divinitus esse praecepta, *ad dilectionem Dei et proximi significando referuntur* '.

[3] *De Civ.* x. 6. Cf. *ib.* xix. 23 : huius [Dei] autem praeclarissimum atque optimum sacrificium nos ipsi sumus, hoc est civitas eius, cuius rei mysterium celebramus oblationibus nostris quae fidelibus notae sunt. *Ib.* xxii. 10 : ipsum vero sacrificium corpus est Christi, quod non offertur ipsis [martyribus] quia hoc sunt et ipsi. *Serm.* 48. 2 : quaerebas quid offerres pro te : offer te. Quid enim Dominus quaerit a te, nisi te ?

sacrament of yourselves that you receive. Be what you receive, and receive what you are.' [1]

Simus quod accipimus : [2] that is the text of all Augustine's Eucharistic preaching. But the attempt to reduce it to a symbolism in which the *res sacramenti*, the thing signified, is incorporation in the Church and nothing more,[3] entirely mistakes the central point of reference. Augustine throughout *assumes* the common faith of the Church in all its realism—that the Eucharist *is* the Christ who gave Himself for us. ' *Because* He suffered for us, He has commended to us in this sacrament His Body and Blood '—that comes first : the application to ourselves follows—' which He has made us also to be. For we are made His own Body : through His mercy we are what we receive '.[4] The Eucharist is a ' sacrament of humility' before it can be a ' sacrament of unity '.[5] If we forget that in order that we might be made one the Body had to be broken and the Blood shed, we shall eat of the food of God's poor, but we shall not be filled. For the feast which the Lord spread was His passion ; and only ' he who imitates is filled '.[6] The ultimate understanding of the ' mystery of that Supper' is the understanding of the martyr, and of all who follow Christ in the martyr's spirit, though they be never called to face the martyr's fiery trial.[7] *Totum exigit te,*

---

[1] *Serm.* 272.   [2] *Serm.* 57. 7.

[3] So Dorner and Harnack, who have been sufficiently refuted by Karl Adam's study, *Die Eucharistielehre des Hl. Augustin.*

[4] *Serm.* 229. Cf. *Serm.* 227 : per ista voluit Dominus Christus commendare corpus et sanguinem suum quem pro nobis fudit in remissionem peccatorum. Si bene accepistis, vos estis quod accepistis.

[5] *En. in Ps.* xxxiii. i. 6 : Unde commendavit corpus et sanguinem suum ? De humilitate sua. Nisi enim esset humilis, nec manducaretur, nec biberetur. *Ib.* i. 10 ; ii. 7.

[6] *Ib.* xxi. ii. 27 ; xlviii. i. 3 : Edunt pauperes et saturabuntur. Quid edunt ? Quod sciunt fideles. Quomodo saturabuntur ? Imitando passionem Domini sui, et non sine causa accipiendo pretium suum.

[7] *Serm.* 304. 1 : Ad illam mensam de qua nobis modo Salomonis proverbia loquebantur, ubi scriptum est : Si sederis cenare ad mensam potentis, cognoscens intellige quae apponuntur tibi ; et sic extende manum tuam, sciens quoniam similia te oportet praeparare. (*Prov.* xxiii. 1 f. (lxx).) Huius cenae mysterium beatus apostolus Ioannes evidenter exposuit, dicens : Sicut Christus pro nobis

qui fecit te. Augustine knows what Christ meant by *with all thy heart*—a total abandonment, an entire devotion, a holocaust in which the whole man is ablaze with love's fire.[1]   If, in discoursing of self-love, he seems to fall short of that, it is to be remembered that what always comes first with him is the convert's sense of sin.   He has seen the ugliness of his own soul ; [2] in the love of God he has lost all value for himself (*coram se viluit*).[3]   He knows that what is past has received the divine forgiveness, but he cannot and will not forget that he is a sinner.   To the Augustine whom Luther esteemed next to Holy Writ, the Lutheran assurance would have spelt deadly peril.   He knows that in the last resort the lover must forget himself ; [4] but he does not speak of self-forgetfulness lightly.   For the Platonist, the soul has indeed forgotten its true self in abandoning itself to the love of the creature.   The self-forgetfulness which love of the Creator brings is love's end and not its beginning.   In comparison with the Supreme and changeless Good, reason can already acknowledge that the finite being is of no account ;   but only in the vision of that changeless Good will love at once confirm and render superfluous the findings of reason :   only when we see God as He is, shall we altogether forget ourselves.[5]

animam suam posuit, sic et nos debemus animas pro fratribus ponere.   Intellexit hoc, fratres, Sanctus Laurentius :   intellexit, ac fecit ;   et prorsus qualia sumpsit in illa mensa, talia praeparavit.   So also *In Jo. Ev. Tr.* 47. 2.

[1] *En. in Ps.* XLIX. 15.

[2] *Serm.* 142. 3 :   arguitur, corripitur, ostenditur sibi, displicet sibi, confitetur foeditatem, desiderat pulchritudinem, et quae ibat effusa, redit confusa.   Cf. *Conf. passim.*

[3] *De Trin.* IV. 1.   Cf. Morin, *Sermones post Maurinos reperti,* Denis xvii. 6 : ipse amator in comparatione rei quae amanda est, vilescere sibi debet.

[4] *Serm.* 142. 3 :   amandus est Deus ita, ut si fieri potest nos ipsos obliviscamur. . . . Oblita est anima se ipsam, sed amando mundum :   obliviscatur se, sed amando artificem mundi.

[5] *C. Jul. Pel.* IV. 28 :   quamdiu non videt sicut videbit in fine summum illud et immutabile bonum, in cuius comparatione se spernat, sibique illius caritate vilescat, tantoque spiritu eius impleatur, ut id sibi non ratione sola sed aeterno quoque amore praeponat.

3. *Neighbour*

There can be no doubt how Augustine would answer the objection that a love of God which can be presented as the true love of self must be egocentric, not theocentric. That must depend, he would say, on your conception of the Supreme Good. If the *Summum Bonum* is by its very nature the *bonum commune*, a good which can be possessed only by being shared, then the desire and pursuit of it can never be the desire and pursuit of a *bonum privatum*. And to Augustine's conception of the *Summum Bonum* the attribute of community belongs no less essentially than the attribute of immutability. The necessity of both attributes he found in the Platonist metaphysic : the αὐτὸ-ἀγαθόν is not only ' always the same ', but it is the universal and not a particular good. But, for incorporation in a Christian philosophy, the divine immutability had to be interpreted in the light of Christian teaching on God's love and man's destiny ; the divine universality had to be translated from the language of metaphysical logic into that of religious ethic, with the aid of the Christian doctrine of the Church. The necessity of the Church —ἡ καθολικὴ ἐκκλησία—for the realisation of Christianity is a standing illustration, a living sacrament, of the universality of the *Summum Bonum*. Goodness is a possession which is not only not diminished by being shared, but is only possessed at all in so far as it *is* shared.[1] Like the apprehension of truth, all spiritual good has this characteristic of not being monopolisable, of not being an object of competition.[2] In the race of love, no runner can desire to be first ; [3] Christ's own love for men was the desire for sharers in His heritage.[4] At every turn, in every variety of context, Augustine recurs to this thought. The story of the Church's rejoicing at the conversion of Victorinus suggests the reflection that ' when joy is felt with many, the joy in each

[1] *De Civ.* xv. 5.
[2] *De Trin.* xii. 15. Cf. *Solil.* i. 22 : Quem modum potest habere illius pulchritudinis amor, in qua non solum non invideo ceteris sed etiam plurimos quaero qui mecum appetant, etc.
[3] *En in. Ps.* xxxix. 11.   [4] *Ib.* xlix. 2.

individual is the fuller '.[1] Fellowship is an essential element in Christian sacrifice.[2] Natural relationships are private and particular ; but she who as a mother is yours only, is sister to every Christian.[3] The preacher cannot be satisfied by ' delivering his own soul ' : *nolo salvus esse sine vobis*.[4] In the Church on earth, ' if you love her unity, whoever has anything in her, has it for you as well ' : the banishment of envy removes the distinctions of *meum* and *tuum*.[5] To acknowledge God's grace in oneself, but to grudge the overflow of its riches to others, is a form of pride no better than the Pelagian.[6] Even the heroic achievements of individual Christians can be ' shared ' by others who are not capable of them : ' so strong a thing is love '.[7] And for the Church in heaven, community is the very principle of the *pax aeterna :* [8] by our desire for the realisation of the City of God, we learn ' to set things common before things private ' ; [9] and though in the ' many mansions ' reward will be proportionate to merit,[10] yet God will so be ' all in all ', that ' charity will make what each possesses common to all. For each one, when he loves in the other what he himself has not, possesses it thus himself : there will be no envy of unequal glory, when the unity of charity shall reign in all.' [11]

Love of neighbour, like love of self, begins with natural instinct. Towards this instinctive affection Augustine's earlier works betray something very like hostility. Let no one say, he writes in the *De Vera Religione,* that Christ's call to ' hate father and mother ' is inhuman. The real ' inhumanity ' is to love a human being not for his relationship to God, but for his relationship to yourself, not for what is ' common ' but for what is ' private '. ' You say, Let me love both ! God says, No : the first and the first alone.' [12] In this treatise and in that on the

---

[1] *Conf.* VIII. 9.
[2] *De Civ.* X. 6.
[3] *Ep.* 243. 4.
[4] *Serm.* 17. 2.
[5] *In Jo. Ev. Tr.* 32. 8.
[6] *En. in Ps.* XLIX. 30.
[7] *Ib.* CXXI. 10.
[8] *De Civ.* XV. 3 ; XIX. 13.
[9] *En. in Ps.* CV. 34.
[10] *De Civ.* XXII. 30.
[11] *In Jo. Ev. Tr.* 67. 2.
[12] *De Ver. Relig.* 88.

Sermon on the Mount, Augustine had suggested that the ties of kinship are no more than consequences of the Fall. In the *Retractations* he peremptorily condemns such a view, and admits only his later interpretation of the Gospel text : namely, that ' hating ' father and mother means only refusal to allow the claim of family affection to set itself against that of the Kingdom of God.[1] In his Sermons on Charity he distinguishes between the ' human ' loves which may be lawful or unlawful, and the ' divine ' love which is ' according to Christ '. The lawful human love for wife and children merits no praise for itself, though its absence is to be condemned. ' Love your children, love your wives, though it be with a worldly love (*etsi saeculariter*). . . . Only, when you love them in this human fashion, see that you love Christ more.' For Christ himself has not ' taken away ', but ' ordered ' this natural love : He said not *He that loveth*, but *He that loveth more than me.*[2]

Here the text has led to a disguising of the real qualitative difference under a difference of degree. Augustine rightly held that the ' care for one's own ' is the first stage in the divinely-ordained hierarchy of peace ; [3] that charity does begin at home, and that common sense assigns its limits to the duty of loving all men alike.[4] But he was equally clear that the love of family and friends can easily be no better than a wider selfishness. The Christian love of neighbour is not an extension of family affection : it is not even, as we might say, its sublimation. For love *secundum Deum* is different in kind from love *secundum hominem*. The charity which is the *end of the commandment* is not *caritas qualis-cumque*. There is a love, real enough in its kind, which can link even ill-doers to one another in the ' fellowship of a lost conscience '. But the charity which is *from a pure heart* must be centred upon God and His righteousness.[5] The storm of grief with which the death of a beloved friend had overwhelmed Augustine in his youth was proof that he had not yet learnt to love men as men

[1] *Retr.* I. 13, 18. Cf. the letter to Laetus, *Ep.* 243.
[2] *Serm.* 349. 7 ; 344. 2.　　　　[3] *De Civ.* XIX. 14.
[4] *De Doctr. Christ.* I. 29.　　　　[5] *En. in Ps.* CXL. 2.

should be loved (*diligere homines humaniter*). The souls that are dear to us must be loved 'in God', in whom alone they are held secure from the touch of change.[1]

The love which is 'according to man' makes man the object of enjoyment. Now Augustine believes that a right love of self can only be relative to the love of God, and that it must therefore be placed in the category of 'use', not in that of 'fruition'. The same should hold of the love of neighbour, who no more than the self is a 'changeless good'. But at the end of the discussion in the *De Doctrina Christiana*, he slips, almost unawares, into speaking of our heavenly reward as the fruition not only of God but of one another 'in God'. True, such fruition will have God rather than man for its real object. The delight which the lover cannot help taking in the beloved is in this earthly life a lodging, a refreshment for the pilgrim. A rightly ordered love will 'pass through' such delight, not 'remaining at rest in it', but 'referring' it to God. 'Not even the Lord Himself, in so far as He deigned to be for us the Way, would keep us holden, but willed that we should pass through'.[2] Like the temporal manifestation of the Christ, the joy of earthly love is sacramental.

Augustine deliberately maintains this qualified extension of the love of enjoyment. While *cupiditas* seeks the enjoyment of self, neighbour, and material goods without reference to God, *caritas* seeks the enjoyment of God for His own sake, and of self and neighbour for the sake of God.[3] And the peace of the Heavenly City is the fellowship of perfect order and harmony in the enjoyment of God and of one another in God.[4] But the

---

[1] *Conf.* IV. 7, 12, 14, 18. Cf. the touching letter to a nun who had lost her brother: *Ep.* 263. 2 : neque enim . . . periit illa caritas qua Timotheus Sapidam dilexit et diligit.

[2] *De Doctr. Christ.* I. 37 f.

[3] *Ib.* III. 16. Cf. *De Trin.* IX. 13 : cum ergo aut par nobis aut inferior creatura sit, inferiore utendum est ad Deum, pari autem fruendum, sed in Deo. Sicut enim te ipso non in te ipso frui debes sed in eo qui fecit te ; sic etiam illo quem diligis tamquam te ipsum. Et nobis ergo et fratribus in Deo fruamur.

[4] *De Civ.* XIX. 13.

perfect fruition of one another, like the fruition of God, is a promise for the life to come. For the act of true love, in this place of our pilgrimage, Augustine has a graphic word. ' *Rape ad eum*—Carry away to God as many as you can. Say to them, " Let us love *Him*, let us love *Him !* " ' [1] That was the *leit-motiv* of all his preaching, all his writing, all his life : *hunc amemus, hunc amemus !* If we desire, as we must, that it shall be well with those whom we love, we shall look for their welfare wherever we look for our own. That is the outward flow of the fountain of living water within us.[2] The true love of neighbour is the will ' that he too may love God with a perfect love : you do not love him as yourself, unless you do all you can to bring him to that good which is your own '.[3]

The attitude of will is so much the most significant element in the love of neighbour that Augustine can pronounce ' benevolence alone ' to be ' enough for the lover '. He acutely observes that ' doing good ' to people can easily produce a feeling of superiority which is fatal to love, and that so far from ' wanting unfortunates ' as recipients of our bounty, we must always ' want equals ', subject with ourselves ' only to Him on whom nothing can be bestowed '.[4] None the less is it in general true that ' love cannot be idle '.[5] And it is just here, in the putting of benevolence into practice, that we most need guidance and enlightenment. ' Would that it were as easy ', says Augustine in the *De Moribus Ecclesiae,* ' to act for our neighbour's good, or to avoid doing him harm, as it is for a well-trained and kindly nature to love him. There good-will is not enough ; we need a method and a wisdom such as no one can have unless God the

---

[1] *Conf.* IV. 18. Cf. *En. in Ps.* LXXII. 34 : si amares aurigam, non raperes ceteros ut tecum amarent ? . . . rape ad unum, et fac unum.

[2] *In Jo. Ev. Tr.* 32. 4.

[3] *De Mor. Eccl.* 26. *Ep.* 23. 1 (to a Donatist bishop) : ' dilectissimo ' autem quod scripsi, novit Deus quod non solum te diligam, sed ita diligam ut me ipsum, quando quidem bene mihi sum conscius et bona me tibi optare quae mihi. *De Doctr. Christ.* I. 30 : velle debemus ut omnes nobiscum diligant Deum, et totum quod vel eos adiuvamus vel adiuvamur ab eis ad unum illum finem referendum est.

[4] *In Ep. Jo. Tr.* 8. 5.   [5] *En. in Ps.* XXXI. ii. 5.

fount of all good give it.'¹ He goes on to describe love in
action, in its two lines of service—works of mercy for the body,
education (*disciplina*) for the soul, and here the activity of
brotherly love is set forth as purely altruistic. But later he
habitually regards the *opera misericordiae* themselves as including
both almsgiving or the relief of bodily suffering in general and
the forgiveness of injuries. This *gemina misericordia* is based on
Luke vi. 37 f., where 'in one and the same place' Christ says
forgive, and it shall be forgiven you : give, and it shall be given to you ; ²
and this text is the authority for that feature in Augustine's
treatment of the whole subject which is most repulsive to our
minds.

He can, it is true, speak with a subtle discernment of the need
for giving not only in the right spirit, but with the 'personal
touch'. 'There should be not only the kindness of a giver,
but the humility of a server. Brethren, I know not how it is,
but when the hand of him who has is laid in the hand of him
who has not, the soul of him who gives to the poor feels as it
were the touch of common humanity and infirmity. Though
one gives and the other receives, the server and the served are
joined together. It is not misfortune but humility that truly
joins us.'³ But the very sympathy which the sufferings of
others excite in us is part of the 'tribulation' of our pilgrimage.⁴
And our efforts to relieve these sufferings, as well as the bearing
of one another's burdens in the forgiveness of injuries,⁵ seem for
Augustine to have their primary, if not their sole justifiable
motive in the securing of ultimate benefit for ourselves. They
are the appointed means of atonement for the venial sin which
no man can avoid : ⁶ the 'baler' with which we are to save
our vessel from being swamped through the leaks of *minuta*

¹ *De Mor. Eccl.* 51.
² *En. in Ps.* CXLIII. 7. Cf. *Serm.* 42 ; 259. 4 ; *Encheirid.* 19.
³ *Serm.* 259. 5.   ⁴ *En. in Ps.* XLIX. 22.
⁵ *Serm.* 57. 11 : the unforgiving spirit is 'horrenda tentatio, quando nobis
tollitur unde ab aliarum tentationum vulneribus sanari possimus.' Cf. *En. in
Ps.* CXXIX. 4.
⁶ *Serm.* 9. 17 ; 42. 1 ; 261. 10.   *C. du. Ep. Pelag.* I. 28.   *Encheirid.* 19.

peccata.[1] The idea of a Christian usury, expressed with a blatancy we find amusing in the words of a familiar hymn, is not ugly in Augustine's eyes.[2]

Here, as elsewhere, his teaching is most un-Christian when he is most assured of following both tradition and Scripture. The notorious treatise of Cyprian, *De Opere et Eleemosynis*, would have been authority enough. But for Augustine the real authority is the twenty-fifth chapter of St. Matthew. Nothing in the Scripture, he says, 'moves' him so deeply. 'Christ says not, Come, receive the Kingdom, for you have lived chastely, have wronged no man, have not oppressed the poor. . . . Not this, but, Receive the Kingdom, *because I was hungry and ye gave me meat.* . . . Again to those on the other side : Depart into eternal fire. . . . How many things He might say to the wicked, if they asked " Why must we depart into eternal fire ? " "You ask, why ?—you, the adulterer, the murderer, the defrauder, the sacrilegious, the blasphemer, the infidel ? " Nothing of all these ; but *because I was hungry, and ye gave me no meat.* . . . I see that you are moved, as I am. . . . We are shown the power of alms for the extinction and blotting out of sins. . . . "You come into my Kingdom", He says, "not because you have not sinned, but because you have redeemed your sins by your alms "." Not only has Augustine read this great chapter in St. Matthew with the text of St. Luke in his mind, but he has forced upon the

[1] *In Jo. Ev. Tr.* 12. 14.   *En. in. Ps.* LXVI. 8.   *Serm.* 56. 11.   *Ep.* 265. 8.
[2] *En. in Ps.* XXXVI. iii. 6.   *Serm.* 38. 8 ; 42. 2 ; 86. 5 ; 239. 5.   Augustine does insist (*De Civ.* XXI. 27 ; *Encheirid.* 19) that almsgiving cannot purge *scelera* or *crimina* without repentance and amendment of life ; but he expressly distinguishes in this respect between *grandia* and *minuta* or *cotidiana peccata*. This distinction was missed by Reuter (*Augustinische Studien*, pp. 410 f.), who quotes on the other side 'Aussprüche evangelischen Klanges' on the need for giving 'from the heart', for recognition that 'we give Thee but Thine own,' and that the Christ present in His poor is far more Giver than Receiver. Reuter concludes : 'Man hat beides neben einander stehen zu lassen und darf doch vermuten, dass das vulgär Katholische in des grossen Mannes Stimmung gereinigt, wenn auch nicht durch die kritische Macht eines vertiefteren ethischen Gedankens überwunden sei'. But the trouble is that the 'vulgär Katholische' is *not* 'gereinigt' but wholeheartedly embraced and commended. No real defence of Augustine is possible in this matter.

latter text the interpretation of Cyprian. ' Forgive, and it shall be forgiven you : give, and it shall be given to you ' has become ' Give, and it shall be forgiven you '. It is amazing that he could fail to see how grossly he was distorting the simplicity of Christ's words. For he goes on in the same sermon to mark that the merit of almsgiving is derived from God's own presence *in pauperibus suis*. ' He wills not that we do good to Him, because He has done good to us. He has need of nothing, and therefore is our true Master. . . . Yet that our works might have direction even to Him, He deigned to be hungry in His poor.'[1] Augustine will never relax the principle that ' those works alone are to be called good works, which are done for the love of God '.[2] But he does not observe that if our good works are done to secure the remission of our own sins, we are making not only the love of neighbour but the love of God a ' means ' to our own advantage : we are attempting to ' use ' not our neighbour only, but God Himself.

We are far from the spirit of *Gratis accepistis, gratis date,* far from the *germana dilectio,* the sincerity of love, which in Augustine's own words ' seeks only the salvation of our brother, looking for no advantage from him '.[3] But when he insists on the impossibility of forgiveness for the unforgiving, he has surer ground in the Gospel. In the teaching of Christ, the divine forgiveness is nothing but God's love for sinful men, and that love is denied access to the heart that will not forgive. Augustine sees in the love of enemies the touchstone of charity, the Christian's wedding garment.[4] To avenge our injuries is to throw away our only claim for pardon ;[5] and it is that because it is the refusal to follow Christ in His example of humility.[6] Forgiveness is the bearing of one another's burdens,[7] the washing of one another's

---

[1] *Serm.* 60. 9 ff.   [2] *En. in Ps.* LXVII. 41.

[3] *In Ep. Jo. Tr.* 6. 4.   [4] *Serm.* 90. 10.   [5] *Serm.* 57. 11.

[6] *Serm.* 123. 1 : ut velint homines vindicari quando laeduntur, superbia facit . . . ideo in omnibus Dominus Christus humiliari dignatus est, praebens nobis viam, si tamen dignemur ambulare per eam. Cf. *Serm.* 5. 3 ; 49. 9 ; 304. 3.

[7] *En. in Ps.* CXXIX. 4.

feet.[1] It is the only expression of love which *cannot* be false. Augustine is realist enough to understand the tremendous difficulty of the task set us. Nothing dies so hard in the human heart as hate.[2] But the forgiving spirit knows that the enmity which inflicts injuries is a sickness of the soul. In your enemy, you are called to love not what he is but what he may be—and that is how God loves the sinner.[3] Christian love is not ' liking ', it is not at the mercy of natural sympathies or antipathies ; but it is the only solvent of antipathies and enmities alike. ' *Rape, rape inimicum : rapiendo non erit inimicus* '.[4] Even so Christ ' became neighbour to us in loving us '.[5]

We begin here to see in what sense Augustine regards love as creative. Creation is the divine prerogative, because only good can create. God's love in forgiveness re-creates His own image in the sinner ; and in so far as the image of God is restored in me, in so far as my love returns to God from whom it came, I begin to share in the creative activity of the divine love. For it becomes possible for me too to forgive, as Christ forgave.

In the Eighth Book of the *De Trinitate*, Augustine sets himself to answer the question, How is love of God possible, seeing that we cannot love what we do not know, and that of God we can have neither the knowledge of immediate acquaintance, nor the knowledge of description based on general terms ? He approaches the problem by considering what we mean when we say that we love e.g. St. Paul. What we love in St. Paul is ' the righteous soul '. With the reality denoted by one term in this description, viz. ' soul ', we are immediately acquainted, for we are aware of the soul in ourselves. But in regard to the other term, ' righteous ', we find that it is not necessary to be righteous ourselves in order to know and love it : we may desire to become righteous and therefore love righteousness when we see or hear of it in another. Yet the knowledge of righteousness which

[1] *In Jo. Ev. Tr.* 58. 5.   [2] *Serm.* 49. 8 ff.
[3] *In Ep. Jo. Tr.* 8. 10.   [4] *Serm.* 90. 10.
[5] *De. Cat. Rud.* 8 : proximum illo iubente et demonstrante diligeret qui non proximum sed longe peregrinantem diligendo factus est proximus.

this desire and love imply is not derived from any external experience. It is a *veritas interior,* present to the soul by intuition : a ' Form ' to which the soul itself can be ' conformed ' only by ' cleaving to it ' in the way of love. The question with which we began, of the knowledge of God, turns out to be the simple question, ' What is love ? ' And the answer is : ' This is true love, by cleaving to the truth to live righteously, and to despise all things mortal for the love of men which is the will for them to live righteously '.[1]

Even in its context, this rigorously ethical definition of a religious ideal is startling. This *amor hominum quo eos volumus iuste vivere* is not easy to resolve into an egocentric desire for a good to be possessed. But when Augustine says that ' he who loves men must love them either because they are righteous or in order that they may be righteous ', he means exactly the same thing as when he says that ' he truly loves a friend who loves God in the friend, either because God is in him or that He may be in him '.[2] The alternative form of phrase reflects the double connotation of *amor,* affective and conative ; but it needs for its understanding the background of the doctrine of the divine image in man, its obscuration and its renewal.

One may be tempted to conclude that Augustine simply *bases* the love of neighbour upon the presence, actual or potential, of the Divine in the human soul. But that will not do justice to his conception of love as a creative energy. In the Homily on St. John xiii. 34, 35,[3] he sees in the words *as I have loved you,* Christ's way of distinguishing the love enjoined in the ' new commandment ' from the ' carnal ' love which is based on the natural relationships whether of family or friendship or of a common humanity. The love of the new commandment *makes new men,* the New People of God, the brothers of His beloved Son. It is to be, like Christ's love for His own, a

---

[1] *De Trin.* viii. 9 f. : Haec est vera dilectio, ut inhaerentes veritati iuste vivamus ; et ideo contemnamus omnia mortalia prae amore hominum quo eos volumus iuste vivere.

[2] *Ib.* Serm. 336. 2. [3] *In Jo. Ev. Tr.* 65.

creative love, loving men not for what they are but in order that they may become, leading them to the goal where God is all in all. In that sense Augustine can say that God is the real object of Christ's love for us, and that all holy love of our neighbour seeks God in him. 'Thus therefore let us love one another, and so far as we can let us by love's pursuit draw one another to have God in ourselves.' For our love of one another is the gift and the creation of Christ's love for us. God is the end as He is the beginning of all true love of neighbour. Righteousness can be called its object because righteousness is the likeness of God in which man's innermost being consists ; and it is love's work to renew, to re-make this likeness.

Augustine never says that we love our neighbour *because* he has a capacity for God ; he says we love him 'in order that God may be in him'. He knows that love's pursuit, the *cura dilectionis,* can transplant the love of God from one soul to another. *Ex amante alio accenditur alius.*[1] Yet because love is never in his thought only a striving, because its beginning and its end is a realised delight in the good, and also because the renewal of the divine image is no sudden transformation but a gradual process, his explanation of love naturally assumes the alternative form which we have noted—'either because they are righteous or in order that they may be righteous'—*aut quia habemus, aut ut habeamus.*[2] Love of a man believed righteous, love of a saint, springs 'from that Form and Truth which the lover sees and comprehends within himself'. The voice of conscience is the 'touch' of the Light of Truth even upon those who turn away from it :[3] the heart of him who 'returns unto the Lord' expands under the Sun of Righteousness, and when he sees the image of God renewing its purity and beauty in the soul of another, he cannot but delight in that which he sees. The 'love of men which is the will for them to live righteously' is realised in the love of neighbour 'in God and for God'.

[1] *Conf.* IV. 21.   [2] *Serm.* 255. 7.

[3] *De Trin.* XIV. 21 : Qui non operatur, et tamen videt quid operandum sit, ipse est qui ab illa luce avertitur, a qua tamen tangitur.

VI

The Love of God

Divine Goodness is an Active and Eternal Principle, stirring up itself without Obligation or reward, to do the best and most excellent Things in an Eternal manner. It is proper only to GOD. Its Excellency is Supreme, its Beauty infinite, its Measure endless, its Nature ineffable, its Perfection unconceivable. It hath no Cause, but it is the Cause of all other Things whatsoever. It is a *Living* and *Eternal Act* of free and undeserved Love, an indeficient Ocean of Bounty, which can never be fathomed, or (by finite Degrees be) wholly received. It is *Invisible* in its Essence, but *Apparent* in its effects ; Incomprehensible, but manifest enough, to be *believed* and *adored*. It is an Infinite and Eternal Essence, which is Good to itself, by being Good to all, infinitely Good to itself, by being without Bound or Measure Good to all its Objects. It is an infinite and Eternal Act, which continually ponders, and entirely intends the Welfare of others, and establishes its own (in a voluntary manner) by that intention : an Act whose Essence is seated in the Preparation of all Delights and the Communication of all its Glories. Its Felicity is Eternal and Infinite, yet seated entirely in the Felicity of others. It doth infinite Good to all its Recipients merely for the sake of the Excellency of the Act of *Doing Good*. It delighteth in the Excellency of that Act, and useth all its power in doing Good, that the Act in which it delighteth might be infinitely perfect. And the perfect Act in which it finally resteth is the Goodness which all adore and desire.

THOMAS TRAHERNE.

VI

WE have reached the centre of our subject—the love of God
to which the universal desire for happiness is an unconscious
pointer, and which has proved to be the necessary condition of
all true love of self or neighbour. In this life of change it is an
unending quest, in the changeless life to come it will be an attained
fruition. But always it is that relation of the soul to God which
is described in the words *haerere, inhaerere, cohaerere*—a union
which to be perfect must be indissoluble. It confers upon the
created human spirit, trembling before the uncertain alternative
of ' To be or not to be ', the security of absolute dependence ;
and thereby are repudiated alike the blasphemy of pantheism
and the dream of apotheosis. Man neither is nor ever will be
God. But he has achieved the victory which no power can
threaten, when he has found in this union with God, not the
means of gaining a satisfaction for himself, but a supreme and
final good which is his own because it is universal. To be
joined to God is the supreme good for man, because there is no
human goodness that is not fruit of the marriage between the
human spirit and the divine.[1] And Charity, the love of God,
is the power that cements and consummates the union. ' *Agglu-
tinata est anima mea post te . . . Ipsum gluten charitas est.*' [2]

But if we are truly to represent Augustine, it is necessary
when we speak of *amor Dei* and *fruitio Dei* to underline not the
first word but the second. The question is not so much whether,
or how, but what or whom we love. For if we become like

[1] *De Civ.* x. 3 : Bonum enim nostrum, de cuius fine inter philosophos
magna contentio est, nullum est aliud quam illi cohaerere, cuius unius anima
intellectualis incorporeo, si dici potest, amplexu veris impletur fecundaturque
virtutibus. Cf. Plotinus, *Enn.* VI. ix. 9 : ' Life in the Supreme is the native
activity of Intellect ; in virtue of that converse it brings forth gods, brings
forth beauty, brings forth righteousness, brings forth all moral good ; for of
all these the soul is pregnant when it has been filled with God ' (tr. Mackenna).
[2] *En. in Ps.* LXII. 17.

that which we love, the fruition of God must derive its ethical quality from the character of the God to whom love joins us. The often-quoted ' Love, and do what thou wilt ', serves in its context but to enforce the moral that true love may be shown in severity as well as in kindness.[1]   *Amor* is *caritas* when it is the love *of God*. It is true enough that in fulfilment of the two great commandments is fulfilled all righteousness. But ' how often do we all offend, because we think that our action is pleasing or not displeasing to the God whom we love ? . . . And why have we not knowledge enough of what pleases Him, but because we have too little knowledge of Himself ? ' [2]

There is summed up the tragedy and the task of all religion, the task to which Augustine devoted all the power of a magnificent intellect, and the tragedy of that intellect's disastrous errors. He tells us that when the heathen peasants of Africa sought admission to the Church, to the question ' What is it you want ? ' they would ' nearly all ' give the same answer—an answer which was as remarkable to Augustine as it is to us. *Dicimus eis, Quid vultis ? Respondent, Nosse gloriam Dei.*[3] ' To know the glory of God.' What, we wonder, was the Bishop wont to reply ? Did he say, as he had said in the *De Moribus Ecclesiae,* that the knowledge of God is the reward of the perfect, not the means of achieving perfection, and that Reason must wait upon Authority, we must first love Him whom we desire to know ? [4] But then arises the dilemma to which he was always returning : how can we love what we do not know ? Neither the Neo-Platonist solution, implied in the invocation of the *Soliloquies*— ' God, whom everything that can love, loves, whether knowingly or unknowingly ' ; [5] nor the ' moralist ' solution, that by loving

---

[1] *In Ep. Jo. Tr.* 7. 8 : the phrase recurs in exactly the same context in Morin, *Sermones post Maurinos reperti*, Frang. v. 3.
[2] *De Spir. et Litt.* 64.   [3] *En. in Ps.* CXXXIV. 22.
[4] *De Mor. Eccl.* 47.
[5] *Solil.* I. 2. Cf. *Enn.* VI. vii. 31 : ἔχουσα τὸν ἔρωτα κἂν ἀγνοῇ ὅτι ἔχει. Erigena, *De Div. Nat.* II. 28 : Eum amant quaecumque amant, sive sciant quia amant sive nesciant : hoc est, sive motu intelligibili rationalive amant, ducente gratia, sive simplici appetitu naturae.

our brother we learn to love God ; nor even the solution of the *fides historica*, that God is fully and finally revealed in Jesus of Nazareth, could wholly satisfy Augustine. Love does not of itself lead to knowledge, nor knowledge of itself to love. God must give His presence to the soul, both as the light that enlightens and as the fire that kindles ; and knowledge and love must grow up together, mutually confirming one another.[1] In other words, God Himself is the condition of *all* human apprehension of Him. We know Him through His gifts, because His gift is of Himself.

The structure of the *De Trinitate* conforms to the rule that Authority takes precedence of Reason. The first half of the treatise analyses and expounds the revelation of God in Holy Scripture. The second pursues that other revelation which according to St. Paul is available to all men. *The invisible things of God, since the creation of the world, are open to sight, being perceived through the things that are made.*[2] It is the aim of Augustine's ' natural theology' to be led ' through the things that are made ' not only to the acknowledgment *that* God is, but to an understanding of *what* He is ; and his method is to concentrate attention, among the things that are made, upon the highest that we know, the soul of man. In the *De Trinitate* Augustine puts forth all his strength to realise the ideal of his *Soliloquies : Deum et animam scire cupio.* His theological masterpiece is not to be read as an attempt to illustrate the mystery of the Godhead by

---

[1] *En. in Ps.* cxviii. viii. 2 : Quapropter ut sciamus diligere Deum, sciendus est Deus ; et ut sciat homo diligere proximum tamquam seipsum, prius debet diligendo Deum diligere seipsum : quod unde poterit, si nescit Deum, si nescit et seipsum ?

De Trin. viii. 13 : Valet ergo fides ad cognitionem et ad dilectionem Dei, non tamquam omnino incogniti, aut omnino non dilecti ; sed quo cognoscatur manifestius, et quo firmius diligatur.

In Jo. Ev. Tr. 96. 4 : sed potius in caritate proficite, quae diffunditur in cordibus vestris per Spiritum sanctum qui datus est vobis ; ut spiritu ferventes et spiritualia diligentes, spiritualem lucem spiritualemque vocem . . . interiore conspectu et auditu nosse possitis. Non enim diligitur quod penitus ignoratur. Sed cum diligitur quod ex quantulacumque parte cognoscitur, ipsa efficitur dilectione ut melius et plenius cognoscatur.

[2] *Romans* i. 20.

psychological analogies. It is the settlement of his account with
Platonist anthropology and ethics as well as with Platonist
theology. We have already spoken of the treatment of the
ὁμοίωσις θεῷ : ' the gist of religion is the imitation of Him
who is worshipped '. The imitation of God is possible for man
because human personality is made on the pattern of the Divine.
In early days [1] Augustine had understood the ' image and similitude ' of *Genesis* I. 26 as meaning the Son, as the ideal or perfect
Resemblance of the Father—a resemblance in which it is our
virtue to partake. But later [2] he insists that the image of the
Tri-Une Godhead is to be found in man himself. The imitation
of God, whether true or ' perverse ', is an imitation of the whole
Trinity.[3] Augustine has perceived that the Neo-Platonist ideal
is an impoverishment of man's nature, just as the nature of God
must be something richer and fuller than the One of Plotinus.
The *imago Trinitatis* in man has been deformed by turning away
from God ; its renewal, which must be the work of grace, will
be the re-direction or re-centring of the soul's trinity upon God
instead of upon self. It is this reformation or renewal for which
Christ is our example, and to which union with Christ enables
us, inasmuch as the grace of God culminates in the Incarnation.
*Induite novum hominem, qui renovatur in agnitione Dei secundum
imaginem eius qui creavit eum*—(*Col.* iii. 10. Cf. *Ephes.* iv. 23).

Thus the knowledge of God, for man, is literally a recognition ; and its beginning is the ' Know thyself' of Greek
wisdom.[4] Like Descartes, Augustine claims that the nature of the
human soul can be truly known only by rejecting every theory of
its constitution that is not based upon the immediate deliveries of
self-consciousness : I can know myself only as *mens* or spiritual
personality.[5] But Augustine insists that introspection yields an
irreducible trinity. I am, I know, I will ; I am a being that

[1] *De Gen. ad litt. imp. lib.* 57 ff. *De Div. Quaest. LXXXIII.* 23.
[2] *De Gen. ad litt. imp. lib.* 61. *Retr.* I. 18.
[3] *C. Secund. Man.* 10.
[4] *Enn.* VI. ix. 7 : ὁ μαθὼν ἑαυτὸν εἰδήσει καὶ ὅποθεν.
[5] *De Trin.* x. 7 ff.

knows and wills ; I know and will my being, my knowledge, and my will.[1] All the Augustinian *vestigia Trinitatis* disclose, on examination, their conformity to this psychological pattern. The ' Nature of the Good ' is seen in the universal participation in *modus, species, ordo*—the principles of individuality or concrete unity, of form or definition, of order or purpose ; [2] and the same three principles appear in the Measure, Number and Weight in which the *Wisdom* writer declares that God has ordered all things.[3] In the Eighth Book of the *De Civitate*, the Platonists are said to be ' nearer to us ' than any other non-Christian philosophers, because, having seen the necessity of a tri-partite division of philosophy into Physic, Logic, and Ethics, they have found in God the *causa subsistendi*, the *ratio intelligendi*, and the *ordo vivendi* : ' the Author of all existences, the Illuminator of all truth, the Bestower of all beatitude '.[4] In this context Augustine is occupied with criticism, and does not point the connection with Trinitarian theology. But when later he comes to trace the origin of the Heavenly City in the story of creation, it is the doctrine of the Trinity which provides the answer to the three questions : ' *Quis fecerit, per quid fecerit, quare fecerit* '. The Creator is God, the instrument His Word, the cause His goodness ; and since God's goodness and His Spirit of Holiness are one, ' therein is the Trinity intimated to us, whence the Holy City has its origin, its instruction, its beatitude. If we ask whence it is, God made it ; if whence it has wisdom, God enlightens it ; if whence it has happiness, God is the end of its fruition. In existence it is determined, in contemplation it is illuminated, in union it is gladdened. It is, it sees, it loves. In God's eternity is its strength, in God's truth its light, in God's goodness its joy '.[5]

God is the Source, the Giver, of all being, all knowledge, all enjoyment, because He is Himself *aeternitas, veritas, caritas*. The problem before Augustine was no longer to maintain the Homo-

---

[1] *Conf.* XIII. 12.   *De Civ.* XI. 26.   [2] *De Nat. Boni* 3.

[3] *De Gen. ad. litt.* IV. 7 : Ille primitus et veraciter et singulariter ista est, qui *terminat* omnia et *format* omnia et *ordinat* omnia.

[4] *De Civ.* VIII. 4 f.   [5] *Ib.* XI. 24.

ousion. The unity of the Godhead is his unquestioned starting-point. The aim of his theology is to show that Godhead *means* Trinity and can be conceived in no other way ; and the danger against which he is constantly on his guard is that of representing the Persons as ' parts ' of an organic whole. If Eternity is ascribed to the Father, Truth to the Son, and Charity to the Spirit, then none of the Three is God ; and for the same reason the Three Persons cannot be regarded as severally the origins of created being, knowledge and love. *Opera Trinitatis ad extra indivisa.* The treatment of the *imago Trinitatis* in men is governed throughout by these considerations. Hence, in the *De Trinitate,* Augustine's emphatic rejection of ' faculty psychology ', of any apparent division of the *mens* or reasonable soul into parts ; hence too his substitution of *memoria* (by which he means very nearly the ' unconscious ') for either *essentia* or *mens* as the first term of the triad. *My* being, indeed, implies knowing and willing, but *all* ' being ' is not inseparable from knowledge and will ; and the term *mens* suggests a substance of which knowledge and will are attributes. Augustine is aware of the audacity of his speculation ; but he will not stop short of seeking in the *imago Trinitatis,* when perfected by grace, an analogue of the inmost being of God, in which the Persons are modes or relationships. In the act of self-knowledge there is ' begotten ', from those latent depths of consciousness which God has never deserted, a true ' word ' or representation of the human spirit, insufficient for itself and wholly dependent on its Maker ; and the act of will which seeks this ' word ' and acquiesces in it when found, is a self-love which is true because it is love of the God from whom it proceeds, and to whom it returns. We may acknowledge, as Augustine acknowledges in the end, that this was to strain human thought beyond its capacity, that it was almost the very attempt to ' expose Truth unveiled ',[1] to ' comprehend God ' and thereby to lose Him,[2] which he himself condemned.

[1] *Ep.* 242. 5 : arbitror te cogniturum tanto minus quemque vestiri lumine veritatis, quanto magis sibi videtur nudam depromere veritatem.

[2] *Serm.* 117. 5 : De Deo loquimur, quid mirum si non comprehendis ? Si enim comprehendis, non est Deus.

But he was none the less sure that the Tri-Une nature of God is to be perceived through the things that are made. Man can aspire to God because He is *not* ' wholly other ', because His changeless Being, perfect Wisdom, and loving Will are even in their transcendence of all things human the marks of spiritual personality, and therefore can claim our worship and invite our love.

The ultimate source of this doctrine of revelation is not in doubt. Life, Light, and Love are not only the key words of the Fourth Gospel ; they are the framework of its marvellously subtle structure. God is revealed in Christ, first as the Life of men in the episodes of Nicodemus, the woman of Samaria, the impotent man, and the feeding of the five thousand ; then as the Light of the world in the discourses of the seventh and eighth chapters and in the healing of the man born blind ; finally as the Love which is communion and atonement, in the upper room and in the Passion. But throughout there is an interlocking of the triple theme, in theological phrase a *circumincessio*, which shows that the Gift is one as well as three. So for Augustine, grace is itself a trinity, and we cannot isolate the Love of God from the Life and the Light which are its fulfilment. If our account of it is not to be maimed, we must let Augustine speak of grace in each of its three modes or aspects.

1. *Being and Life*

' When we say that God has life, we mean that He is life, and gives life to men.' [1]   The Being of the Creator is changeless, and this changelessness is defined in the formula *est quod habet*. God *is* His Life, His Wisdom, and His Righteousness. But the God whose Name is *I am that I am* is also the God of Abraham, Isaac, and Jacob. The Very Being will not withhold itself from mankind.[2]   Existence itself is the Creator's primal gift, a ' grace '

---

[1] *In Jo. Ev. Tr.* 48. 6.
[2] Serm. 7. 7. : sic sum quod sum, sic sum ipsum esse . . . ut nolim hominibus de-esse. Cf. Morin, *Sermones post Maurinos reperti*, Denis ii. 5 : Audisti

which is ' common ' or ' general ' ; [1] the omnipresent energy of God sustains the whole creation, and the words of the opening prayer in the *Confessions*—' I should not be, wert not Thou in me . . . or rather, were I not in Thee ' [2]—are as true of the humblest living thing,[3] as true even of stick and stone. 'Everything that is, possesses at least the minimal goodness which Being, the gift of God, has conferred on it. Life, in any form, adds a higher degree of likeness to the Creator ; and when life is conscious, it has an enhanced value to which animal instinct testifies./ The ills of human life were not less in the fifth century than in the twentieth, and Augustine, we know, was not inclined to minimise them. Yet he attributes, not only to the instinct of self-preservation, but to the conscious love of life, an intensity and force much greater than the modern temper is disposed to allow.[4] He believes that the beggar would ' jump for joy ' at the promise of immortal beggary ; [5] and he will not even admit that eternal damnation is necessarily worse than non-existence.[6]

None the less, he will say that it is ' not a great thing to live, or even to live for ever, but only to live happily '.[7] And *beata vita* is different in kind from both animal and rational existence. The soul is the principle of life to the body, because through it

quid sum ; audi quid capias, audi quid speres. . . . Non potes capere nomen substantiae meae ; cape nomen misericordiae meae. Ego sum Deus Abraham et Deus Isaac et Deus Jacob . . . Hoc mihi nomen est in aeternum. Aeternum nomen esse non posset Deus Abraham et Deus Isaac et Deus Jacob, nisi in aeternum viverent Abraham, Isaac et Jacob.

[1] *Serm.* 26. 4 ff. : excepta illa communi gratia naturae, qua homines facti sumus, nec digni fuimus, quia non fuimus.

[2] *Conf.* I. 2.

[3] *In Jo. Ev. Tr.* 34. 3 : qui salvum facit te, ipse salvum facit equum tuum, ipse ovem tuam ; ad minima omnino veniamus, ipse gallinam tuam.

[4] Yet G. K. Chesterton remembered his grandfather saying : ' I should thank God for my creation, if I knew I were a lost soul '. (*Autobiography*, p. 19.)

[5] *De Civ.* XI. 27. Cf. *Serm.* 297. 3 f. : utique natura refugit mortem . . . habet istum sensum genus humanum. . . . Non reprehendimus, non accusamus, etiamsi vita ista ametur.

[6] *C. Jul. Pelag.* V. 44, in reference to the ' levissima damnatio ' of unbaptised children.

[7] *Serm.* 127. 2.

God raises matter to a higher degree of being. But that in the soul which gives life to the body is not that which gives life to the soul. The analogy which Augustine constantly draws between the soul as the life of the body and God as the life of the soul,[1] only becomes clear when we remember the double function which he ascribes to the soul in relation to the body. It is not only to animate, but to dominate. Obedience to God means freedom from servitude to the body, restoration of the true ' order ' of spiritual-material existence, in a word fulfilment of personality.[2] Righteousness is the ' higher life ' of the soul, because it is a fuller participation in the Life of God, in which Being and Righteousness are identical.[3]

Here we must recall the Neo-Platonist ontology from which Augustine sets out. ' There is no life ', he had said in the *De Vera Religione,* ' which is not of God, since God is the highest life and the source of life ; nor is any life evil as life, but only as it inclines towards death. Now the only death of life is naughtiness (*nequitia*) which is so called from being a " thing of naught" (*ne quidquam sit*). . . . The life which wilfully falls away from its Maker, whose Being it enjoyed, and desires in a manner contrary to God's law to enjoy the bodily things to which God made it superior, inclines to nonentity.'[4] For death, he goes on to explain, means a loss of being, though not necessarily a complete loss : there are degrees of death—' the less things *are*, the more they die '—and material things as such have less being than any living principle : they are ' nearer to nothing '.[5] This is Augustine's version of Plotinus's theory of the hierarchy of existence and the gradual ' fading-out ' of Being into Not-Being ; it is a Christianised version, in that the origin of evil is not placed, with Plotinus,[6] in the ' formlessness ' of the

---

[1] E.g. *En. in Ps.* LXX. ii. 3. *Serm.* 62. 3 ; 65. 5 ; 156. 6 ; 161. 6.

[2] *In Jo. Ev. Tr.* 23. 5 (quoted above, p. 27).

[3] *Ep.* 120. 18 f.   [4] *De Ver. Relig.* 21.   [5] *Ib.* 22.

[6] *Enn.* I. viii. 3. In a later chapter (11) of the same book, Plotinus actually presents and dismisses a theory, closely resembling Augustine's, of moral evil as the privation of good in the soul itself—a theory which would make it superfluous to seek for an evil reality in the external world. His argument

ultimate matter, but in the voluntary act of spirit. Augustine had not abandoned his Platonist principles when, many years later, he wrote to answer the philosophical enquiries of Dioscorus. He still held that ' the stability of the soul is in proportion to its union with God who supremely Is ; and that this supreme Being belongs to God because He can change neither for the better nor for the worse, whereas for the soul itself a change for the better, towards more perfect union with God, is to be desired : change for the worse, or falling away, is to be condemned. All falling away (*defectus*) inclines towards extinction : though it may not be apparent whether that term is ever reached, it is apparent to all that extinction means the ceasing to be of what was.' [1]

But the logical implication of this theory of degrees of being or life, dependent on righteousness or union with God, should certainly be that the sinful soul is capable of infinite approximation to nonentity. For the being of the soul is *not* a ' changeless ' being : a life in unrighteousness is its death, and when through the grace of Christ it is revived, it becomes sharer in ' another ' life which is not its own.[2]

Nygren[3] has laid stress upon the fact that the Christian Apologists of the second century were acutely conscious of the cleavage between the Greek philosophical and religious belief in the natural immortality of the soul, a divine substance entangled in the world of matter, and the Christian gospel of a resurrection which is the redemption of body and soul alike. He sees in this the theocentric ' Agape-motive ' asserting itself against the ' Eros-motive ' of Hellenistic religion, dominant in

against this theory is that the soul cannot be supposed ' to produce vice within itself by the operation of its own principle ', for that principle is life and therefore good. Plotinus cannot conceive the possibility of a sin which is the essential act of soul.

[1] *Ep.* 118. 15.

[2] *In Jo. Ev. Tr.* 19. 11. Cf. *De Nat. et Grat.* 25 : mors animae quam deseruit vita sua, hoc est Deus eius, quae necesse est mortua opera faciat, donec Christi gratia reviviscat.

[3] *Eros und Agape II.* (G.T.), pp. 67 ff.

Gnosticism, with its confidence in the native power of the soul to reascend to its own place. Justin Martyr came to Christianity from Platonism, and both he and Irenaeus declare, in opposition to the Gnostics, that since the soul is a thing created, it cannot be immortal ' in its own right ', but can subsist only so long as its Creator wills. They reject the Platonic argument that the soul is the principle of life and that ' life itself ' cannot die ; the soul receives or participates in life, which is therefore separable from it. But they agree with Plato that the ' life ' of the soul is not to be identified with righteousness, since unrighteousness does not destroy it ; God's justice requires a life after death, not only for righteous souls, but for unrighteous, ' so long as God may will their being and their punishment to endure '.[1] Justin and Irenaeus repeat without question the orthodox teaching that this punishment in fact will be without end ; though it is remarkable that Justin records an express affirmation, by the ' old man ' who converted him from Platonist errors, that the soul will have life no longer, will cease to be, when God so wills.[2]

Augustine is at one with the Apologists and at variance with Platonism in denying that the soul has life ' in itself '. There is no divine *Seelengrund* which cannot die : eternal life is the gift of God. But he does hold that the life of the soul is righteousness ; and the difficulty for him is to find any room within his Christian Neo-Platonism for the Catholic dogma, which he accepted for his own part, like Justin and Irenaeus, as a postulate of belief in God's justice. He writes to Optatus that amid much uncertainty about the soul, he is at least sure ' that the soul is a creature partly mortal, in so far as it can suffer deterioration and estrangement from the life of God . . . partly immortal, since it cannot lose the consciousness whence its weal or woe after this life will be derived '.[3] He sees, in fact, that

---

[1] Justin, *Dial.* 4 ff. Irenaeus, *Adv. Haer.* II. 56 (Harvey).   [2] *Dial.* 6.
[3] *Ep.* 202A. 17. Cf. *ib.* 120. 18 : animarum licet immortaliter vita qualicumque viventium verior et maior vita iustitia est. *De Civ.* XIII. 24 : anima creata est immortalis, quae licet peccato mortua perhibeatur carens quadam

the soul's 'real immortality' can be nothing but a participation in the eternal life of God, that there can be no such thing as an eternity of evil ; and it follows that the soul *potest mori, potest occidi* : there may be a 'dead soul' in a living body.[1] But he was obliged to maintain an inherent incorruptibility even of the most depraved soul ; and for that he had recourse, in the early *De Immortalitate Animae*, to the Platonic argument which deduces the soul's immortality from its character as the perceiving subject of an eternal object, of Truth itself.[2] The soul is immortal because the Light which it receives is also Life ; and it is implied that no degree of failure in the love of God can altogether deprive the soul of the divine illumination. Yet we are told [3] that if 'death cannot separate us from the love of God', it is because 'that wherewith we love God cannot die except when it ceases to love God ; since death itself is, not to love God'.

There is indeed a remarkable contrast between the later argument for immortality in the *De Trinitate,* where the whole burden of proof rests on faith in the risen Christ,[4] and the dialectics of the early treatise, in which, as the *Retractations* show plainly enough, Augustine had come to lose all interest.[5] But the breach in his theology which Scripture or tradition required is scarcely disguised. It was dogma that the soul is created immortal ; and he did not see that on his own principles this is a contradiction in terms more ultimate than the idea of a 'dead soul'. Platonism could assert the soul's immortality without

vita sua . . . tamen propria quadam, licet misera, vita sua non desinit vivere, quia immortalis est creata. *De Gen. ad litt.* VII. 43 : immortalis secundum quemdam vitae modum, quem nullo modo potest amittere. *In Jo. Ev. Tr.* 23. 9 : immortalis dicitur anima : est quidem, quia vivit semper anima, et est in illa quaedam vita permanens, sed mutabilis vita.

[1] *Serm.* 65. 4 f. Of the 'dead soul' the Orphic saying is true, that the body is its sepulchre : *En. in. Ps.* LXXXVII. 11.

[2] Cf. Plato, *Phaedo,* 78 B ff. ; Plotinus, *Enn.* IV. vii. 8.

[3] *De Mor. Eccl.* 19 : written not many months after the *De Immortalitate Animae.*

[4] *De Trin.* XIII. 12.

[5] *Retr.* I. 5 : sic obscurus est ut fatiget cum legitur etiam intentionem meam vixque intelligatur a me ipso.

such a contradiction ; for Platonism did not know what creation means. It was Augustine's belief that God has created man with a ' capacity for eternity ', and that the realisation of this capacity is contingent upon grace. The love of life which we have by nature is a love of being for ourselves, a being which is of necessity mutable and imperfect. Grace can lift our being up to the Being of God, because it can lift our love.

2. Truth and Knowledge

This is life eternal, to know Thee.[1]—' Add truth to life, and you get happiness ; for as no one wishes to die, so no one wishes to be deceived.' [2]   The desire to know is as much a part of man's nature as the desire to be.[3] But we have just been reminded that Augustine believes that not only life but knowledge has been conferred on man by the Creator's gift. In line with the early Apologists, he holds that the Logos does indeed enlighten every man coming into the world : we may turn away from the light of truth, but we are all ' touched ' by it.[4] His peculiar theory of knowledge was worked out in the *De Magistro* shortly after his return to Africa in 387, and was never abandoned or modified.[5] The same facts on which Plato relied to support his theory of ἀνάμνησις, were for Augustine evidence that there is no such thing as teaching, in the sense of conveying knowledge from one mind to another. We are to call no one ' master ' upon earth : all that the teacher can do is to admonish the pupil to learn from the *magister interior* who is also the ' Master in heaven '.[6]

The truths to which Augustine believes that we thus have access are those intuitive judgements which he calls *regulae* or

---

[1] *John* xvii. 3.   [2] *Serm.* 306. 9.

[3] *De Civ.* XI. 27 : nosse quantum ametur quamque falli nolit humana natura, vel hinc intelligi potest, quod lamentari quisque sana mente mavult quam laetari in amentia.

[4] *De Trin.* XIV. 21.   [5] Cf. e.g. *De Pecc. Mer.* I. 37.

[6] *De Magist.* 46. It is hardly necessary to point out how this ancient doctrine foreshadows the principles of modern educational theory.

' norms '—of which both the propositions of mathematics and
the ultimate value-judgements are examples, and upon which in
the *De Libero Arbitrio* he builds his most typical ' proof' of God.
They are not ' innate ideas ' : they do not ' belong ' to the mind,
as part of its constitution. When it is said that such truths are
' seen in the light of God ', what is meant is that the same omnipresent energy of God which maintains the world in being, is
in the mind of man as it were incandescent, so enabling us to
see that these things are so. The mind cannot criticise them as
it does the deliverances of the senses : it simply finds them and
accepts them : its judgements are made not upon them but
according to them.[1] We remember how Augustine tells in the
Confessions that it was through pondering on the source of these
intuitions, through asking himself whence came the light in
which he saw that the changeless is better than the changing,
that he attained his momentary but overwhelmingly immediate
experience of the reality of God. That experience is irresistibly
recalled to our minds, when at the summit of his long argument
in the *De Libero Arbitrio*, having fulfilled his promise to his
interlocutor by showing in the *regulae veritatis* the existence of
something ' more sublime ' than the reasoning soul which takes
knowledge of them, he breaks suddenly into his great encomium
of ' Truth itself', as that of which alone the possession can satisfy
us.[2] But this Truth is not, like the *regulae*, to be seen in the light
of a spiritual sun ; it is the Sun itself, upon which the soul's eye,
if it be strong enough, will seek to gaze direct.[3] It is a ' Beauty
of Truth and Wisdom ', to which access can never be impeded
by the throng of devotees. ' For all who turn to the love of
it, throughout the world, it is at hand ; for all it endures for
ever ; in no place, yet nowhere lacking ; admonishing without,

---

[1] *De Lib. Arb.* II. 34 : iudicamus haec secundum illas interiores regulas
veritatis, quas communiter cernimus ; de ipsis vero nullo modo quis iudicat.
Cum enim quis dixerit aeterna temporalibus esse potiora, aut septem et tria
decem esse, nemo dicit ita esse debuisse, sed tantum ita esse cognoscens, non
examinator corrigit sed tantum laetatur inventor. Cf. *Enn.* v. iii. 4 : τὸ δια-
νοητικὸν . . . κρίνει ἃ κρίνει τοῖς ἐν αὐτῷ κανόσιν, οὓς παρὰ τοῦ νοῦ ἔχει.
[2] *De Lib. Arb.* II. 35.   [3] *Ib.* 36.

instructing within ; transforming to good all that behold it, never losing its own goodness.'[1]

Truth so glorified can be nothing less than the living Wisdom which, as the Church teaches, is the co-equal Son of the Eternal Father, the Word or wholly adequate representation of the one supreme spiritual Reality.[2] So Augustine appropriates to his purpose the *Nous* of Plotinus, in which knower and known are one. The divine Ideas or Thoughts are not identified with but are reflected in the ' numbers ' or mathematical correspondences which give form to the created universe, and in the ethical axioms which govern men's valuation of the world.

It does not follow, however, that because we recognise the ' norms of truth ' we are able to fix our eyes upon the Sun in whose light we have seen them. For that we need, not the power of intellect, but the ' constant will ' (*perseverans voluntas*).[3] Again and again Augustine dwells upon the transitoriness of that apprehension of God which can be reached by intellectual effort.[4] It is never to be forgotten that the Augustinian ' intellect ' is not the discursive reason but the mind at worship. But his own experience had been that he ' lacked the strength to fix his gaze ' ;[5] and it was his firm conviction that this inevitable ' relapse into the common world ' is a sign of moral and not merely intellectual weakness : it is because of ' the perverse will by which things lower are loved better '.[6]

But the typical passage in the *Confessions* to which reference has been made ends with a significant phrase. ' There was left ', he says, ' only a loving memory (*amantem memoriam*).' The Augustinian *memoria* is not, like the Platonic ἀνάμνησις, a latent retention of things seen in an earlier, celestial existence. It is that deep of the soul in which is treasured not only the consciousness of the self, but a consciousness of God sufficient at least to stir our will to the search of recollection. It is the sphere of the *Magister interior*. No one can love the absolutely unknown. Knowledge can be pursued only because our desire has been called

---

[1] *De Lib. Arb.* II. 38.   [2] *Ib.* 39.   [3] *Ib.* 38.
[4] See above, pp. 33 f.   [5] *Conf.* VII. 23.   [6] *De Lib. Arb.* II. 37.

forth by something known—whether it be the universal which
elicits desire of acquaintance with the particular, or an intuition
of some absolute value to which the knowledge we seek is
instrumental, or even knowledge itself—the desire of knowledge
' for its own sake ' being always the thirst for *more* of that which
we already possess in part.[1] ' Tu ne Me chercherais pas, si tu
ne M'avais déjà trouvé.' Just as self-consciousness makes it
possible to ask questions about the self, to achieve the self-
knowledge by which we may be convinced of our true place
in the world as spiritual personalities, so the latent ' memory of
God ', reinforced by every conscious act of devotion, enables us
to approach the explicit and permanent *recognition* of Him as the
Lord of our being, which is what Augustine means by ' adhering
to the Truth '.

The knowledge of God to which the method and assumptions
of the *De Trinitate* lead us is a mode of apprehension conceived
on the analogy of our knowledge of ourselves. God is *not far
from each one of us; for in Him we live and move and have
our being.* But though God is with us always, we are not
always ' with Him ' : [2] it is ' man's great woe, not to be with
Him without whom he cannot be ',[3] to be conscious of nothing
but loneliness and limitation, shut up within the walls of a
phantom prison. Through grace, we are shown that the prison
is of our own building ; and through grace, as St. Paul taught, we
become what we are, the children of God's House, stones in a
living temple. *Incipis sentire Deum.*

For this profoundly personal apprehension of God, the term
' vision ' is indeed inadequate. The prominence of the term in
the language of Augustine, as in that of Christian piety in general,
is not only a heritage of Platonism. No other metaphor drawn
from sense perception could serve to convey at once the nearness

[1] *De Trin.* X. 1 ff.
[2] Cf. Plotinus's simile of the choir and the Conductor : ἀεὶ μὲν περὶ αὐτό,
οὐκ ἀεὶ δὲ εἰς αὐτὸ βλέπομεν (*Enn.* VI. ix. 8).
[3] *De Trin.* XIV. 16.

and the remoteness of the divine Object of spiritual experience. But to the Greeks and to the Greeks alone had been given that extraordinary combination of visual sensitiveness and intellectual passion which led to the discovery that if truth is to be worshipped, then truth is beauty. And here Augustine was a Platonist not by adoption but by nature. When he argued in the *De Musica* that we can love nothing but the beautiful, he was repeating the theme of his rhetorician's essay written in the early days at Carthage, long before he read Plotinus.[1]

He was not the only Christian Father who had an acute sense of the beauty of nature. But for him as perhaps for no other writer of antiquity, the beauty of nature is ' numinous ', overwhelming : it is an ' almost unspeakable' beauty, that must ' fill with awe everyone who contemplates it '.[2] And the *species* or ' form ' which is the secret of this beauty is the unity of design, a unity in multiplicity, that speaks the One Designer, the voice by which the mute creation proclaims its Maker.[3] ' We see the fabric of the world, . . . and because of the greatness and the beauty of this fabric, though as yet we see not, yet already we love the inestimable greatness and beauty of its Craftsman. For He whom our heart cannot yet behold in purity, has not failed to set His work before our eyes, that in seeing what we can see we may love what we cannot see, in order that one day through the merit of that love we may be enabled to see.' [4]

But if the heavens declare the glory of God, much more does the ' beauty of righteousness ' which is the perfection of His image in the inner man,[5] and which shines through the

---

[1] *De Mus.* VI. 28. Cf. *Conf.* IV. 20.

[2] *En. in Ps.* CXLIV. 15 : omnia haec nonne omnem consideratorem terrent ? . . . et hic vivunt . . . in ista pulchritudine propre iam ineffabili, hic vivunt tecum et vermiculi et mures.

[3] *De Ver. Relig.* 59 ff. Cf. *Ep.* 18. 2.

[4] *En. in Ps.* CIII. i. 1.

[5] *Ep.* 120. 20 : quid est aliud iustitia . . . quam interioris hominis pulchritudo ? et certe secundum hanc pulchritudinem magis quam corpus sumus ad imaginem Dei.

mutilated limbs of the martyr and the bent body of the aged saint.[1] For ' charity itself is the soul's beauty ', bestowed on it by ' Him who is ever beautiful ', and whose love for men creates in them a beauty like His own.[2] The beauty of the Bride of Christ is the Bridegroom's gift ; for He is ' lovely in heaven, lovely upon earth ; lovely in the womb, lovely in His parents' arms ; lovely in His works of power, lovely under the scourge's blow ; lovely in bidding men live, lovely in scorn of death ; lovely yielding up His life, lovely taking it again ; lovely on the Tree, lovely in the tomb, lovely at last in heaven '.[3] The Beauty which at long last had won the love of the writer of the *Confessions* was a Beauty old and yet new. The ' beauty of Truth and Wisdom '[4] was not only the theme of Augustine's Neo-Platonist enthusiasm. Always it was ' the fair beauty of the Lord ' that his heart worshipped : the *Retractations* echo the *Soliloquies,* and at the end of his life his love of truth was still what it had been at Cassiciacum : *illius pulchritudinis amor.*[5] What the *Sero te amavi !* of the *Confessions* tells us is that the changeless Beauty which he had long pursued only ceased to be a mirage when it took the human form divine of the Incarnate Redeemer. Drawn by the cords of a man, Eros must at last recognise in Agape the perfect loveliness which can transform its lovers into its own image.

3. *Love*

Dr. Inge maintains that the God of Neo-Platonism is not the One but *Nous* or Spirit ; for ' it is only as Spirit that the God-head is known to us as a factor in our lives '. *Nous* is the *Deus revelatus,* the One the *Deus absconditus.* Arnou is surely more accurate when he says that in the system of Plotinus the One corresponds most nearly to *our* idea of God as the sole absolutely independent principle : it is in speaking of the Supreme, and

---

[1] *En. in Ps.* XXXII. ii. 1.　*In Jo. Ev. Tr.* 3. 21.
[2] *In Ep. Jo. Tr.* 9. 9.　　　　[3] *En. in Ps.* XLIV. 3.
[4] *De Lib. Arb.* II. 38.
[5] *Solil.* I. 22.　*Retr.* I. 1. 3.　*Ep.* 118. 23.

then only, that Plotinus uses the unmistakable language of religious devotion.[1] But it is true enough that Augustine's Neo-Platonism finds its Trinity in Spirit. For of Spirit Plotinus was able to predicate not only Being and Knowledge, but Love. But his Spirit is love because it is not itself the Good, but in continued tension towards the Good upon which it depends. For Augustine therefore the problem was not only to eliminate the distinction between Spirit and the Good, but at the same time to give a meaning both to the divine Goodness and to the divine Love consonant with the removal of this distinction ; to find in Goodness Love's source as well as its satisfaction, to widen or transform the Eros which strains ever inwards and upwards into the Agape which not only creates but cares for its creatures and therefore redeems.

He begins with a conception strange to Plotinus but based immediately on St. John. God is to be loved *because* He is love. *Amor amoris*, the love of love, must then be an article on which the Christian faith stands or falls. And first, *amor amoris* is an

[1] Inge, *Philosophy of Plotinus* (3rd ed.), vol. ii. pp. 82 f. Arnou, *Le Desir de Dieu dans la Philosophie de Plotin*, pp. 128 ff. When Inge enumerates passages in which ' *Nous* is formally identified with God ', he is ' misleading his readers ' more seriously than the ' modern critics who habitually speak of the Neoplatonic Absolute as God '. Here is one of these passages in Mackenna's translation :—

' Thus we have here one identical Principle, the Intellect, which is the universe of authentic beings, the Truth : as such it is a great god, or, better, not a god among gods but the Godhead entire. *It is a god, a secondary god manifesting before there is any vision of that other, the Supreme which rests over all*, enthroned in transcendence upon that splendid pediment, the Nature following close upon it. The Supreme in its progress could never be borne forward upon some soulless vehicle, nor even directly upon the soul : it will be heralded by some ineffable beauty : before the great King in his progress there comes first the minor train, then rank by rank the greater and more exalted, closer to the King the kinglier ; next his own honoured company, until, last among all those grandeurs, suddenly appears the Supreme Monarch himself, and all—unless indeed for those who have contented themselves with the spectacle before his coming and gone away—prostrate themselves and hail him.' (*Enn.* v. v. 3 : my italics.)

The whole point is that when Plotinus says θεός he does *not* mean what we mean by ' God '. If Inge were right, Plotinus would not be a monotheist. Plotinus is a monotheist. *Ergo.*

observable fact of experience. It is as much man's nature to love love as to love being or knowledge. We are not more certain of our existence and of our self-consciousness than we are of an energy of will which approves and affirms our existence and our knowledge ; and this *amor* or active will is itself no less an object of approval and affirmation.[1] Further, as we cannot but desire that our being should be the most perfect of which our nature is capable, that we should know what is true, so we cannot but desire that our will should be directed to what is absolutely good. The life of intelligence would not be desirable if it were lacking in all affective element,[2] but ' we should love the love of what ought to be loved, even as we should hate the love of what ought not to be loved '.[3] This is most clearly seen in our estimation of love in others. ' In men who are loved most deservedly, it is their love that is loved the most. For the right to be called a good man belongs not to him who knows what is good, but to him who loves it.' [4] *Nec faciunt bonos vel malos mores nisi boni vel mali amores.*[5] Above all, ' what is it that we love in Christ ? The crucified body, the pierced side, or charity itself ? When we hear that He suffered for us, what is it that we love ? Our love is for His charity.' [6] True love is nothing else but the will to a life of righteousness, for ourselves and our neighbours ; and since the life of righteousness means ' adhering in love ' to the Truth or Pattern of Righteousness, the love of neighbour is itself the love of love, the desire that the love of God be multiplied.[7]

' God is Love. Why then should we go harking to the topmost heaven or the nethermost earth, seeking for Him who is with us, if but we would be with Him ? Let no man say, I know not what I am to love. Let him love his brother, and he will love that same love. He knows the love wherewith he loves his brother, better than the brother whom he loves. See, God may be held more known than a brother—more known

[1] *De Civ.* XI. 26. [2] *De Div. Quaest. LXXXIII.* 35.
[3] *En. in Ps.* CXVIII. viii. 4. [4] *De Civ.* XI. 28.
[5] *Ep.* 155. 13. [6] *En. in Ps.* CXXVII. 8. [7] *De Trin.* VIII. 10.

because more present; more known because more inward;
more known, because more sure. Embrace the love which is
God: through love embrace God. He is that very love that
links in the bond of holiness all the good Angels and all the
servants of God, that joins us and them to one another in obedience to Himself.' The love which we are to love would not
indeed be love, had it no object; and that is why St. John is
able to teach us that the love of the brethren ' not only is from
God, but is God '.[1]

A passage like this is not to be dismissed as an example of
Augustine's rhetorical fervour. It is not only here, nor only in
preaching on the great texts of St. John's Epistle,[2] that he bids
us see in our love of one another the very presence of God.
On the other hand, St. Thomas will rightly remind us that he
speaks as a Platonist and can only mean that charity in us is
a ' participation ' of the divine Love.[3] The love that dwells in
us is no more than the gifts of eternal life and knowledge of the
truth, ' something uncreated in the soul '.[4] It is a part of the
divine likeness.

How then does Augustine conceive the divine Exemplar?
Is love in God only the love of love, the love of Himself? Yes,
and No.

Augustine follows Plotinus unreservedly in his denial that
the Supreme Good can have ' need ' of anything whatsoever.
Bonorum meorum non eges.[5] God *needs* neither the world He has
created,[6] nor the service,[7] the worship,[8] or the love [9] of man.
The primary object of His Will as of His Knowledge is His own
Being with which both are identical. Hence Augustine's preoccupation with the self-direction of knowledge and will in the

---

[1] *De Trin.* VIII. 11 f.   [2] E.g. *In. Ep. Jo. Tr.* 9. 10.

[3] *Summa Theol.* IIª IIªᵉ q. 23, a. 2.

[4] Cf. *In Jo. Ev. Tr.* 102. 5 : amorem itaque nostrum pium quo colimus
Deum, fecit Deus et vidit quia bonum est.

[5] *Ps.* xvi. 2.   [6] *Conf.* XIII. 2, 5.   *De Civ.* XI. 24.

[7] *Conf.* XIII. 1.   *Ep.* 138. 6.   *En. in Ps.* LXIX. 7.

[8] *De Civ.* X. 5, 17.   *Ep.* 102. 17.   *En. in Ps.* CII. 4 ; CXXXIV. 1.

[9] *Serm.* 34. 8 ; 117. 5.   *En. in Ps.* XXXII. ii. 18.

imago Trinitatis. In a famous passage, Plotinus himself speaks of
the Supreme Unity as 'love's object and love's self, love of
Himself'; and his way of insisting that the One is altogether
causa sui is to repeat that He is 'sovereign of Himself' . . . that
He is not 'as He happened to be' but 'as He willed to be'.[1]
But the measure of such phrases can only be taken from their
author's consistent refusal to the Supreme of self-consciousness
in any form. 'Self-Eros' is for Plotinus a term of paradox,
indicating the transcendence of subject and object, of seeker and
sought. The Christian Platonist, of course, holds as firmly
that God *wills* not only His own Goodness but all the manifold
good which He has called into being. The love of God for us
His creatures is incomparably greater than our love for Him; [2]
and it is shown in the act of creation and in the work of
redemption.

(*a*) *Creation.*—In Plotinus, creation is eternal, and in the sense
of being implicit in the nature of God, necessary. 'The One
could not be alone'.[3] But in creation God has no monopoly:
it is a graded process which begins with the Supreme and
extends itself outwards and downwards throughout the universe.[4]
The principle of creation is love—not the love of the higher for
the lower, but the love of each creature for what is above itself,
reproducing images of the object of its contemplation.[5] Such is
the creativity of the artist, whose vision embodies itself in an
essentially inadequate material. But such cannot be the mode of
creativity in the Supreme Good; and Plotinus has to fall back

---

[1] *Enn.* VI. viii. 15 *et saepe.*

[2] *En. in Ps.* CIII. i. 13.   [3] *Enn.* IV. viii. 6.

[4] *Enn.* II. ix. 3 : 'it is of the essence of things that each gives of its being
to another'; II. ix. 8 : 'the Intellectual could not be the last of things, but
must have a double act, one within itself and one outgoing'; v. ii. 1 : 'it
repeats the act of the One in pouring out a vast power'; IV. viii. 6 : 'in the
same way the outgoing process could not end with the souls, their issue stifled :
every Kind must produce its next' (tr. Mackenna).

[5] *Enn.* III. viii. 4 : (Nature says) 'I gaze, and the figures of the material
world take being as if they fell from my contemplation'. See Inge, *op. cit.*
vol. i. 195 f., ii. 121.

upon the argument that since all the perfection we know is generative, the Supreme Good through imitation of whom all lesser things become perfect must be held to generate also.[1] Spirit *is* the creative vision of the One,[2] and Spirit is the real Demiurge.[3]

Both Plotinus and Augustine can speak of creation as the act of divine self-giving in which God's nature is manifested. But there are two fundamental differences between the Neoplatonist idea of creation and Augustine's, or any Christian, doctrine. First, while Plotinus sees the process beginning in the hierarchy of ' things divine ' and completing itself in the external world of sense, Augustine draws his line firmly and finally between the one Maker and the many things made. And second, Augustine is able to accept less ambiguously than Plotinus the motive for creation assigned in Plato's own myth. ' Let us declare then,' says Timaeus, ' for what cause Nature and this universe was framed by him that framed it. He was good, and in none that is good can there arise jealousy of aught at any time. So, being far aloof from this, He desired that all things should be as like unto Himself as possible. This is that most sovereign cause of nature and the universe which we shall most surely be right in accepting from men of understanding.' [4] Augustine believes that Plato either is here dependent on the Book of Genesis, or has discovered for himself the cause of creation signified in the words *God saw that it was good*, namely ' that by the good God might be wrought good works '.[5] In his own commentary on *Genesis*, he puts the Platonic argument succinctly. ' If God were unable to create good things, there would be no power in Him ; if He were able and yet created them not, there would be great jealousy (*invidia*). Since therefore He is all-powerful and good, He has created all things " very good ".' [6]

But when it is said that God's goodness is the sole cause of creation, what is meant is precisely that creation is *free* and in no

---

[1] *Enn.* v. iv. 1.
[2] *Enn.* v. i. 7.
[3] *Enn.* v. ix. 3.
[4] *Timaeus* 29 DE (tr. Archer-Hind).
[5] *De Civ.* XI. 21.
[6] *De Gen. ad litt.* IV. 27.

sense the outcome of need. ' By saying, *God saw that it was good*, it is made plain enough that God made what was made not because of any necessity, not because of any need for some advantage of His own, but because of His goodness solely.' [1] It is ' out of the fulness of God's goodness ' that there has been brought into existence a good which adds nothing to His perfection, without which He would still have lacked nothing.[2] Man is driven by his necessities to make houses and clothing, to cultivate the soil ; the creative activity of God is wholly free, and man comes nearest to such freedom in the act of worship which he performs not ' of necessity ', but ' because it pleases him '.[3] Nothing could show more clearly Augustine's sense of the difference between the ' spontaneous goodness ' (*gratuita bonitas*) [4] which is God's love, and man's love which even when it is the love of neighbour is always the search for God. In worship alone all search, all desire is transcended. For God's creative love the word *bonitas* is accordingly preferred to *caritas* or *amor*. But the Good of Plotinus, beyond willing and knowing, towards which we move but which makes no movement towards us,[5] has become the Goodness of active, outgoing Love.

The classical passage on creation as the expression of God's love occurs in the first book of the *De Genesi ad litteram*.[6] When Scripture says that ' the Spirit of God moved over the waters ', we are to understand that ' there is in God a benignity supreme,

---

[1] *De Civ.* XI. 24.

[2] *Conf.* XIII. 2, 5. Plotinus has a harsher tone. *Enn.* V. v. 12 : ' Not that God has any need of His derivatives : He ignores all that produced realm (πᾶν καὶ ὅλον ἀφεὶς τὸ γενόμενον), never necessary to Him, and remains identically what He was before He brought it into being. So too, had the secondary never existed, He would have been unconcerned (οὐδ' ἂν ἐμέλησεν αὐτῷ μὴ γενομένον) ' (tr. Mackenna).

[3] *En. in Ps.* CXXXIV. 10 f. : Invenimus aliquid quod libera voluntate faciamus ? Invenimus plane, cum ipsum Deum amando laudamus. Hoc enim libera voluntate facis, quando amas quod laudas ; non enim ex necessitate sed quia placet.

[4] *De Civ.* XII. 18 *ad fin.* This is what Nygren calls ' uncaused ' Agape.

[5] *Enn.* VI. ix. 8.

[6] Augustine marked its importance by transcribing it some years later as a reply to one of the Questions of Dulcitius (*De Octo Dulc. Quaest.* 8).

holy, and righteous ; and a love (*amor*) proceeding not from indigence but from bounty towards His works '.[1] ' Needy and unsatisfied love (*amor*) is naturally *subject* to the things it loves (*diligit*) ; . . . the Spirit of God in Whom we apprehend His holy benevolence and love (*dilectio*) is said to " move *over* " the waters, lest God be thought to love (*amare*) the works He should create through the compulsion of need rather than through the overflow of benevolence.'[2] And *God saw that it was good*, because ' that same benignity which was pleased to create was pleased with what was created. For there are two effects of God's love (*amat*) for His creation : its coming to be and its continuing in being. That there should be a world to continue, the Spirit moved over the waters ; that it should continue, God saw that it was good.'[3]

Here we see what creative love is as well as what it is not. It is not compelled by a want, but it is the expression of a will. On the one hand, the ' need ' or ' necessity ' which Augustine is concerned to exclude from the conception of God's activity is just that element in Eros which makes it dependent upon a good external to itself—the same element which Plotinus would exclude by calling the One ' Self-Eros '. Neither Augustine nor Thomas will regard creation as implied in the idea of the divine goodness. It is ' fitting ', but not ' necessary '.[4] Augustine indeed finds in the uniqueness of creation, in the fact that Christian doctrine rejects the supposition of a world or worlds without beginning or end, a proof that the eternal goodness of God requires no external embodiment or completion ;[5] and Thomas, though he doubts whether it can be proved that the world had a beginning, agrees that if it had, the ' excess of the divine goodness ' would thereby be the more vividly demonstrated.[6] On the other hand, creation is no arbitrary *fiat*. Augustine no more than Plotinus

---

[1] *De Gen. ad litt.* I. 11.   [2] *Ib.* 13.   [3] *Ib.* 14.
[4] Cf. for St. Thomas, *Contra Gentiles*, II. 28, 31.
[5] *De Civ.* XII. 18.
[6] *Contra Gentiles*, II. 35, 38. Bréhier, in his note on *Enn.* II. ix. 7 (the treatise *Against the Gnostics*) goes so far as to say, of the question of the eternity of the world : ' C'est le point capital qui sépare l'hellénisme du christianisme '.

ascribes to God a freedom which is not the expression of His changeless nature : he confutes Pelagian indeterminism with the argument that if freedom be so understood, then God is not free.[1] God makes the world not only because He is good, but because it is good that a world should be. His love is *not* ' uncaused ' self-giving, but the joy of Supreme Goodness in the realisation of all lesser goods—as Thomas says, in the ' multiplication of likenesses of Himself'.

It is a foundation-stone of Augustine's religious philosophy that there is no creation but the bringing into being of good, and that good can be created by God alone. ' What is more worthy of the good God,' he asks, ' than the making of good things, which none but God can make ? '[2] For man to claim such power for himself is the ' perverse imitation of God ' which is the sin of Pelagianism. But the greatest of all created goods is the capacity of finite spirit for union with God ; and what we miss in Augustine is a full sense that God's creation of man in His own likeness is the great token of His love, *because* it is the creation of children destined for love's fellowship with their Father. That is of course implicit in the doctrine of the *imago Trinitatis,* and it may well seem explicit in *fecisti nos ad Te.* But the common translation ' Thou hast made us for Thyself' is inaccurate as well as ambiguous : the words mean ' Thou hast made us to be toward Thee, to know and love Thee'. Augustine in his zeal for the divine self-sufficiency is too fearful of representing the loving will of God as a real seeking of our human love. Perfect love must be eternally in the Holy Trinity. God is *not* ' organic to the world ', as He is in Neo-Platonism and in much modern theism. A creation which was ' necessary ' could not (so Augustine maintains) be the product or expression of goodness, and a free Creator cannot ' need ' His creatures. But *we* need God, because all our good is derived from Him and depends on Him : we ' grow from God ', not He from us.[3] There must therefore be an irreducible difference between God's

---

[1] *C. Jul. op. imp.* III. 120.   [2] *Ep.* 166. 15.
[3] *En. in Ps.* CXLIX. 4.

love for the creature and the creature's love for God—a difference which at once emerges when Augustine attempts in the *De Doctrina Christiana* to describe God's love in terms of use and fruition. If fruition means ' cleaving to something for its own sake ', and use means ' referring what is to be used to the obtaining of what is loved ' ; if ' the object of fruition makes us happy ' and ' the object of use helps us on our way to happiness ',[1]—it would seem evident that the categories of use and fruition alike are applicable only to beings dependent for their happiness on something outside themselves. Yet Augustine asks whether God loves us ' that He may use us, or that He may enjoy us '. The second alternative is immediately dismissed : ' if God enjoys us, then He needs a good which is ours—what no sane man could maintain. For all our good is either Himself or from Himself ; and who can fail to see that the light has no need of the brightness of those things which itself has illumined ? ' [2] On the other hand, while use in man implies reference to his own advantage, and in this sense God ' uses ' nothing ; yet we may say that He ' uses ' us in that His love ' refers ' the being and goodness which He has conferred upon us to His own goodness—and therefore to our advantage though not His.[3] The embarrassment in which Augustine is here involved by his own conceptions might well have led him to a franker admission that love was not to be confined within such Procrustean limits. But we can see what he means—that God's perfection makes His love wholly ' unselfish ', wholly ' disinterested ', the ' pure Agape ' to which creation witnesses.

The Spirit ' moving over the waters ' recalled to Augustine the *supereminens via,* the ' more excellent way ' of love, the *supereminens scientiae charitas Christi,* the ' love of Christ that passeth knowledge '.[4] There *is* a ' way ', in which we may rise above the ' needy and unsatisfied love ' of the creature ; because the Spirit that moved over the waters is a Spirit that has been *given* to us. At the end of the meditations on the first

[1] *De Doctr. Christ.* I. 3 f. [2] *Ib.* 34.
[3] *Ib.* 35. [4] *De Gen. ad litt.* I. 13.

verses of *Genesis* which fill the last Books of his *Confessions,*
Augustine glances for the last time at the Manichaean ' ravings '
of a creation that was not free but forced and limited by the
intractability of a pre-existing matter and the hostility of a rival
power. ' They speak this madness, because they see not Thy
works through Thy Spirit, nor recognise Thee in them. But
for those who see the world through Thy Spirit, it is Thou who
seest in them. When they see that Thy works are good, it is
Thou who seest that they are good : it is Thou who pleasest
in whatever pleases for Thy sake : what pleases us through Thy
Spirit, pleases Thee in us.' [1] The recognition of God in His
creation, that ' seeing that it is good ' which is creative love's
return upon itself, is always a divine act. ' All these things we
see, and they are very good ; because Thou seest them in us,
Thou who hast given us the Spirit wherewith to see them and
to love Thee in them.' [2] But this is love at worship—*non ex
necessitate sed quia placet.*

(*b*) *Redemption.*—The race of man, so made for fellowship
with its Maker, has sold its birthright and separated itself from
God. God's love cannot change, but *for man* it is no longer
a present reality ; for he is fastened by sin either in presumption
or in despair.[3] So the act of God by which sin is overcome must
consist in a revelation of the love in which sinful man cannot
believe. This is the one purpose of Christ's coming—*ad demon-
strandam erga nos dilectionem Dei*—to show the love of God ; and
when Augustine writes for his deacon Deo-gratias a manual of
elementary religious instruction, that is where he begins. He
appeals first to a series of the great New Testament texts,[4] and
proceeds to argue at length from common human experience
that ' there is no stronger invitation to love than to be beforehand
in loving '. The power of love to call forth love is seen alike
in sensual passion and in pure friendship. But nothing can

---

[1] *Conf.* XIII. 45 f.   [2] *Ib.* 49.
[3] *Serm.* 20. 3 ; 87. 10 f.   *En. in Ps.* CI. 10 ; CXLIV. 11.
[4] *Romans* v. 6 ff., viii. 32, xiii. 10 ; I *John* iii. 16, iv. 10.

kindle my love so strongly as the knowledge that I am loved
by a better than myself : above all, ' if I had no hopes that such
love for me was possible ', and ' that other deign of his own
accord to show how much he loves me '.[1] That is how the
Bishop of Hippo's faith and experience led him to present the
Catholic truth of the Incarnation to the intelligence of the convert ;
and the fact is noteworthy. But what he put first in the order
of elementary Christian teaching, he puts first also in his most
advanced theological disquisition. The Fourth and Thirteenth
Books of the *De Trinitate* contain Augustine's *Cur Deus homo ?*
In both places the first answer to the question is the same : ' first
we needed to be assured of God's great love for us, lest through
despair we might not dare to lift ourselves up to Him '.[2]

It has been said that in regard to the Atonement Augustine
has no characteristic doctrine of his own, and does no more
than take up current or traditional lines of thought.[3] In fact,
what is always uppermost in his mind when he speaks of Christ's
Incarnation and Death—and for Augustine in his maturity the
Manger and the Cross are not to be divided—is the love of
God shown forth therein ; and, conversely, when the love of
God is in question, he can but point to Christ's Incarnation and
Death. ' It is the shining proof of God's love towards us, that
He sent His Only begotten Son to die for us.' [4] ' The proof of
God's great love ' is ' that He sent to us His Word, His only Son,
by whose taking flesh to be born and suffer on our behalf we
might come to know for how much man counts to God (*quanti
Deus hominum penderet*).' [5] ' He who made man from the dust
and gave him life, has given His Only Son to death for this
thing of His making. The greatness of His love for us (*quantum
nos amet*) who can explain, who can even worthily imagine ? ' [6]

---

[1] *De Catech. Rud.* 7.   [2] *De Trin.* IV. 2 ; cf. *ib.* XIII. 13.
[3] See Rashdall, *The Idea of Atonement in Christian Theology,* pp. 330 ff.
[4] *Ep.* 127. I.   [5] *De Civ.* VII. 31.
[6] *Serm.* 57 ad fin. Cf. *Serm.* 215. 5 : quantus ergo Dei amor erga homines
et qualis affectio, sic amare etiam peccatores ut amore eorum moreretur !
En. in Ps. CXLIII. 10 : *Quid est homo, quoniam innotuisti ei ? aut filius
hominis, quoniam aestimas eum ? . . .* Aestimatio enim est, quanti pretii sit

But if *quantum nos Deus dilexerit* is the first great lesson of the Incarnation, *quales dilexerit* is the second.[1] Not sin's despair only, but sin's presumption was to be overcome ; and for that we must ' learn how we have been loved in our unloveliness . . . before there was anything in us worthy to be loved '.[2] God's love for sinners can be expressed only in that paradoxical form. ' You were loved first, that you might become worthy to be loved.'[3] It is true that the paradox is such only *sub specie temporis*. ' The love of God is incomprehensible, but it is unchangeable. He has not begun to love us since we have been reconciled to Him through the blood of His Son. He loved us before the foundation of the world, so that we too might share sonship with the Only-Begotten, before we were anything at all. We may not therefore so understand our reconciliation to God through the death of His Son as though the Son had enabled Him to begin to love those whom He had hated. . . . Rather He to whom we are reconciled was loving us already, though we were at enmity with Him because of sin '.[4] The enmity is man's work : the love of God is eternally given to His own. If Augustine had represented the work of redemption as nothing more than the showing forth in time of an eternal truth, he would have been not only more Platonist than Christian, but more Pelagian than Augustinian. But it is not so. God's love in the Word Incarnate has the same creative power as when through the Word Eternal it brought heaven and earth into being. ' Our Maker is our Re-maker.'[5] Of the love that

quidque. Quanti aestimavit hominem, qui pro eo Unici sanguinem fudit. . . . Quoniam tanti eum pendis, tanti eum aestimas, pretiosum quiddam esse ostendis.

[1] *De Trin.* IV. 2. *Serm.* 336. 2.   [2] *Serm.* 142. 5.

[3] *Ib.* Cf. *In Jo. Ev. Tr.* 102. 5 : displicentes amati sumus, ut esset in nobis unde placeremus. *En. in Ps.* XLIV. 3 : [sponsa] amata est foeda, ne remaneret foeda.

[4] *In Jo. Ev. Tr.* 110. 6. Cf. *De Trin.* I. 21 : tales nos amat Deus, quales futuri sumus, non quales sumus. Quales enim amat, tales in aeternum conservat. *Ib.* V. 17 : quod amicus Dei iustus esse incipit, ipse mutatur : Deus autem absit ut temporaliter aliquem diligat, quasi nova dilectione quae in illo ante non erat.   [5] *Ep.* 231. 6 : qui fecit, refecit.

inspires Christian worship, Augustine can say that ' God made
it and saw that it was good : God has loved the love He has
made because it is He that made it ' ; though His creation of
this love *in* us proceeds from His eternal love *for* us.[1] Redemption
is in the fullest sense a new creation, restoring in sinful man the
love toward God which he had lost.

And how is the restoration accomplished ? ' Because nothing
is more contrary to love than envy, and the mother of envy is
pride, the Lord Jesus Christ, the God-Man, is both the proof
of God's love towards us, and the pattern of the humility which
befits us men ; so that the gross tumour of our sickness might
be healed by the antidote of a medicine more potent. Great
is the wretchedness of man's pride ; but greater is the mercy of
God's humility.' [2] These sentences from the *De Catechizandis
Rudibus* are of course typical of a hundred others ; and they
raise the question of what is generally recognised, in Harnack's
phrase, to be the ' pith and sinew ' of Augustine's Christology.
Harnack's judgment has indeed been disputed, and Augustine
has been charged with wavering, as in the passage quoted, between
a ' rationalist ethic ' which would regard the *humana humilitas* of
Jesus, his life of self-sacrifice, as the perfect example of morality,
and an ' unethical dogmatic ' which sees in the *Deus humilis* the
Eternal Word who humbles Himself in the taking of our flesh.[3]
The dilemma is false. The humility of Jesus is redemptive
because it is the humility of the Mediator, the God-Man, and
therefore has the divine potency of creation. That Christ is our
example is what every Christian teacher, whether Augustinian
or Pelagian, must keep in the forefront of his exhortation. But
it was the ' virus ' of Julian's heresy to place the *gratia Christi* in
Christ's example and not in His gift, to seek righteousness by the

---

[1] *In Jo. Ev. Tr.* 102. 5.

[2] *De Catech. Rud.* 8. Cf. *Encheirid.* 28. *De Trin.* xiii. 22. *De Agone
Christ.* 12. *De Pecc. Mer.* ii. 27. *Ep.* 232. 6. *En. in Ps.* xviii. ii. 15 ; xxxiii.
i. 4 ; cxviii. ix. 2. *In Jo. Ev. Tr.* 25. 16 ; 55. 7. *Serm.* 77. 11 ; 142. 2 ; 189, 3 ;
etc., etc.

[3] O. Scheel, *Die Anschauung Augustins über Christi Person und Werk*,
pp. 347 ff.

imitation of Christ instead of through the Holy Spirit which leads men to that imitation.[1] Augustine found his Platonic exemplarism confirmed by the Pauline and Catholic doctrine of Christ's mystical Body. The members of Christ are not only called to imitate—they are made partakers of His Cross and of His Resurrection. And so the ' humility ' of Christ's Incarnation and Death is not only the medicine for the healing of our pride, for which no human example of humility could suffice, but the profound mystery (*altum sacramentum*) by which the chain of sin is loosed.[2]

The ' humility of God ', therefore, is not to be understood in the sense of the *communicatio idiomatum,* as a predicate applicable properly to the Incarnate Christ only. It is the ' down-coming ' of divine Love, the literal ' condescension ' of God which at once demands and makes possible in men the response of acceptance ; and it is embodied in the loving self-sacrifice of Christ's Life and Death. ' God is over all : you lift yourself up, and you touch Him not ; you humble yourself, and He comes down to you.'[3] And, conversely, ' it is your weakness that is the reason of Christ's humility : . . . because you could not go to Him, He comes to you '.[4] For us, humility has a double aspect. We are called to ' partake ' in the ' divine humility ' of self-giving love ; but we can do so only in the ' human humility ' proper to the creature, which simply receives the divine gift, acknowledging that of itself it has nothing. Even here, Christ is our pattern ; for the assumption of human nature by the Person of the Word is the supreme instance of unmerited grace. When we profess our faith in Christ ' born of the Holy Spirit and of the Virgin Mary ', we must understand that it was by God's free grace that a Son of Man from the very beginning of his natural existence was the Son of God ; for the Holy Spirit is the Gift of God, God's Gift of Himself.[5]

[1] *C. Jul. op. imp.* II. 146.   [2] *De Trin.* VIII. 7.
[3] *En. in Ps.* XXXIII. ii. 23.   [4] *Serm.* 142. 2.
[5] *Encheirid.* 12.

(c) *Love and the Holy Spirit.*—No part of Augustine's Trinitarian doctrine has had a more profound or more lasting influence upon Christian thought than his 'appropriation' of the divine Love to the Person of the Holy Spirit. He himself claimed no originality for this doctrine. It was based upon two ideas, of which one, that of the Spirit as the Gift of God, was scriptural and traditional, while the other, that of the Spirit as the 'link' between the Father and the Son, appears to have been suggested to him by the Platonist Victorinus. In any case, he refers in the *De Fide et Symbolo*, a work of his early years in the priesthood, to both these ideas as current.[1] In the *De Trinitate* he endeavours to combine them.

In the name 'Gift' he finds the relational character which his argument has postulated as the necessary constitutive of Personal distinction in the Trinity. As Gift, the Holy Spirit is related both to the Father and to the Son, from whom the Gift proceeds : as 'Spirit', the Gift is 'a kind of communion of the Father and the Son', for Both are Spirit.[2] But here there arises a difficulty of which Augustine is only partly conscious. When Scripture and tradition had called the Spirit the Gift of God, what was meant had always been a gift to men ; and it was Augustine's object to understand the Persons of the Trinity as internal relations within the Godhead. If gift implies giver, it as certainly implies recipient ; and then the nature of God seems to require an external relation to the existence of the created world, which Augustine denied. He might have sought a solution by representing the 'communion' of the Father and the Son as the mutual 'self-giving' of love ; and in one passage, where he is commenting upon a phrase of Hilary—'eternity in the Father, form (*species*) in the Image, use in the Gift'—something of the kind is certainly suggested. 'The ineffable relation', he says, 'as it were the embrace, of Father and Image, cannot lack perfect fruition, love, joy ; and this love, delight, happiness or beatitude—human words cannot worthily express it—is what Hilary denotes as "use".' But he passes immediately to

[1] *De Fid. et Symb.* 19.　　　　[2] *De Trin.* v. 12.

the external relation. 'In the Trinity the Holy Spirit, not Himself begotten, is the sweetness (*suavitas*) of Begetter and Begotten, with the profusion of a vast bounty flowing out over all creatures according to their capacity to receive, that they may observe their order and rest in the places assigned to them.' [1] But where he is expressly dealing with the difficulty in question, he declares only that the Spirit is 'eternally Gift, though temporally given'; inasmuch as before we the recipients came into being, the Spirit 'eternally so proceeded as to be givable (*donabile*)' : [2] an explanation which leaves the difficulty, for his own theology, untouched.

So far he has been dealing with those relational distinctions which forbid the 'confounding of the Persons'. In the next stage of his discussion, he shows that the terms 'Wisdom' and 'Power', which Scripture applies to God the Son, are *not* relational but 'substantive', and must therefore hold of the indivisible essence of the Godhead ; and he proceeds to maintain the same position with regard to the term Love. When St. John says 'God is love', he is speaking of the substance of the divine Being, in which all Three Persons are equal. We may conceive the Spirit as the unity, as the holiness, as the mutual love of the First Two Persons ; but this 'communion', this love is 'consubstantial' : it belongs to the essential nature of Father and Son, and it is not that which makes the Spirit a 'Person'.[3]

There the matter is left in the first part of the treatise. In the second part, the series of psychological *vestigia Trinitatis* provide in the second term of each triad an analogy for the Personal or distinctive being of the Son, as the Word or Image of the Father ; but the third term always consists, not in the idea of Gift by which the Person of the Spirit has (in the first part) been distinguished, but in that of love or will as the active relating of object to subject. So, when Augustine comes in the final Book to review his whole argument, he has much to say of the inadequacy of the analogies which he has drawn in respect to the Second Person of the Trinity : as compared with the Eternal

---

[1] *De Trin.* VI. 11.   [2] *Ib.* V. 16 f.   [3] *Ib.* VI. 7.

Word of God, the human *verbum interius* or unspoken thought, the human act of self-knowledge, is no more than an *aenigma in speculo*, a blurred and imperfect reflection. But when he passes to the doctrine of the Spirit, the only question is whether and in what sense the Spirit, as the ' communion ' of Father and Son, is to be called Love. It is premissed that as the Three Persons are One God, so are They One Wisdom and One Love ; and it finally becomes clear that in the last resort Augustine will justify the ' appropriation ' of the term Love to the Spirit, as of the term Wisdom to the Son, by nothing else than the authority of Scripture. He appeals to the First Epistle of St. John, where we read that *love is of God*, that *God is love*, that *whosoever abideth in love, abideth in God and God in him*, and that *hereby we know that we abide in Him and He in us, because He hath given us of His Spirit*. ' The Holy Spirit, proceeding from God, enkindles the man to whom He has been given with the love of God and of his neighbour, and Himself is love.' [1] St. Paul has told us that love is the supreme Gift ; and we may conclude that ' the love which proceeds from God and is God, is properly or especially that Holy Spirit through whom the love of God is spread abroad in our hearts, the love of God *through which the whole Trinity makes Its dwelling within us*. Wherefore most rightly is the Holy Spirit, God as He is, called the Gift of God ; and to that Gift what special meaning can we give but love, which leads to God, and without which there is no gift of God whatever that can lead to Him ? ' [2]

In the *De Trinitate*, as it stands, we see not the fruit but the process of fifteen years' meditation. Augustine knew that he had achieved no consistent or systematic exposition of these high mysteries ; [3] and his doctrine of the Holy Spirit, as we have seen, is tentative and imperfectly integrated. But certain points are clear. The acceptance of the term ' Gift ' as *differentia* of the Third Person involved the concentration of attention upon the

---

[1] *De Trin.* xv. 31. [2] *Ib.* 32.

[3] Cf. his dedicatory letter to Aurelius : ' emendatos non ut volui sed ut potui '.

Spirit as immanent. He insists expressly that the ' gift of the Spirit ' is the Spirit Himself, that it has no other content ; [1] and he is so far from feeling the need to distinguish the love of God which the Spirit ' spreads abroad in our hearts ' from the love which is in God Himself both the principle of communion or unity between the Persons and the principle of creative and redemptive activity, that his phrases tend rather to obscure than to mark any such distinction.   And if this is so in the *De Trinitate,* it is certainly not less so in the *Sermons* and *Homilies.*   That the love of God, our love for God, is God's gift, was his final reply to the Pelagianism which saw in the Incarnation only the *demand* of God's love that we should love Him in return.[2]   *Amare Deum, Dei donum est.*[3]   As the reply to Pelagianism, that would have been enough.   But Augustine goes beyond it.   ' He whom we have loved has given us Himself : He has given us that from which our love derives *(dedit unde diligeremus)* ' ; for the presence in us of the Holy Spirit means that we love God ' through God ' *(amemus Deum de Deo).*[4]   Or, more boldly still : ' that you may love God, let Him dwell in you and love Himself through you *(amet se de te)* '.[5]   There follows indeed an explanatory clause : ' that is, let Him stir you, kindle you, enlighten you, arouse you, to the love of Him ' ; but it is an explanation, not a qualification of what precedes.

The clue to Augustine's meaning must be sought in his central conception of union with God. *Mihi bonum est adhaerere Deo.   He that is joined to the Lord is one spirit,* says St. Paul ; and Augustine will not have forgotten the context of that saying when he applies it to the destiny of man's soul.   When the image of the Trinity is renewed in it, ' when it shall cleave utterly and wholly to God, it will be made *one spirit* . . . entering into participation of the divine Nature, Truth, and Bliss '[6] St. Paul speaks in the present or perfect tense, Augustine in the future ; for he cannot forget that the soul as known to itself

[1] *De Trin.* xv. 36.　　　　[2] *C. Jul. op. imp.* I. 94.
[3] *Serm.* 297. I.　　　　[4] *Ib.* 34. 2 f.
[5] *Ib.* 128. 4.　　　　[6] *De Trin.* XIV. 20.

here and now has not risen above the sphere of change.[1]   But
St. Paul too knows that union with God has the aspect not only
of a reconciliation once for all accomplished, but of a sanctification which is continually in process, that the inner man is renewed
from day to day.[2]   So for Augustine the earnest of the Spirit is
a unity which is ' unity because it is love, and love because it is
holiness '.[3]   And this unity is not Plotinus's flight of the alone
to the Alone.   ' Through that which is common to the Father
and the Son, They have willed that we should have communion
with one another and with Them, that we should be brought
together into one through That one Gift which is of Them
Both—the Holy Spirit, God and God's Gift.   By that Gift are
we reconciled to the Divine and made to delight therein.' [4]
Because sin is the separation of men from God and their division
from one another, the forgiveness of sins in which Satan's
' kingdom of division ' is overthrown, and the fellowship of
the Church's unity, within which alone the forgiveness of sins
is assured, are alike the special work of the Holy Spirit who is
' as it were the Fellowship of the Father and the Son '.[5]   *Extra
Ecclesiam nulla salus.*   Behind all the misconstruction and abuse
of that principle there remains the truth that neither sin or forgiveness can be comprehended in terms of a relation of ' the
alone to the Alone '.   The solitary soul *cannot* be ' in Christ '.
It is not the individual who is called to be ' a Christ ', to imitate
or reproduce the union of human nature with the Word ; for
the love of God cannot exist apart from love of the brethren.
But in the Communion of Saints love is a ' theandric activity ',
Emmanuel, God with us—*unus Christus amans se ipsum.*

Conclusion

Christianity came into the Hellenistic world as the Gospel of
the Resurrection, the promise to mortal man of everlasting life.[6]

[1] *De Trin.* xiv. 20 : se ipsam vero nunc quando videt, non aliquid
immutabile videt.   [2] Cf. *ib.* 23.
   [3] *Ib.* vi. 7.   [4] *Serm.* 71. 18.   [5] *Serm.* 71. 28, 33.
   [6] Harnack may have exaggerated his thesis, and his use of the word
' physical ' is certainly misleading.   But the thesis itself is indisputable.

For the Greek mind, immortality meant divinisation : the word
θεός denoted, not the one Creator and Ruler whom Israel
worshipped, but a *kind* of being whose most important difference
from humanity was freedom from death. The datum of Greek
theology was thus the assumed fact that through Christ the
individual man becomes θεός—divine. Its problem was the
interpretation of this fact in accord with the ethical monotheism
which was wholly foreign to Greek religion and for which the
Greek language was without any adequate expression. The ambiguity of the word θεός was not only the source and strength
of Arianism ; it lurked in the formulas by which orthodoxy
sought to defend itself. Nothing could really be settled by the
argument that if ' in Christ ' man's mortal nature is made to
partake of the divine privilege of immortality, then Christ
Himself cannot be less than God, so long as it was not clear that
God is far more than an immortal being. ' Because of His
immeasurable love He became what we are, that He might fit
us to be what He is.'[1] 'He entered into humanity, that we
might be made divine.'[2] Are the great sentences of Irenaeus
and Athanasius founded upon a *quid pro quo* ?

Augustine possessed the enormous advantage of beginning
with the real monotheism to which Greek theology had needed
to find its way. The unity and the uniqueness of God were his
postulates, and for all his Neo-Platonism he shrinks from the
language of ' deification '. Not that such language had for his
ears the sound of blasphemy :[3] in the *De Natura et Gratia* he
states soberly his belief that the perfection of man's righteousness
will never make creature equal to Creator. ' Those who think ',
he adds, ' that we shall be brought so far as to be changed into the
substance of God, and be made altogether what He is, must support their opinion as they may ; for my part I do not believe it.'[4]

---

[1] Irenaeus, *Adv. Haer.* v. praef.

[2] Athanasius, *De Incarn. Verb.* 54.

[3] Cf. *Serm.* 166. 4 : Deus deum te vult facere : non natura, sed . . .
adoptione. . . . Sic totus homo deificatus, etc.

[4] *De Nat. et Grat.* 37.

Redemption has indeed for him its 'physical' connotation. Where the Greeks had thought of mortality and immortality, where the scholastics were to think of nature and super-nature, Augustine thinks of change and the changeless. But change is wider than death, and Platonism made it an ethical and not merely a physical conception. We have seen what was Augustine's equivalent for the Greek thesis of the divinisation of human nature through the Incarnate Word. *Aeterno Creatori adhaerentes, et nos aeternitate afficiamur necesse est.* The superiority of his understanding of Christianity lies in the sureness of his conviction, first, that 'cleaving to God' must be the personal union of love, and second, that this union is neither cause nor effect of a transformation of man's nature, but is itself that transformation. The *De Incarnatione* of Athanasius views the work of Christ in two aspects only : Being and Knowledge. Christ has saved us from the death to which sin had doomed us, and revealed to us the truth of God to which sin had blinded us. Augustine knows that if the *gratia Christi* has brought knowledge and immortality to man, it is because it has brought into men's hearts the love of God. The theologians of the Eastern Church who had given so much wealth of meaning to the doctrine of our union with Christ in His mystical Body were certainly not ignorant that there can be no true membership of Christ without love ; but their concern to vindicate a 'real' as against a 'merely moral' union arose from the Pelagian assumption that love is of man, not, or not only, of God. Augustine taught the Church that she is 'really' one with Christ only in the measure in which she 'realises' the love which is shed abroad in our hearts through the Holy Spirit which is given to us.

VII

Sin and Punishment

Behold, all ye that kindle a fire,
That gird yourselves about with firebrands :
Walk ye in the flame of your fire,
And among the brands that ye have kindled.

THE BOOK OF ISAIAH.

The wrath of God is revealed from heaven against all ungodliness and un-righteousness of men . . . for that they exchanged the truth of God for a lie, and worshipped and served the creature rather than the Creator. . . . For this cause God gave them up unto vile passions . . . receiving in themselves that recompence of their error which was their due. And even as they refused to have God in their knowledge, God gave them up unto a reprobate mind.

ST. PAUL.

Das Strafgesetz ist ein kategorische Imperativ . . . wenn die Gerechtigkeit untergeht, so hat es keinen Werth mehr dass Menschen auf Erden leben.

IMMANUEL KANT.

VII

'NOTHING can possibly be conceived, in the world or even out of it, which can be called good without qualification, except'— union with God, *adhaerere Deo*. The love of God which is God's gift of Himself, is the one all-sufficient motive of the Christian life. We have now to look at the dark reverse of this serene and splendid doctrine, at the theory of evil for which most of all, as we may think, Augustine needs the famous prayer of the *De Trinitate :* 'If aught that I have said comes from myself, may it have pardon from Thee and from Thy Church'.

The gravamen of the charge against Augustine is not that he has exaggerated the evil of sin : for the Christian who has once knelt in spirit before the Crucifix, that is impossible ; nor that he ascribes the extent of this evil to a corruption of human nature for which as a fact of history the narrative of *Genesis* may appear insufficient evidence. The present state of mankind is what it is, however it has been reached ; and Christian faith in God can be combined at least as easily with belief as with disbelief in the Fall of man. It is Augustine's account, not of the origin of moral evil, but of its consequences, not his mistaking of a myth of the *Urzeit* for history, but the eschatology which he professes to deduce from it, his dogmas of the *Endzeit,* that have alienated men from the Catholic faith. Because it is impossible for us to love a God who condemns to eternal fire all those of His children who have never heard the Gospel message, it is impossible for us to believe that such a God exists. What we are now to consider is the relation of Augustine's doctrine of sin to his doctrine of the *Summum Bonum,* and its connection or lack of connection with his theories of punishment. We may reject his teaching on Judgement, without thereby passing a verdict upon his teaching on Sin.

1. *Sin*

(*a*) *The Act of Will.*—It was the problem of evil which had made Augustine a Manichaean.[1] He began his career as a Christian theologian by asserting the reality of human responsibility against the Manichaean attempt to escape from this responsibility by postulating a superhuman principle of world-evil. The Pelagians were not unnaturally provoked by the doctrine of original sin in its specifically Augustinian form into denouncing its defender as a Manichaean himself, and their denunciation has been echoed by modern critics. For Augustine, this was mere unintelligent abuse : from beginning to end he had maintained that sin can *arise* from nothing but the free choice of a spiritual being. In the *Retractations* he deals very carefully with the *De Libero Arbitrio,* upon which the Pelagians had specially fastened as inconsistent with his later theories ; but he does not find it necessary to add any safeguards to the definition of sin which he had given in that treatise. He had shown that neither the objects of our bodily affections and impulses, nor the will by which we exercise our power of choice between one object and another, are evil in themselves. But the ' proper and primal ' good for man, at once his virtue and his happiness, is the soul's ' adherence ' to the changeless and universal Good ; the power of will which a man *must* use for the attainment of this end stands midway in the scale of value between the end itself and the external world of sense which he *can* use aright, if he will.[2] Since, then, our good is God's will, ' the human will sins when it turns aside from the changeless and universal Good, and turns towards its own private good, or to goods remote from, or beneath itself. It turns to a private good when it wills to be in its own power ; to a good outside its proper range, when it seeks the knowledge of what belongs to others or concerns not itself ; to an inferior good, when it loves bodily pleasure. Thus a man, given over to pride, curiosity, or wantonness, finds himself in another life, which in comparison with the higher life is death, yet which is ruled by the

---

[1] *De Lib. Arb.* I. 4.   [2] *Ib.* II. 50, 52.

government of divine providence, ordering all things in the
places appropriate to them and assigning unto every man his
own (*sua cuique*) according to his deserts. . . . What is evil is
the will's aversion from the changeless Good and its conversion
to the goods that are changing ; and this aversion and conversion,
being voluntary and not compelled, is followed by the fit and
just punishment of misery.' [1]

In this definition, Augustine's view of the nature of sin is
seen to be the direct corollary of his view of the *Summum Bonum.*
Negatively, it is the failure to love God ; positively, it is the
inevitable transference of love to objects which, though good
because God's creatures, are goods less than the highest.[2] As the
love of the Tri-Une God acknowledges Him as source of Being,
Knowledge, and Goodness, so sin displays itself in the perversions
of *superbia, curiositas,* and *lascivia,* the ' pride of life ', the ' lust
of the eye ', and the ' lust of the flesh ' which were the three
temptations which Christ overcame in the wilderness.[3] Not the
being of the self, nor its desire to know and enjoy, are evil : its
preference of its own being and of the knowledge and enjoyment
of things temporal, to the one eternal Good, is what constitutes
sin. It is the ' lie in the soul ' ; for good, true or apparent, is the
motive for every act of will, and we cannot prefer the lesser to the
greater good unless we are deceived.[4] But the deception is our
own act, and we are accountable for its consequences. As the
love of God is (in scholastic terms) both formal and material
cause of union with Him, so is sin both formal and material
cause of that separation from God which nothing else can bring
about.[5]

[1] *De Lib. Arb.* II. 53.

[2] Cf. *De Nat. Boni* 34 : Non malam naturam homo appetivit . . . sed id
quod melius erat deserendo, factum malum ipse commisit.

[3] Cf. *De Vera Relig.* 69 ff. *En. in Ps.* VIII. 13. *De Trin.* XII. 14. *Conf.* X.
41 ff. We may find it difficult to regard ' curiosity ' as anything but a virtue ;
and no doubt the significance here given to it is largely schematic and artificial.
But for the age of Augustine there were still things that man was never
meant to know.   [4] *De Civ.* XIV. 4.

[5] *Ib.* X. 22. *De Pecc. Merit.* I. 34. *De Spir. et Litt.* 42. *En. in Ps.*
CXXXVII. 2.

In the concept of sin both ethics and religion are involved. From the strictly ethical point of view, no action is sin for which the agent cannot be held personally responsible; and, as we have seen, it was precisely in order to establish the strictly ethical point of view that Augustine wrote the *De Libero Arbitrio*. Both the norm of conduct and the accountability of the individual agent are expressed in the 'eternal law', which both requires the subordination of lower to higher values and asserts the dependence of happiness upon the will's free acceptance of this principle of order. 'Merit' is in the will.[1]

The ethical condemnation of an action becomes religious when the law is identified with the Lawgiver, when it becomes possible for the guilty soul to cry: *Against Thee only have I sinned.* For Augustine's religious philosophy it is not easy to make this confession. He is certain that 'nothing can hurt God' or 'disturb the order of His rule'.[2] Sin is indeed disobedience, and that primarily.[3] God is the Lord, the Master to whom we belong; but He is the absolute Master because He has no need of our service,[4] and all His commands are the commands of love, 'for our benefit, not for His'.[5] Because God is love, the transgression of His command is an offence against man. Because God is love, no man who offends against his brother can dare to say that he is 'sinning' *only* against a man.[6] But for the same reason—because God is love, and the fulfilment of His will is our union with Him, there can be no sin that does not separate the sinner from God. Whether the sinner be aware of it or not, the separation is a fact which must endure until love has broken down the barrier in forgiveness; and for Augustinian religion this enduring state of separation from God is the *pondus peccati*, the weight of sin.

---

[1] *De Lib. Arb.* I. 15, 18, 30.   [2] *Conf.* III. 16 ; XII. 11.

[3] *En. in Ps.* LXX. ii. 7.   *De Pecc. Merit.* II. 35.

[4] *Ep.* 138. 6.   *En. in Ps.* LXIX. 6.

[5] *En. in Ps.* XXXVI. ii. 13 : quid exigit Deus nisi quod tibi prosit ? *Ib.* CII. 4 : laudari se vult Deus ; et hoc, ut tu proficias, non ut ille sublimetur. *Ep.* 102. 17 : nobis prodest colere Deum, non ipsi Deo.

[6] *In Ep. Jo. Tr.* 7. 5.

Of course, ethical philosophy has recognised since Aristotle the distinction between 'act' and 'habit', and the fact that habit is not easily reversible. But the only 'state' to which the moral philosopher will assign ethical significance is that condition of the individual which is the product of his own voluntary and purposeful activity—his self-determined character. Experience seemed to Augustine to make the 'strictly ethical' point of view untenable. All the struggles of his later thought were forced upon him by the realisation that in the *De Libero Arbitrio* he had been describing man's ethical nature in the abstract; that for the concrete human beings we know and are, *sin has made a difference;* that as a fact of experience we do not begin with 'adherence to God', but in a state of separation from Him which is marked by two fundamental differences from the act of sin as ethically defined. First, the state of sin is *involuntary* in the sense that the subject of it cannot escape from it by his own will; and second, it is a state which *cannot* be said to arise only as the consequence of the subject's own voluntary activity.

(b) *The Involuntary State.*—Already in the *De Libero Arbitrio* these questions are being raised, and the tendencies of thought which reach their issue in the anti-Pelagian treatises are discernible. The origin of moral evil has been placed in the will; and when his interlocutor Evodius seeks to go a step further back, to find a 'cause of the will itself', Augustine refuses the question. If the will has a cause to which resistance is impossible, moral responsibility disappears, and sin with it. 'Who can be said to sin in an act which cannot be avoided? But sin is a fact, and avoidance of it is therefore possible.'[1] When Pelagius quoted that sentence against him, Augustine replied that sin can indeed be avoided, though only with the help of grace.[2] But in the *De Libero Arbitrio* the statement leads at once to the consideration that in man *as he is* we find states of ignorance and infirmity of which it must be allowed that the victim 'has it not in his power to be good'.[3] And the conclusion is immediately drawn that

---

[1] *De Lib. Arb.* III. 50.   [2] *De Nat. et Grat.* 80.
[3] *De Lib. Arb.* III. 51.

this condition is ' not the nature of man as he was made, but the punishment to which he has been condemned. When we speak of the freedom of the will to do right, the freedom of which we speak is that in which man was made.' [1]

There already is the sharp distinction between sin which is sin simply, sin without qualification, and sin which is also *poena peccati*—the distinction on which Augustine was to rely for his refutation of Julian thirty years later.[2] Julian too had quoted a definition of sin from an early anti-Manichaean treatise : ' the will's pursuit of an end forbidden by the moral law (*iustitia*), and from which there is freedom to abstain '.[3] For a state to which we have been condemned, that definition is manifestly inapplicable : all punishment is willy-nilly. When man knew the law of God, and while there was as yet in him no lusting of the flesh against the spirit, he was free to do right. But *that* freedom is his no longer. Man has fallen *sponte*, by his own act ; his own act cannot raise him again.[4] He is *sold under sin*. If, instead of allowing that such a condition is no longer to be called sin, Augustine insists on retaining the name in a modified sense, it is because he regards sin as still rooted in the will, though it be a will enslaved.

' Divine grace lending its aid to the human will, man *can* in this life be without sin. If I am asked why then he is not, I might answer most easily and most truthfully, " Because men will not " ; but if I am asked " Why will they not ? " the answer is a longer matter. . . . Men *will* not do what is right, either because the right is hidden from them, or because they take no delight in it. For the strength of our will to anything is proportionate to the certainty of our knowledge of its goodness, and the ardour of our delight in it. Thus ignorance and infirmity are failings which hinder the will from being moved to a good action or to abstinence from a bad one. But that what was hidden may become known, what delighted not may become

---

[1] *De Lib. Arb.* III. 52. Cf. *Retr.* I. 9. 5.
[2] *C. Jul. op. imp.* V. 59 ; VI. 17 *et sæpe*.
[3] *Ib.* I. 44. [4] *De Lib. Arb.* II. 54.

sweet, belongs to the grace of God, by which He helps the wills of men.'[1] So, in the picture of the 'earthly hell' drawn in the last book of the *De Civitate*, it is the 'profundity of men's ignorance', and the 'love of things vain and harmful', the universality of error and perverse desire, which mark the penal condition of the life to which the whole human race has been 'condemned'.[2] And in the *Encheiridion*, Augustine's latest summary of Christian doctrine, ignorance and infirmity are named without qualification as 'the two causes of sin', against which we must pray for the grace which illuminates as well as confers the 'delight in righteousness'.[3]

It is clear that these two 'causes of sin', the failure of intellect and the failure of will, are but the negative aspects of the mis-direction of both faculties, the *curiositas* and *lascivia,* which in the definition of the *De Libero Arbitrio* and the discussions of the *De Vera Religione* Augustine, faithful as always to his Trinitarian pattern of thought, had ranked after *superbia* as making up the soul's three-fold defection from the love of God. But as ignorance and infirmity come to stand more and more in his view for the fallen condition in which man suffers under the penal deprivation of his true liberty, so pride takes its place more distinctly as the ultimate origin of sin, the *radix omnium malorum*.[4] Pride is itself the Fall, of man as of angels : *ipsum quippe extolli, iam deici est.*[5] It is the pursuit of that 'perverse exaltation' in which man seeks 'to become and to be a principle to himself, abandoning the one Principle to which the soul should cleave '.[6] *Jerusalem is built as a city, whereof the participation is in the Self-Same (cuius participatio in idipsum).* The 'Self-Same' is the mystic title of God as the changeless *I am ;* nothing subject to change ' has of itself the Self-Same ', and the name of Israel—*est videns Deum*—signifies that man has being only according to the measure of his vision or participation of God. 'The proud

---

[1] *De Pecc. Merit.* II. 26.   [2] *De Civ.* XXII. 22.

[3] *Encheirid.* 22.   Cf. *Serm.* 182. 6.

[4] *De Gen. ad litt.* XI. 19.   In *Jo. Ev. Tr.* 25. 16.   *En. in Ps.* XVIII. ii. 15 ; LVII. 18.

[5] *De Civ.* XIV. 13.   *En. in Ps.* XCIII. 15 f.   [6] *De Civ.* XIV. 13.

therefore is not Israel ; for his participation is not in the Self-Same : he wishes to be the Self-Same for himself. . . . The participator in the Self-Same is he who confesses that he is other than God, that he has from God all the good he can have.' [1]

Because man has fallen through pride, he can be raised again only through humility. ' Unto man, borne above himself by pride, God in His mercy came down humbly, commending His evident and manifest grace in that very man whom He took to Himself with love beyond his fellows. Not even that man himself, so joined to the Word of God that by the joining one and the same person should be Son of God and Son of Man, wrought it by any precedent merits of his own will. . . . This then especially is commended to us, this, I dare to think, especially is taught and learnt in the treasures of wisdom and knowledge which are hidden in Christ. For this reason each one of us at one time knows and at another knows not how to begin and carry to fulfilment a good work, at one time he takes delight in it, at another he does not ; that he may learn that his knowledge or his delight comes not of his own power but of the divine gift, and thus be healed from the vanity of self-exaltation, and know how true is the saying, not of this earth but in a spiritual sense : *The Lord shall give sweetness, and our earth shall give its increase.*' [2] It is Christ who shows fallen man what is good, it is the Holy Spirit who enables him to desire it and accomplish it ; and thus are removed the blindness of heart and the weakness of will which have resulted from man's attempt to secure for himself an impossible independence, to be in Julian's phrase ' emancipated from God '. The way of redemption is ' first, humility, second, humility, third, humility '.

(*c*) *Original Sin.*—The *peccatum originale,* the sin of Adam, is pride, the false self-love which makes the self its own end. If we ask why Augustine did not teach that this same tendency of the self to rebellion against the love of God is what the children of Adam inherit, the answer must be sought in his conception of the sinful state in which we are born as the ' punishment ' of

---

[1] *En. in Ps.* CXXI. 6, 8.　　　　[2] *De Pecc. Merit.* II. 27.

sin rather than as sin in the 'strictly ethical' sense. That he found the *poena peccati* in concupiscence, the lusting of the flesh against the spirit, is certainly due to the seventh chapter of the Epistle to the Romans, and not to a particular theory of the manner of sin's propagation.

The attempt to extract anything like a logically consistent doctrine from the confusion of the controversy with Julian must be pronounced hopeless. Julian's rationalist ethic, for which every natural impulse is morally neutral, provoked Augustine to identify concupiscence with the natural impulses themselves, and to ask how the 'enemy' we have to fight can at the same time be a 'neutral'. But in the main he did avoid the Manichaeanism with which Julian so constantly taunted him. The evil of concupiscence is the war in our members, and this war is a fault, a *vitium*, but it is not, properly speaking, sin : it is only 'called' sin because it is both the effect and the occasion, the 'daughter' and the 'mother' of sin.[1]

Augustine's difficulties arise from the premiss of his anti-Manichaean argument : namely, that all human evil is either sin or punishment.[2] The state in which we are born is evil. But if this evil is punishment rather than sin, what of the guilt (*reatus*) which punishment implies ? The only possible answer seemed to be that we bear the 'guilt' of a sin which we have not our-selves committed : the 'innocent' child is at the same time 'guilty'. But then guilt ceases to be ethically intelligible. It stands for the fact that man comes into the world 'without God', severed from the love which is his life.

As in Adam all die, even so in Christ shall all be made alive. The supposed unity of the race in Adam serves but ill for the understanding of our unity in Christ. For Christ came to create a real unity where unity was lacking. 'In Adam' mankind

---

[1] *De Nupt. et Concup.* I. 27. *C. du. Ep. Pelag.* I. 27. Even in *C. Jul. op. imp.* Augustine will (on occasion) make the distinction. Cf. II. 71 : Aliud est peccatum, aliud concupiscentia peccati, cui non consentit qui per gratiam Dei non peccat : quamvis et ipsa concupiscentia peccati *vocatur* peccatum, quia peccato facta est.

[2] *De Vera Relig.* 23. *De Gen. ad litt. imp. lib.* 3.

was not and never could be one. There is doubtless profound truth in Schleiermacher's words : ' sin is in each the work of all, and in all the work of each '.[1] The moral solidarity of mankind is a far more adequate explanation of the world we know than any ethic of individual responsibility. But the cry of the Crucified—*Why hast Thou forsaken me ?*—is the cry of innocence, not of guilt. It is the cry of souls innumerable who have been separated from God by the sin of others. Augustine could only understand it as the ' sacrament ' of our death to sin, the voice in which the Head speaks for all His sinful members.[2] The doctrine of original sin cannot be rationalised ; and when the attempt was made by means of it to rationalise divine justice and eternal damnation, it ceased to represent the mystery of iniquity, and stood out naked as an invention of the devil.

2. *Justice*

The pride of man is evil because it is the ' privation of good ', self-severance from the love of God : it is punishable because it is revolt against the universal Order. The faith of Israel, the assurance that ' the Lord is King, be the people never so impatient ', nourished by the atmosphere of Roman law and imperial polity, and reinforced in different ways by Stoic and Neo-Platonist thought, is for Augustine the necessary pre-supposition of any Christian theodicy. ' Nothing happens in the world of sight and sense, without either command or permission from the inner, invisible and spiritual Court of the Supreme Emperor, according to the ineffable justice of rewards and punishments, graces and retributions, in this great and boundless polity of the whole creation.' [3] That the justice of God's government of the world is *so far* comparable to the justice of human law as to

[1] Quoted by F. R. Tennant, *The Origin and Propagation of Sin*, p. 71.
[2] *De Trin.* IV. 6. Cf. *En. in Ps.* XL. 6 : In illo eramus, cum dixit, Deus meus, Deus meus, ut quid me dereliquisti ? In ipso enim psalmo ubi in capite hic versus est, consequenter dicitur ' Verba delictorum meorum '. Quorum delictorum in illo, nisi quia vetus homo noster simul crucifixus est cum illo ?
[3] *De Trin.* III. 9.

manifest itself in the distribution of reward and punishment, is the postulate of the whole argument of the *De Libero Arbitrio*.

Augustine assumes the current definition of justice as ' giving every man his due '.[1] But he interprets the juristic concept in the Platonic sense.[2] The *notio aeternae legis* is that ' justice consists in the perfect ordering of all things ' ;[3] and order means the subjection of lower to higher, of the lesser to the greater good.[4] The soul that ' knows itself' will seek ' to be ordered according to its own nature, beneath that to which it should be subject, above those things to which it should be preferred '.[5] Justice in us men lies in submission to God, and in ' owing no man anything but to love another '.[6] The *ordo universi* is Plotinus's grand hierarchy of existence, in which all things have their place according to their share of good ; and Augustine can without hesitation present this cosmology of the *Enneads*[7] as a truth of which ' we are persuaded by the Christian faith '. The Cosmos is good in virtue of the principle of sub-ordination which gives it unity—a law manifested alike in the physical order of the external world, the regular sequences of nature ; in the order of value, exemplified in the superiority of the spiritual to the material ; and in the order of ' desert ' by which the spiritual world itself is subject to the rule of punishment and reward.[8]

Human law is necessarily variable ; but through all its variations its ground is in the immutable decree of the *lex aeterna*, that ' the wicked merit a life of misery, the good a life of blessedness '.[9] The fundamental difference between the

---

[1] *De Lib. Arb.* I. 27. *En. in Ps.* LXXXIII. 11. *De Civ.* XIX. 21. But when Julian gives, for divine justice, the same definition (*C. Jul. op. imp.* I. 35), Augustine confronts him with the inscrutable destinies of children and with the parable of the Labourers in the Vineyard.

[2] *De Civ.* XIX. 4 : Quid iustitia, cuius munus est sua cuique tribuere (unde fit in ipso homine quidam iustus ordo naturae, ut anima subdatur Deo et animae caro, ac per hoc Deo et anima et caro), nonne demonstrat in eo se adhuc opere laborare potius quam in huius operis iam fine requiescere ?

[3] *De Lib. Arb.* I. 15. [4] *Ib.* 18. [5] *De Trin.* X. 7.
[6] *En. in Ps.* LXXXIII. 11. [7] See esp. *Enn.* III. ii. 7 ff.
[8] *C. Secund. Manich.* 10. [9] *De Lib. Arb.* I. 15.

' temporal' order of human society and the eternal *ordo universi* is that human laws can be broken, while the law of God is inviolable and inviolate. No man's sin can ' disturb the order of God's empire'.[1] ' Let a man choose for himself what he will. The works of the Lord are not so constituted that a creature in the freedom of choice which has been given him may overcome the will of the Creator, even though he act against the Creator's will. God wills not your sin; for He forbids it. But if you have sinned, think not that a man has done what he would and that to God has happened that which He would not. As He wills that man should not sin, so He wills to spare the sinner that he may turn again and live ; so in the end He wills to punish the man who persists in sin, that his contumacy may not escape the power of justice. Whatever you choose, the Almighty will not lack the means to fulfil His will in you.' [2] ' If all existences should observe the limit, form, and order proper to them, there will be no evil ; but if any will to use these goods amiss, not even so does he overcome the will of God, who knows how to order justly the unjust ; so that if they by the pravity of their will have used His goods amiss, He by the justice of His power uses their evil well, ordering aright in punishments those who have ordered themselves perversely in sins.' [3] The saying of Plotinus that it is ' a mark of the highest power to be able to use evil well ',[4] is a commonplace in Augustine ; [5] but he commonly employs it in reference to the power of God to bring good out of evil, as in the supreme instance of the betrayal by Judas. In the passage just quoted, which is closely reproduced in the Letter-treatise of the year 412, *On the Grace of the New Testament,* the punishment itself is the method of the divine ' using'. So elsewhere God's omnipotent goodness is said ' to do good with things evil, either by pardoning, or by healing, or by conversion to the advantage

---

[1] *Conf.* XII. II.
[2] *En. in. Ps.* CX. 2. Cf. *De Spir. et Litt.* 58.
[3] *De Nat. Boni* 37. Cf. *Ep.* 140. 4. [4] *Enn.* III. ii. 5.
[5] E.g. *Serm.* 214. 3. *In Jo. Ev. Tr.* 27. 10. *C. Jul. op. imp.* V. 60.

of the pious, *or even by a most just punishment* '.[1] Augustine shrinks no more than Plotinus from the assertion that the punishment of sin is itself a positive good—good *because* it is just.[2] And when he has to comment on the Psalmist's maledictions, and on the martyrs' prayer for vengeance in the *Apocalypse*, his explanation is that while the Christian must always desire the correction rather than the punishment of the wicked, yet when they are punished he must acquiesce and rejoice, not in the punishment of a man whom he does not hate, but in the justice of God whom he loves.[3]

The metaphysic of Plotinus is not pantheist in intention ; but his theodicy took the aesthetic form to which every variety of pantheism inclines. The world's course is conceived as a great dramatic poem which owes its beauty to conflict, and to which the bad *dramatis personae* are as necessary as the good.[4] Not merely the punishment, but the presence of evil is justified on these lines. It is in the earliest writings of Augustine, as we should expect, that this wholly un-Christian theodicy is most prominent : it appears at its worst and most reminiscent of Plotinus in the *De Vera Religione*.[5] Augustine never indeed abandoned it. There are isolated comparisons in the strongly Platonist Eleventh Book of the *De Civitate*, of the *ordo saeculorum* to a lovely poem with its contrasts, and of the universe, ' fair even with its sinners ', to a picture with its light and shade.[6] Even in the *Encheiridion* the ' ordering of evil ' is said to make its own contribution to the ' marvellous beauty of the universe '.[7] But these are echoes rather than re-affirmations. The gradual hardening of Augustine's attitude to sin, a hardening which was accentuated though not initiated by the Pelagian controversy, made it impossible for him to maintain with the old conviction those aesthetic defences which satisfy the pantheist only because of his inadequate sense of the reality of the world's evil. The rigid

[1] *De Contin.* 15. [2] *Ib.* Cf. *De Civ.* XII. 3.
[3] *En. in. Ps.* LXXVIII. 14. [4] *Enn.* III. ii. 15 ff.
[5] *De Vera Relig.* 43 f., 76 f. Cf. *De Ord.* I. 18 ; II. 11 ff. *De Lib. Arb.* III. 24 ff.
[6] *De Civ.* XI. 18, 23. [7] *Encheirid.* 3.

Augustinianism of the *Encheiridion* is driven by its own refusal of any dualistic solution to assert that faith in God's omnipotence —'the beginning of our confession'—requires us to *believe* that in the last resort it must be good for evil as well as good to exist.[1] But this is faith, not understanding. The reason can go no further than to vindicate the goodness of just punishment.

Augustine is certain that retributive justice is an attribute of God, because he believes that the human idea of justice is one of the *regulae virtutum* or ultimate moral principles, the existence of which is his principal reason for believing in the existence of God Himself. Even man's instinctive tendency to avenge an injury, *an eye for an eye and a tooth for a tooth,* may be called ' a justice of the unjust : not because it is inequitable that every man should be treated as he has treated others, . . . but because the lust of vengeance is vicious, and it is rather for the judge to decree such retribution as between others than for a good man to seek it for himself'.[2] ' Shall I not avenge myself, you say, when the laws are on my side ? It is just that you should avenge yourself : it is permitted, because it is just. Only see first whether you have not that in you which calls for vengeance, before you take your own. You speak as though God would suppress the justice of vengeance, and not rather quench the pride of the avenger.'[3] Even when Augustine comes to formulate that theory of the *massa peccati* which *prima facie* is irreconcilable with belief in God's justice, he appeals to a principle ' observable in our human business and mundane contracts ; did we not retain in them the print of certain vestiges of the higher justice, our weak view could never rise and fix itself in the most holy and pure sanctuary of spiritual commands '.[4] The principle is the right of the creditor at his sole discretion not to demand payment of a debt ; and Augustine forgets that this is precisely what justice is not, that with the remission of debts justice *qua* justice has nothing to do. The returning of good for evil is a mark not of God's justice but of His goodness.[5] The conception

[1] *Encheirid.* 24. [2] *En. in Ps.* cviii. 4. [3] *Ib.* cii. 11.
[4] *De Div. Quaest. ad Simpl.* i. ii. 16. [5] *De Grat. et Lib. Arb.* 43, 45.

of forgiveness as a remission of debt rests upon a too superficial interpretation of Christ's parable.

Augustine's deeper thought upon the relation of forgiveness to punishment is very different. It is that forgiveness is ultimately possible only when the sinner takes upon himself in penitence his own punishment. ' *Virga directionis, virga regni tui.* . . . God cannot so act as not to punish sin. Sin is to be punished : otherwise it were not sin. . . . God withholds His hand from your sins ; withhold not your own. Turn yourself to the punishment of your own sins, since it is not possible for sin to be unpunished. The punishment must be at your hands, or at His. Do you acknowledge, that He may forgive.' [1] So, in a great chapter of the *Summa contra Gentiles,* St. Thomas lays it down that the only punishment which is *satisfactoria* is when the sinner ' exacts the penalty from himself'. The more intense is the sinner's penitential love, the less is any other punishment needed. ' Vicarious ' punishment, therefore, implies the bond of love between its bearer and the sinner, whose punishment is real in so far as he really suffers with his suffering friend—' suffering the more, insomuch as he knows himself to be the cause of his friend's suffering '.[2]

Doubt of God's justice is to Augustine the sure road to atheism. But such doubt may spring not only from intellectual perplexity but from moral dishonesty, and he deals with both kinds of doubt.

(*a*) With those whose faith is shaken by the apparent injustice of the world's order, his method is to ask the critics whence they derive the standards for their criticism. The condemnation of iniquity implies a vision of justice. But man does not make his

---

[1] *En. in. Ps.* XLIV. 18. *Ib.* LVIII. i. 13 : iniquitas omnis, parva magnave sit, puniatur necesse est, aut ab ipso homine poenitente, aut a Deo vindicante. Nam et quem poenitet, punit se ipsum. . . . Et ideo tui miserebitur Deus, quia iam te operantem aequitatem invenit Deus. Quid est, operantem aequitatem ? Quia hoc in te odisti, quod et ille odit ; ut incipias placere Deo, dum hoc in te punis quod displicet Deo. Cf. *Ep.* 153. 6 ; *Serm.* 278. 12. The abuse and perversion of this principle in the penitential system does not depreciate its value. [2] *Contra Gentiles,* III. 158.

idea of justice : it comes to him from the *fons iustitiae* which is God, and how can Very Justice be unjust ? It is our human ignorance that prevents us from seeing the how and the why of particular manifestations of God's justice. 'We imagined this or that to be unjust : we should believe that it is just, because it is the act of God.' [1] The danger of this line of argument is manifest, and Augustine does not escape it by his appeal to the one instance of an indubitably innocent Sufferer, where the counsel of God, so often hidden, is known to us. He is obliged in the end to shift his ground and to declare that human and divine justice are incommensurable. 'Divine justice, as it is higher than human, is so much the more inscrutable and so much the further removed from ours. What just man permits the perpetration of a crime which he has in his power to prevent ? Yet God permits these things, God who is incomparably more just than any just man, incomparably greater than any human power. Think of that, and do not compare the judgement of God with that of men ; for we cannot question that God is just, even when He does what seems to men unjust, and what a man would be unjust if he should do.' [2] 'I call God just, for lack of a better word ; for He is beyond justice. . . . Scripture calls Him just ; but that is even as Scripture speaks of His repenting or being ignorant.' [3] Augustine stops short on the verge of a great discovery. What if the power of God, of which Scripture also speaks, be a power no less different from men's common thought of power ? The chasm in his reasoning is unbridged. He has based belief in God's justice, in God Himself, on human recognition of the rightness of retributive punishment ; but when confronted with the problem of justifying the ways of God, he tells us that God's justice is transcendent, that our standards are inapplicable to it, and that our ignorance should compel us to stop short with *O altitudo !* The human conscience will always revolt against such a method of silencing its questions. If it is true that our basic moral ideas have an ultimate validity

[1] *En. in Ps.* LXI. 21 f.
[2] *C. Jul. op. imp.* III. 24. Cf. *C. Jul. Pel.* v. 14.   [3] *Serm.* 341. 9.

which is itself our surest ground for belief in God, to belittle the deliveries of conscience is to cut at the roots of that belief. When we are required to believe that what appears irreconcilable with our idea of justice, may be just ' in a higher sense ', what reason remains for clinging to our conviction that ' judgement is unjust, is not judgement at all, if every man receive not his deserts ' ? [1]

(*b*) Yet this conviction has in fact for Augustine the value of absolute truth, and it is upon it that he relies in dealing with the second kind of doubt as to God's justice, the moral refusal to face the consequences of sin. In the evil life which implies the belief that ' God is pleased with iniquity ', that ' Christ will come and show indulgence to us all ', he finds the real denial of God.[2] To those who revolt against the idea of a God who punishes, he retorts that this is to wish God as unjust as ourselves. ' God will make you to be like Him, and you try to make Him like you. Be pleased with God as He is, not as you would have Him to be.' [3] ' That man pleases God, whom God pleases. . . . You see how many there are who dispute against God, who are dissatisfied with His works . . . preferring the accomplishment of their own will to that of God's, they would bend God to their will, instead of mending their own by His.' [4] Such men, adds Augustine, find the ' quick-change-artist ' more to their liking than God—*facilius placet pantomimus quam Deus*. ' We cannot search out men's consciences, but let us keep a true and sure conviction *about things themselves* . . . let us love justice, and hate injustice—not the justice and the injustice which we devise for ourselves in error, but those which we faithfully behold in the truth of God as to be sought or shunned. . . . How should they who hold the truth in hatred, love the Father of truth (*John* xv. 23) ? For they refuse the condemnation of their deeds ; and truth has it that such deeds are condemned. They hate the truth therefore inasmuch as they hate the punishment of themselves which truth imposes upon all such.' [5]

---

[1] *En. in Ps.* xcviii. 6.   [2] *Ib.* lii. 2, 4.   [3] *Serm.* 9. 9.
[4] *En. in Ps.* xxxii. ii. 1.   [5] *In Jo. Ev. Tr.* 90. 2, 3.

Amor Dei

The wrath of God is revealed from heaven against all ungodliness and unrighteousness of men. The ethics of naturalism are always at bottom Manichaean. The existence of evil is admitted, but only as an external fact of nature : moral evil is no more than a ' physical ' phenomenon. When we say that wrongdoing is to be condemned, we mean no more than that it is to be disapproved. Responsibility and accountability are empty terms, for they do not mean that a man ought to ' answer ' for his actions, ought to ' render ' account for them. Punishment is justified only as a method of education, adapted to man's inability to distinguish right and wrong save by their consequences. The concept of justice is deprived of all retributive connotation, and reduced to the distributive *suum cuique*,—the ' right ' of the individual to have his share in the good life of this world. The ' sense of sin ', like religion itself, is regarded as a delusion, whether the delusion be held still to serve a purpose in the present stage of civilisation, or to have outlived its usefulness, or to have been at all times pernicious.

In Augustine's Christianity, the sense of sin is the narrow gate through which all must pass who would see the truth. *Let God be true and every man a liar.* No one can say, ' Evil, be thou my good ' : the lie that every man utters in the moment of sin is that evil *is* his good. *Non possumus hominum indagare conscientiam.* It is a mournful fact that the philosophy of determinism, so far from enforcing the maxim ' tout comprendre, c'est tout pardonner ', appears to encourage the most violent condemnation of others, the most obstinate refusal either to understand or to pardon. Unconvinced of our own sin, we are ready to take our seat on the judgement throne which belongs to God. The Christian penitent must always fear to judge ; but he must also have *de ipsis rebus claram certamque sententiam.* Knowing that Christ died *for him,* he must see sin as what it is : he must accept the revelation of the wrath of God.

3. *Suffering and Punishment*

Δράσαντι παθεῖν.—*The soul that sinneth, it shall die.* If
Augustine had gone no further than to re-affirm the profoundest
conviction of Hebrew and Greek religious thought, he would
not indeed have established a Christian theodicy, but he would
have retained the sympathy of more than one great moralist of
modern times. If we ask how he was led to develop a system
which Christian and non-Christian thinkers alike have not only
rejected, but rejected with horror, we shall find the answer in
a double failure on his part. He failed first to reach anything like
a Christian solution of the problem of suffering ; and, secondly,
to maintain consistently a theory of the true nature of punishment
to which he himself had made contributions of the highest value.

(*a*) *Suffering.*—Augustine constantly speaks of the Old
Testament dispensation as a necessary stage in the moral training
of mankind.[1] Its promises and threatenings alike are ' carnal ' :
the people of Israel are encouraged to obedience and deterred
from disobedience by hope and fear, both alike directed to this
life, to outward prosperity and disaster. We recognise that it was
just this limitation of outlook which made the sufferings of the
righteous so intolerable a burden upon the thought of later
Jewish piety. Once only, in the Book of Job, we see a mind
of exceptional power and originality rejecting the premiss that
all suffering is the punishment of sin ; but we can hardly be
surprised that Augustine did not appreciate the significance of
a book which even now we are only beginning to understand.
He found the same burning question exercising the minds of
many of the Psalmists, and in his *Expositions of the Psalms* he
gives a picture of the religious attitude to suffering which differs
little if at all from that of Job's comforters. ' Between the true
heart and the corrupt heart there is this difference. Every man
who assigns all that he suffers against his will, afflictions, sorrows,
toils, humiliations, to nought but the just will of God, not taxing
God with unwisdom, as though He knew not what He did in

[1] Typical passages are : *De Catech. Rud.* 40. *De Civ.* X. 25. *En. in Ps.*
XXXIV. i. 7 ; LXXIII. 2. *De Gest. Pel.* 14. *C. du. Ep. Pelag.* III. 13.

chastening one and sparing others—he is the true of heart. But they are perverse of heart, corrupt and crooked, who say that all the evils they suffer, they suffer unrighteously, taxing with unrighteousness Him through whose will they suffer ; or else, when they dare not tax Him with unrighteousness, denying His government.' [1] ' We find that Scripture calls true of heart those who endure the world's evils without accusing God. Look you, my brethren : it is a rarity that I speak of (*rara avis ista quam loquor*). I know not how it is, that when any evil happens to a man, he hastens to accuse God, though it should be himself. You praise yourself when you do any good ; when you suffer any evil you accuse God. That is the crooked, not the true heart.' [2]

But the evils of the world loom large : there is indeed much to be accounted for, and no man may know all God's judgements ; but we may hold it certain that ' without the judgement of God no one is slow in mind or crippled in body '.[3] And so the principle is extended until the position is reached that ' the whole life of mortal man is a punishment ' : [4] ' there is nothing that we suffer in this life, but comes of that death which by the first sin we merited ' ; [5] and there can be no release from misery ' in this present age, which in its entirety God has willed to have the nature of punishment for men '.[6] The servants whose eyes are upon the hands of their master are those who are ' commanded to be beaten '. . . . ' Our Master has commanded us to be beaten . . . the whole of this mortal life is our stroke. . . . In all that have been born since the beginning of the human race, Adam is chastised . . . many have grown so callous as not to feel their strokes. But to those who have been made sons, has been given the sense of pain : they feel that they are chastised, and they know who has commanded their chastisement.' [7] The world's gladness is but wickedness unpunished.[8] All who know God to

---

[1] *En. in Ps.* XXXI. ii. 25. Cf. *ib.* LXIII. 18 ; CXXII. 10.
[2] *In Jo. Ev. Tr.* 28. 7.   [3] *En. in Ps.* CXVIII. vi. 2.
[4] *De Civ.* XXI. 14 f.   [5] *En. in Ps.* XXXVII. 5.
[6] *C. Jul. op. imp.* II. 119.   [7] *En. in Ps.* CXXII. 6.
[8] *Serm.* 171. 4.

be their Father will find in His chastening the proof of His Fatherhood.[1]

Origen's pessimistic doctrine of creation, ' not for the bringing into being of good but for the restraint of evil ',[2] had been repudiated by Augustine, and no doubt he continued to feel that his own view was more in accord not only with Scripture and tradition, but with the glory of God. We may find it easier to believe with Origen that the material world would never have existed but for the fall of souls, than with Augustine that man's sin could so turn upside down the work of a good Creator. But there can be no doubt that Augustine offers his doctrine of original sin as the only tenable explanation of the facts of human suffering. Men's misery proves their guilt.[3] Apart from Scripture and the Church's practice of infant baptism, his argument against Julian rests almost entirely upon the sufferings of children too young ' to have sins of their own '. We can see from the pathetic letter [4] in which he urges upon Jerome the difficulty of justifying on the creationist theory of the soul the damnation of unbaptised infants, that the sufferings of children were to him no mere theological argument but a heartrending fact. Yet in that letter he speaks of these sufferings as *parvulorum poenae :* so deeply rooted in his mind is the idea of the penal character of *all* suffering, to which he had first been led by the necessities of his defence of Catholic truth against Manichaeanism. ' What is the pain which we call bodily ', he had said in the *De Vera Religione,* ' but the momentary loss of well-being (*corruptio repentina salutis*) in that part of our nature which the soul by misuse has exposed to decay ? and what is the pain we call mental, but the lack of those changeable objects which the soul enjoyed or hoped it could enjoy ? And this is the whole of what we call evil, namely, sin and the punishment of sin.' [5]

Naturally, Augustine finds that the suffering which is of its

---

[1] *En. in Ps.* LXXXVIII. ii. 3 f. ; XCIII. 17.   [2] *De Civ.* XI. 23.
[3] *C. Jul. op. imp.* VI. 27 : ideo convincuntur rei esse, quoniam sunt miseri.
[4] *Ep.* 166. 16 f.
[5] *De Vera Relig.* 23.   Cf. *C. Secund. Manich.* 19.

nature a punishment can be and is *used* by God for purposes of good other than the punishment itself. ' The evils which the faithful piously endure are profitable either for the amendment of sin, or for the exercising and testing of righteousness, or for the demonstration of the wretchedness of this life, in order that the life whose blessedness will be true and unbroken may be longed for the more ardently and the more urgently sought after.' [1] Not the pain but the cause makes the martyr. God is no sadist : His pleasure is in our righteousness, not our torments.[2] Suffering is to be judged not by its own character but by the character of him who bears it.[3] Once even we find Augustine telling his hearers that ' all the misery in which the world groans . . . is a healing pain, and not a penal sentence ' ; but he drops back next moment into speaking of the *dolor medicinalis* as a *poena flagelli*.[4] He does not deny that suffering *can* purify, that there are men who are made better by punishment. But that suffering does not normally have this effect, he thinks too evident to permit of our supposing that all human suffering is intended to be purgative.

A genuinely Christian view of suffering must be based upon a deeper understanding of the significance of Christ's Cross than Augustine was able to reach. He does of course hold firmly what Dr. Aulen has called the ' classical ' theory of the Atonement. In Christ's victory over the devil he sees the deliverance of mankind from sin and sin's consequences ; and when he teaches, like Irenaeus, that the victory was gained *non potentia, sed iustitia,* he means by *iustitia* the obedience unto death of Him who knew no sin. Because the Sufferer was innocent, His suffering was victorious.[5] But Augustine no more than any of the Fathers could take the further step which is imperatively demanded, and discover in the sufferings of Christ God's final answer to Job's questionings. *Neither did this man sin, nor his parents, that he was*

---

[1] *De Trin.* XIII. 20. Cf. *Ep.* 130. 25 : ad sanandum tumorem superbiae vel ad probandam exercendamve patientiam . . . vel ad quaecumque flagellanda et abolenda peccata.

[2] *Serm.* 285. 2.

[3] *De Civ.* I. 8 : interest non qualia sed qualis quisque patiatur.

[4] *En. in Ps.* CXXXVIII. 15.   [5] *De Trin.* XIII. 16 ff.

born blind; but that the works of God should be manifested in him.
The ' explanation ' of suffering must lie not in its beginning but
in its end. It is no more the supreme evil than is pleasure the
supreme good ; but Christianity can be content to preach
neither a Stoical indifference to pain and pleasure alike, nor an
Epicurean humanitarianism which aims only at the alleviation of
the one and the increase of the other. The love which brings
happiness in refusing the pursuit of pleasure can transfigure pain
without denying its painfulness or stifling the movement of
compassion. Out of that suffering which unites the sufferer to
God, the evil has been wrung ; yet the sharer in Christ's Passion
will never meet another's suffering with the bare exhortation to
endure.

In this matter Augustine does not come beyond the occasional
approach, the momentary glimpse. In one remarkable passage
we find the suggestion that God's answer to Job out of the
whirlwind is spoken ' in the person of Christ ', in whom Omnipotence itself was to stoop to the ' obedience of suffering '.[1] And
it was impossible that the principle of exegesis followed throughout the *Expositions of the Psalms*, the doctrine of Christ's unity
with His members, should not often lead to reflections upon
suffering in which the penal conception is almost forgotten.
' When the Head begins to speak, separate not the Body from
Him. If the Head would not separate Himself from the words
of the Body, shall the Body dare to separate itself from the
sufferings of the Head ? Suffer in Christ. . . . As He willed that
our sins should be His own for His Body's sake, so let us will
His sufferings to be ours, for the sake of our Head.' [2] The
' filling-up of that which was lacking in the sufferings of Christ '
is the contribution which each of His members can make to
the ' universal Passion '. Yet even here Augustine disfigures the
thought of St. Paul by comparing the sufferings of Christ's

---

[1] *De Pecc. Merit.* II. 16 : intelligat ergo quam debeat aequo animo tolerare
quae pertulit, si Christus in quo peccatum, cum propter nos homo factus esset,
omnino nullum fuit, et in quo Deo tanta potentia est, nequaquam tamen
passionis oboedientiam recusavit.

[2] *En. in Ps.* XXXVII. 16.

members to a 'property-tax' due from all citizens of His empire according to their means, and pointing forward to the final day of reckoning when all accounts will be balanced.[1] It is significant that we are brought nearest to Christ in a context where there is no explicit mention of the Greater Sufferer. 'Let charity abound in you, and you will suffer the more for the sinner. The greater is your love, the deeper will be the pain to you from him whose wrongdoing you endure—a pain not of anger against him, but of suffering on his behalf.'[2]

(*b*) *Punishment.*—We may feel that Augustine could not have rested in a view of suffering which the revelation of God in Christ has made untenable, if he had allowed himself to think out the implications of his own spiritual and devotional experience. But he did not do so. Convinced as he was that all the material evils, as well as a great deal of the spiritual disablement, with which human beings are afflicted, are before anything else the punishment of sin, he was unable to carry out with consistency that theory of punishment which is alone appropriate to his philosophy of the *Summum Bonum*.

Prima et maxima peccantium est poena peccasse, said Seneca ;[3] and Platonism had shown Augustine the way to a grounding and development of what we may call the 'internal' theory of punishment, which went far beyond Seneca. The sanctions of human law are effective only for the lovers of this world : they have no terror for a man whose heart is not set on those goods of which he can be deprived against his will.[4] If the supreme good for man is *adhaerere Deo*, the only real evil which man can suffer is that very separation from God in which sin consists. No external or temporal pains and penalties can add anything to the evil of a condition which belongs to the inner and eternal being of the soul. As the soul can have life which is life indeed only by participation in the life of God, so it can have vision only

[1] *En in Ps.* LXI. 4 : quas icanonem passionum . . . pariatoria plenaria.
[2] *Ib.* XCVIII. 12. [3] *Ep. ad Lucil.* 97. 14.
[4] *De Lib. Arb.* I. 32 f.

when it is ' turned towards ' the Truth. ' The beginning of the
punishment which God inflicts upon the soul that turns away
from Him is blindness itself. For he who turns away from the
true Light which is God, is thereby made blind. He does not
feel his punishment, but already he has it.' [1] And so it is with
the soul's love. The ' disordered soul ' is ' its own punishment '.[2]
The *De Libero Arbitrio* begins with a definition of moral evil as
the domination of *libido*, and Augustine in an eloquent passage [3]
compels Evodius to recognise that this domination in itself is
' no small punishment '. Here he follows, of course, the lines
laid down for all time by Plato in the *Republic* and the *Gorgias*.
Purely Platonic, again, is his comment on Psalm LVI. ' Every
man who prepares a pit for his brother, must of necessity fall
into it himself. Observe, my brethren, have Christian eyes. . . .
You see a man exulting in wrongdoing : his exultation itself is
his own pit. Better is the unhappiness of him who suffers, than
the rejoicing of him who inflicts the wrong '.[4] But what is more
important is to observe that Augustine's whole representation of
concupiscence as *poena peccati* is based on the same principle.
The spirit of man, the ' rational creature ', has a place in the
universal order which is maintained by submission to the higher
and control over the lower. ' Man has received a body to be
his servant. . . . Having the Creator above it and a thing created
below it, the rational soul, set in a middle station, has been given
the rule of cleaving to its Superior and ruling its inferior. It
cannot govern its inferior unless it be governed by its Better.
That it is dragged captive by its inferior shows that it has deserted

---

[1] *Serm.* 117. 5. Cf. *ib.* 180. 8 : tu praesentem Deum ultorem putas, si ille
qui te iuratione falsa deceperit continuo exspiret. . . . Peieravit, exclusit spiritum
quo vivebat anima. Exspiravit, sed nescis ; exspiravit, sed non vides. . . .
Credo ergo, adhibe oculos fidei. Nemo periurus impunitus, prorsus nemo :
cum illo est poena sua.

[2] *Conf.* I. 19.

[3] *De Lib. Arb.* I. 22.

[4] *En. in Ps.* LVI. 14. Cf. *ib.* XXXIV. i. 11 : Nemo malus non sibi prius nocet
. . . malitia tua ut alteri non noceat fieri potest : ut autem tibi non noceat
fieri non potest.

its Better.'[1]   The point on which all turns is that man's power
to rule is not inherent in him but is derived from and wholly
dependent upon his being ruled.   'By refusal to serve, men
avoid only the service of a good Master, not service altogether ;
for he who will not serve charity must of necessity serve iniquity.'[2]
Augustine has taken the thought of St. Paul in *Romans* vi, and made
it the central point of his own ethical system.   It belongs, we
remember, to his definition of Christianity, that the soul must
'serve its Master, lest it be trodden down by its own servant.'[3]
And the Fall of man means that his servant has trodden him down :
he has lost control of his natural desires.

Augustine has not been alone in giving to one of these desires
an exaggerated prominence.   It was disastrous, if not unnatural,
that in seeking to give an account of the propagation of sin, he
should have made the use he did of the instinct by which the
species itself is propagated.   He committed himself in controversy with the heretic to a theory which in his discussion with
the orthodox he recognised to be inadequate : unless soul is
body, as Tertullian thought, or a function of body, conditions of
physical propagation can never explain a spiritual fact.   But he
observed in the sexual instinct a peculiar disassociation of activity
from purpose which made it for him the chief though by no
means the only instance of the penal ' disorder ' of man's nature.
Here, as elsewhere, concupiscence is simply the loss of spirit's
rule over flesh—a punishment, but not an external or arbitrary
punishment.   What is evil in it is not the desire itself, but the
desire's ' disobedience ', its a-moral force ;[4]   but considering
the facts of Augustine's psychological history, we can hardly
wonder at his failure to keep these two things distinguished in

---

[1] *En. in. Ps.* CXLV. 5.   *Serm.* 30. 4 : carnem [Deus] animae subdidit,
animam sibi.   Si semper illa staret sub Domino suo, semper et ista obediret
dominae suae.   Noli ergo mirari, si ea quae deseruit superiorem, pœnas
patitur per inferiorem.   Cf. *De Serm. Dom. in Mont.* I. 9 ; *Serm.* 152. 5, etc.

[2] *En. in Ps.* XVIII. ii. 15.

[3] *In Jo. Ev. Tr.* 23. 5.   Cf. *supra*, p. 27.

[4] *C. Jul. Pelag.* IV. 7.

the heat of the lamentable argument with Julian.[1] Confusion
was inevitable, because the naturalism of Julian would not accept
Augustine's mythical Eden or the depravation of man's nature
which was what Augustine understood by the Fall ; and
Augustine could not accept Julian's view of *libido*, as we now
experience it, as both natural and innocent. Julian's peculiarly
'modern' attitude to sex was untenable, as Augustine very
clearly saw,[2] without a rupture which Julian himself was not
prepared to make with the whole Catholic tradition of the
superiority of continence to marriage. Augustine demanded
an admission that Christians must recognise a punishment in the
fact of man's being 'compared to beasts that have no understanding' : that it is for man a 'misery' which beasts cannot
know to be the field of struggle between spirit and flesh : that
'by the deterioration of man's nature through sin, what is
appropriate to the animal nature has become matter of punishment
for man ; and in the evil of the flesh's lusting against the spirit
there is the greater cause for shame, in that between two powers,
both belonging to our nature, of which the one should command
and the other serve, there has arisen a discord not only painful
but disgraceful '.[3]

[1] Yet cf. e.g. *C. Jul. op. imp.* IV. 49, where Augustine allows that there
might have been 'concupiscentia nuptialis' in Eden, 'etiamsi nemo peccasset'.

The *Opus Imperfectum* makes melancholy reading ; but it is not easy to
understand how the most cursory perusal of it could have given Dr. Rashdall
the impression that Julian was a 'comparatively decent controversialist',
while Augustine's own part of the dialogue is 'filled with the rudest and
coarsest vituperation' (*Idea of Atonement*, etc., p. 347), or led Prof. Raven to
say that Julian 'makes his points with courtesy', while Augustine betrays
'the streak of coarse sensuality' which in him 'became increasingly evident
with age' (*Jesus and the Gospel of Love*, p. 363). Neither antagonist is sparing
of vituperation, but of coarseness Julian has a monopoly. Samples of Julian's
'decency' and 'courtesy' may be found in cc. 9, 11, 22, 45, 58, 98 of the
first Book—to go no farther. No one, after reading Julian's abominable
piece of sarcasm upon what Augustine had told of his mother in the *Confessions*,
and Augustine's rejoinder (*op. imp.* I. 68), can think that the younger man
shows 'more of the spirit of Christ' than the older.

[2] *C. Jul. Pelag.* IV. 9.

[3] *C. Jul. op. imp.* IV 38, 43. We are told nowadays that Augustine's whole
religious development is to be understood as an affair of repressed sexuality :

All this is, it will be seen, in no way dependent on any theory of the propagation of guilt. It is no more than a particular application of the general doctrine stated in lapidary phrase in the Fourteenth Book of the *De Civitate* : ' It is a just condemnation . . . that man who by keeping the commandment would have been spiritual even in the flesh, should become carnal even in the spirit : that he who in his pride had taken pleasure in himself, in the justice of God should be made over to himself— not so as to be altogether in his own power, but so that in dissension even with himself, under that power to which he consented in sinning, he should find his lot in a cruel and wretched slavery instead of in that freedom which he coveted '.[1] ' When God punishes sinners, He inflicts no evil of His own upon them, but leaves them to that which is theirs.' [2] . . . ' To every man his own sin is made the penalty, and his iniquity is turned into punishment ; that we may not suppose that the great Peace and ineffable Light of God brings forth from Himself the means for the punishment of sins : rather He so orders the sins themselves that what had been delights to the sinner become the instruments of the Lord's chastisement.' [3]

that the mystic ardour of his maturity no less than the cruel logic of his old age has its roots in this pathological clay. It seems to be forgotten that between the ages of sixteen and thirty-two he lived an unimpeachably 'normal' sexual life; and there is not the least ground for supposing that it was unduly 'inhibited' by religious scruples. The fact is that a 'normal' sexual relationship did not make him—any more than it will necessarily make any man or any woman—happy. And we may take leave to doubt whether he would have been either a happier or a better man, if (*per impossibile*) he had settled down to married life with the mother of Adeodatus after his conversion. It was not religious scruple that drove him to what seems to us the one really base action of his life—his desertion of this woman who had given herself to him and whom he had loved; nor did he need the modern censure to tell him that the action was vile: 'Interea peccata mea multiplicabantur' are the words with which he records it (*Conf.* VI. 25). We can recognise that he was wrong—disastrously wrong—in identifying his sexual impulses with the barrier that separated him from the love of God. But 'love of the divine Beauty' was at no time with him a surrogate for sexual desire. We have no right and we should not have the presumption to say that when he rose from his knees in the Milan garden he was not altogether a 'new man'.

[1] *De Civ.* XIV. 15.   [2] *En. in Ps.* V. 10.   [3] *Ib.* VII. 16.

In this conception of punishment as ' internal ', of the sinful state as the Divine judgement on the sinner, Augustine as we have said is not original : Irenaeus had in part anticipated him, and Plotinus here too is his master.[1]   As we shall see, it is the logical counterpart to his teaching about reward, and if he could have maintained it fully and consistently it would have saved him from his worst errors.   That he was not able to do so was due to the influence of two other strains of thought on the subject, neither of which was it possible for him wholly to disallow.

(i) There was the Platonic tradition which had shaped (almost to the exclusion of any other) the views of Clement and Origen, and which remained dominant in the Eastern Church. For the great Alexandrians, the primary if not the sole function of punishment was remedial—the correction of the wrong doer. As is well known, Origen could not bring himself to believe that even in the world to come the punishment of sinners would not

---

[1] Irenaeus, *Adv. Haer.* v. 27 : ' To all that hold fast the love of God, He gives fellowship with Himself ; and fellowship with God is life and light and the fruition of God's good things.   Upon all that deliberately turn away from God, He imposes separation from Himself ; and separation from God is death, separation from light is darkness, separation from God is the loss of all His good things.   Those therefore who by their apostasy have lost these blessings, being deprived of all good, fall into the state of punishment—a punishment which is not so much the direct act of God as the consequence following upon the privation of all good.'

Plotinus, *Enn.* IV. iii. 24 : ' The space open to the soul's resort is vast and diverse ; the difference will come by the double force of the individual condition and of the justice reigning in things. No-one can ever escape the suffering entailed by ill deeds done : the divine law is ineluctable, carrying bound up, as one with it, the fore-ordained execution of its doom. The sufferer, all unaware, is swept onward towards his due, hurried always by the restless driving of his errors, until at last, wearied out by that against which he struggled, he falls into his fit place, and by self-chosen movement is brought to the lot he never chose.' *Ib.* IV. iv. 45 : ' Anyone that adds his evil to the total of things is known for what he is, and in accordance with his kind, is pressed down into the evil which he has made his own ' (tr. Mackenna).

Plotinus generally presents the ' divine law of justice ' in the half-mythical form of spatial transmigration which Plato had given it, especially in the Tenth Book of the *Laws* (903 ff.) : ' like goes to like '.   Augustine, in dropping spatial metaphor and seeing the punishment entirely in the inward state of the sinner, is not the less true to Plato's intention.

be directed to this end. Augustine, though rejecting, gently but firmly, the heresy of Origen,[1] recognised that the corrective aim is indispensable for the due administration of human justice, and constantly affirmed that God ' uses ' the evils which men have brought upon themselves to ' cure ' their infirmities. He might have avoided the difficulties arising from a confusion of two really incompatible theories,[2] if he had refused to allow the name of punishment to action which is corrective or remedial ; and he comes very near to doing this in the distinction which he frequently draws between punishment and correction.[3] But this way out was excluded for him.

(ii) For there was another complex of ideas too deeply in-grained in his mind for any escape from it to be possible—the ideas of the ordinary man, and especially of the ordinary Roman citizen, drawn from the ordinary assumptions of legal justice. In the laying down of penalties for social offences, the principle assumed by the criminal law is precisely that a man must *not* be ' left to himself '. He must be shown that wrong-doing does not pay, and the only way of ensuring this demonstration is by the infliction of an external pain which if ' left to himself ' he would not have suffered, and which generally will ' fit the crime ' only in the sense of being roughly proportionate to its gravity. Needless to say, these common-sense notions were not only part of the mental heritage of the ordinary Catholic in Roman Africa, but had become more inseparable than ever from his religious convictions in consequence of the enormous influence of men like Tertullian and Cyprian. It is of course part of the secret of Augustine's power that after the vagaries and experi-mentings of his youth he submitted himself with his whole heart to the ' common Catholicism ' of the Church : had he not made this great *kenosis*, he would have been a lesser man. But it had —*inter alia*—the fatal effect of dooming his philosophy of punish-

---

[1] *De Civ.* XXI. 17 : cum misericordibus nostris . . . pacifice disputandum.

[2] Cf. e.g. *C. Jul. op. imp.* VI. 36 : quid est iuste, nisi merito peccatorum, *vel examinatione virtutum ?*

[3] *Ep.* 104. 8. *En. in Ps.* LXXVIII. 14. *De Serm. Dom. in Mont.* I. 63.

ment to hesitations and contradictions. God is assimilated to a human judge : instead of being Himself the eternal Law whose workings are above all violation, He becomes the executor of a code which is protected from too frequent violation only by the application of external ' sanctions '. The God whose ' just judgement' is at one moment described as ' leaving the transgressor (*relinquere delinquentem*), so that he to whom God had been true felicity may be his own punishment ',[1] is at another still asserted in the prophet's words to ' create evil ',[2] to be indeed the author of the evil which man suffers, though not of that which man does.[3] The ' wrath of God' is not His outraged holiness, but His ' righteous vengeance '.[4] And all the outward hardness of our mortal life, the toil and pain, the body's death, which Christ's example has taught us to endure as *not worthy to be compared with the glory that shall be revealed*,[5] take on the terrible significance and weight of retribution for the world's sin.

We have seen how Augustine attempted to unify these diverse elements in his thought. The bodily creation, he says, which is good in itself though a good of the lowest rank, if it usurps the love which the soul owes to God, ' becomes penal to its lover ' : loved with the love which would enjoy instead of use, ' it becomes corruptible, disintegrates and deserts its lover, because he by such love has deserted God '.[6] It is a heroic attempt at rationalisation, but it can hardly be saved from collapse before the facts of our experience, in which health and disease make no distinction of persons, and the lightning as well as the rain falls upon just and unjust,—even by the violent reduction of the human race to ' one single lump of sin '.

But for our present purpose the worst effect of the confusion in Augustine's teaching about punishment is not his theory of original sin : it is rather to be found in the resulting confusion of ethical motive. In the denotation of punishment he has to

[1] *C. Jul. op. imp.* IV. 33. [2] *Ib.* III. 203.
[3] *De Lib. Arb.* I. I. [4] *Ep.* 184. 2.
[5] *De Ver. Relig.* 31. Cf. *Serm.* 217. 3 : commendavit nobis Dominus Jesus Christus in passione sua labores et contritiones praesentis saeculi.
[6] *De Ver. Relig.* 40. 23.

make room, side by side with what is comprehended in the sinful state itself, the *peccatum* which is also *poena peccati*, for an external and as it were detachable consequence of sin towards which the Christian attitude must be radically different. Once religion has lent its sanction to an association of sin and suffering of the same character as the legal association of crime and punishment, it is likely that men will regard suffering as more to be avoided than sin, or will at least regard sin as to be avoided because of the suffering to which it leads, and from which it is essentially distinct. Fear and not love will become the motive for serving God.

4. *Fear and Love*

Augustine says that he has known very few cases—perhaps none at all—of conversion to Christianity in which fear has played no part.[1] We may believe him either the more or the less readily, because of his confessing for his own part, not only that it was the fear of death and judgement to come which alone held him back in his youth from complete abandonment to the pleasures of the flesh,[2] but even that he will not as a preacher encourage any ' evil security ' in his hearers, because he himself is not secure. *Timens terreo . . . ego ignem aeternum timeo.*[3] Experience of what he honestly believed to be the good effects of the use of force against the Donatists seemed to him to legitimate in certain cases the motive of fear ; and in the notorious letter to Vincentius he supports his argument, that the divine threatenings issue from the divine love, by an exegesis, almost incredible as coming from him, of the text *No man cometh unto me, except the Father draw him.*[4] He maintains the traditional opposition of the Law and the Gospel : God's ' lesser precepts ' were given ' to the people who still needed to be bound under fear : the greater, through His Son, to the people who were to be freed by love '.[5] The fear of punishment can break the strength of evil habit,

---

[1] *De Catech. Rud.* 9.   [2] *Conf.* VI. 26.   [3] *En. in Ps.* LXXX. 20.
[4] *Ep.* 93. 5 : quod fit in cordibus omnium qui se ad eum divinae iracundiae timore convertunt.
[5] *De Serm. Dom. in Mont.* I. 2.   Cf. *En. in Ps.* XC. ii. 8.

encourage a ' habit of goodness ', and so prepare a place for the
perfect love that casts out fear.[1]   It is the needle which pricks an
entry for the thread of love, the surgeon's knife which makes
healing possible.[2]   Fear has its proper place in that stage of our
spiritual training when we have not yet learnt the ' sweetness of
religion ', when as yet the ' beauty of goodness does not delight
us ' ; [3] and it can safely be cast out by love, but by love only—
not by pride, heedlessness, or moral insensibility.[4]   There is
nothing praiseworthy in avoiding sin ' because you fear to burn
in eternal fire ' ; yet Augustine will not say that such fear is evil,
for Christ Himself has ' vehemently urged' it upon us : *fear
Him who has power to cast soul and body into hell : yea, I say unto
you, fear Him !* We do well to fear even when we cannot be
sure that if we could sin unseen and unpunished we should not
sin ; fear itself may be our safe escort to love.[5]

But when love enters and casts out that servile fear, she
brings a companion with her—the *fear of the Lord* which *is
clean and endureth for ever.* The slave fears his master's punishments so long as the master's eyes are on him : the righteous man,
who alone is truly free, ' if he could hear God saying to him
" I see thee sinning, I will not condemn thee, but thou art displeasing to me "— . . . yet he must fear, not condemnation,
punishment or torment, but lest he hurt his Father's happiness,
lest he displease his Lover's eyes '.[6]   Here the *castus timor* is
altogether without self-regard. When Augustine comes to
speak of *castus amor,* the nuance changes. ' If your love is for
the vision of your God, if in this pilgrimage you breathe the
sighings of that love, see how the Lord your God will prove you,
as though He said to you, " Do what thou wilt, fulfil thy lusts,
. . . count all thy likings lawful : I will not punish thee for that,
I will not send thee into hell, only I will deny to thee My Face ".

---

[1] *Ep.* 140. 45.   *En. in Ps.* cxxvii. 7.   Yet Augustine was doubtful of the
value of human punishment as a deterrent. *Ep.* 95. 3 : impendentem vindictam
metuentes, quae ab hominibus metuitur, nescio utrum plures correcti sunt
quam in deterius abierunt.

[2] *In Ep. Jo. Tr.* 9. 4.   [3] *De Div. Quaest.* LXXXIII. 36.   *Serm.* 9. 8.
[4] *Serm.* 348. 2.   [5] *Ib.* 161. 8.   [6] *Ib.* 9.

If those words strike you with terror, you have known love (*si expavisti, amasti*) : if at the saying " Thy God will deny to thee His face ", your heart has trembled, if not to behold your God is great punishment in your eyes, then you have loved freely (*gratis amasti*).' [1]   How little Augustine saw need to distinguish between ' disinterested' fear of offending God's love and the ' interested' fear of separation from his presence, is well shown by yet a third passage where both are combined. The aim of Christian progress, he says in the *De Catechizandis Rudibus,* is for the love of God to be stronger than the fear of hell ; then ' even if God should say " Enjoy for ever thy carnal pleasures, sin all thou canst : yet thou shalt not die nor be sent into hell, *but only shalt not be with me* " : at such words the Christian would shudder, and sin not at all, no longer that he may not fall into that which he used to fear, *but lest he offend the God whom he so much loves*'.[2]

But after all, ' this is punishment for the lover, not for the despiser'.[3] Until we have discovered that blessedness is not an external or separable reward for loving God, but simply that love's fruition, we shall not understand what it means to say that sin is its own punishment ; and meanwhile, ' penalties must put fear into the man who cares not for rewards'.[4] For Augustine, whose deeper and more spiritual view of punishment did not prevent him from accepting the ' external' theory of hell-fire as well, it was natural enough to hold that the threatenings of the Law had not been superseded by the promises of the Gospel— that the Law may still be a schoolmaster to bring us to Christ. What for us has changed the situation is the general decay of faith in God ; and the question we are bound to ask ourselves is how far the failure of Christianity to find a Christian solution of the problem of punishment may have contributed to that decay and may hinder the restoration of that faith.

---

[1] *Serm.* 178. 11. Cf. *En. in Ps.* XXVI. ii. 16 : *Quaesivi vultum tuum ; vultum tuum, Domine, requiram. Ne avertas faciem tuam a me : ne declines in ira a servo tuo.* Magnifice, nihil dici divinius potest. . . . Posset illi forte responderi hoc modo : Quid times, ne declinet a te in ira ? Magis si a te declinaverit in ira, non in te vindicabit. . . . Opta ergo potius ut declinet a te in ira. Non, inquit. Novit enim quid desiderat. Ira eius non est nisi aversio vultus eius.

[2] *De Catech. Rud.* 27.   [3] *En. in Ps.* XLIX. 7.   [4] *Ib.*

VIII

Grace and Reward

We cannot enjoy God by any external conjunction with Him : divine fruition is not by a mere kind of apposition or contiguity of our natures with the divine, but it is an internal union, whereby a divine spirit, informing our souls, sends the strength of a divine life through them ; and as this is more strong and active, so is happiness itself more energetical within us. It must be some divine efflux running quite through our souls, awakening and exalting all the vital powers of them into an active sympathy with some absolute good, that renders us completely blessed. It is not to sit gazing upon a deity by some thin speculation ; but it is an inward feeling and sensation of this mighty goodness displaying itself within us, melting our fierce and furious natures, that would fain be something in contradiction with God, into a universal compliance with itself, and wrapping up our amorous minds wholly into itself, whereby God comes to be all in all to us.

JOHN SMITH (*Cambridge Platonist*).

VIII

THE gaps and contradictions in Augustine's theory of punishment are most apparent in his teaching about baptism. All children are born in the state of separation from God which is at once guilt or liability to punishment, and punishment itself in the form of the moral disorder of concupiscence. In baptism the guilt is removed, and therewith the liability to punishment in the world to come, eternal separation from God. But the 'punishment' which consists in the disorder of concupiscence is *not* removed: here the punishment outlasts the guilt,[1] and is therefore detachable from it. The revolt of flesh against spirit continues in the baptised, though it is not 'reckoned as sin':[2] its penal character is shown in the moral struggle 'in which we are in jeopardy' as long as we live.[3] Yet infant baptism is not a mere form, effective only in the event of death before the child can understand what was involved in it. The grace of baptism is an earnest of the grace without which neither forgiveness of actual sin [4] nor ultimate victory in the fight against concupiscence is possible. The baptism of the infant, like the original sin which it purges, is the 'work of others'.[5] The faith of the Church in presenting the child is a 'sacrament' of the faith which the child must make his own when the time comes for him to enter on his warfare.[6] For he can be victor 'in truth and sincerity, only through delight in true righteousness; and true righteousness is in the faith of Christ. . . . Faults are to be accounted overcome only when their conquest is through the love of God, which none but God Himself gives, nor otherwise than through the Mediator of God and men, the man Christ Jesus. . . . Whosoever therefore desires to escape eternal punishment, let him not only be baptised but also justified in Jesus

---

[1] *In Jo. Ev. Tr.* 124. 5 : productior poena quam culpa.
[2] *De Nupt. et Concup.* I. 27 f. Cf. *De Pecc. Mer.* II. 45 f. ; *C. Jul. Pel.* VI. 60 ff.
[3] *De Civ.* XXII. 23.   [4] *De Nupt. et Concup.* I. 38.
[5] *C. Jul. Pel.* VI. 29 : alienum opus.   [6] *Ep.* 98. 5.

Christ.'[1] By justification, Augustine means the progressive restoration of the rule of spirit over flesh. It is to be achieved ' in Christ ', because it can only be achieved through the gift, by Christ's mediation, of that *delectatio iustitiae* which is a part of *amor Dei*. The gift of grace is simply the love of God appearing in us as the ' delight in righteousness '.

1. *Delectatio Iustitiae*

Augustine's general argument for grace is always an *a fortiori* argument based on the admitted fact of Creation, of man's dependence on God for his being. ' My being was Thy work : was not my goodness Thy work too ? . . . If Thou hast given me being and another has given me goodness, the giver to me of goodness is better than the giver to me of being.'[2] ' Boast yourself, and say " I am rich ". With what riches ? " If I will, I am righteous : if I will not, I am not. I have it in my own power to be righteous or not." . . . Then God has given you flesh, God has given you sense, soul, mind, understanding ; and you give yourself righteousness ? Would not all those other gifts, if righteousness were lacking to them, count only for punishment ? You are so rich, that God having given you the lesser things, you give yourself the greater ? '[3]

To this general argument Pelagianism, ancient and modern, has never found an adequate reply. St. Paul's question—*What hast thou which thou hast not received ?*—the question which no one has ever pressed home so relentlessly as Augustine, is answerable only in one way by all who confess that man has a Maker. Pelagius claimed that a full recognition of God's creative grace need go no further than to acknowledge that human nature has received from its Maker, in the power of undetermined choice, the ' possibility ' of avoiding sin ; and that the realisation of this possibility in the good will and the good action which are *ours* and not God's, is ' aided ' by God's revelation of what is good in

---

[1] *De Civ.* XXI. 16.   [2] *En. in Ps.* LVIII. ii. 11.   Cf. *ib.* CXLIV. 10.
[3] *Serm.* 290. 7.

the ' law and the teaching ' which culminate in Christ's example, His pattern of a holy life.[1]   The shallowness of such an account of moral activity must always be manifest to anyone who like Augustine has known in himself the agony of moral impotence and the divided self.   The young man who prayed ' Give me chastity, but not yet ', had heard ' the law and the teaching ' : he was already *consenting unto the law that it was good*.   But for him the ' possibility ' of fulfilling the law was not power to fulfil it.   And when he asked himself why, he could only confess that chastity was unattainable for him because he did not really want it, because his desire for it was not sincere, whole-hearted —*non ex toto vult*.[2]   ' It does not follow that we shall strive for that which we have recognised as worth our striving, unless we delight in it in the measure in which it is proper to be loved.' [3]

The Pelagian controversy compelled Augustine to go beyond the general argument of *Quid habes quod non accepisti ?*, and develop a psychology of grace, an account of the actual working in the human heart of God's redemptive love.   The keyword of this anti-Pelagian psychology is ' delight in righteousness '.   It begins with *amor amoris,* an Eros of frustrate desire : ' Often we see what we should do but do it not, because the doing does not delight us ; and we desire that it may delight us '.[4]   We recognise our lack of love, and we confess that by no effort of our own can we make good the deficiency.   No man can ever make himself take pleasure in what is good.   *Dominus dabit suavitatem,* says the Psalmist.   *No man cometh unto me, except the Father that sent me draw him.*   The Father's ' drawing ' is a ' violence done to the heart ', but ' not a rough or painful violence. . . . It is sweet, its very sweetness draws.' [5]   So far from being a drawing without or against our will, it is a drawing ' by pleasure '. *Trahit sua quemque voluptas,* wrote Virgil.   The ' heart's pleasure ' of the Christian is the ' delight in the Lord ', the delight in that truth, blessedness, righteousness, eternal life, of which Christ is

---

[1] *De Grat. Christi* 4 ff.
[2] *Conf.* VIII. 21.
[3] *De Spir. et Litt.* 63.
[4] *En. in Ps.* CXVIII. viii. 4.
[5] *Serm.* 131. 2.

the sum.[1] Charity is the *cupiditas boni,* the desire of the good ;
and ' the good begins to be desired (*concupisci*), when it begins
to be sweet. . . . Therefore the *blessing of sweetness* is the grace
of God, whereby we are made to delight in and to desire, that
is, to love, what He commands us.' [2] Christ's burden is light,
His yoke is sweet (*suave*) through the love which He inspires.
Amanti suave est : non amanti, durum est.[3] And so the whole
argument of the *De Spiritu et Littera* is summed up : ' We say
that the human will is divinely assisted to work righteousness in
such manner that, besides man's creation with the endowment
of free will, and besides the teaching by which he is instructed
how he ought to live, he receives the Holy Spirit, whereby there
arises in his soul the delight in and the love of God the supreme
and changeless Good. . . . When the right action and the true
aim has begun to appear clearly, unless it be also delighted in and
loved, there is no doing, no devotion, no good life. And that
it may be loved, the love of God is spread abroad in our hearts,
not by the free will whose spring is in ourselves, but through the
Holy Spirit which is given us.' [4]

It will be remembered that in examining Augustine's usage
of the word *amor,* we observed that while generally applying it
to the direction of the will, as that which gives character to
moral activity in the widest sense, he includes in it both affective
and conative elements, and that sometimes one and sometimes
the other of these elements is uppermost in his mind. Love is
both quest (*appetitus*) and enjoyment (*fruitio*). Clearly, when he
speaks of ' delectation ', he is simply isolating for the moment the
affective aspect of *amor.* His *non amatur nisi quod delectat* [5] is not
a hedonist formula : it does no more than affirm, in agreement
with the modern psychologist, that feeling is the indispensable
pre-supposition of conation, that the affective state evoked by

---

[1] *In Jo. Ev. Tr.* 26. 4.
[2] *C. du. Ep. Pelag.* II. 21. 　　　　　　　　　[3] *Serm.* 30. 10.
[4] *De Spir. et Litt.* 5. Cf. *ib.* 51 : per fidem confugiat ad misericordiam Dei,
ut det quod iubet atque inspirata gratiae suavitate per Spiritum Sanctum faciat
plus delectare quod praecipit quam delectat quod impedit.
[5] *Serm.* 159. 3.

awareness of an object, as well as the awareness itself, are necessary springs of voluntary activity. But if charity as a voluntary activity is the gift of God, we cannot hesitate to admit that those conditions of its birth in us in which the soul is evidently more passive than active, are God's gift too. In the *De Diversis Quaestionibus ad Simplicianum,* the work in which the Augustinian doctrine of grace first appears full-fledged, he emphasises the passivity of both presentation and feeling. ' Who has it in his power either that an object be presented which can please him (*delectare*), or that when presented it shall please ? . . . But the will can by no means be set in motion unless an object be presented which delights and attracts.' [1] Just as the doctrine of grace could not stop short at the act of faith, could not allow that our embracing of God's revelation is something which God leaves altogether to us, so was it impossible that in the gift of love should not be included the gift of that delight in righteousness which is the presupposition of all active charity. ' The man with whom God deals graciously (*facit suavitatem*) is he in whom God inspires delight in the good—and that is, to speak more plainly, he to whom God gives the love of God.' [2] Augustine could call delectation, like love itself, the 'soul's weight'.[3] But he could not have *identified* love with delectation without compromising his fundamental conception of human love as unsatisfied, questing will. Least of all does he regard either the delectation or the love of which it is a part as a force external to the will. In the words which he used in the *Retractations* of faith and works : ' both are ours, but both are given '.[4]

How easily this psychology of grace could be perverted into a psychological hedonism was shown in Jansenism. Augustine had constantly described the moral struggle as a struggle between the ' heavenly delectation ' which is ' delight in righteousness ', and the ' earthly delectation ', the inordinate desires which lead to sin.[5] Since the text of *Romans* vii. 22—*I delight in* (συνήδομαι,

---

[1] *De Div. Quaest. ad Simpl.* I. ii. 21 f.
[2] *En. in Ps.* cxviii. xvii. 2.   [3] *De Mus.* vi. 29.   [4] *Retr.* I. 23.
[5] *Serm.* 159. *De Gen. ad litt.* x. 20. *Encheirid.* 22, etc.

condelector) the law of God after the inner man—seemed clearly to speak of the *delectatio iustitiae* in which the presence of grace is manifested, he had found himself obliged to correct his earlier interpretation of this chapter as an account of man's condition ' under the law ' [1]—a change which was the easier for him because on other grounds he had become convinced that the Christian ' under grace ' is not exempt from the fight against concupiscence, the contrary ' law in the members ' whose power accordingly became that of a rival delectation. The two delectations are simply the rival ' loves ' of the *De Civitate*, only regarded as affections rather than as wills. Resistance to temptation, then, is possible only inasmuch as the ' delight in the law of God ' is the stronger ; for ' our activity must be directed in accordance with that which delights us the more '.[2] This gave Jansen his text ; and he represented Augustine [3] as teaching that the ' essence of Christ's healing grace ', of the *gratia efficax*, is nothing but the *delectatio victrix*, the ' heavenly delight ' which opposes and subdues the ' earthly '. The love of God is the product or fruit of this victorious delectation, which is itself needed not because of the will's nature but because of its weakness. It is ' the medicine of a diseased and prostrate will, not a help for a will sound and erect ' : in short, pleasure is an unpleasant necessity. Jansen calls it in so many words the ' lubricant ' of the will.

Yet even Jansen did not maintain so artificial an isolation of the affective from the conative element in love as this would suggest ; for his definition of delectation is ' a vital, indeliberate act of love *and desire,* preceding consent of will '. Among ' the acts of the soul ' he distinguishes the ' primary complacency ' by which man's heart is initially ' adapted ' to the good as fitting and ' connatural ' to itself, and to which he gives the name of *amor,* both from the actual movement of desire (*desiderium*),

---

[1] *C. du. Ep. Pelag.* I. 22. Cf. the series of Sermons on *Romans* vii. and viii. *Serm.* 153-159, esp. 154. 11 and 155. 3.

[2] *Exp. Ep. ad Gal.* 49.

[3] See the *Augustinus* (Rouen ed. 1652) Tom. III. pp. 167-188.

and from the final state of ' rest ' or ' joy ' (*quies, nempe gaudium seu delectatio*) in which the movement terminates. This ultimate ' delectation ', he is careful to point out, is obviously not the Augustinian *delectatio victrix*, which rather corresponds in part to the ' primary complacency ' and in part to the appetitive movement or desire. He appeals to St. Thomas's doctrine that love in the sense of desire carries with it an immediate delectation which increases with the progress of the movement towards its goal : there is progressive anticipation of the ' rest ' in which the movement terminates and desire is satisfied. And in this sense he would interpret Augustine's frequent sayings to the effect that love makes God present to the soul. Jansen thus regards delectation not as the bare feeling of pleasure but as including a conative element. By insisting that both the desire and the complacency are ' indeliberate ', he keeps delectation and volition apart, and is able to speak of this ' vital act ' as ' sent from heaven into the will '. Thereby ' the soul is so sweetly and delectably carried away in pursuit of the good, that the will consents to it *freely* ', and its love of the good increases in intensity in proportion to the strength of the delectation which moves it.

Jansen, therefore, no more than Augustine, makes the love of God co-extensive with the ' delight in righteousness '. But Augustine does not, as Jansen does, separate the delectation from the devoted will. Nor does he derive the motive power of the delectation from an associated desire for the delectation's increase. Augustine, rightly understood, is hedonist in psychology as little as he is hedonist in ethics. He no more believes that pleasure is the object of all human activity than that pleasure is the supreme good. The hedonism of Jansen is betrayed not only in his treatment of the *delectatio victrix* but in his failure to distinguish the ' good ' which is the object of the will from the subjective state of ' rest ', the ultimate delectation of the satisfied soul. That is the essential anthropocentrism, which *uses* God for the end of human happiness, instead of proclaiming that the union with God which brings happiness is unattainable unless God is loved ' for His own sake '—the paradox of hedonism in its religious form. Neither Augustine nor Thomas was ever in danger of this degradation of man's true end into a means.

Nothing, on the other hand, could be more un-Augustinian than the Jansenist theory that delight is given only as the medicine of a will diseased. In Augustine's thought, the love of God is inseparable from delight because it is the gift of the Holy Spirit who in the Trinity is 'love, delight, happiness, beatitude '.[1] In the divine Love there is no striving or want ; and when the Holy Spirit is given to us, we receive more than a pledge (*pignus*) of something to be enjoyed in the future : we receive an ' earnest ' (*arrha*), a foretaste, realised here and now.[2] Needless to say, this gift of the Spirit is ours *by measure* only : we still feel love as a need, because that which we love is not always present with us.[3] Grace in this life is never more than the ' earnest ' of the Spirit. But its character determines its source. It is so far the highest good of which we have any experience that not to acknowledge it as God's gift means its destruction. ' Your belief that you have so great a possession of yourself, is proof to me that you have it not ; for if you had it, you would know whence you had it.' [4] We know that charity is not of ourselves because we know that to delight in God is the *Donum Dei, Deus quia ex Deo*. And in the struggle between flesh and spirit, between the earthly and the heavenly delectations, it is the Spirit of God ' that fights in you against you, against that which is against you in yourself'.[5]

2. *Grace and Freedom*

St. Thomas held that to identify charity with the immanent operation of the Holy Spirit—an identification for which Peter Lombard had claimed the authority of Augustine—was to destroy the nature of charity as a voluntary and meritorious act of the will.[6] In fact, it was not easy for the doctrine of grace to find accommodation in a frame of ethical thought which

[1] *De Trin.* VI. 11.   [2] *Serm.* 156. 16.
[3] *De Trin.* X. 19.   [4] *Serm.* 145. 4.
[5] *Serm.* 128. 9.   [6] *Summa Theol.* IIa IIae. q. 23, a. 2.

persistently assumed that man's destiny hereafter will depend upon his deserts. If there is a Judgement to come, there must be merit or demerit to be judged; and merit presupposes freedom. Augustine himself poses the dilemma to the monks of Adrumetum. ' If there be no such thing as God's grace, how can He be the Saviour of the world ? If there be no such thing as free-will, how can He be its Judge ? ' [1]

Augustine believed that the dilemma was not insuperable, and that his own doctrine in no way impaired the responsibility of the moral agent. It is not really true that he confused the problem by ambiguity in his use of the term ' freedom '. He did in fact distinguish very clearly two quite different senses of the word ; and though he was not careful to be consistent in his language, there is seldom any doubt as to his meaning.[2] By freedom (*libertas*) he means the power, which man's fallen nature obviously does not possess, to choose and to accomplish the good. But the loss of *libertas* does not involve the loss of *liberum arbitrium*, which is not the *libertas indifferentiae,* the absolute power of choice between alternatives—that was the mistaken idea of Julian —but the spontaneity, the self-determination inherent in the will as such. *Cogi velle,* ' to be compelled to will ', is a contradiction in terms : ' if I am compelled, I do not will '.[3] All choice is free choice, all will is free-will. What Augustine had said in the *De Libero Arbitrio*—that ' nothing is so entirely in our power as the will itself'—he repeated and upheld in the *Retractations*. When we say that this or that is ' in our power ', we mean precisely that we do it when we will.[4] The mistake of the Pelagians was to forget that the will does not move in a vacuum, that it is

[1] *Ep.* 214. 2.

[2] The *Encheiridion* is little if at all later than the *C. duas Epist. Pelagianorum.* When therefore we read in the *Encheiridion* (c. 9) : libero arbitrio male utens homo et se perdidit *et ipsum,* we must interpret the epigram in the light of *C. du. Ep. Pel.* I. 5 : quis nostrum dicat quod primi hominis peccato perierit liberum arbitrium de genere humano ? *Libertas* quidem periit per peccatum ... liberum arbitrium usque adeo in peccatore non periit ut per ipsum peccent maxime omnes qui cum delectatione peccant et amore peccati et hoc eis placet quod eos libet.

[3] *C. Jul. op. imp.* I. 101.   [4] *Retr.* I. 22.

' determined ' by motives, and that our motives are in part the product of our environment and of the whole complex series of presentations and impressions over which we have no control. For the truth which must so far be allowed to ' determinism ', Augustine's constant formula is a text from *Proverbs : praeparatur voluntas a Deo*.[1] Were this ' preparation of the will ' by God not a fact, there could be no meaning in prayer and no truth in St. Paul's saying that *God worketh in us to will* as well as *to do*. But it is as certain that when we will, the will is our will, as that when we act the action is our action.[2] God is our Helper, and ' the very name of Helper tells you that you yourself are active '.[3] That is a thought which recurs constantly in Augustine's preaching. In the temple of God there are no stones ' that have no motion of their own—lifted and laid by the Builder ' : we are ' living stones '.[4] St. Francis de Sales is in perfect accord with Augustine when he compares the soul under grace to the *apodes*, the birds who cannot of their own strength lift themselves into the air to fly, but who when lifted by the breezes must use their wings or fall to earth again.[5] Augustine is clear that the indwelling of the Holy Spirit can never be an encroachment upon human personality. *Qui fecit te sine te, non te iustificat sine te*.[6] The supreme instance of grace is the Incarnation, and we may be certain where Augustine would have stood in the Monophysite and Monothelite controversies. Neither in Christ nor in the redeemed humanity of which He is the Head, could he have allowed any question of an extinction of the individual human will.

God's working in men's hearts, says Augustine, is never a compulsion : it is not ' so that they believe against their will, but so that they become willing instead of unwilling '.[7] But this ' becoming willing instead of unwilling ' is itself the critical decision of faith ; and the turning-point in the development of Augustine's doctrine of grace was the moment at which he

---

[1] *Prov.* viii. 35 (LXX.).   [2] *De Grat. et Lib. Arb.* 32.
[3] *Serm.* 156. 11. Cf. *En. in Ps.* LXXVIII. 12 ; CXLIII. 6. *In Ep. Jo. Tr.* 4. 7.
[4] *Serm.* 156. 13.   [5] *Traité de l'Amour de Dieu*, II. 9.
[6] *Serm.* 169. 13.   [7] *C. du Ep. Pel.* I. 37.

perceived that man cannot claim ' emancipation from God '
even for the act of faith. What vitiated his later treatment of
the whole matter was his wavering reaction to the Pelagian
Entweder-oder—either God's work, *or* ours ?—a dilemma which
before the controversy began he had accepted without scruple.
The attempt to distinguish between what we do ourselves and
what God does for us must always involve our thinking about
grace in tangles which are inextricable. And so we find that
Augustine will first attribute the forthcomingness of the act of
will (*ut velimus*) *both* to God's calling *and* to man's response,
while ascribing the right action and the eternal happiness, to
which the will is directed, to God's gift alone ; but that in the
end the pressure of controversy will make him assert that it is
the forthcomingness of will which God works in us ' without
us ', and only when the will is formed and active can we say
that He works with us in the grace that makes perfect.[1] Midway
between these two comes the apparently unambiguous statement
of the *De Spiritu et Littera :* ' To consent to the calling of God
or to refuse it belongs to our own will : which, so far from
conflicting with the text *What hast thou which thou hast not
received ?* , does even confirm it. For the soul cannot receive
and possess the gift there spoken of but by consenting. *What*
the soul is to possess, *what* it is to receive, pertains to God : the
receiving and possessing, necessarily to him who receives and
possesses.'[2] But what, we may ask, is this receiving of God's
gift, but the very attitude and act of faith itself, the ' will to
believe ' which in the same context Augustine has expressly
distinguished from ' consent to God's calling ', and ascribed to

[1] The first distinction occurs in the decisive pre-Pelagian work *De Div.
Quaest. ad Simplicianum* of 396 (I. ii. 10) : ut velimus, et suum esse voluit et
nostrum : suum vocando, nostrum sequendo. Quod autem voluerimus,
solus praestat, id est, posse bene agere et semper beate vivere. The second is
in the *De Grat. et Lib. Arb.* of thirty years later (*c.* 33) : ut velimus, sine nobis
operatur : cum autem volumus, et sic volumus ut faciamus, nobiscum co-
operatur. The two distinctions are not, it is worth noting, diametrically
opposed (as H. Jonas, *Augustin und der Paulinische Freiheitsproblem*, p. 53, seems
to think) ; for *quod voluerimus* is not the same as *cum volumus.*

[2] *De Spir. et Litt.* 60 (of 412).

the divine working through the mediate presentation of that calling to men's minds ? [1] There would have been no need for any such distinction if the question of faith's origin—God's work or ours ?—were not still presenting itself to him as a genuine dilemma. The *Retractations* prove that at the end of his life he was capable of seeing through it. He had written, in the days before he became bishop : ' That we believe, belongs to us ; that we perform what is good, belongs to Him Who gives the Holy Spirit to the believer '. ' I should certainly not have said that ', is his comment, ' if I had known then that faith itself is found among God's gifts, which are given *through the same Spirit. Both therefore are ours,* because of our will's free choice, and yet both are given, through the Spirit of faith and love.' [2]

If the reality of the consent to receive, and the possibility of refusal, be denied, there is an end of any understanding of grace as a loving relation between persons. Love is ' irresistible ' only in the sense that to overcome the resistance of pride, the pride whose essence is the refusal to receive, is possible to love and to love only. But ' irresistible grace ' in the Jansenist sense, is as much a contradiction in terms as *cogi velle*. And Augustine never realised that his own conception of grace required nothing less than a revolution in his thought of the divine omnipotence. It is true that not even in the last years of his life, in the final hardening of his predestinationist doctrine, do we find him losing sight altogether of man's response to the call of God. He still affirmed that the Spirit's leading does not annul but evoke the activity of man. *Aguntur ut agant, non ut ipsi nihil agant.*[3] Even when he says that no human will can resist the will of God,

---

[1] *De Spir. et Litt.* 60 : His ergo modis (the Gospel message ' from without ', the mysterious promptings of conscience ' within ') quando Deus agit cum anima rationali, ut ei credat—neque enim credere potest quodlibet libero arbitrio, si nulla sit suasio vel vocatio cui credat—profecto et ipsum velle credere Deus operatur in homine, et in omnibus misericordia eius praevenit nos ; consentire autem vocationi Dei vel ab ea dissentire, sicut dixi, propriae voluntatis est, etc.

[2] *Retr.* I. 23.   [3] *De Corr. et Grat.* 4.

he is thinking not of an ' irresistible grace ', forcibly impelling to action, but of the Almighty providence which rules the issues of all human willing. ' God does what He will with those who do what He wills not.' [1] Not even in the *De Correptione et Gratia* is the Augustine of the *Confessions* altogether unrecognisable. The ' will that all men should be saved ', which he could not see how to ascribe directly or absolutely to God, was still for him a necessary implication of the love which God inspires in us : to reprove, to exhort, to pray for the sinner is a duty, because love may despair of no man.[2] But nearly all that Augustine wrote after his seventieth year [3] is the work of a man whose energy has burnt itself out, whose love has grown cold. The system which generally goes by the name of Augustinianism is in great part a cruel travesty of Augustine's deepest and most vital thought.

The free will of man is a good, because it is part of God's creation. But its place is among the *media bona* which it is man's task to use, and which he can use well or ill.[4] The gnostic theodicy of Berdyaev,[5] which would have freedom rooted in the ' non-being ' which preceded creation, and thus relieve God from the responsibility for its existence, goes back for its formal expression to the Augustinian creation ' out of nothing '. But Berdyaev does just what Augustine refused to do : he makes the ' nothing ' into a ' something ' endowed with definite and fatal quality ; and on the principles of Augustine he is therefore fundamentally Manichaean. Creation *de nihilo* is not for Augustine the origin of free-will, but the metaphysical ground for the possibility of evil. God's creation is limited not by a mysterious ' meonic abyss of freedom ', but by His own nature. God is One and cannot multiply Himself : mutability is inseparable from crea-tureliness.[6] But Berdyaev derives from his ' uncreated freedom ' not only the free-will of man with its potentiality for evil, but

---

[1] *De Corr. et Grat.* 43. [2] *Ib.* 46 f.

[3] The most important of these writings are the *De Gratia et Libero Arbitrio,* the *De Correptione et Gratia,* the *De Praedestinatione Sanctorum* and *De Dono Perseverantiae,* the *Retractations* and the *Contra Julianum opus imperfectum.*

[4] *De Lib. Arb.* II. 49 f. [5] See esp. his *Destiny of Man.*

[6] *C. Jul. op. imp.* V. 42.

the 'creativeness', the power to co-operate in the work of God, upon which his ethical system is centred. And this 'creative freedom' is not far from Augustine's *libertas*—the liberty of the sons of God which is power and life.

For *this* freedom is not a legal concept : it is not, like *liberum arbitrium*, a postulate of judgement, reward and punishment. The starting-point, indeed, is the passage in the Epistle to the Romans in which St. Paul, speaking ' after the manner of men ', illustrates the Christian position both ' under law ' and ' under grace ' from the status of legal servitude. *Know ye not that to whom ye present yourselves as bondmen unto obedience, his bondmen ye are whom ye obey—whether of sin unto death, or of obedience unto righteousness ?* As sin's bondmen we were ' free in regard to righteousness ', owing no recognition to God as our master. ' Made free from sin, we become the bondmen of God.' [1] Augustine's characteristic literalism makes real categories out of the figurative language of St. Paul. We have seen how his whole ethic is framed in the forms of mastery and service. The moral choice is a choice of ruler : [2] only in serving God does man escape servitude to the flesh. But there are two kinds of service, willing and unwilling. The service that is delighted in transforms itself into freedom. *Praeceptum liber facit qui libens facit.*[3]

Thus four possible conditions arise. Either ' sin ' or ' righteousness ' may be served willingly or unwillingly. The worst sin is that in which the sinner delights, doing vileness for the love of vileness ; and in such sin there is attained a perverted, diabolic freedom—' the freedom from righteousness '.[4] But most men have motives for transgressing or obeying the moral law, other than the transgression or the obedience itself. Either they ' do the evil they would not ' because concupiscence is too strong in them, or they ' do the good ' from hope or fear of

---

[1] *Rom.* vi. 16-22.
[2] *En. in Ps.* cxlviii. 2 : in unoquoque hominum intus est imperator . . . in tuo autem arbitrio Deus esse voluit, cui pares locum, Deo an diabolo ; cum paraveris, qui possidebit, ipse imperabit.
[3] *De Grat. Christ.* 14.   [4] *C. du. Ep. Pelag.* I. 5.

consequence. Both these kinds of action are strictly and entirely ' servile '. Only the ' delight in righteousness ', the doing of good because it is good, confers the divine enfranchisement, the liberty which is liberty indeed, upon the will. So, when Julian maintains that freedom can only exist where the will is ' carried captive ' neither to righteousness nor to iniquity, Augustine replies that no word but captivity can describe the state of him who does the evil that he would not. But the ' delight in the law of God ' is not a captivity : the will is ' drawn to its Liberator by the sweetness of a free spirit's love, not by the cramping fear of a slave '.[1]

In the *De Spiritu et Littera*, after quoting at length from the seventh chapter of *Romans*, Augustine makes the comment : ' If the law's command is performed through fear of punishment, not through love of righteousness, it is performed slavishly, not freely, *and therefore is not performed at all.* For there can be no good fruit that does not ripen from the root of love. And if we have the faith that works through love, we begin to delight in the law of God according to the inner man, a delighting which is the gift not of the Letter but of the Spirit.'[2] The comment is not the less instructive for its irrelevance to the text. Augustine well understood the meaning of St. Paul's attack on legalism at its root, as man's hopeless effort to establish a claim of his own, to put himself in the right with God. But here he is developing the Apostle's *obiter dicta* into a psychology of freedom. The *spirit of bondage unto fear,* and the *delighting in the law of God according to the inner man,* are not cardinal principles in St. Paul ; but they suggest to Augustine the motives which decide the quality of all moral action. As we have already seen, he could not bring himself to deny all value to fear, at least as a propaedeutic. That would have been to despise the threatenings of the Gospel : it was too manifest that in the New Covenant as well as in the Old men are made afraid. But the law of the New Covenant is written on the heart, and nothing is done from the heart that is

[1] *C. Jul. op. imp.* III. 112.   [2] *De Spir. et Litt.* 26.

done for fear of punishment.[1]   The obedience of fear is always
a servile obedience, and the obedience of hope is no better ; for
he who obeys because he fears or hopes, would act otherwise if
he dared.[2]   The commandment remains a force external to his
own will.   But the paradox of the command to love is that if it
be obeyed because it is commanded, it is not obeyed—*ideo nec fit.*
To delight in the law of God is to delight in God, and in that
delight to be free : *libertas enim delectat.*[3]   The law of love is the
law of liberty :[4] it is the ' very presence of the Holy Spirit ', the
' finger of God ' writing His Law in our hearts, spreading abroad
in them the love which is the fulfilling of the law.[5]

The *delectatio iustitiae* is thus not only that which gives freedom
to the captive and power to the impotent will.   It is the solvent
of legalism, the end of passive obedience to law as a moral norm
imposed from without.   Freedom is no longer a condition of
legal merit.   It is the emancipation, progressively realisable, from
fear of punishment and hope of reward alike.   Augustine does
not envisage any sudden or complete release from moral servitude : delight in the law of God does not immediately extinguish
the law in the members.   But it is the *earnest of the Spirit,* the
promise of deliverance from the *body of this death.*   It is not
' autonomy ' of the will ; for though the gift of God becomes
our own when we love what we have received,[6] we lose it the
moment we forget that we have received it.   It is equally
remote from the ' heteronomy ' whether of desire for pleasure
or of desire for personal perfection ; for it is the life-giving ' joy
in the Lord ' which lifts us out of ourselves and enables us to
rejoice even in tribulation.   It is the heart's delight in the divine
presence ' as the beloved in the lover ', which finds expression
both in the sober words of St. Thomas on the ' friendship of God '
which sets men free from passion and from fear,[7] and in the
mystic rapture of *My beloved is mine and I am His.*

[1] *En. in. Ps.* LXXVII. 10.
[2] *Ib.* XXXII. i. 6 ; CXVIII. xi. 1.   *De Spir. et Litt.* 13, 56.
[3] *In Jo. Ev. Tr.* 41. 10.   [4] *Ep.* 167. 19.
[5] *De Spir. et Litt.* 36.   [6] *Serm.* 166. 3.
[7] *Contra Gentiles,* IV. 22.

3. *Grace and Merit*

The reality of human freedom, both 'under the law' in the limited sense that our will and our actions are our own, and 'under grace', when Christian life consists in growth towards true liberty, is one of Augustine's most positive assertions. Much less unambiguous is his attitude towards the idea of merit. For here he was conscious of a critical change in his own understanding of Christianity. The 'victory of God's grace' befell him in the year 396, when he recognised the truth that faith is no more, if no less, a human achievement than the good works which follow it.[1] But the nature of the crisis is obscured by the famous phrase of the *Retractations—laboratum est quidem pro libero arbitrio voluntatis humanae; sed vicit Dei gratia*.[2] The real loser in Augustine's mental fight was not, as we have seen, the 'human will's free choice', but man's claim to have deserved the gift of grace by his unaided act of faith.

For the shackling of Latin theology in the chain of 'works' and 'merit', Tertullian has commonly been made to bear most of the blame ; but it is a question whether the Latin language itself was not a more powerful influence than the Roman lawyer who used it. The Latin *meritum* is a participial form of the verb *mereri*, while in Greek there is no verb 'to deserve'. The Greeks thought of merit or worth adjectivally, as a quality of persons or things. The Latins ask what a man has *done* to make him worthy. For the Greeks, desert is a matter of estimation, for the Latins a matter of fact. Thus, while ἀξία means 'value' or 'dignity' as often as 'desert', *mereri* properly denotes the act by which the agent earns either a stipulated payment or a legal punishment ; though it is naturally extended to cover 'moral' desert also. When Augustine speaks of *merita naturalia* in reference to the values or dignities of things in the scale of being,[3] or Julian of *meritum innocentiae* as a goodness independent of the will and so by definition 'unearned',[4] both are adopting a usage which is decidedly exceptional. The plural *merita*, unlike our 'merits',

---

[1] *Retr.* I. 23.   [2] *Ib.* II. I.
[3] *C. Secund. Man.* 10.   [4] *C. Jul. op. imp.* VI. 19.

normally indicates so many distinct actions of positive or negative value ; and it is to be observed that while positive value generally attaches to economic or contractual activity, negative value is chiefly in view when the associations are those of public law ; for the law provides punishments but not rewards. The influence of this distinction is evident when the notion of merit is applied to religion : the good Christian is the labourer who is worthy of his hire ; the bad is the criminal who has incurred penalty.

The Greek language could only supply its lack of an active verb meaning ' to deserve ' by the periphrasis ' to be worthy ' (ἄξιος εἶναι), or by the passives ἀξιοῦσθαι, καταξιοῦσθαι, which denote not the subject's ' right ', but the estimate in which he is held by another. So St. Paul prays that the Thessalonians may be ' counted worthy ' of their calling, of the Kingdom of God.[1] For the ideas of payment, reward, requital, Greek has of course an ample vocabulary ; and here we find that the commonest words are associated not with the juridical but with the economic sphere. μισθός, the New Testament ' reward ', means ' payment for services ' : ἀνταπόδοσις and its cognates, common in Aristotle and in Biblical Greek, signify primarily the rendering of due μισθός or payment. Thus, while the Latin ' merit ' regards both the claim for payment and the liability to punishment from the point of view of the claimant or person liable, the Greek tendency is to regard punishment and reward objectively as the discharge of payment.

These linguistic facts throw light on the differences between Eastern and Western moral theology. Greek patristic thought could not throw over the New Testament. *It is a righteous thing with God to recompense* (ἀνταποδοῦναι).[2] But the natural correlate of ἀνταπόδοσις was μισθός—*Call the labourers and give them their hire* (ἀποδὸς τὸν μισθόν) ; and neither the warning in Christ's parable, that God's recompense is not based on the principle of ' equal wages for equal work ', nor the presence of metaphor in ' the wages of sin ', could easily be forgotten. The recompense is God's sovereign act rather than man's ' earning '.

---

[1] 2 *Thess.* i. 5, 11.   [2] 2 *Thess.* i. 6.

The Latin *mereri* placed man's act in the foreground. ' To merit ', writes Hilary, ' is predicable of the person whose own act is origin of the acquisition of merit for himself.' [1] ' The good deed ', says Tertullian, ' puts God in debit.' [2] Cyprian and Ambrose transmit to Augustine the ugly theory of alms-giving as the stipulated price of forgiveness. And Augustine himself began with the Latin idea of merit in its double connota-tion—contractual and juridical—as what a man ' acquires for himself '. When in the *Soliloquies* he ' rejects the error of those who think that souls have no merits in God's sight ',[3] no doubt he has in mind the Manichaean denial of human responsibility. In the *De Libero Arbitrio,* starting from the certainty of God's just judgement, he reaches the fundamental position that ' merit is in the will ', that ' by the will alone we *merit and live* a life either of worthiness and happiness, or of shame and misery '.[4] Here there is as yet no postponement of the judgement and requital to another life : we are still in the atmosphere of Cassiciacum. In principle, this conclusion of the *De Libero Arbitrio* anticipates Abélard and Kant. Moral goodness is in the ' good will ', not in the outward ' work ' : there are not ' merits ', but ' merit ', which lies in the inward unity of personal intention. But in practice, Augustine never ceased to speak of faith, prayer, and ' good works ' as so many distinct ' meritings '. His sermons harp, unabashed, upon the ' Christian usury '.[5] *Beata vita* is *merces bonorum :* ' goodness is the work, blessedness the wages. God commands the work, and offers the pay. He says, Do this, and this shall you receive '.[6] ' God wills that we be as it were in commerce with Him : He makes an exchange with us.' [7] This is popular homiletic, in the style learnt from Ambrose ; but Augustine was not a man who preached ' down ' to his congre-gations, or sanctioned motives which he could not himself approve. He speaks in a private letter of his own ' passionate desire ' to follow Christ's counsel to the rich young man—*sell all*

[1] *De Trin.* XI. 19. [2] *De Paenit.* 2. [3] *Solil.* I. 3.
[4] *De Lib. Arb.* I. 28, 30. [5] E.g. *Serm.* 42. 2 ; 123. 5.
[6] *Serm.* 150. 4. [7] *Serm.* 177. 10.

that thou hast, and give to the poor, and thou shalt have treasure in heaven. 'Not by my own strength', he professes, 'but with the help of His grace I have so done.' And he adds, with no sense of inconsistency, 'it will none the less be set to my account (*imputabitur*) because I was not rich '.[1]

Not until the Pelagian controversy had sharpened the issue of grace and merit, does he appear to have discovered the sense of St. Paul's great antithesis : *the wages of sin is death, but the gift of God is eternal life.* In a letter of about the year 419 he urges the full weight of that text against the thesis of Caelestius that grace is given ' according to merits '. But his argument is not that eternal life may not truly be called ' the wages of righteousness ', that it is not truly the reward of merit : if the Apostle did not say this, it was because he would make it plain that the merit of righteousness is itself given.[2] The text is expounded in the same way in the *Encheiridion* and the latest treatises. Eternal life is *grace for grace*, a gift which crowns the gifts already given ; but it remains assuredly ' the reward of good works '.[3]

No phrase of Augustine's has stamped itself more permanently upon Catholic theology than his *hominis bona merita, Dei munera.* ' When God crowns our merits, He crowns nothing but His own gifts.' [4] ' No man deserves to receive aught of good from the Father of lights from whom cometh every perfect gift, save by receiving what he deserves not.' [5] The Council of Trent, for its own purposes, inverted the formula, and wrote : ' So great is God's goodness towards all men, that He wills His own gifts to be their merits '. But in effect the Counter-Reformation was sweeping aside the doubtful scholastic classification of *de congruo* and *de condigno* in favour of the simple paradox of Augustine.

Augustine certainly meant his paradox to be accepted as such. It was far from being a disguised equivalent of the Lutheran denial of all human merit. Given that all good, and therefore

<hr/>

[1] *Ep.* 157. 39.   [2] *Ep.* 194. 19 ff.
[3] *Encheirid.* 28.   *De Grat. et Lib. Arb.* 19 ff.   *De Corrept. et Grat.* 41.   Cf.
In Jo. Ev. Tr. 3. 9.   [4] *Ep.* 194. 19.   [5] *Ep.* 186. 10.

all good will, is of God, all evil will of ourselves, Augustine could not escape his conclusion that God's ' hardening ' of sinners is always merited, His ' justification ' never.[1] But that was not to say that ' the righteous have no merits. They have indeed, since they are righteous. But to be made righteous, they had none ; for their justification is *gratis per gratiam.*'[2] ' The grace of God is not given according to our deservings ; for we see that it was given and is given every day, following not only upon no good deserts, but upon many evil. But, assuredly, when it has been given, there begin to be good deserts of our own, yet through grace.'[3]

There was more than one reason for Augustine's upholding the compatibility of grace and merit. It was certainly not a politic concession of the *doctor gratiae,* made to save his cause in face of the conservatism of tradition. Scripture, as always, was his primary authority, and it dictated the form of his solution. If St. Paul, who owed all that he was to the grace of God, yet knew that because he had fought a good fight, there was laid up for him a crown of righteousness—a crown of which he ' could not have been worthy, had not grace been given to his unworthiness '[4]—then we may not doubt that God will ' crown His gifts ' to every man.

But God's spiritual gifts are never external objects, separable possessions of the recipient. God's gifts ' become our own when we love what we have received ' : that is, they enter into the texture of our being and transfigure it. Grace not only respects, but intensifies and enlarges our freedom. The ' help ' of grace means no division of labour : it does not mean that part of the work is ours, and part God's. Cardinal Bellarmine wrote that ' in the good work which we do by God's help, there is nothing of ours that is not God's, nor anything of God's that is not ours. God does the *whole* and man does the *whole* '.[5] That is genuinely

---

[1] *Ep.* 186. 20.   *De Grat. et Lib. Arb.* 43.   [2] *Ep.* 194. 6.
[3] *De Grat. et Lib. Arb.* 13.   [4] *De Gest. Pelag.* 35.
[5] Bellarmine, *De Justificatione,* v. 5. I owe this and some other references in the present section to the article on *Mérite* by J. Rivière in the *Dictionnaire de Theologie Catholique.*

Augustinian. The activity of love is theandric : it springs from the *one spirit* in him who is *joined unto the Lord*. Augustine does not speak of the 'merits of Christ', and the realism of his doctrine of the mystical Body excludes all possibility of nominalist 'imputation'. But as member of Christ, though in myself I am *poor and needy*, I look for the Head to 'strip away my rags and cover me with His robe '.[1] In proud humility I must dare even to know that *I am holy*, because Christ's holiness sanctifies His Body in every part.[2] We may not separate ourselves from that righteousness in respect of which the world must be convicted in Christ's *going to the Father* : because *we* are risen with Christ, we may become *the righteousness of God in Him* : the Christ who goes to the Father is 'the whole Christ with us (*totus nobiscum*) ',[3] the Christ to whose wholeness we belong.

And the reality of the righteousness which belongs to Christ's Body is a reality of merit, inasmuch as it is of the nature of grace that *to him that hath shall be given*. Grace must always *abound;* for it is the fecundity of the divine love,[4] continually proceeding to ever new creation, as the barriers to its acceptance, one by one, fall away. But Augustine does not believe that in this life we can ever say that no barrier remains. In the last resort, his belief in the reality of merit is the consequence of his belief that our life on earth is always and to the end a pilgrimage. The assurance of God's love can never be the assurance of our personal salvation. And therefore the whole purpose of this temporal existence is ' to win the merit whereby we may live in eternity '.[5] There the word ' merit ' has escaped from its Latin fetters. Our real need is to become *fit* for the vision of God. Here on earth we can never surpass the ' lesser righteousness ' which ' works merit '. That ' fullness of perfect righteousness ' which is the enjoyment of God's presence will be given, like the resurrection

[1] *En. in Ps.* XXXIX. 27.

[2] *Ib.* LXXXV. 4 : non est ista superbia elati, sed confessio non ingrati.

[3] *Serm.* 144. 6.

[4] Cf. *En. in Ps.* LV. 17 : Deus . . . verus et verax animae maritus, ad prolem sempiternae vitae fecundans et steriles nos non esse permittens.

[5] *Ep.* 130. 14.

of the dead, *in ictu oculi*—not as an ideal to be pursued through obedience, but as a reward to those who have been obedient here : [1] not a reward of external felicity to men who have already achieved moral perfection, but a *merces perficiens,* a reward which consists in the perfecting of the imperfect—given to those who by their hunger and thirst after righteousness have ' deserved ' to be filled.[2]

But this means that grace and merit are inseparable ; for hunger and thirst after righteousness is nothing else than that love of God with all our heart, with all our soul, and with all our mind, which Christ has taught us is the way to inherit eternal life. *This is life eternal, to know Thee the true God.* And that is ' the whole reward in whose promise we rejoice ; but the reward cannot precede the deserving of it, nor be given to man before he is worthy '.[3] So Augustine had written shortly after his baptism, and so he believed after all the controversies of the years that followed. It was life more than controversy that taught him to understand how both the faith which makes love possible, and the love which energises faith and ' merits ' eternal life, are the gifts of God.

4. *Love and Reward*

Over against the follies and the filth of paganism, Augustine sets the *salubritas* of the Christian religion. Christians flock to the churches, to hear ' how they must live well in this present time, in order that after this life they may deserve to live happily and for ever '.[4] The *De Catechizandis Rudibus* gives us a vivid picture of the common human material with which the African priest of A.D. 400 was called to deal. Augustine knows too well that many seek admission to the church for the sake of nothing but worldly convenience. Such persons will almost certainly not give a true answer to the catechist's preliminary enquiry

---

[1] *C. du. Ep. Pelag.* III. 23.
[2] *De Perfect. Justit.* 17. Cf. *Ep.* 186. 10 : non gratiam Dei aliquid meriti praecedit humani, sed ipsa gratia meretur augeri, ut aucta mereatur et perfici.
[3] *De Mor. Eccl.* 47.   [4] *De Civ.* II. 28.

into motives. But let us assume, says the Bishop, that the candidate has been asked whether it is for any advantage in this present life, or for the hoped-for rest hereafter, that he desires to be a Christian ; and that he replies ' For the rest to come '. Take him at his word, and improve the occasion. ' *Deo gratias, frater :* I give you great joy, I rejoice for you, that in all the perilous storms of this world you have bethought you of a security that is real and certain '.[1] There follows a discourse on the vanity of worldly desires, and on the urgent need for sincerity ; and then comes the conclusion. ' He who will become a Christian for the sake of the everlasting happiness and rest perpetual promised after this life to the saints, that he may not go into eternal fire with the devil, but enter with Christ into His eternal Kingdom, he is a Christian indeed—wary in all temptation, lest he be corrupted by prosperity or broken by adversity, moderate and self-restrained in abundance of worldly goods, brave and patient in tribulations. Such a man will yet go forward and attain a better state, in which he will love God more than he fears hell ; so that even if God should say to him, " Enjoy carnal delights for ever, sin all thou canst ; yet thou shalt not die nor be sent into hell, but only shalt not be with me "—he would stand aghast and sin not at all, no longer lest he fall into that which he feared, but lest he offend the God whom he so loves.' [2] We observed before, in quoting these last sentences, how plainly they show that Augustine does not distinguish between the ' holy fear ' of exile from God's presence,—an ' interested ' fear —and the fear of sin as a violation of love, in which all thought of reaction upon the self is absent.

The rest of Augustine's sample instruction of the catechumen is largely occupied with a sketch of Bible history adapted to enforce the same moral. The manifestation in Christ to all nations of the ' spiritual grace known before only to a few patriarchs and prophets,' was to the end ' that no one should worship God save freely (*gratis*), desiring from Him not the visible rewards of service and felicity in the present life, but

---

[1] *De Catech. Rud.* 24. [2] *Ib.* 27.

eternal life alone, in which God Himself is to be enjoyed. . . .
For then is the Law also fulfilled, when all God's commandments
are performed not in the covetous desire of things temporal, but
for the love of Him who commanded them.'¹ Here once more
we must recognise that *amor illius qui praecepit* is identified with
the ' desire of eternal life in which God Himself is to be enjoyed '.
The motive of Christian worship and life is not presented as a
' disinterested ' love of God : we are not to desire nothing for
ourselves, but the right thing, the ' one thing needful '. ' The
promises of the Old Testament are earthly . . . but now what is
promised is a good of the heart itself, a good of the mind, a
spiritual good.'² ' The everlasting reward of justification is not
that land from which the Amorites were driven, . . . but God
Himself, to whom it is good to hold fast ; so that God's good
thing which men love is God Himself whom they love.'³

Preaching on the anniversary of his ordination, the bishop
exclaims : ' What shall I return unto the Lord for all that He
hath done unto me ? If I say that I make Him a return in feeding
His sheep, even that is done not by me, but by the grace of God
with me. . . . Yet for our loving Him freely (*gratis*), for our
feeding His sheep, we do seek a reward. And how can this be ?
How can we say at the same time " I love freely that I may
feed ", and " I demand a reward because I feed " ? That would
be impossible, reward could by no means be sought from Him
who is freely loved, unless He who is loved were Himself the
reward.'⁴ By ' pure love ' of God, Augustine means a love of
which God alone is the object, not a love free from any element
of desire. ' The heart is not pure ', he says, ' if it worships God
for a reward. What then ? shall we have no reward for the
worship of God ? Assuredly we shall, but it will be God Himself, whom we worship : His own self will be our reward, in
that we shall see Him as He is. . . . If you do not love Him,

¹ *De Catech. Rud.* 39.
² *De Spir. et Litt.* 36. The ' intelligibile bonum ' is a good of ' cor, mens,
spiritus '.
³ *Ib.* 42. ⁴ *Serm.* 340. 1.

that is not enough ; but if you love Him, if you worship freely Him who freely wrought your undeserved redemption, if when you consider His goodness towards you, your heart sighs and is restless with longing for Him, then seek not from Him anything outside Him : He Himself suffices you.' [1]   Once again, it is not God, the absolute Good, but the merciful and loving Redeemer of mankind, who calls forth an answering love.   God is *gratis amandus, gratis colendus;* and God is *ipse nobis praemium.*   The first of these thoughts is for Augustine so far from excluding the second that it necessarily implies it.   There is no theme to which he more constantly returns in his Sermons and Homilies ; and always the pre-supposition is that the love of God is the love of Him who is for us men the Supreme Good.   In the long series of passages to be quoted—and nothing but quotation can convey the full significance of what is the very heart of Augustine's religion—the emphasis is sometimes negative, sometimes positive : sometimes on the motives which ' pure love ' excludes, sometimes on the one motive which it requires ; but in the substance of the thought there is no variation whatever.

' God will be worshipped freely (*gratis*), He will be loved freely, that is, purely : He will be loved not because He gives anything apart from Himself, but because He gives Himself. . . . To call upon God (*Deum invocare*) is to call Him in to yourself. . . . When you say, ' God grant me wealth ', your desire is that wealth, not God, may come to you. . . . If you called upon God, He Himself would come to you, He Himself would be your wealth.' [2]   ' See how the Psalmist has loved Him, and shown the purity of his heart.   *He is the God of my heart, God is my portion for ever.*   The heart is pure : God now is loved freely, no other reward is sought from Him.   He who seeks from God another reward, and for that will serve God, makes that which he will receive more precious than God from whom he will receive it.   What then ?   Has God no reward ? None, save Himself: the reward of God is God Himself.' [3] ' What does the sacrifice of Abraham teach us ?   In brief, not to

[1] *En. in Ps.* LV. 17.   [2] *Ib.* LII. 8.   [3] *Ib.* LXXII. 32.

prefer to God that which God gives. . . . Not even a great good received at His hands may you prefer to the Giver ; and when He sees fit to withdraw it, esteem Him not the less. For God is to be loved freely : what sweeter reward can come from God than God Himself ? ' [1] Religion (*pietas*) is ' to love God freely, and not to set for oneself apart from Him any reward to be expected from Him. For there is nothing better than Him. Of what price can be anything that is sought from God by the heart in which God Himself is held cheap ? ' [2] The soul's love of God must be like that of a wife for her true husband, ' loving Him freely, not desiring to receive from Him that which may delight her, but setting Himself before her eyes, to delight in Him alone. . . . God loves me, God loves you. . . . He says to us, " Ask what you will ". . . . You will find nought more precious, nought better to ask for, than Himself who has made all things. Ask for the Maker Himself, and in Him and from Him you will possess all that He has made.' [3] Good works are the *breadth*, perseverance in them the *length ;* but the *height* is ' to think on God and to love Him, to love freely the God who is our Helper, who watches our contending, who crowns our victory, who bestows the prize—in fine, to count God Himself the prize, to expect nothing from Him but Himself. If you love, love freely : if you love in truth, let Him whom you love be your reward.' [4] The Psalmist does not ask God what He will give him for an inheritance. ' He says, " Be Thou Thyself my inheritance ! I love *Thee*, love Thee with all my being, love Thee with all my heart, all my soul, all my mind. What to me will be anything that Thou mightest give me, apart from Thyself ? " This is to love God freely, to hope from God for God, to haste to be filled with God, to be satisfied only with God Himself.' [5]

In these passages there is no explicit eschatological reference. The dominant thought is that the knowledge and love of God is religion's all-sufficient motive, and that the intrusion of any

[1] *Serm.* 2. 4.   [2] *Ib.* 91. 3.   [3] *En. in Ps.* XXXIV. i. 12.
[4] *Serm.* 165. 4.   [5] *Ib.* 334. 3.

245

other desire must corrupt it. In those that follow, the pilgrim note sounds clearer : the lover looks forward, the reward is to come. Yet we shall find no difference in the description of it. There is the same restraint, the same deliberate monotony of language, the same refusal of any attempt to explicate the *fruitio Dei* in categories of temporal experience.

' Pure love ' is nothing else but ' the longing for the vision of God '.[1] ' Nothing that God can promise is of any worth, apart from God Himself. God could by no means satisfy me, did He not promise me Himself. What is all the earth, the sea, the sky, the stars . . . the hosts of Angels ? For the Creator of them all I thirst, for Him I hunger, to Him I call—*With Thee is the well of life.*'[2] It is ' servile work ' only that violates the ' spiritual sabbath ' ; ' whatever a man does, if it is with intent to pursue an earthly advantage, his work is servile. . . . For God is to be loved freely, and the soul cannot rest save in that which it loves. But eternal rest is given to it only in the love of God, who alone is eternal.'[3] The morbid longings of a sick man are banished by the restoration of health ; so, when our souls attain their perfect health which is immortality, ' we shall feel need no longer, and therein will be our happiness. For we shall be filled, filled with our God, who Himself will be to us all that our longings make us count most desirable here.'[4] ' He who has given the promise, is Himself the end of our longing. He will give Himself, because He has given Himself. He will give His own immortal being to our immortality, because He gave Himself as mortal to our mortality.'[5]

Se ipsum dabit, quia se ipsum dedit. In those words Augustine concentrates all his eschatology of love. The God who is Love has given Himself to man in the sacrifice of Christ, and of that gift, itself a calling, He will not repent.[6] Divine Love is grafted in the body of death : eternity is even now at work in time, and we feel the tension of its working in the restlessness of our hearts. Faith is the recognition that love contains the promise of

[1] *Serm.* 178. 11.   [2] *Ib.* 158. 7.   [3] *Ib.* 33. 3.
[4] *Ib.* 255. 7.   [5] *En. in Ps.* XLII. 2.   [6] *Romans* xi. 29.

its own fulfilment, that God will not fail to ' crown His gifts '. For ' it is He whom we long to receive, who makes us ask ; He whom we desire to find, who makes us seek. . . . And when He has been received, He still works in us an asking and a seeking, that He may be received more abundantly.'[1] The text *Seek His face evermore* was one that Augustine loved to ponder. God always comes to meet the seeker, the search is continuously rewarding, though it but disclose the infinite perspective beyond our attainment.[2] Does the seeking belong to this life only, in which ' faith already finds Him, hope still seeks Him, and love finds Him through faith, yet seeks to possess Him through sight ' ? Augustine is not sure. It may be that even when we see Him as He is, He will yet be *sine fine quaerendus quia sine fine amandus :* if there be no end to love's increase, love's seeking, the deepening of its apprehension, may well be infinite.[3]

In this affirmation that God Himself is the reward of the love which He inspires, that love accepted is love gained, Augustine's conviction of the essential continuity binding this life to the life eternal has overcome far more completely than in his thought of sin and its punishment the legal concept of retribution. The reward of heaven is not compensation in another kind—happiness for virtue : the next world is not ' called in to redress the balance ' of this. The delight in righteousness is one with the joy of heaven, and God is sought ' for the sake of ' heaven's joy as little as righteousness on earth is sought ' for the sake of ' the *delectatio iustitiae*. There is no trace of religious hedonism in Augustine's reiteration of *Deus ipse praemium*. Nor can it be

---

[1] *En. in Ps.* cxviii. xiv. 2.

[2] *De Trin.* xv. 2 : cessandum non est, quamdiu in ipsa incomprehensibilium rerum inquisitione proficitur, et melior meliorque fit quaerens tam magnum bonum, quod et inveniendum quaeritur et quaerendum invenitur.

[3] *En. in Ps.* civ. 3 : ut non huic inquisitioni qua significatur amor, finem praestet inventio, sed amore crescente inquisitio crescat inventi. But compare *In Jo. Ev. Tr.* 63. 1 : satiat quaerentem in quantum capit ; et invenientem capaciorem facit, ut rursus quaerat impleri, ubi plus capere coeperit . . . donec ad illam vitam veniamus, ubi sic impleamur ut capaciores non efficiamur, quia ita perfecti erimus ut iam non proficiamus. Tunc enim ostendetur nobis quod sufficit nobis.

said that his hope of reward is selfish or individualistic, that his love of God is not God's love because it is not the love of man. At the end of his sermon on the 73rd Psalm—a sermon in which he 'forgot how long he had been speaking'—he comes to his beloved text *Mihi bonum est adhaerere Deo*. 'This is the whole good', he exclaims. 'Would you have more? If you would, I grieve for you. (*Vultis amplius? Doleo volentes.*) Brethren, what can you want more? When we see Him face to face, nothing can be better than to be joined fast to Him. But *now*, here in my pilgrimage, when the fulfilment is not yet, what is my good? *Ponere in Deo spem meam.* So long as you are not yet fast joined to Him, set there your hope. . . . Cleave to Him in hope. And here, setting your hope in God, what will you have to do? *Ut annuntiem omnes laudes tuas in atriis filiae Sion.* What will be your work, but to praise Him you love, and to make others share your love of Him?'[1] 'The reward for which true religion looks is in the fellowship of holy men and Angels, that God may be all in all.'[2] The peace of heaven is not the rest of the solitary soul. God will be 'a common vision, a common possession, a common peace'.[3] The gift, the love, the worship, will be shared.[4] And this means more than that in the heart of each and every citizen of the Heavenly City God will be enthroned. For 'the peace of the Heavenly City is the perfectly ordered, perfectly united fellowship in the fruition of God and of one another in God';[5] and this fruition of God and of one another in God is the supreme reward.[6] The separation of man from God, in this fallen world, has for its consequence the separation of men from one another. The burden of sin is loneliness, *nescire cor alterius*, the 'stern necessity' which compels each of us in our earthly pilgrimage to 'carry his own heart', which 'shuts the door of every heart to every other'.[7] So deeply did Augustine feel the misery of this mutual ignorance

[1] *En. in Ps.* LXXII. 34. [2] *De Civ.* XIV. *ad fin.*
[3] *En. in Ps.* LXXXIV. 10. [4] *De Civ.* XXII. 30.
[5] *Ib.* XIX. 13. [6] *De Doctr. Christ.* I. 35.
[7] *En.* 2 *in Ps.* XXX. i. 13. *En. in Ps.* LV. 9.

which divides us, that it could seem to him that 'most of the
evils of mankind have no other cause but false suspicions' : [1]
could we but *know* one another, we should be less tempted to
say to ourselves 'I alone am good'.[2] But in the City of God
'the peoples will acknowledge themselves' (*populi confitebuntur*),
because 'the hearts of all will be transparent, manifest, luminous
in the perfection of love' : the Holy City will at last know herself throughout and entirely, no part hidden from the whole.[3]
For God's light will shine upon the hidden things of darkness,
and in that light each to each will be *quanto notior, tanto utique
carior*—the better known, the better beloved.[4]

That is the 'fruition of one another in God'. But the final
word of the *De Civitate*, the keynote of all the lyric hymns of
the life to come which so often turn Augustine's preaching into
music, is not fruition. It is not rest, nor vision, nor even love,
but praise. *Vacabimus, et videbimus; videbimus, et amabimus;
amabimus, et laudabimus.*[5] The blessedness of the dwellers in
God's House is to be alway praising Him ; and even in this the
continuity which we have marked is not broken. For the
praise of God was the Christian's work in this world, the work
through which he was to win his fellows to God's love. The
praise of God is man's highest work ; if all his works are not the
praise of God, they draw him down to the love of himself.[6]
All good life is praise : the voice of praise is never silent but
when we fall from righteousness. And this work of praise is
our schooling for the perfect praise of the Heavenly City.[7] The

---

[1] *Serm.* 306. 8. [2] *Ib.* 249. 2. [3] *En. in Ps.* XLIV. 33.
[4] *Ep.* 92. 1 f. Cf. *Encheirid.* 32. We may compare Plotinus, *Enn.* v.
viii. 4 : ἐκεῖ . . . ὁρῶσι τὰ πάντα . . . καὶ ἑαυτοὺς ἐν ἄλλοις · διαφανῆ γὰρ
πάντα καὶ σκοτεινὸν οὐδὲ ἀντίτυπον οὐδέν, ἀλλὰ πᾶς παντὶ φανερὸς εἰς τὸ
εἴσω καὶ πάντα · φῶς γὰρ φωτί.
[5] *De Civ.* XXII. *ad fin.* [6] *En. in Ps.* XLIV. 9.
[7] *Ib.* CXLVIII. 2 : Tunc desinis laudare Deum, quando a iustitia et ab eo
quod illi placet, declinas . . . cum laudatis Deum, toti laudate : cantet vox,
cantet vita, cantent facta. *Ib.* CXLVI. 2 : Laudas cum agis negotium, laudas
cum cibum et potum capis, laudas cum in lecto requiescis (Augustine has gone
out of his way to say that the Christian marriage-bed glorifies God), laudas cum
dormis ; quando non laudas ? Perficitur in nobis laudatio Dei, cum ad illam

life of love may be founded in those fleeting glimpses of the eternal, those ' beginnings of contemplation ' which are possible for us here through faith. But when that which is perfect is come, our ' whole business ' (*totum nostrum negotium*) will be the praise of God.[1] *Tota actio nostra, Amen et Alleluia erit.* ' Because our vision of the True will be without satiety, in perpetual delight, because our contemplation will have the perfect assurance of immediacy,—kindled, then, by the love of Very Truth, cleaving to Him in the pure embrace of spirit, our spirit's voice will praise Him and say Alleluia. Uplifting one another to the same praise, in most fervent love to one another and to God, all the citizens of that City will say Alleluia, inasmuch as they will say Amen.'[2]

Patiently Augustine strives to meet the natural apprehension of wearisome futility which he knew that all such pictures of the worship of eternity are apt to arouse. It is only, he repeats, because we lack love, that we can fear lest praise should make us weary ; it is only because in our imagination we transfer ourselves as we are to the choir of heaven, that such activity can seem to us empty and unreal. ' When we see Him as He is, we shall be like Him ; and being like Him, how should we fail, by what should be distracted ? Let us rest assured, my brethren. We shall not be wearied by the praise of God, nor by His love. If your love should fail, so would your praise ; but if love will be everlasting, because the Beauty of God will be uncloying, inexhaustible, fear not that you will lack power ever to praise Him, whom you will have power ever to love.'[3]

If now we turn again to those antitheses of the Here and the Hereafter in which Augustine framed his ideal of human happi-

---

civitatem venerimus, etc. Cf. *Serm.* 33 and 34, on the ' New Song ' : 34. 6 : Laus ipsius estis, si bene vivatis.

[1] Typical passages are *En. in Ps.* LXXXIII. 8 ; LXXXV. 24 ; LXXXVI. 9. *Serm.* 243. 8 ; 252. 9 ; 255. 1.

[2] *Serm.* 362. 29.   [3] *En. in Ps.* LXXXIII. 8.

ness, *beata vita,* we can better understand why he found the category of reward still appropriate to the relations of eternity and
time. The Christian warfare looks forward to the peace which
is to be won ; the labour of love to which our neighbour's need
compels us looks forward to the ' rest of God ', the rest which
is not idleness but a ' tranquil activity ',[1] the contemplation in
which all love's needs are met and transcended ; the faith through
which we accept God's promise in Christ looks forward to the
sight, the presently apprehended reality, in which that promise
will be fulfilled. Warfare, toil, and faith, are for the sake of
God, the means which we have to use to reach the end of fruition.
But though as means they are relative, significant only in view
of the end, they are not as means indifferent, they are not ' means
and nothing more '. They are more than the vehicles of our
pilgrimage, they are the pilgrim's journeying itself, in which at
every moment our salvation is nearer than when we believed.
Even in this life, though there is always work before us, our
reward is truly with us.

Augustine often marks the double sense of the word ' end ' :
it can mean ' either the ceasing to be of what was, or the perfecting of what was begun ', either *consumi* or *consummari*. Christ
is the ' end of the law ', but as *finis non consumens sed perficiens :
non qui consumat sed qui consummet.*[2] And in this sense the life
eternal is this life's end : in the vision of God our love is not
consumed but made perfect.[3] If eternal life is the ' reward that
makes perfect '—*merces perficiens*—that is to say that in it alone
all the strivings of our imperfect existence can be stilled. It is
at the same time to remind each one of us that *for him* the fulfilment is not inevitable ; but *Deus ipse praemium,* understood as
Augustine meant it to be understood, does not encourage but
forbid self-centredness. For God will not reward our service by

---

[1] *Ep.* 55. 17 : in illa requie non desidiosa segnitia sed quaedam ineffabilis
tranquillitas actionis otiosae.

[2] *En. 2 in Ps.* XXX. i. 1 ; LVI. 2. *In Ep. Jo. Tr.* 10. 5.

[3] *Serm.* 53. 6 : hic est finis amoris nostri—finis quo perficiamur, non quo
consumamur.

becoming the servant of our desires. God will be eternally *Himself*, eternally to be worshipped, the King and not the Kingdom. The ' possession ' of God is the knowledge of Him and the love of Him as He is, not as we in our sinfulness might wish Him to be. *Ipsi gloria in saecula saeculorum.*

IX

Pure Love

O Deus, ego amo Te !
Nec amo Te, ut salves me,
Aut quia non amantes Te
    Aeterno punis igne.
Tu, tu, mi Iesu, totum me
    Amplexus es in cruce ;
Tulisti clavos, lanceam,
Multamque ignominiam,
    Innumeros dolores,
    Sudores, et angores,
Ac mortem, et haec propter me,
    Ac pro me peccatore.
Cur igitur non amem te ?—
O Iesu amantissime !—
Non ut in caelo salves me,
Aut ne in aeternum damnes me,
Sed sicut Tu amasti me—
Sic amo, et amabo Te :
Solum quia Rex meus es,
Et solum quia Deus es.
                          Amen.

                    St. Francis Xavier.

IX

'THE chief end of man is to glorify God and enjoy Him for ever.' We have seen that the religion of Augustine ends in the subordination of all else to the glory of God. Man is made for worship. But the starting-point was the question posed by a pagan ethic, namely, What is the Good *for man*? How shall *I* win happiness? 'The Christian command of love gives the final answer to ancient philosophy's enquiry for the *Summum Bonum*. That the Christian idea of love comes off the loser, is a simple consequence of the fact that the ancient view of life has put the question.'[1] So Nygren summarises and comments upon the Augustinian 'synthesis'; and it is evident enough that Augustine's method of approach was determined by the form of the question he had set himself to answer. 'When I seek Thee, my God, I seek for happiness.'[2] The happiness of man is in the fruition of God. It was not easy, on such principles, to save either ethics from egocentrism or religion from anthropocentrism. He accepted from Cyprian without question the selfish motive for Christian works of mercy; and from the same authority he took his interpretation of the first three petitions of the Lord's Prayer. When we pray that God's Name be hallowed, His Kingdom come, His will be done, we are praying 'for ourselves and not for God'—'that it may be well with us'.[3] Karl Holl condemned Augustine as a 'corrupter of Christian morality': do not his Sermons on the Lord's Prayer contain something like a corruption of the Christian religion?

Holl's judgment is directed against the doctrine of 'right self-love', a self-love which is identified with the love of God. As we have seen, the 'false self-love' which is the spirit of the Earthly City is not so much egoism as atheism: it is *amor sui*

[1] Nygren, *Eros und Agape II*, p. 315.
[2] *Conf.* x. 29.   [3] *Serm.* 56-59.

usque ad contemptum Dei, the self-centredness which is end as
well as beginning, the pride which puts self in the place of God.
For Augustine the question of 'disinterestedness' never arose
at all. Pure love, *castus amor,* is the desire of God only, but it
is the desire of God. God is *gratis amandus,* but He is *ipse nobis
præmium.*

But for the whole history of the mediaeval doctrine of
Christian love, the question of disinterestedness is nothing less than
central. In this matter, Luther, the Quietists, and Fénélon were
not innovators : they were dealing with a problem as familiar to
the scholastics as to the mystics of the middle ages. Neither
schoolmen nor mystics were satisfied with the doctrine of *caritas*
which they had inherited ; and it is interesting to note that their
dissatisfaction was not caused merely by a sense of the inadequacy
of Augustine's 'synthesis' of pagan and Christian motives, of
Eros and Agape. The disturbing factor was Philia, and the
problem was the relation of Philia to Caritas. Aristotle's *Ethics*
were not re-discovered till the thirteenth century, but Cicero
had never been lost, and in his *De Amicitia* there was the strongest
possible assertion of the essentially disinterested character of the
love of friends. True friendship, says Laelius, must be sought
not in hope of reward or of any advantage accruing from it,
but because ' the whole fruit of it is contained in love itself ' ; [1]
and the true ground of that love is the 'likeness in virtue' [2]
which enables the friend to see his friend 'as another self' [3] and
which leads to the union of pure minds, to a mingling of soul
with soul, so that out of two they are as it were made one. [4]

Augustine of course knew his *De Amicitia,* and these leading
thoughts of Cicero's treatise were familiar to him. [5] But a love
that is grounded on 'likeness in virtue' could for him have no
place in the relations of man and God ; and in fact he scarcely

[1] *De Amicit.* 9.   [2] *Ib.* 14.   [3] *Ib.* 21.

[4] *Ib.* : cuius animum ita cum suo commisceat, ut efficiat paene unum ex
duobus.

[5] *Conf.* IV. II. : ille alter eram . . . sensi animam meam et animam illius
unam fuisse animam in duobus corporibus. *Ep.* 155. I : inde manat vera
amicitia, non pensanda temporalibus commodis sed gratuito amore potanda.

ever speaks of a ' friendship ' with God.[1] In the twelfth century
the Ciceronian influence is traceable not only (where we should
expect it) in the ' enfant terrible ' of the Schools, Abélard, but
in the mystical theology of the Cistercians. Abélard is the first
of the mediaevals to claim that men should love God as a friend
loves a friend : that Christ's example requires us to love God
not because He is ' Himself our reward ', not even ' because He
first loved us ', but for His absolute goodness, ' whatever He
may do with us '. The love of God must be *amor amicitiae* and
nothing else : all *amor concupiscentiae,* all desire for possession and
for possession's joys, must be excluded.[2]

Abélard's argument was at once challenged by Hugo of St.
Victor, who maintained (like Augustine according to Nygren) that
all love desires good, that we cannot desire any good for God
in whom all good is present, and that to invite us to love God
yet not to seek the ' possession ' of Him is to say that we may
love without ' caring '.[3] But Abélard's implied assumption, that
the love of God can be understood in terms of the love of man,
that the standard of judgement valid for the relations between
man and man must hold all along the line of the relations between
man and God, had already been disallowed by the Cistercian
William of St. Thierry : love of God is union with God and

---

[1] Once in the early *De Gen. c. Manich.* I. 4 ; and cf. p. 170, n. 4.

[2] *Expos. in Ep. Pauli ad Rom.* III. (Migne, *P.L.* CLXXVIII, c. 892) : Si Deum
quia me diligit diligam, et non potius quia quicquid mihi faciat talis ipse est
qui super omnia diligendus est, dicitur in me illa Veritatis sententia : *Si enim eos
diligitis qui vos diligunt, quam mercedem habebitis ?*—Abélard goes on to urge
the real disinterestedness of a father's love for an undutiful son, of the love of
a ' chaste wife ' for the husband who makes her suffer. Professor Gilson has
shrewdly observed that Héloïse as much as Cicero was Abélard's teacher here.
' Concupiscentia te mihi ', she had written to him, ' potius quam amicitia
sociavit, libidinis ardor potius quam amor.'—' Elle vient de lui faire comprendre quelque chose. Voulez-vous aimer Dieu ? nous dit-il : ne l'aimez pas
comme j'aimais Héloïse, mais comme Héloïse m'a aimé' (*Theologie Mystique
de St. Bernard,* pp. 186 ff.).

[3] *De Sacramentis* II, Pars xiii. 8 (Migne, *P.L.* CLXXVI, c. 534). It is not
certain that the *De Sacramentis* is later than Abélard's commentary on the
Epistle to the Romans ; but Hugo is certainly replying to some one who had
argued like Abélard (' dicunt hoc stulti quidam ').

cannot but bring blessedness with it.[1] And Bernard himself, though he does not directly impugn Abélard on this score, develops from the Ciceronian account of pure friendship a very different doctrine of love.

1. *St. Bernard*

The *De Diligendo Deo* begins, indeed, with a short answer to the questions, Why and How is God to be loved ? ' The cause for loving God is God : the measure of it is to love Him without measure.' That, says Bernard, is *sat dictum sapienti;* but he will descend to the level of the *insipientes,* the ' slow of understanding ', and in what follows the love of God ' for His own sake ' is shown, in the Augustinian manner, to be grounded first upon God's ' deserving ' (*merito suo*), and secondly upon our ' advantage ' (*commodo nostro*). God ' deserves ' to be loved for His manifold goodness to us in creation and redemption ; and the love of Him brings its reward. And at this point Bernard suddenly shows his hand. ' The love of God ', he writes, ' is not unrewarded, though it must be without regard to the reward. True charity cannot be void of good (*vacua*), yet she is no hireling, for she seeketh not her own. Charity is an affection, not a contract, neither gained nor gaining on terms of a bargain. It takes the heart freely and makes it free (*sponte afficit et spontaneum facit*). True love is satisfied by itself : it has a reward, but its reward is that which is loved . . . it seeks not, yet merits, reward.' [2] Is Bernard conscious here that he is going beyond Augustine ? One cannot be quite sure. The Augustinian *habet praemium, sed id quod amatur* is only equivalent to *Verus amor se ipso contentus est* if *id quod amatur* is equivalent to *amor ipse.* But in the 83rd Sermon on the Song of Songs, no doubt is possible. ' The soul that loves, loves, and *knows naught else.* . . .

---

[1] *De Contemplando Deo,* VIII. (Migne, *P.L.* CLXXXIV, c. 375) : Quid autem est absurdius uniri Deo amore et non beatitudine ?—For the approximate dates of the relevant works of Abélard, William, and St. Bernard, see Gilson, *op. cit.* pp. 15 f.

[2] *De Dilig. Deo,* VII. (Migne, *P.L.* CLXXXII, c. 984).

Love suffices of itself, pleases of itself and because of itself. Love is its own merit, its own reward. Apart from itself it needs neither cause nor fruit. Its fruit is its exercise. I love because I love, I love that I may love.'[1] In other words, the fruition of God cannot be distinguished from the love of Him ; for love has ceased to be a desire that seeks satisfaction, and become a passionate ardour that excludes everything which is not itself.

Charity seeketh not her own is Bernard's favourite text. Abélard argued from it to the necessity of creation : God's love must have an object ' outside ' the divine Being. God must ' go out of Himself' to the creature.[2] For Bernard too the ' undefiled ' law is the law of love which' keeps for itself nothing of its own '; but he finds this same law at the heart of God's Being in the love which is the bond of the Tri-Une life.[3] Charity does not *seek* ' her own ', because she already possesses it : *non quaerit quae sunt sua, profecto quia non desunt.*[4]

It is only because man is fallen that the love which naturally should serve nature's Author, begins as self-love with the service of the body's needs ; yet because it is made for God it cannot rest in the finite, and thrusts the soul upon an unending pursuit of worldly pleasures that can never satiate its longing. The first check upon self-love is that natural sympathy with the needs and sufferings of others which teaches us to love our neighbour ; and in common experience we discover our need of God's help and protection, and so learn, without ceasing to love ourselves, to love God also, first for His benefits and at length ' for His own sake ', because we have tasted and seen that the Lord is good.[5] But there is a higher stage to reach, in which nothing will be loved but for God's sake ; and that is the *excessus*, the

---

[1] *In Cant. Serm.* LXXXIII. 3, 4 (Migne, *P.L.* CLXXXIII, cc. 1182 f.) : with ' fructus eius, usus eius ', compare Cicero's ' omnis eius fructus in ipso amore inest '.

[2] *Theol. Christ. lib.* IV. (Migne, *P.L.* CLXXVIII, cc. 1299 f.).

[3] *De Dilig. Deo,* XII. (Migne, *P.L.* CLXXXII, c. 996).

[4] *In Cant. Serm.* XVIII. 3 (Migne, *P.L.* CLXXXIII, c. 860).

[5] *De Dilig. Deo,* VII.-IX. (Migne, *P.L.* CLXXXII, cc. 985-990).

rapture in which the soul, 'forgetting itself, as a broken vessel, passes wholly to God (*totus pergat in Deum*), and cleaving unto God is made one spirit with Him'. It is the experience of this ecstasy, rather than its essential significance, that Bernard describes as 'losing oneself', 'being unconscious of self', 'emptied of self', 'as it were brought to nothing' (*paene adnullari*). In this life it comes only to a few, and to them as a rare and transient moment of exaltation. But the perfection of charity is man's final destiny. 'Because the Scripture says that God has made all things for Himself, the thing made will assuredly one day be brought into conformity and accord with its Maker. One day we must cross over into that same affection of will : even as God willed all things to be for Himself, so we must will that neither ourselves nor aught else have been or be save equally for God— that is, for His will alone, not for our pleasure. We shall know delight indeed, but not so much because our need is stilled, our happiness won, as that His will shall be seen accomplished in us and upon us.'[1]

In this account of the 'heavenly ecstasy' there is no word to suggest the loss of conscious personality. It is a definition of Pure Love to which Fénélon himself will be able to add nothing. But it is a pure love in which self remains entire, in which the love of self indeed is consummated, because the self is loved *propter Deum*, as God loves it. In the complete adherence of the human will to the divine, there survives no taint of the *proprium*, of that which isolates and separates ; and in that sense Bernard can say : *sic affici, deificari est*. But he shows what he means by the similes he employs, especially the beautiful comparison of the air which in the sunbeam *seems* 'not so much illumined as light itself'. He says expressly that the 'substance' of the created soul 'will remain, only in another form, another glory, another potency'.[2]

The key to the understanding of Bernard's reconciliation of self-love with the pure love of God is to be found, as Gilson has

[1] *De Dilig. Deo*, x. (Migne, *P.L.* CLXXXII, cc. 990 f.).
[2] *Ib.*

shown clearly, in his doctrine of the divine similitude.[1] The soul's essential nature, as Augustine taught, is to be an image of God. The fall of man was the obscuring of the divine image by a dissimilitude, an ' unlikeness' superimposed upon it. But the image itself is indestructible : every man retains his ' capacity for the eternal '. Through the knowledge of Christ, the Word, the perfect Image, he learns to know himself in humility as an image disfigured ; through the Holy Spirit, his love is weaned from self in charity and compassion.[2] The so-called ' annihilation' of self is the doing-away of the unlikeness ; and since the image of God in becoming unlike God became unlike itself, the love which restores the divine similitude restores the soul to itself. In that restored likeness we shall know even as we are known, love as we are loved ; for the likeness of God, the love of God, the vision of God, are all one. *Caritas illa visio, illa similitudo est.*[3]

Love is the divine likeness, because in no way but by love can man respond to God with an affection *of the same kind.* God's sovereignty calls forth our obedience, His wrath our fear, His judgement our adoration ; but ' when God loves, He wills naught else but to be loved : His love has no other purpose but to be returned, for He knows that those who have loved Him are made blest by that love itself'.[4] And God's own love—this is Bernard's final word, the truth that Augustine had seen and that Pascal re-discovered—is always and everywhere prevenient. In the restoration of the divine likeness we can never claim that love in us is a ' work' of our own : the love whereby we are ' made righteous ' is a *righteousness of God;* for its very existence is effect and evidence of God's love for us. ' When I love, I can no more doubt that I am loved than that I love.' [5] *Ipse fecit ut desideres.*[6] Eros itself is the creation of Agape. We could

---

[1] See esp. *In Cant. Serm.* LXXX-LXXXIII. And Gilson, *op. cit.* pp. 139 f., 150 ff. ; *Spirit of Mediaeval Philosophy,* c. XIV.

[2] *De Grad. Humil.* VII. (Migne, *P.L.* CLXXXII, c. 953).

[3] *In Cant. Serm.* LXXXII. 8 (Migne, *P.L.* CLXXXIII, c. 1181).

[4] *Ib.* LXXXIII. 4 (*ib.* c. 1183).   [5] *Ib.* LXXXIV. 6 (*ib.* c. 1187).

[6] *De Dilig. Deo,* VII. (Migne, *P.L.* CLXXXII, c. 987). The words are Augustine's : Morin, *Sermones post Maurinos reperti,* Wilmart xi. 9.

not seek Him were He not already seeking us. The miracle
of the divine love is its penetration of the sinful heart. ' Who
can but stand amazed ', cries Bernard, ' before the love of a God
contemned and yet recalling ? '[1]

Magna res amor. But the secret of love's greatness, of its
power for good, lies as Bernard insists in its ' having recourse to
its beginning, returning to its origin, flowing back to its source
and continually renewing thence its never-ceasing stream '.[2]
There is the difference between Cistercian mysticism and the
' one-way ' theory of love. Bernard knew as well as Augustine
that the love that does not flow out, like God's, into the parched
and thirsting world of men, is no true love. But he would never
believe that God has made us to be mere ' channels ' of His love.
The metaphor is his own. The Church, he says, has too many
' pipes ', too few ' cisterns '. The cistern flows over because it is
full, even as God's love for men is the overflow of that Fountain
of life that has filled heaven from all eternity.[3]

St. Bernard is perhaps the most conspicuous example of the
mystic's power to combine the contemplative life with a manifold
and absorbing practical activity. That he felt the tension between
' religion ' and the world, between the ' Paradise of the cloister '
and the stress and struggle of secular affairs which *caritas fraterna*
imposed upon him, is not surprising. But it is a mistake to
interpret this tension as a ' competition ' between love of the
brethren and love of God. It is the voice of the Beloved that
says *Arise and hasten*—that is, to work for the good of souls : it
is the sign of contemplation's truth and purity that the spirit
which has been enkindled by the divine flame be filled ever and
again with zeal to win for God others to love Him in like manner.[4]
The spiritual marriage cannot be barren, and the *breasts* from
which the Bride nourishes the children whom she brings forth
are *better*, that is, more necessary, than the *wine* of contemplation.[5]

All this is in substance Augustinian doctrine ; but the form

[1] *In Cant. Serm.* LXXXII. 8 (Migne, *P.L.* CLXXXIII, c. 1181).
[2] *Ib.* LXXXIII. 4 (*ib.* c. 1183).   [3] *Ib.* XVIII. 3 (*ib.* c. 860).
[4] *Ib.* LVII. 9 (*ib.* c. 1054).   [5] *Ib.* IX. 8 (*ib.* c. 818).

is new. It is usual to find Bernard's most original contribution to Christian piety in the warmth of his personal devotion to the Incarnate Christ ; and it may be true that this, which he himself was rather inclined to depreciate as a ' carnal love ', a necessary but inferior stage in the school of charity, was the real nutriment and strength of his love for God. But the nuptial mysticism which he drew from the Song of Songs must be recognised as a synthesis of Eros and Philia whose influence upon mediaeval Christian thought was scarcely less important than that of Augustine's synthesis of Eros and Agape. For it broke through the traditional *reverentia*, the over-emphasis of the divine ' self-sufficiency ', which stood in the way of recognition and acceptance of a real mutuality in love between God and man. The Bridegroom *delights* in the Bride, as she in Him. And though the peculiar tension of which we have spoken led Bernard to think that the perfect union of spirit between lover and beloved can be looked for only in the life to come, and on earth at most anticipated, *raro raptimque,* in the mystic *excessus*, it is certain that he meant to encourage not only his monks at Clairvaux but any and every faithful Catholic (*quivis in Ecclesia constitutus*) to apply to himself and seek to realise in his own person the words of the Bride, the Church his mother—*Dilectus meus mihi, et ego illi.*[1]

2. St. Thomas Aquinas

We have seen that Bernard's mysticism depends upon the faith that man is made in the image of God. The same faith rules the thought of the great system-makers of the thirteenth century ; and to link the mystic of Clairvaux with the Angel of the Schools, we cannot do better than quote a passage from St. Thomas's *Summa contra Gentiles.*

' An effect (or thing caused) must move towards its end in the manner in which its agent (or cause) acts for the end. Now God, who is the Prime Agent of all things, does not act as acquiring anything by His action, but as by His action bestowing

---

[1] *In Cant. Serm.* LXVIII. 4 (Migne, *P.L.* CLXXXIII, c. 1110).

something (*aliquid largiens*) ; since He is not in potency, so as to be able to acquire, but in perfect act out of which He can bestow. The ordering of things towards God is therefore not to an end *for* which something is to be acquired, but in order that they may in the manner possible for them attain God Himself at His own hands ; seeing that He Himself is their end. In that created things acquire the divine goodness, they become like God. If therefore all things move towards God as to their last end, in order that they may attain His goodness, it follows that the last end of things is to be made like unto God. . . . All things created are as it were images of the Prime Agent, God. For the action of an agent is like himself : [1] the perfection of an image is to represent its exemplar through likeness to it. . . . All things therefore exist for the attaining of the divine likeness as their last end.' [2]

The theology of St. Thomas is the Platonist theology of Augustine, shaped into a closer philosophical consistency by the use of two or three fundamental principles derived from Aristotle, and resting ultimately upon the Hebrew-Christian doctrine of creation, accepted and thought through with a more radical completeness than ever before.[3] Creation means the absolute dependence of creaturely existence upon the divine Agape, and this absolute dependence constitutes an irreducible *unlikeness* between creature and Creator. On the other hand, creation, as the production of a real effect by a real cause, of beings by Being, means that creature must be *like* Creator : *omne agens agit sibi simile.* In willing Himself, God wills other things. What we love for its own sake, we desire to see multiplied as far as possible ; and God's Being can be ' multiplied ' only so far as many things share in His likeness.[4] And it is the dignity, at once splendid and

---

[1] Omne agens agit sibi simile—one of Thomas's most constant formulæ, which comes not from Aristotle but from Plotinus : *Enn.* IV. iii. 10 : κοινὸν τοῦτο παντὶ τῷ ὄντι εἰς ὁμοίωσιν ἑαυτῷ ἄγειν.

[2] *C.G.* III. 18 f.

[3] See A. E. Taylor, *Philosophical Studies*, pp. 238 ff. ; and E. Gilson, *Spirit of Mediaeval Philosophy*, cc. III. and IV.

[4] *C.G.* I. 75. *S.T.* I. q. 19, a. 2.

tragical, of that image of God which is the human soul, to resemble its Maker so far as to be itself a *cause* and not an effect merely—to be a free agent and not a mechanical instrument. Thus, beside the absolute dependence upon God which man shares with the whole created world, Thomas insists—and his highest distinction in the history of Christian thought is to have so insisted—upon man's relative yet real independence. In the tendency of Augustinianism to ' detract from the perfection of the creature,' he sees a danger of ' detracting from the perfection of the divine power '.[1] In Gilson's words, ' with St. Thomas, the divine likeness sinks for the first time into the heart of nature ' : as a created cause, man is summoned ' to exert a finite participation in the infinite fecundity of the creative act '.[2] ' Nothing is nearer to divinity ', said the Areopagite, ' than to be made a fellow-worker with God.'[3] But to imitate the divine causality is to imitate the divine self-giving. ' There is truth in the saying ', writes Thomas, again quoting Pseudo-Denys, ' that good is diffusive of itself in so far as it is good : the better anything is, the wider will be the compass to which the diffusion of its goodness will extend. God, who is most perfect in goodness, and diffuses His goodness most universally, is therein the exemplar of all other beings that diffuse goodness.'[4]

Agape, then, is unquestionably for St. Thomas the principle not only of God's creative activity, but of the divine likeness in man. But in his psychology of love as a natural passion, Aristotelian assumptions are dominant to such an extent that the problem of egoism, unfelt by Augustine, becomes for Thomas extremely acute. The most important of these assumptions are the metaphysical theory of matter and form, potency and act, and the ethical theory that all love is based upon self-love,[5] that a friend is ' another self '.

Natural love is a *passion*, because the appetitive ' power ' of

---

[1] *C.G.* III. 69.   [2] Gilson, *op. cit.* pp. 141, 131.
[3] *C.G.* III. 21 : a citation of Ps.-Denys.   [4] *Ib.* 24.
[5] Aristotle, *Eth. Nic.* IX. 4 (in the mediaeval version) : amicabilia quae sunt ad alterum venerunt ex amicabilibus quae sunt ad seipsum.

the soul, to which it belongs, is as matter to a form acting thereon. When the ' appetite ' is ' informed ' by the good appropriate to it, the act resulting is a ' complacency ' or feeling of pleasure in the good so presented. This complacency is what Thomas understands by love in the strict sense ; [1] and when he says that love is ' nothing else than a kind of transformation of the affection into the thing loved ',[2] we can recognise in a new dress Augustine's doctrine that we become like that which we love.[3] But the complacency in which my love consists is satisfaction in an object as *my own good*. The good which all things seeks is their own perfection.[4] Only that form of good to which I am potentially adapted can actualise my complacency : the good for each thing is what is ' akin and proportionate to it '.[5] This ' likeness ', ' connaturalness ', or correspondence of natures, is the necessary pre-supposition or postulate of that union between *amans* and *amatum*, lover and beloved, which love itself formally involves, as the affective counterpart of the union of matter with appropriate form.

The affective union of love does not of itself or necessarily imply any ' movement ' of desire, any conative or volitional activity, though it naturally leads to such. But Thomas has to make place in his psychological scheme for Aristotle's definition of the act of love (τὸ φιλεῖν) in terms of benevolence—the willing of a person's good for his own sake.[6] He can understand God's own love in no other way : if God loves His creatures, He wills their good for their sake, although, unlike our human love which is effect not cause of the goodness in its object, the divine love is creative—*infundens et creans bonitatem in rebus*.[7] Benevolence, wishing some one well, has a double object—the good which is willed, and the person, whether self or another, for whom it is willed ; and Thomas distinguishes these two directions

---

[1] *S.T.* I^a II^{ae}. q. 26, a. 2. [2] *In Sent.* III. 27. I. I.
[3] *De Div. Quaest. LXXXIII.* 35 : id quod amatur, afficiat ex se amantem necesse est.
[4] *S.T.* I. q. 5, a. 1. [5] *S.T.* I^a II^{ae}. q. 27, a. 1.
[6] *Rhet.* II. 4. *Eth. Nic.* VIII. 2. 4. Cf. *S.T.* I^a II^{ae}. q. 26, a. 4.
[7] *S.T.* I. q. 20, a. 1, 2 ; *C.G.* I. 91.

of benevolence by the not very happy pair of terms which he had inherited from his predecessors : *amor concupiscentiae* and *amor amicitiae*. Since the good desired is desired for the sake of the recipient, *amor concupiscentiae* must be regarded as secondary to *amor amicitiae*. It is the latter only which is love *simpliciter*, in which the object is loved ' for itself' and not ' for the sake of anything else '.[1] By means of this analysis Thomas is enabled to connect with the purely affective condition of complacency which is his own strict definition of love, the benevolence which is properly a consequence of it. And he proceeds to observe [2] that the ' likeness ' upon which *amor amicitiae* is founded must be an actual likeness ; if it indicated a quality actual in the loved object but in the lover potential only, the resulting love would be *amor concupiscentiae*.

Here, then, we encounter just that feature in the Aristotelian account of Philia which seems most incompatible with the character of Agape in the Christian sense—the love which is so little dependent upon likeness as to show its nature most fully in forgiveness. St. Thomas, however, has chosen to follow Aristotle ; and since grace is the perfection and not the destruction of nature, we are prepared to find this same basic principle of an actual likeness as the postulate of love, in his doctrine of the Theological Virtue of Charity. Charity is a friendship between man and God ; and all friendship is founded *super aliqua communicatione*, upon the fact that something is possessed in common. Κοινὰ τὰ τῶν φιλῶν. That we are ' called into the fellowship of the Son of God ' means, says Thomas, that God gives us a *share* in His own beatitude ; and it is this communion established between God and man that is the ground of the mutual benevolence, the friendship, which is charity.[3] The divine beatitude is simply the life of God in its affective aspect : God *is* His beatitude.[4] That man should share in the very life of God is something that exceeds all his natural powers. Such communion must be a *donum gratuitum*, belonging to the sphere not of Nature

[1] *S.T.* I^a II^ae. q. 26, a. 4. [2] *Ib.* q. 27, a. 3.
[3] *Ib.* q. 65, a. 5 ; II^a II^ae. q. 23, a. 1. [4] *C.G.* I. 101.

267

but of Grace ; and that is why the love which is founded upon it must itself be an activity of ' super-nature ', of the New Man, the higher potency to which humanity has been raised 'in Christ'. *The love of God is spread abroad in our hearts through the Holy Spirit which is given to us.*[1] Thomas will not disallow Augustine's ' Platonist mode of speaking ' : he agrees that charity is ' a kind of participation of the divine love ' ; but he will not follow the Master of the Sentences in his inference that as the *immediate* working of the Holy Spirit charity is itself ' not a human love at all ', but ' something uncreated in the soul ' : if it is not an activity of the free human will, it is nothing.[2] It is an ' infused ' and not a ' natural ' activity, only in the sense that its operation is proof that nature has been transformed by grace.

Thomas exposed himself to misunderstanding by his frequent statement that the specific character of charity is to be seen in its relation to the divine Good *in quantum est beatitudinis obiectum.*[3] Nothing is further from his intention than to equate charity with the desire of beatitude. On the contrary, charity is the most excellent of the Theological Virtues just because, while Faith and Hope look to God as the source whence come knowledge of the truth and acquisition of good, Charity attains to God Himself ' in order to rest in Him, and not that something may accrue to us from Him '.[4] Both faith and hope connote a certain ' distance ' separating them from their object : faith is of truth not seen, hope of good not possessed ; charity implies a union with the same good, already won. *Amor caritatis est de eo quod iam habetur.*[5] And this union is more than the *unio affectus,* without which, as we have already seen, no love can exist. It is a real presence. Among the effects of natural love, Thomas ranks first the desire for the presence of the beloved, and second, the mutual indwelling by which lover and beloved are in one another's hearts and minds.[6] So, through the gift of grace, the omnipresent God makes the

[1] *S.T.* II^a II^{ae}. q. 24, a. 2.   [2] *Ib.* q. 23, a. 2.

[3] *S.T.* I. q. 60, a. 5 ; I^a II^{ae}. q. 109, a. 3 ; II^a II^{ae}. q. 23, a. 4 ; q. 26, a. 1, 2, etc.

[4] *S.T.* II^a II^{ae}. q. 23, a. 6.   [5] *S.T.* I^a II^{ae}. q. 66, a. 6.

[6] *Ib.* q. 28, a. 1, 2.

soul His temple ' in a new way '. The Holy Spirit is *given* to ' abide in us ', ' as the known in the knower, the beloved in the lover '.[1] God, dwelling in us, vouchsafes to be possessed and enjoyed as a *persona convivens, a* familiar friend.[2] That is what Thomas means when he says that charity even in this present life (*caritas viae*) is *immediately* united to God, and only through the mediation of that union passes to the world of men.[3] And here, evidently, he is at one both with Bernard and with Augustine. *Caritas non quaerit quae sunt sua—profecto quia non desunt.* Through charity, *tota nos inhabitat Trinitas.*

St. Thomas's doctrine of love, both natural and supernatural, is governed by the idea of unity. From Pseudo-Denys he took the maxim that love is a ' unitive power ', and reconciled it with the egoism of the Aristotelian theory that self-love is the ' form and root of friendship ', by the argument that the unity of the individual must be the principle of union—the less complete unity realisable between one individual and another.[4] The same argument reappears when Thomas is defending his most flagrantly un-Christian thesis : ' that a man should love himself in charity more than his neighbour '. ' Because unity ranks before union, a man's own share in the divine good must rank higher as a motive of love than the association of another with him in that sharing.'[5] The true line of Thomas's thought points rather to union as the higher unity, to escape from the ' illusion of the closed individual ' in a widening of the boundaries of the self ; and we may doubt whether he would have committed himself to an argument as fallacious as it is revolting to Christian conscience, if he had not allowed the crude individualism of Aristotle to impair his own deeper intuition of the Agape which takes a man, even as it has taken God, ' out of himself '.

But to the other question—' Whether a man should love God in charity more than himself '—his reply is an *a fortiori* argument,

[1] *S.T.* I. q. 43, a. 3.
[2] The phrase comes from the Thomist commentator John of St. Thomas (quoted by Gardeil, *Structure de l'Âme et l'Expérience Mystique*, vol. ii. p. 85).
[3] *S.T.* ii[a] ii[ae]. q. 27, a. 4.   [4] *Ib.* q. 25, a. 4.
[5] *Ib.* q. 26, a. 4.

from nature to grace.[1] The ' nature ' in which he believes it
feasible to study the possibility of a ' disinterested ' love of God
is not, of course, the empirical human nature in which Bernard
saw self-love as the consequence of sin. It is nature taken in
abstraction both from the *un*natural—the Fall and its results, and
from the *super*natural—grace and its healing infusion. Of this
ideal nature, covering the whole natural world, both inanimate
and animate, Thomas asserts that the fact of creatureliness, of
existential dependence, necessarily imposes a subordination of
creature to Creator, of the dependent good or fulfilment of the
particular being, to the Sovereign Good, the universal End which
is the Being of God. He illustrates the effect of such dependence
by the natural self-subordination of part to whole both in the
organism and in society.[2] But he is conscious of the inadequacy
of this illustration : the good of the individual is not a part of the
Supreme Good, any more than man is a part of God. ' The
higher entity is compared to the lower ', he says, ' as whole to
part, in so far as the higher possesses in perfection and totality
what is possessed by the lower only imperfectly and partially.'[3]
It is the old ambiguity of Plato's terminology, wavering between
the concept of participation, of the Idea's immanence in the
particular, and that of imitation or resemblance, which better
safeguards its transcendence. Thomas, as we know, could only
interpret the participation of the individual in universal Being
in the sense of ' a certain degree of assimilation to it ',[4] ' the likeness of analogy which things originated bear to their origin '.[5]
' The tendency of any being towards its own good is a tendency
towards the divine likeness ; for in so far as it is good, it is being
made like to God. . . . It tends to its own good *because* it tends
to the divine likeness, *and not conversely.*'[6] If it is the perfection
of natural existence to represent in finite mode the infinite
goodness, then man can only seek his own perfection ' for the
sake of God ' : if he should love himself more than God, he

[1] *S.T.* iia iiae. q. 26, a. 3.   [2] *S.T.* i. q. 60, a. 5.
[3] *In De Div. Nom.* 4. 9.   [4] *S.T.* i. q. 6, a. 4.
[5] *C.G.* iii. 24.   [6] *Ib.*

would be preferring image to Exemplar. He must love himself,
for his being and its perfection are the will of God ; but he can
love himself only as ' belonging to God ', *pertinens ad Deum*.[1]

All this, we are to remember, follows from that dependence
upon God which is the natural good of man as part of the created
world. Man, as God made him, has a natural love of God
above all things, for he knows that his nature is to be an image
of God, and therein he possesses already the *unio similitudinis,* the
likeness which love postulates. But the *friendship* of God, as we
have seen, is grounded by Thomas upon ' supernature ', upon
a sharing in the divine life which exceeds the powers conferred
upon humanity in creation. In the love of charity, God is loved
' inasmuch as He is the Good which imparts universally to all
who receive it a supernatural beatitude '.[2] The grace of charity
perfects nature, because in it there is more than a recovery for
man of the natural love of God which he has lost through sin.
Since God's Son has taken our nature upon him, we are become
' partakers in the divine nature,' adopted into a ' spiritual fellowship '[3] in which we receive the high privilege of being called
the friends of God.

St. Thomas's doctrine of love is the attempt of the greatest
Christian thinker since Augustine to give coherent form to
Augustine's own conviction that man fulfils himself in finding
God. The love of God is a different thing from the desire for
happiness ; for what men universally desire is only to be happy :
there is no universal desire for happiness in what Thomas calls
its ' specific notion ', no agreement about the object external to
the self in which happiness is to be attained.[4] Pleasure is a real
good, and Thomas sees no reason to underrate it : ' in a certain
sense ' he calls it the greatest good that man can experience.[5]
But while happiness is that condition of soul in which ' appetition
is at rest in the good attained ', delight is no more than an effect
or concomitant of happiness.[6] Men desire it ' by reason of the

---

[1] *S.T.* ii[a] ii[ae]. q. 25, a. 4.
[2] *S.T.* i. q. 60, a. 5.
[3] *S.T.* i[a] ii[ae]. q. 109, a. 3.
[4] *Ib.* q. 5, a. 8.
[5] *Ib.* q. 34, a. 3.
[6] *Ib.* q. 4, a. 1.

good ',[1] and the last end of man is neither pleasure nor the fruition upon which it attends, but God.[2]

3. *Duns Scotus*

Yet this clear distinction between happiness in its subjective reference as a creaturely condition, and the uncreated Object which is the real goal of all human endeavour, was not enough to acquit Thomas's doctrine, in the eyes of his greatest follower and acutest critic, from the charge of eudaemonist egoism. The criticisms of Duns Scotus are to no small extent based on misunderstandings, but the positions which he desired to substitute for those criticised are of extraordinary interest and importance.

Scotus agrees that a natural love of God above all things is possible. But he puts his finger on the weak points in Thomas's use of the subordination of part to whole in order to explain the capacity of natural man to set God above himself. In the case of an organism, it is not the part that sacrifices itself, but the whole that sacrifices the part ; and only pantheism can regard man as a part of God. In the case of a society, it is indeed true that an individual will devote himself for the good of the community ; but Scotus points out that when this individual is a pagan with no hope of immortality, his heroism is in fact absolutely disinterested : he chooses self-annihilation for the sake of a greater good in which *no* part will be his ; and Scotus draws the inference that for the sake of the divine Good the natural man has both capacity and obligation to will his own non-existence. And this is but an instance of the general principle which the Franciscan moralist formulates in terms which anticipate Kant. The natural reason is able to see that a supreme good demands a supreme love, and the natural will must be capable of responding to that insight. *Nihil potest intellectus recte dictare, in quod dictatum non possit voluntas naturalis naturaliter tendere.*[3] There is a categorical imperative of the practical reason, and ' I ought ' implies ' I can '.

---

[1] *S.T.* Iª IIᵃᵉ. q. 2, a. 6.   [2] *Ib.* q. 11, a. 3.
[3] *Comment. Oxon. in Sent.* III. dist. 27, q. 1 n. 13 f.

But if the natural love of God above all things is thus cleared from all suspicion of interestedness, Thomas's account of the supernatural virtue of charity, as Scotus understands it, appears inconsistent with the very argument *a fortiori* by which it is reached. When Thomas says that charity is the love of God *ut obiectum beatitudinis,* he means, as we saw, that this beatitude is charity's condition. Scotus, like Bossuet after him, interprets the phrase as if it defined not the condition but the motive of charity, and, so understood, he condemns it roundly.[1] Charity, he maintains, has one primary motive and one only—the absolute goodness of God, and not the relation of that goodness to any created being. It is true that God's infinite goodness is not the only *cause* of our love for Him. The knowledge that ' this Goodness has loved me and given Itself to me ', precedes and evokes the act of charity ; and this act is accompanied or rather followed by recognition that the Goodness to which it is directed is the source of beatitude.[2] But both these latter considerations are ' accidental ', secondary. The love of God, says Scotus, can be pure *amor amicitiae* only when it regards Him as infinitely good in Himself, *not* as ' good to me or to you '.[3] Charity must tend to God in virtue of His absolute perfection, ' even if *per impossibile* all benefit to the lover were cut away from it '.[4] And the love of God ' above all things ' will indeed be an affection more intense than that which any other object can inspire ; but its intensity will be in the strength of active self-devotion rather than in the tender warmth, the passive ' sweetness ' of feeling, which is sometimes a reward that love may receive but cannot expect, sometimes the nourishment wherewith God feeds His ' little ones ' lest they faint by the way.[5]

That charity exceeds the natural powers and must be infused through grace, Scotus admits as *de fide.* But he thinks it is easier to see the ' congruity ' of the doctrine than to establish it rationally. He is not interested in finding a ground in super-

---

[1] ' Impropriissime dicunt.'   [2] *Ox.* III. dist. 27, q . I n. 7 ff.
[3] *Report. Paris. in Sent.* III. dist. 27, q . I n. 8 f.
[4] *Ox.* III. dist. 27, q. I n. 2.   [5] *Ib.* n. 16 f.

nature for the possibility of friendship between man and God, because in fact it is not for him as it was for Thomas the essential nature of charity to be a friendship with God. Scotus prefers to define charity, in a phrase recalling Augustine, as the *affectio iustitiae,* the 'passion for righteousness'. The terms *amor amicitiae* and *amor concupiscentiae* are in his usage equivalent to *affectio iustitiae* and *affectio commodi,* disinterested love and selfish desire, respectively ; and the 'love of friendship', the passion for righteousness, is itself the fruition of God in which beatitude consists. Beatitude is strictly an act of the will, and since the fruition of God according to Augustine's definition is ' to cleave to Him in love for His own sake ', it is attainable in a measure in this life, in so far as the Christian pilgrim, seeking nothing for himself, delights in the infinite goodness of God, willing only that God be what He is.[1] In this life, it is only the condition of mortality that excludes perfect beatitude.[2]

Like Augustine, Scotus absorbs within the love of God the love both of self and of neighbour. We cannot love God without willing that God be loved : ' by the same act, I will God, and will that you should love God : I love you in charity, in willing for you the good of righteousness '.[3] Scotus does not deny that self-love comes before the love of neighbour ; but the reason is simply that every man is for himself the immediate appointed instrument for directing a pure love towards God.[4] The desire of charity—Augustine's *amor amoris*—whether for self or for neighbour is wholly subordinate to the self-less love of God ' for His own sake '.

Against the endeavour of St. Thomas to justify and safeguard from abuse the eudaemonist form which Christian ethics had received from Augustine, the work of Duns Scotus stands out as a resolute refusal to compromise. *Amor concupiscentiae* is to have *no* place in the love which fulfils the first great commandment. Self-interest must be *wholly* excluded, and this can only be if in the last resort the self can cease to will even its own being.

[1] *Ox.* IV. dist. 49, q. 5 n. 4. [2] *Ib.* q. 12.
[3] *Ib.* III. dist. 28, q. 1 n. 3. [4] *Ib.* dist. 29, q. 1 n. 2.

Quilibet debet velle se non esse propter bonum divinum. In his zeal for pure love, Scotus is compelled to eliminate not only Eros but Philia—not only the desire of perfection, but the delight of a realised intercourse between persons ; for the friend can only be loved as *my* friend, my *alter ego,* and therefore as a good *for me.* When we consider what is left, we see that it is no more than that absolute self-prostration before transcendent goodness, that uttermost acceptance of God's holy will, which we call worship.

4. *Luther* [1]

To assert that the mediaeval doctrine of *caritas* bears throughout the mark of *amor concupiscentiae,*[2] that it is always based upon the love of self ; [3] to claim that Luther found Christianity egocentric and left it theocentric [4]—this is (to say no more) to do scant justice to Luther's scholastic master. When Luther says that ' every act of concupiscence towards God is an evil, a fornication of the spirit ' ; [5] when he speaks of the *profundissima infectio* of original sin, ' whereby even in God Himself through love of concupiscence man seeks those things that are his own ',[6] he is giving characteristically vivid and violent expression to what he had learnt from Duns Scotus. When he wrote : ' those who truly love God, in filial love and friendship, . . . offer themselves freely unto every ordinance of God's will, even to hell and death eternally, if God should so will—be but His will fully performed ',[7]

---

[1] In order to learn at first-hand what the Schoolmen have to say about Charity, the student is fortunately not required to know their voluminous writings *in extenso ;* and for the general theological background against which their particular doctrines must be set, there is no lack of reliable guidance. With Luther the matter is not so easy. But since our immediate concern is only to indicate his attitude towards the Augustinian doctrine of *amor Dei,* we may best avoid misrepresenting him by borrowing our citations from an authority not likely to have erred on the side of under-estimating Luther's originality—Karl Holl, in his *Gesammelte Aufsätze zur Kirchengeschichte.*

[2] Nygren, *Eros und Agape II.* (G.T.), p. 506.

[3] *Ib.* p. 531.   [4] *Ib.* p. 504 *et passim.*

[5] *C. Schol. Theol.* Th. 22 (Weimar ed. I. p. 225) : quoted by K. Holl, *op. cit.* vol. i. p. 210.

[6] *In Epist. ad Romanos* (ed. J. Ficker), II. p. 155 : Holl, p. 63.

[7] *Ib.* II. p. 217 : Holl, p. 56.

he may have been influenced more immediately by Tauler and the *Theologia Germanica*, but he was only drawing the last logical conclusion from what Duns had maintained of *amor amicitiae* and the absolute negation of self which it requires. Above all, Duns is the source of Luther's teaching upon the true nature of beatitude. 'Blessedness is in this, to will the will of God and His glory in all things, and to desire nothing of one's own either in this world or the next.'[1] The Scotist doctrine, that heaven itself is nothing but perfect union with the divine will, was enough to dissolve all the perplexities of the Lutheran 'assurance'. If we cannot be certain of our election, we can yet be certain of our salvation ; for 'those who will what God wills, even if He should will them damned and reprobate, would suffer no harm' (*non haberent malum*) ;[2] nay, for those who conform themselves to the will of God, 'it is impossible that they remain in Hell, for it is impossible that a man who has cast himself into the depths of God's will, should remain outside of God'.[3] *Impossibile est ut extra Deum maneat qui in voluntatem Dei sese penitus proiecit.* With that magnificent 'impossibility' Luther drew the sting from predestination itself ; and we should not fail to observe that at the same time the sting is drawn from that very 'abdication of beatitude' which Scotus and the German mystics had taught him to demand from a pure love of God. He has come back, almost against his will, to Augustine's *ibi ero, ubi non pereo*.

Nor is it only the voluntarism of Scotus that joins Luther to the Schools. Nygren places upon the title-page of his second volume a quotation from the Heidelberg Disputation : *Amor Dei non invenit sed creat suum diligibile. Amor hominis fit a suo diligibili.* He does not seem to be aware that in these words Luther was simply paraphrasing the *Summa Theologiae*,[4] and that the distinction is no less vital for the theology of St. Thomas than for that of Luther. Luther of course means, as Thomas did not, to refuse all value to the human love which is 'created by its

---

[1] *In Epist. ad Romanos* (ed. J. Ficker), II. p. 217 : Holl, p. 57.
[2] *Ib.* II. p. 223 : Holl, p. 152.   [3] *Ib.* II. p. 218 : Holl, p. 152.
[4] *S.T.* I. 9. 20, a. 2 (cf. *supra*, p. 266).

object '. In the accepted Aristotelian theory that the powers of the soul are ' passive, matter (awaiting form), acting by receiving ', he sees proof of the ' contrariety ' to theology of the philosophy which ' in all things seeks its own and receives good rather than imparts it '.[1] He forgets that his own *theologia crucis* has placed man under the inescapable obligation to ' receive ' in faith the good which God alone ' imparts '. We need not depreciate the significance of Luther's protest against the practical Pelagianism, the taint of ' works-religion ' with which mediaeval Christianity had been infected. But his polemic against *fides caritate formata,* his expulsion of love from the faith that justifies, proves only that he never understood St. Thomas. Charity no more than Faith is in Thomas's doctrine a ' work ' by which man's effort achieves the fellowship with God. Both belong to that goodness which the love of God ' creates and infuses '. Charity is the activity of the New Man. And the Luther who was wont to say that only he who is already ' selig ', *beatus,* has the power to do good, was nearer than he knew to the great Schoolman, who taught that man's power to respond in charity to the divine love springs from that participation in the blessed life of God which is membership in the mystic Body of Christ.

5. *St. Francis de Sales*

Forty years after Luther's death, a young French nobleman, finishing his education at Paris in the study of classics and philosophy ' to please his father ', and of theology ' to please himself ', suddenly realised the full horror of predestinationism. If Augustine were right, and the great mass of mankind had been created only to demonstrate the divine justice, then it was not only possible but by all odds most probable that he himself was damned. For a few weeks the boy (he was not yet twenty) was in agony, clinging to the resolution ' to love and serve God with all his strength during his life, all the more that in eternity this was to be impossible for him '. Then one day he knelt before

---

[1] The passage quoted in *Eros und Agape II.* (G.T.), p. 547.

the Black Virgin in the church of St. Étienne-des-Grès, and said the prayer posted by the altar. When he rose, ' he found himself perfectly and entirely healed : the trouble had fallen from him like the scales of a leprosy '. To him as to the patriarch on Mount Moriah, in and through the act of sacrifice, had come the revealing word. He would have glorified God by the acceptance of his own perdition ; he learnt that such glory is not sought for the Name *qui non est damnator sed Jesus*.[1]

The young man was François de Sales, who was to spend his life as Bishop of a diocese not altogether unlike Augustine's. To the Calvinists of Geneva the appeal of Francis was the same as Augustine's appeal to the Donatists of Hippo. ' Tout est à l'amour, en l'amour, pour l'amour, et d'amour en la sainte Église.'[2] But time had brought its revenges : at Geneva there was not schism only but heresy, and the heresy with too much reason could claim Augustine for its authority. Francis met it with the ' devout humanism ' in which Brémond has so well described the genius of his Christianity. He is the Clement of the seventeenth century, convinced like Clement of the essential beauty, goodness, and loveableness of the human soul. But the gentleness, the ' douceur ' of Francis, is rooted in a severity which is as far from Clement's asceticism as the religion of the Cross from the wisdom of Epictetus—' le bon Epictète '. ' Mount Calvary is the Academy of Love.'

That is the title of the last chapter of the *Traité de l'Amour de Dieu*, the finest fruit of the Counter-Reformation—a book which Dom Chapman called ' the greatest work of genius in theology since St. Thomas '. Its author professed that he had said nothing in it which he had not learnt from others ; but he had not learnt from books only. Much as he owed to Augustine, Bernard, and Thomas, he owed more to his spiritual daughter and beloved friend Madame de Chantal. In her and the contemplative sisterhood which he led her to found, Francis saw the teachings of St. Teresa at work. In the *Traité*—' our book ' as he always

[1] See Brémond, *Histoire Littéraire du Sentiment Religieux en France,* vol. i. pp. 86 ff.　　　　　[2] *Traité de l'Amour de Dieu :* Preface.

spoke of it to her—Madame de Chantal recognised the portrait of its saintly author : it is as certain that Francis in writing it had Sainte Jeanne de Chantal and not himself for his model.

The 'mystical theology' of union with God in prayer is indeed the centre of the *Traité;* but it is no more than the centre, and the Salesian text, 'Toutes choses sont créées pour l'oraison' is only not misleading as a summary of the Salesian doctrine if 'l'oraison' be taken to qualify the entire content of a God-directed life. 'What can it profit the soul', exclaims Francis, 'to be ravished unto God by prayer, while in her life and conversation she is ravished by earthly and base affections ? '[1] Of love towards God, there are 'two principal exercises, the one affective, the other effective : by that we affect or love God and what He loves, by this we serve God and do what He ordains. That joins us to God's goodness, this makes us execute His will . . . the one makes us pleased in God, the other makes us please God ; by the one we conceive, by the other we bring forth.' [2] Prayer is the first of these exercises, a part and not the whole of the Christian love whose ' birth, progress, decay, operations, properties, advantages, and excellencies ' [3] Francis set himself to represent.

The psychological foundations are laid in the first book of the Treatise ; and what is here most noteworthy is that while the general scheme and the terminology are scholastic, the underlying thought is nearer to Augustine than to Thomas. The will or 'reasonable appetite' has a natural affinity to good such that its nature and that of the good can only be understood in reference to one another. This affinity ' produces the complacency which the will takes in feeling and perceiving good ; this complacency moves and spurs the will forward to good ; and this movement tends to union '.[4] But Francis places the essence of love not, with St. Thomas, in the complacency which is the ' first stirring or emotion which good causes in the will ', but in the ' movement,

[1] *Traité*, VII. 7. Quotations are from the English translation by H. B. Mackey in the *Library of St. Francis de Sales.*
[2] *Ib.* VI. 1.   [3] *Ib.* Preface.   [4] *Ib.* I. 7.

outpouring, or advancement of the heart towards good '. Complacency is the ' great motive ' of love, its *causa efficiens* : love itself is the ' great movement ' of complacency.[1] It is Augustine's *pondus animi,* with the double character, affective and conative, which Augustine gave to it. Francis accepts the scholastic distinction of *amor concupiscentiae* and *amor benevolentiae* (or *amicitiae*), in the Scotist sense of interested and disinterested love. But in *all* love, selfish or unselfish, he finds both delight in a present good and striving for a good unattained ; and his terms for these two elements as they appear in a ' disinterested ' love are ' complaisance ' and ' bienveuillance '. In God's creative love, ' benevolence ' precedes ' complacency ' : His loving will calls the creature into existence, and in His Sabbath rest He ' sees that it is good '. In our love of God, the order is reversed.[2] In the love of complacency, the soul cries : ' It suffices me that God is God, that His goodness is infinite, that His perfection is immeasurable : whether I die or live matters little to me, since my Well-Beloved lives eternally an all-triumphant life '.[3] As one lute tuned to another will sound in accord when the second is played, the delight in God brings us into conformity with Him. ' Our heart, together with the pleasure which it takes in the thing beloved, draws unto itself the quality thereof.' [4] And so complacency leads to benevolence, the heart into which God has been drawn casts itself into God. ' We have taken delight in the sovereign excellency of God's perfection, and thereupon we desire that He be sovereignly loved, honoured and adored.' [5] Delight and desire, the activities of heart and will, are the *systole* and *diastole* in which the life of love consists, and charity needs both for its full realisation. ' Man's heart is never so much disquieted as when the motion by which it continually opens and shuts itself is hindered, never so quiet as when its motions are free ; *so that the heart's quiet consists in its motion.* It is the same with the love of the Seraphim and seraphical men ; for this has its repose in its continual movement of complacency, by which

[1] *Traité,* v. 1.   [2] *Ib.* v. 6.   [3] *Ib.* v. 3.
[4] *Ib.* VIII. 1.   [5] *Ib.* VIII. 2.

it draws God into itself, as if shutting itself, and of benevolence, by which it opens itself and throws itself entirely into God.' [1]

In this account of love's essential nature, the evident aim of Francis is to retain the warmth and fervour of Augustine's 'delighting in the Lord', while purging it of the last traces of self-reference. As though anticipating the hedonist perversion which the *delectatio iustitiae* was so soon to undergo at the hands of Jansen, he makes all pursuit of personal righteousness completely subordinate to the adoring acceptance of the righteousness of God. But his own Augustinianism goes further than this. It is not only in the definition of love that he modifies the teaching of St. Thomas. Thomas, we remember, had required for the 'affinity' of nature upon which love's complacency is grounded, a real likeness between lover and beloved. Francis, having re-established the movement of desire as an essential part and not merely a consequence of love, is enabled to see its ground rather in a 'correspondence' or mutual relation 'which makes things apt to unite in order to communicate to one another some perfection'.[2] Between God and the soul there is a real affinity of likeness ; but there is also 'an incomparable correspondence between God and man, for their reciprocal perfection : not that God can receive any perfection from man, but because, as man cannot be perfected but by the divine goodness, so the divine goodness can scarcely so well exercise its perfection outside itself, as upon our humanity. The one has great want and capacity to receive good, the other great abundance and inclination to bestow it. . . . The meeting of abundance and indigence is most sweet and agreeable, and one could scarcely have said whether the abounding good have a greater contentment in spreading and communicating itself, or the failing and needy good in receiving and drawing to itself—until our Saviour had told us that *it is more blessed to give than to receive.* Now where there is more blessedness there is more satisfaction ; and therefore the divine goodness receives greater pleasure in giving than we in receiving.' [3]

[1] *Traité,* v. 12.   [2] *Ib.* I. 8.   [3] *Ib.* I. 15.

Here once more are Eros and Agape—man's need met by God's abundance, the potency of the human soul and the divine Act. But neither Augustine nor Thomas dared to bring Eros and Agape so near together, to bind them in so organic a unity. Augustine too believed that creation is the overflow of God's eternal bliss. But Francis has all but said that God's perfection *needs* man's poverty. To understand his thought we must take into account his theology of the Incarnation. Francis, like Duns Scotus, will not allow that the union of God and man in Christ has place only in the scheme of redemption : it is not primarily God's remedy for sin, but the expression of God's love, the end for which the world was made. *All things have been created through Him, and unto Him.*[1] ' Toutes choses sont créées pour l'oraison '—yes, but only because the Christ, in whom the creature is united to the Creator, is Himself the one perfect prayer. ' Our great Saviour ', says Francis, ' was the first in the divine intention . . . in view of this desired fruit the vine of the universe was planted, and the succession of many generations established, which as leaves or blossoms proceed from it as fore-runners and fit preparatives for the production of that grape which the sacred spouse so much praises in the Canticles, and the juice of which rejoices God and men.'[2]

The Agape whose end is Incarnation cannot be understood as ' uncaused self-giving ', as the simple outflow of creative goodness. It is the Creator's will to *unite* Himself to the creature. Everywhere Francis sees proof of God's ' extreme desire to be loved '.[3] He is ' the divine Lover at the gate '. His calls for our love are constant, the means which His providence has offered for us to love Him are ' rich and abundant ' ; and that is why it would be ingratitude and disloyalty were we not to will and desire the salvation which God desires for us, and to accept ' with an absolute resolution ' the graces which He has provided for its attainment.[4] The ' abdication of beatitude ' can never mean the

---

[1] *Coloss.* i. 16.
[3] *Ib.* II. 8.
[2] *Traité*, II. 5.
[4] *Ib.* VIII. 4.

desire ' to *be* cast off and deprived of God's grace, for this cannot holily be desired '.[1]

It follows that in his view of the relations of nature and grace, Francis is at the opposite pole to Luther. The ' natural ' love of God above all things is for him no abstract possibility. He accepts the scholastic account of it,[2] but he sees in it the real link between nature and grace. Like a spark under the ashes, the *inclination* to love God remains with us even after the power to realise such love has been lost by sin. Its presence forbids us to say that our nature is completely or hopelessly corrupt ; for this natural inclination is the ' handle ' by which God holds us and draws us to Himself.[3] Luther, with his startling candour of self-exposure and his rush to generalise, said that everyone who is honest with himself—as honest as Martin Luther !—must confess that in his heart of hearts he would rather there were no moral law. To talk of a natural love of goodness and hatred of sin is a hypocrisy, clean contrary to the immediate deliveries of conscience and the ' vital pulse of experience '.[4] ' The entire observance of God's commandments,' writes Francis, ' is not within the bounds of human strength, yet is it within the stretch of the instinct of the human spirit, as being most conformable to natural light and reason ; so that, living according to God's commandment, we are not outside our natural inclination.' [5] As decisively as Luther, Francis rejects the Aristotelian theory that ' the love which we have for others proceeds from the love of ourselves '.[6] But Luther agrees with Aristotle that man lies under an inborn necessity of loving self above all things : there is no ' higher self ', no *Fünkelein* or *Seelengrund* such as the mystics fancied. The whole man is one ; self-will is at once the very foundation of his being and the *summa omnium vitiorum*.[7] Francis follows the mystics, but not all the way. His *fine pointe* or ' summit of the spirit ' is not the ' uncreated spark ' in which

---

[1] *Traité*, X. 16.   [2] *Ib.* X. 10.   [3] *Ib.* I. 16 ff.
[4] Weimar ed. VII. 115 : Holl, *op. cit.* p. 63.
[5] *Traité*, VII. 6.   [6] *Ib.* X. 10.
[7] *In. Epist. ad Romanos*, II. 75 : Holl, *op. cit.* p. 61.

Meister Eckhart and his disciples perceived the essential divinity of the human soul. It is not grace itself, but the point where grace enters. In the 'lower part' of the soul Francis includes all its active powers, both animal and rational; and in this whole sphere self-assertion is dominant. The *fine pointe* is nothing more than man's inamissible capacity for saying 'Yes' to the grace of God : it is utterly human because utterly receptive. Its response to grace is made by the 'simple acquiescings' of faith, hope and charity : faith 'by which we acquiesce in the truth of the mysteries which we do not understand', hope 'by which we acquiesce in the promise of the goods which we see not', charity 'by which we acquiesce in the union of our spirit with God, which we scarcely perceive'. Of these 'supernatural affections', stirred in us by the operation of the Holy Spirit, 'the true and natural dwelling is in this supreme region of the soul, from whence as from a happy source of living water, they run out by divers conduits and brooks upon the inferior parts and faculties'.[1] So Francis brings faith and love together : faith is a loving complacency in the beauty of divine truth, and love a trusting acceptance of the divine embrace.

Acquiescence, submission, is the secret alike of union with God in prayer and of conformity of life with His will. In the prayer of quiet, the will 'works not save by a simple acquiescence in the divine good-pleasure, willing to be in prayer without any other aim than to be in the sight of God according as it shall please Him'.[2] And the rapture which is the crown of prayer is justified and sealed by the 'ecstasy of act and life'. *Ye are dead, and your life is hid with Christ in God.*[3] In the ecstatic life there is both doing and suffering ; for the will of God is both His 'signified' will in commandment and counsel, which He has made us free to follow or resist—and here love transforms obedience into joy ; and what Francis calls God's absolute will or 'good-pleasure', known to us only by the event—and here 'the loving heart will love God's good-pleasure not in consolations only but in afflictions also : yea, it loves it better upon

[1] *Traité*, I. 12.   [2] *Ib.* VI. II.   [3] *Ib.* VII. 6.   *Coloss.* iii. 3.

the cross in pains and difficulties, because the principal effect of
love is to make the lover suffer for the thing beloved'. In
suffering, ' there is nothing to receive our affection save the will
of God only '.[1] The ' holy indifference ' which Francis preaches
is to extend to the spiritual as well as to the natural life : it is
an indifference to the ' comforts ' of religion as well as to all
worldly comfort. Francis forestalls the quietist exaggerations
of this teaching. Indifference, he says, does not mean that we
are to ' care for nothing, and abandon our affairs to the mercy
of events '. On the contrary, we should ' omit nothing which
is requisite to bring the work which God has put into our hands
to a happy issue, yet upon condition that if the event be contrary,
we should lovingly and peaceably embrace it '.[2] And the soul
that has stripped itself of all its natural affections, even of the
desire for personal progress in virtue and holiness, is never called
to remain naked : it will put on again new affections—' perhaps
the very same which it has renounced and resigned '—but it
will walk none the less *in newness of life,* seeking things that are
good not for its own adornment and contentment, but because
' the Saviour's name is sanctified in them, His Kingdom advanced, His good-pleasure glorified'.[3] The supreme pattern
of holy indifference is always for Francis the *Fiat voluntas tua*
of Gethsemane and the *Pater, in manus tuas* of Calvary. There
was the acquiescence of the *fine pointe* in the Father's will, above
the experienced agony and darkness of *Transeat calix iste* and
Quare me dereliquisti ?

There is an extraordinary beauty in the passage of thought
which leads Francis from Calvary to Bethlehem, from the self-
surrender of the Crucified into the Father's keeping to the abandonment of the child Jesus in his mother's arms—' going not
but by her steps, willing not but by her will '.[4] It is the same
beauty which makes the *Traité de l'Amour de Dieu* glow all
through with a wonderful chiaroscuro. Francis himself is a
' once-born ' soul, for whom the love of God is joy and peace
in believing, for whom ' never does any love take the heart

[1] *Traité,* IX. 2.   [2] *Ib.* 6.   [3] *Ib.* 16.   [4] *Ib.* 14.

from God, save that which is contrary unto Him '.[1] His book would not have been what it is had not he himself been born again in the spiritual travail of an *alter ego*. From Jeanne de Chantal he learnt the lesson of the Cross : that ' all love that takes not its beginning from our Saviour's Passion is frivolous and dangerous '. In that Passion ' love and death are so mingled that we cannot have the one in our heart without the other. . . . Except there, all is either eternal death or eternal love ; and all Christian wisdom consists in choosing rightly '.[2]

In François de Sales the various elements contributed by the Christian thought and experience of the Middle Ages towards the correction of Augustinianism are formed into a coherent system, in which the Augustinian *amor Dei* is transformed—yet not out of recognition. As strongly as Scotus or Luther, Francis held that the Christian is called to a fruition of God in this present life—a fruition which consists in union with Him through the grace of contemplative prayer and acceptance of His will in the life of action. His chief concern is to combat the self-centredness and self-seeking which are as fatal to the ' affective ' exercise of love to God in prayer as to the ' effective ' exercise of the same love in external activity. Prayer is not prayer if it is the pursuit of ' religious experience ', just as service is not service if it aims at any kind of self-satisfaction. Francis emphatically refuses to take happiness, in the sense of a psychical condition, for the end of religion. The true destiny of man, as St. Thomas had said, is not beatitude but God.

6. *Bérulle and Condren*

In Brémond's great history of French Christianity in the seventeenth century, Francis is the vanguard of attack upon ' panhedonism ', or what we might more recognisably call sentimentalism, the degradation of religion into a cult of enjoyable emotions. But it is to the ' École Française ', of which the chief figures are the Oratorians Bérulle and Condren, that Brémond

---

[1] *Traité*, x. 3. [2] *Ib.* xII. 13.

ascribes, not the 'Copernican revolution' in religion which Nygren would claim for Luther, but the decisive re-affirmation of a religious attitude in comparison to which that of Luther might more aptly be called pre-Copernican. For the Catholic writer, the centrality of God as thus re-affirmed by the French School has a meaning quite different from that which it bears for the Protestant. In Nygren's view, God is at the centre when He is in undisputed possession of the stage upon which the drama of human salvation is enacted : God, and God alone, is *for* man. Brémond sees the theocentrism of the Oratorians in their rigorous concentration upon the glory of God rather than the salvation of man : man is *for* God, and God alone. In the teaching of Bérulle, the true spirit of prayer as of all religion is reverence and adoration for the sovereign majesty of God, 'for what He is in Himself rather than for what He is in regard to us '. ' Il faut premièrement regarder Dieu et non pas soi-même.' [1] But this worship of God 'in Himself', a worship which should include both an adequate mental concept of the Object of adoration and an absolute submission of will to the Supreme Good so conceived,[2] is beyond the reach of the finite human being. The worship of God in spirit and in truth is only made possible for men through the perfect Worshipper, the God-Man whose whole incarnate life was a realisation of religion : we can only worship God by 'adherence' to the Christ in us. 'Our being ', says Bérulle, ' is a thing defective and imperfect, a void needing to be filled. . . . Our first movement must be towards Jesus as our fulfilment, and in this seeking for Jesus, in this adherence to Jesus, in this continual and profound dependence upon Jesus, is our life, our rest, our strength and all our power of working.' [3] The human spirit is no more than a ' pure capacity ' for Christ ; and grace annuls (*anéantit*) our own being, constituting us nothing but a ' relation ' to Him.[4] For Bérulle the Incarnation is not

[1] Brémond, *Histoire Littéraire du Sentiment Religieux en France*, vol. iii. pp. 24-33.
[2] *Ib.* p. 118.
[3] Bérulle, *Oeuvres*, pp. 1180 f. Brémond, *ib.* pp. 84 f.
[4] Brémond, *ib.* pp. 86 ff.

an event 'past and done with', but 'living and present'. It is 'a mystery binding God to man and man to God, and we must bind ourselves to that mystery',[1] suffering the Christ to reproduce in us as He wills those inward 'states' of worshipful relation to God of which all the passing acts of Jesus were significant.[2]

The Christocentrism of Bérulle kept his theocentrism for all its austerity balanced and sane. In Condren, neither the saintliness which made so extraordinary an impression upon his contemporaries, nor the extravagant encomiums of Brémond,[3] can obscure the fact that theocentrism took a form in which the Incarnation is robbed of half its meaning. In his boyhood, Condren passed through a mystical experience which Brémond rightly compares to those which Augustine set down in the Seventh Book of the Confessions and Pascal in his Memorial. 'Suddenly, his spirit was enveloped in a marvellous light, in the brightness of which the divine majesty appeared to him so immense and so infinite, that he felt that beside that pure Being nothing else should subsist, and that the whole universe should be destroyed for His glory. . . . One could not love Him enough, but by willing to lose oneself, with His Son, for the love of Him.' 'The purity and the power of that light' fixed upon Condren's soul 'a point of death which never faded'.[4] For the rest of his life, worship meant immolation, *anéantissement;* and with a disastrous contraction of Bérulle's thought, he narrowed down the sacrificial significance of Christ to His death upon the Cross, the one immolation worthy of God. For the infinity of the Eternal Father can receive no adequate praise but in the confession 'that not only the universe but His own Son must be *destroyed* before Him'.[5] Adherence to Christ is therefore adherence to *anéantissement;* and, as Brémond insists, this demand for 'annulment' of our being is a consequence not

---

[1] Bérulle, *Oeuvres*, pp. 582, 494. Mersch, *Le Corps Mystique*, vol. ii. p. 311.

[2] Brémond, vol. iii. pp. 64 ff.

[3] Cf. *ib.* p. 358 : 'le plus haut génie religieux des temps modernes'.

[4] D. Amelote, *La Vie du P. Ch. de Condren*, I. 41 ff. Brémond, *ib.* p. 342.

[5] *Ib.*

of the Fall but of the Creation.[1]   It is not only sin, it is creaturely
existence as such which is an offence to Condren.   Religion is
' the spirit of purity which cannot endure that anything but
God should live '.[2]   In taking possession of Christ's members,
the divine Spirit ' remains Himself in such holiness and purity
that He remains in perfection in the Father, in the Word, and
in Himself, without any going-out therefrom, without addition
to what He is . . . because in giving Himself to men, He brings
them to nothing in the gift, and thus His gift consumes its very
self, so holy is it, so impossible for it to suffer anything of the
creature.'[3]   And Christian self-immolation will culminate in
adoring the Judgement to come, ' even were it our own damnation ' ; for Christ will come then ' not for men but for God,
to do Him justice for the outrages that men have committed '.[4]

It is hardly possible to conceive a more complete contrast to
the ' devout humanism ' of François de Sales than this sombre
deformation of the religion of sacrifice.   Condren has eliminated
anthropocentrism from the Christianity of Augustine only by so
exclusive an emphasis upon Augustine's doctrine of the divine
self-sufficiency as to make creation altogether unintelligible.
Why should God have brought out of nothing a world which
can glorify Him only by a voluntary return to nothingness ?
How could He be pleased with the ' destruction ' of that which
He Himself made and saw that it was good ?   The mysticism
that seeks escape from creatureliness ceases indeed to be Christian
mysticism.   The glory of God is eternal and infinite ; but no
good can come of the deliberate attempt to isolate that glory from
His creation of finite spirits that they might enjoy Him for ever.
God is ' in Himself ' such as the work of creation and redemption
has revealed Him to be.   ' God creates, not that there may be
witnesses to render Him His due glory, but beings who shall
rejoice in it as He rejoices in it Himself, and who, participating

---

[1] Brémond, vol. iii. p. 362.
[2] Condren, *Lettres,* pp. 149 f.   Brémond, *ib.* p. 360.
[3] *Ib.* pp. 104-108.   Brémond, *ib.* p. 375.
[4] *Ib.* pp. 44-53.   Brémond, *ib.* p. 402.

in His Being, participate at the same time in His beatitude.' [1]—
That, according to Gilson, is the teaching of the mediaeval theologians. And we know that for St. John, the glory of Christ's
Passion, the glory that His disciples were to behold and share, is
that same glory which the Son had with the Father before the
world was.[2]

7. *Fénélon*

In the controversy between Bossuet and Fénélon, a pedantic
revival of Augustine's ethical eudaemonism was met by the
whole weight of seven centuries of Christian experience. The
controversy was lamentable and futile, because Bossuet's own
religion was tinged scarcely less deeply than Fénélon's with the
theocentrism of the Oratorians. The question at issue had
already received its answer. François de Sales had written that
' the Holy Spirit, dwelling in our hearts by charity, makes those
same works which are wholly ours still more wholly His. *He
does them for us as we do them for Him.* . . . We give God the
glory of our praise, and He gives us the glory of possessing
Him.' [3] Brémond comments that these words contain the
solution of the ' panhedonists' everlasting imbroglio'. ' Love's
power to beatify is in proportion to its disinterestedness. . . . It
is for our happiness that the Holy Spirit makes us act : God
becomes as it were anthropocentrist—*qui propter nos homines*—
and the better to attain that end, enables us to theocentrise
ourselves.' [4]

Fénélon was able to quote at least one quite unambiguous
statement of St. Thomas to the same effect : that the soul is
' by so much the more blessed, the more sincerely it loves God
because of the goodness which is His very nature and not because
of its participation in blessedness itself '.[5] But, as we have seen,
St. Thomas's loyalty to Aristotle as well as to Augustine had

[1] Gilson, *Spirit of Mediaeval Philosophy*, p. 104.
[2] John xvii. 5, 22, 24.   [3] *Traité*, xi. 6.
[4] Brémond, vol. vii. p. 70 n.
[5] St. Thomas, *Opusc.* lxii. : quoted in Fénélon's *Dissertatio de Amore Puro*.

imposed upon his doctrine of charity a general form only too
easy to misinterpret; and Bossuet found it possible to appeal to
him for support of the two indubitably Augustinian articles of
faith, that ' the search for God is the search for happiness ', and
that God is ' Himself our reward '.

Fénélon took his stand on the distinction clearly drawn by
St. Thomas between the two senses of the phrase ' man's last end '.
Objectively, man's end is God, the *divina bonitas;* subjectively,
it is attainment of the end, personal beatitude. Fénélon argued
that the subjective end, a created and finite good, must on
Augustinian principles be ' referred ' to the uncreated and infinite
good which is God. To Bossuet's not inaccurate summary of
Augustine's eudaemonism—' vouloir être heureux, c'est con-
fusément vouloir Dieu : vouloir Dieu, c'est distinctement
vouloir être heureux '—he presented the dilemma : Do we seek
God's glory for the sake of our own beatitude, or our own
beatitude for the sake of God's glory ? To seek what can really
make us happy, and to seek it for that reason, are not one and
the same thing ; and if Augustine's *castus amor* is the desire of
God and of nothing else beside Him, it is not the desire of
personal beatitude.[1] It could never have occurred to Bossuet
that he might refuse the dilemma and assert roundly that the
glory of God consists in that revelation of Himself to His
children which is consummated in the beatific vision. Instead,
he admitted the distinction ; he admitted even that the ' principal
and specific motive ' of charity is God's goodness ' in itself ' ;
but he insisted that the desire of our own beatitude, though a
' secondary ' motive, is essential and inseparable, and that, God's
perfect goodness implying His benevolence towards men, the
desire of beatitude is always implicit if not always explicit in the
love of God.[2]

Fénélon was not slow to claim that this was to surrender the
whole eudaemonist position. Orthodox theology maintained
that beatitude is a *donum gratuitum,* and not a benefit which man

---

[1] *IIIe Lettre à M. de Meaux.*
[2] Bossuet, *Summa Doctrinae* and *Schola in Tuto.*

has any right to expect from God's goodness : as the Roman Catechism put it, ' God could have compelled us to serve His glory without any reward '. To suggest that God would not have been lovable if He had not given to mankind the promise of the vision of Himself, is to confuse nature and grace. Fénélon himself agreed that the ' secondary motive ' was *inseparable : that the Christian is always impelled to the love of God ' both in the acts of charity by the motive of the divine Beauty, and in the acts of hope by the motive of beatitude, as his own personal good '.[1] But that abstraction of this secondary motive was possible, he found proved beyond all doubt by the experience of the saints. The Thirty-Third Article of the Issy Conferences, signed by Bossuet as well as Fénélon, had approved as ' an act of perfect abandonment and pure love ', ' the submission and assent to the will of God, even under the impossible supposition that God should withdraw the eternal goods promised to righteous souls, and keep them in eternal torments, though not deprived of His grace or His love '. The supposition indeed is to our minds not so much impossible as nonsensical : to speak of eternal torments in which the sufferers are deprived neither of God's grace nor of His love, is to utter words which have meaning only in the context of a grossly external and unspiritual conception of hell. But the experience which underlies such extravagant language is nothing less real than that ' inclination to the Cross ', that sharing in Christ's Passion to the uttermost, in which the Dominican Fathers Chardon and Piny,[2] with all the saints, had found the length and breadth and depth and height of love.

Fénélon's book had been condemned because its statements appeared to exclude from Christian perfection all desire for personal beatitude as a reward. His defence was that the intention of the book had been to show that the love of charity is and must be independent of the motive of reward, although the virtue of hope will always exercise its proper function of aspiration to beatitude ; but, when charity is dominant, the acts of hope which charity itself ' commands ' as in accord with God's will, ' pass

[1] Fénélon, *Diss. de Amore Puro*.   [2] Brémond, vol. viii.

over into the form of charity '—that is, we hope for beatitude no longer from the motive of natural self-love, but for the sake of God's glory.[1]

It is generally taken for granted that Fénélon was right in his claim that love itself means something incompatible with self-seeking, and that his only mistake was to treat ' pure love ' as a state of perfection reserved for a few. But what is not always observed is that in keeping a place even in Christian perfection for the hope of reward, he displays a crudely individualist conception of the reward which is hope's object. His *beatitudo* is always *privata beatitudo*. He shows no sign of realising that Augustine's finest achievement was the demonstration that there can be no such thing—that *privata beatitudo* is a flat contradiction in terms. In one passage [2] he appeals to St. Thomas's doctrine that the ' part ' naturally desires the common good more than its own particular or ' private ' good : the Fall, as Augustine taught, was the corruption of human nature just because it was the pursuit of a ' private good ' instead of the *bonum commune*. But Fénélon proceeds to identify this *bonum commune totius universi* simply with the *beatitudo aut gloria Dei*. He says nothing of God as being the good *of all*, nor draws any distinction between the desire for our own personal good and the desire for the good of the whole family of God. On the contrary, he finds that *privata beatitudo* remains the proper object of Christian hope, though not of Christian charity. This degradation of Christian hope into an expectation of reward in heaven which is only saved from pure egoism inasmuch as it is ' commanded ' or ' informed ' by the charity which seeks God's glory, was a result of the controversy the more unfortunate that it remained uncontroverted. Fénélon did not see that hope is not Christian at all unless it is hope *for all*—hope for the victory of good over evil everywhere, hope as free from the limitations of individual self-interest as the most perfect charity.

[1] Fénélon, *Epist. II. de Amore Puro.*   [2] *Ib.*

8. *Bishop Butler*

' Everybody knows, you therefore need only just be put in mind, that there is such a thing as having so great a horror of one extreme as to run insensibly and of course into the contrary ; and that a doctrine's having been a shelter for enthusiasm, or made to serve the purpose of superstition, is no proof of the falsity of it. . . . It may be sufficient to have mentioned this in general, without taking notice of the particular extravagances which have been vented under the pretence or endeavour of explaining the love of God, or how manifestly we are got into the contrary extreme, under the notion of a reasonable religion—so very reasonable as to have nothing to do with the heart and affections.' [1]

The authors of the particular extravagances of which the young preacher at the Rolls Court Chapel, afterwards famous as Bishop Butler, was thinking, no doubt included Fénélon as well as Madame Guyon. And the Fifteen Sermons may seem indeed to advocate a religion ' so very reasonable ' that their place is in the literature of philosophic ethics rather than of piety. Yet the *Sermons* are really addressed *ad hominem* no less than the *Analogy*. Butler found himself living in an age whose distinctive ' vice or folly ' was ' to profess a contracted spirit and greater regard to self-interest than appears to have been done formerly ' ; and he assured his hearers that he would accordingly make ' all possible concessions to the favourite passion ', ' treat it with the utmost tenderness and concern for its interests '.[2] The philosophic student or historian can easily fail to appreciate the Bishop's irony, and suppose that his serious intention hardly went further than to confirm the coincidence of virtue and happiness, conscience and self-love, intuitionism and eudaemonism. He has thus been taxed with failure to provide a single criterion of morality. At one time he will say that ' it is manifest that nothing can be of consequence to mankind or any creature but happiness ' ;[3] at another that, ' were the Author of Nature to propose nothing

[1] Butler, *Sermon* XIII. *ad init.*
[2] *Sermon* XI. *ad init.*
[3] *Sermon* XII.

294

to Himself as an end but the production of happiness, were His moral character merely that of benevolence, *yet ours is not so* '.[1] He will assert in the strongest terms the natural supremacy of conscience over self-love as well as all ' particular affections ' ; [2] yet when he ' sits down in a cool hour ', he finds that even ' the pursuit of what is right and good as such ', can be justified only if it is clearly not inconsistent with happiness.[3]

But the two Sermons upon the Love of God ought not to be read as a religious excrescence upon a sober discussion of ethical questions. The prayer with which the Twelfth Sermon, On the Love of Neighbour, closes [4] makes it clear enough that Butler's aim has been not so much to reconcile a due self-love with a due benevolence as to establish the reality of disinterestedness in the normal affective life of man, and so to clear the ground for a presentation of the religious motive in terms which recall neither Fénélon nor Bossuet, but the Augustinianism of François de Sales. Having proved that ' the very notion of affection implies resting in its objects as an end ', he can go on without fear of ' enthusiasm ' to describe a love of God free from ' any other regards, how reasonable soever, which respect anything out of or besides the perfection of the divine nature ', and to call ' the question whether we ought to love God for His sake or for our own, a mere mistake in language ' ; for ' it is a great mistake to think you can love or fear or hate anything from consideration that such love or fear or hate may be a means of obtaining good or avoiding evil '.[5] The love of God is the response evoked in us by a righteousness which we can trust because it is everlasting and changeless. The religious life is the outcome of

[1] *Dissertation on the Nature of Virtue.*
[2] *Sermon* II.   [3] *Sermon* XI.
[4] ' O almighty God, inspire us with this divine principle ; kill in us all the seeds of envy and ill-will ; and help us, by cultivating within ourselves the love of our neighbour, to improve in the love of Thee. Thou hast placed us in various kindreds, friendships, and relations, as the school of discipline for our affections ; help us, by the due exercise of them, to improve to perfection ; till all partial affection be lost in that entire universal one, and Thou, O God, shalt be all in all.'
[5] *Sermon* XIII.

a resignation to the will of God which is perfect ' when our will is lost and resolved up into His '—a temper which embodies itself in worship, ' the highest exercise and employment of mind that a creature is capable of '. So Butler passes from the consideration of love to God in our present ' state of imperfection ' to the hope of its fulfilment when we shall see Him face to face ; and his stately eloquence enlarges, often in the same words, upon those same themes on which the changes had been rung so often in the cathedral of Hippo thirteen hundred years before : man's insufficiency to himself, his weary pursuit of things that can never satisfy, of means mistaken for ends. Happiness lies not in property and possessions, but ' in a faculty's having its proper object '. If ' all the common enjoyments of life are from the faculties [God] hath endued us with, and the objects He hath made suitable to them ', ' He may Himself be to us infinitely more than all these : He may be to us all that we want '. The vision of God will be the contemplation of the Beauty, Wisdom and Goodness that is cause of all things lovely, true, and good ; it will be the ' perception of His presence with us ' after the manner of ' the presence of a friend ', but ' in a nearer and stricter way ', as the life of our life, our strength and our portion for ever.[1]

Bishop Butler is perhaps the last great Christian thinker who is content to regard religion primarily as belief in God's ' moral government ' of the world, a government so exercised that ' every one at length and upon the whole shall receive according to his deserts '.[2] The argument of the *Analogy* rests as firmly as that of the *De Libero Arbitrio* upon the premiss that a righteous God must reward righteousness and punish unrighteousness in men. But in Butler, though he is as sure as Augustine that sin is not sin because it is punished but punished because it is sin, the religious intuition that it is good for man to hold him fast by God has *almost* given way to an ethical theory that virtue and happiness are generally coincident ; and that theory does not save him from a view of punishment which is almost wholly

---

[1] *Sermon.* XIV. [2] *Analogy*, Part II. c. 4.

'external'. Yet it gives the more weight to his quiet confession that when we are commanded to love God, 'somewhat more must be meant than merely that we live in hope of rewards or fear of punishments from Him'.[1] It remained for Kant to enthrone the 'Stern Daughter of the Voice of God' as a Lawgiver that neither threatens nor promises. But Butler knew, as Kant did not, that the love of God is 'somewhat more', even than obedience.

[1] Preface to *Sermons, ad fin.*

X

Epilogue : The Analogy of Love

Amari nec Deus nec aliqua creatura dedignatur vel respuit : immo laetanter se diligi omnes fatentur et amore iocundari.

RICHARD ROLLE.

He courts our love with infinite esteem,
And seeks it so that it doth almost seem
Even all His blessedness.   His love doth prize
It as the only sacrifice.

'Tis death, my soul, to be indifferent ;
Set forth thyself unto thy whole extent,
And all the glory of His Passion prize,
    Who for thee lives, who for thee dies.

There is no goodness nor desert in thee
For which thy love so coveted should be ;
His goodness is the fountain of thy worth.
    Oh ! live to love and set it forth.

Thy love is nothing but itself, and yet
So infinite is His, that He doth set
A value infinite upon it.   Oh !
    This, canst thou careless be, and know ?

THOMAS TRAHERNE.

X

It is not only the disciple of Luther to whom all consideration of man's love to God is apt to seem a waste of time, or worse. When Dom Chapman of Downside, sketching out in a letter to a Jesuit his ample theory of Catholic truth, came to speak of Charity, he marked it as ' God's, not ours, which is not worth considering '.[1] *Herein is love, not that we loved God, but that He loved us.* Yet if we can say nothing at all of God but in the forms of our human thought and experience, that confession itself can have no meaning apart from the whole human context within which love has been understood or misunderstood.

There are two possible ways of understanding or misunderstanding it. We may either attempt to reduce the complexity and vagueness of the term to a single ' clear and distinct idea ', by analysing, isolating, defining : this and this and this is called love, is confused with love, but Love itself, Auto-Agape, is none of these, it is That and That alone. Or we may, provisionally, acquiesce in the multiplicity, the apparent hotch-potch of dissimilarities which strive to cover themselves with Love's mantle, and ask whether after all they may be parts of an organic whole, aspects of a single spiritual reality.

Let us follow this second course. In whatever sense love may be taken in common usage, it will be in some relation to good. (a) Love may be subordinate to good, created, caused, or evoked by good ; or (b) the relation may be reversed, and love may be the cause, good the effect ; or (c) love and good may coalesce : love may be a kind of good, there may even be no way of explaining good except as love. The spiritual development of the ordinary human being does in fact seem to disclose, successively or concurrently, these three relations between love and good.

The child begins its life in complete dependence. Its needs are few but insistent, and it is helpless to satisfy them : it cannot

---

[1] *Spiritual Letters of Dom John Chapman*, p. 226.

even find its way to its mother's breast. What is ' good ' for it is to be fed, warmed, and washed ; and it ' loves ' all three processes. Very soon it is more than a little animal. The mind, its distinctive humanity, awakes and grows—an awakening and a growth only in part determined by the actual human environment. The physical needs remain, but they are no longer the only needs : the child wants not only the breast or the bottle, but its mother, and it wants, more generally, to be amused. Still, all its good comes to it from outside : if it ' enjoys itself ' at all, that is because it has been given what it needs. Its love is purely reactive to external sources of gratification, to the ' not-self ' which answers to desire and gives delight.

But sooner or later comes the new stage, in which memory and imagination turn the passive recipient into an active originator. The child makes the great discovery that he need not always be asking for what he wants, that he has in himself a certain power of realising the good which from its station in the outside world has stepped in the form of an idea across the threshold of his mind and become at home within him. In fancy or in fact, in the endowing of a toy with life and character or in the building of houses in the sand, he can reproduce for himself the imagined good. The observer can become the artist, the enjoyer a quasi-creator. He is still dependent upon the given, for his creative activity presupposes vision. It is not true that he seeks to ' express himself ', or that he makes just for the sake of making. He seeks to express something which is *not* himself, to make something that he has seen and that has value for him. Apart from its value he would not want to make it. The making is at first a travail, a struggle with difficulties, and only when a certain degree of mastery over the material has been achieved does the actual process of creation become enjoyable. But in the process love, without losing its old form, has taken on a new one. It is no longer *only* a reaction to presented good, but also a *causa efficiens*, summoning new good into existence.

Now it is true that the creative impulse opens a door of escape from self-centredness, inasmuch as in creation there is activity of the self *for* a good to be realised, instead of more or less passive intake of all good as *for* the self. But the new impulse can and at first does accentuate egoism rather than diminish it. What I have made is mine, and no one else has a right to its enjoyment. Before the self can begin to take its place in a wider world, the consequences must be drawn from another discovery. At first other people were so many objects in an environment upon which the child depended for the satisfaction of his needs. But he does not take very long to find that some of these objects (and one of them in particular) have a peculiar interest in him which he can turn to good account. They show a concern for him which is not unlike his own concern for his own product or possession. They behave as though he were valuable to them, and he proves that he is aware of the fact by his ingenuity in trading upon it. But his parents' love is much more than a convenience to be used, more even than a value to be enjoyed. It evokes response in kind, and he finds himself loving them because they first loved him, and impelled continually to reinforce the bond which makes them his as he is theirs, by the little displays of love, of pure delight in pleasing, which are the sweetest of all parenthood's rewards. Love itself has become a peculiar good, a thing as precious as it is fragile—for faults and failures on either side can interrupt it. Moreover, it contains within itself, no less than the creative impulse, the seeds of mischief. The child, in realising his own value to another, is led for the first time to a conscious attribution of value to himself. He becomes an important person in his own eyes—a *more* important person than the visitor, the nurse, or the brother or sister, whom his parents do not or must not be allowed to love as well as him. Through the very experience that begins his emancipation from self-centredness, he becomes infected with the pride which is a far more serious obstacle than natural egoism to the progress and the perfection of love.

Let us suppose that our child is growing up as he should in a society of fellow-children. He is constantly confronted by the claims of partnership, and he assumes the validity of the axiom :

' the more there is of yours, the less there is of mine '—an axiom which is true enough of the particular kind of good which at this stage has most apparent value for him. Daily experience of an enjoyment which is in fact the keener for being shared fails to convince him that he would not be happier if he had all the good things to himself. Daily experience of the discomfort of quarrelling fails to prove that peace is better secured by concession or compromise than by victory. For the jealousy which is pride's inseparable companion is actually stronger than the desire of good things themselves. He does not ' want equals ', and he cannot understand that the struggle for superiority is a waste of the energies which should be directed towards creation and enjoyment. Fellowship in love, a natural growth between child and parent, manifests its value much less easily between brother and sister. But this manifestation is the indispensable condition for the security of all other values. The lesson has to be learnt, not only that jealousy poisons creation, that sharing intensifies enjoyment, but that brotherly love is to be sought for its own sake, and that its enemy is not the desire for any other competing good, but the pride which is in declared and deliberate opposition to the unity of the Spirit in the bond of peace.

The lesson is too large to be learnt in the nursery : indeed the measure of its appropriation is the measure in which the child has become the man. Spiritual growth means, first, the testing and correction of childhood's values, the recognition that abiding good is not to be found in anything which cannot be shared or is diminished by participation. It means, next, the purification of the creative impulse, so that the maker is moved not by the attraction of novelty nor to satisfy a conceit of power, but simply by the call of good to be let into the world through any door that can be opened to it. And it means, above all, the discovery of supreme power in humility, in the charity which seeketh not her own, is not easily provoked, hopeth all things, believeth all things, endureth all things. That discovery is never made by taking thought : it is never a deduction from abstract principles. The truth to be found has always to be seen somewhere in actual embodiment. We learn the possibility and the loveliness of love only when it is at work before our eyes in concrete and visible form.

So much may serve as an outline, commonplace enough, of the developing functions of human love. It appears first as reaction to the given good, then as impulse to embody the good idea, and finally as purpose to be served in patient devotion. If we now attempt to trace a corresponding pattern in the love which is God's own nature, it will be in the faith common to St. Augustine and St. Thomas, that His invisible things are understood through the things that are made, that there is a relation not of identity but of analogy between the natural and the supernatural, between the changing and the changeless Good.

For all human apprehension, the good is in some sense a thing given. The noblest achievements of human creativity are never ' out of nothing ' : the richest soil is barren until the seed of the ' word ' has fallen upon it. God's grace is everywhere prevenient ; and that is why our creating is at most an analogue of His. He is the only true Creator, for He alone needs no model, no vision of a good that is not His own : He alone is dependent upon no imperfect medium. In all that is good, there is a likeness of Him : the orders of space and time reveal His glory ; and if for us to whom the revelation is given there is one glory of the sun, another of the moon, another of the stars, if to our partial vision there is more of God here than there, now than then, the apparent inequalities are grounded in the Revealer's design to keep us on tip-toe, to nourish our thirst for Himself. It is good for us that our reach should exceed our grasp, that enjoyment should never quench desire. But for the Creator we may surely believe that His ' ancient rapture ' is eternal : that the universe in all its tragi-comic magnificence reflects a divine self-enjoyment in which God will have us share whenever we look into the tiniest corner of His creation and see that it is good. Not all the suffering through which love must pass to be made perfect should blind us to the truth that love is consummated in delight ; for greater than the pain of childbirth is the joy that a man is born into the world. And a thought of the infinite love of God which gives no place to delight can hardly claim kinship with the mind of One who traced that love in the glorious arraying of the lilies. There must be a sense in which what-soever things are lovely are lovely *for* their Maker as well as, nay far more than, for us to whom they reveal Him.

But they would not be so, were not He Himself revealed in them. And if it is true that no solitary enjoyment is perfect, that no good is equal to the good of fellowship, it will follow that the love which unites men to one another, the *vinculum perfectionis,* must also and pre-eminently have its analogue in the love of God. God has made men apt to find their completion in communion, because such communion is a likeness of the mutual love in which and through which Three Persons are One God. We could conceive of a divine Agape that was nothing but a sheer giving of itself, only if God's existence were wholly dependent on the existence of the world, and His Kingdom, not Himself, were the Supreme Good. What St. Augustine's doctrine of the Holy Spirit means is that the perfection of love is spiritual κοινωνία or fellowship, that love belongs to the eternal Being of God because the divine Life is itself not bare unity but community, and that love can have no other purpose, as it can have no other source, but the mutual ' inherence ' of persons, life in one another.

What then are we to say of the charity which endureth all things ? If our deepest insight into the divine purpose shows us the will of God to unite us to Himself as children to their Father, and if there is nothing but sin that separates us from God, no obstacle to communion but pride, we must acknowledge our responsibility for the Cross. We cannot say that *all* suffering is the consequence of sin. It may be true that part of the pain in which the whole creation groans and travails together is an in-evitable accompaniment of creation as such ; that to make a world at all, a world that should be *other* than God, involved a self-limitation of the Infinite of which pain, and pain of which

He could not and would not escape the burden for Himself, is a necessary aspect. We do not know enough to speak confidently of these mysteries ; though we could not love the Creator of such a world as this, were we not sure of His compassion, of His presence in the sparrow that falls to the ground as well as in every crying child that is the victim of man's wickedness. But we do know that nothing but the sight of the anguish it inflicts upon love has power to break down pride.

The love which endures, which offers itself to the unloving, is always the servant of its own high purpose—not to rest till the sundered fellowship is restored, till rejection is changed to response. Calvary is for the sake of Pentecost : *It is expedient for you that I go away :* the Body of Christ is broken in the Eucharist, to be made whole in its partakers. So long as there is sin in the world, the breaking must go on : membership of Christ must mean communion in His sufferings. The ' mercifulness ' which is literally *com*-passion is the way in which we are called to imitate the divine perfection in a world still to be redeemed. Yet suffering can be the end neither for God nor man. We are not yet come to the Perfect Man ; but that is the unseen reality on which we lay hold in faith, the consummation to which we look forward. Charity believeth all things, hopeth all things ; and its faith and hope no less than its endurance are creative of that unity of the Spirit which is its end.

If perfect love is spiritual communion, a definition of charity which would restrict its proper activity to a ' one-way ' relationship, a giving without receiving, seems strangely inadequate. It is true that the unity of the Spirit is a good that awaits the re-creation which is redemption, and that love as redemptive energy must pour itself out like the rain of God upon the unthankful and the evil. *If ye love them that love you, what reward have you ?* It is indeed the *test* of a love which would be like God's, that it is all-embracing ; but we may be certain that Christ did not mean either that it is better to have enemies than friends, or that any outward act of beneficence can be a substitute for the inward disposition of heart which would make a friend out of the enemy. The reluctance to see Christian love in its purity except where it is not returned cannot justify itself by the Sermon on the Mount. It is rather a consequence of the tendency to follow Kant in belittling the ethical significance of the so-called ' pathological ' love, supposed to depend upon a feeling of attraction beyond the will's control. Moberly, for example, wrote in *Atonement and Personality* that ' while we cannot altogether help verbally using [the word "love"] for that yearning of person towards person which hideously travesties the true spirit of love, we yet educate ourselves towards true insight of soul by protesting that this is the libel not the truth, nor part of the truth, of what love really means '.[1] Even if ' yearning of person towards person ' is here intended as a euphemism for sexual desire isolated from its spiritual potentialities, the verdict is suggestive of Augustine at his Manichaean worst rather than of a sanely Christian acceptance of our bodily nature. To tell men that the experience in which, whether they will or no, they recognise at least the possibility of the highest of this life's goods, has no right to the name by which they will certainly not cease to call it, is to perform a doubtful service to morality. And the religion of grace ought not to take offence at any love because it has to confess itself altogether a gift.

' Pathological ' love is not of course limited to the sphere of sex : it is the basis of all natural friendship. But marriage most clearly illustrates that feature in such relationships which is commonly contrasted with Christian love's essential characteristic—namely, their exclusiveness. The love of the Good Samaritan is no universal philanthropy—there is no talk in the Gospels about loving men because they are men—but it is a love that goes out to meet need without respect of persons. The love of friend and friend, still more the love of husband and wife, is a love of conscious preference ; and there is apparent discontinuity between an affection concentrated upon this particular person

---

[1] *Atonement and Personality*, p. 52.

because he is what he is, because he is found more lovable than another, and an intention to help, an impulse to do good without regard to anything in the nature or character of the person who is to receive it, but governed solely by his *condition*.

Yet it may be that the discontinuity is less than it seems. The two kinds of love certainly cannot be opposed to one another as pure taking to pure giving, as enjoyment to creation. If you are really ' in love ', you are not pre-occupied with the satisfaction of your own need. You believe that you have found something supremely worthy to receive the best that you can give, something that demands from you a complete devotion ; and that very belief has idealised the object of your love, has given to it a value which others could not perceive in it, but which love's exchange can at the least begin to realise. The love of a man and a woman for one another is a creative act in which through mutual self-giving each is born anew. Two persons are no longer solitary units, admitting in theory at most the claims of others to equal shares in life. They have committed themselves to a vital affirmation of one other being's absolute value. That affirmation was made possible by a compelling vision. The vision may fade, but it remains the task and the glory of life in one another to maintain its reality in testing and purifying faith. If they have faith, they need never again be the egoists they once were.

There may of course be an egoism *à deux*. Every unity wider than the individual, that is not in Augustine's phrase ' referred to God ', is exposed to the danger of self-deification. The nationalism which is the most destructive force in the world to-day is rooted in the perversion of lesser loyalties. But it is gratuitous to suppose that either married love or the love of friends tends to become a wider selfishness in proportion to the completeness with which the partners have given themselves to one another. On the contrary, such a tendency indicates that the partnership has been unequal, that on one side or the other the Ego has asserted its domination and spoilt the purity of the union. If the new unity-in-duality has been found by a real surrender of the separate, self-assertive will on either side, it will be more and not less capable of inclusion and subordination in the service of a greater good.

Christian charity is not an *extension* of the love which has linked two persons together because of the good they were able to see in one another. The growth of charity does not take the form of a progressive removal of landmarks, an expanding circle of ever wider comprehensiveness. Charity grows intensively not extensively. It is the measure of an active conviction that unity in love is the greatest of all good things, expressing itself in the effort to overcome all hindrance to that unity. And therefore no one altogether incapable or ignorant of Philia, of love received as well as given, is in a way to have Agape. The love which has been enjoyed as a gift provides the motive for the love which is to give itself to others : the need which Agape goes out to meet is always in the end the need for love and for nothing else. That is why loveless pride will always refuse the ' charity ' which is just ' the bestowing of goods to feed the poor ', a charity in which it sees patronage and not love.

Reduced to its simplest terms, the existence of love in a human being means that the eye of the spirit has opened to the sunshine of good. A man has seen that which is good, and seeing it has delighted in it. His delight is acceptance, and what is accepted is a gift ; he must ask who is the giver and why should anything have been given to *him*. The only answer to that question is love. He *sees* that the gift of good can be nothing but the expression of love, and that love itself is greater than any or all of the gifts in which its activity is displayed. If greater, then more to be desired ; and if he can desire above all things the gift of love, if he can truly cast out of his heart all that is contrary to love, then love will be given to him, and he will have power to return it to the giver. In such fruition of a supreme good there is supreme delight, and the delight itself is radiant, ' diffusive of itself ', creative.

If this is some approximation to a true account of happenings that we know, we can go on to say that if love of man for God is possible it will be nothing but the effect of God's revelation of Himself to man as the Giver who is Love. In the great religious tradition which we have been studying, the love of God is reducible neither to a ' pathological ' emotion, nor to a creative potency, nor to a sense of moral obligation. Its range and its efficacy are no narrower than the whole life of the spirit : it is delight, desire, and devotion. Delight, because beauty in all its form and colour is the garment of God's loveliness ; desire, because the great deep of God's truth is a constant reminder of man's lack of knowledge and a constant call to exploration and adventure ; devotion, because God's goodness cannot be worshipped except by sacrifice. And the claim of God is incommensurable with the claims of our fellow-men ; for the love of Him is more, though it is never less, than personal love. No Christian philosophy can think of God as ' a person ' among others, whom we may come to know and add to the number of our friends. The irreverence which we immediately perceive in any such thought consists in its implied pretence to equality between creature and Creator. We can only speak of friendship with God without danger, if we remember at every moment its *un*likeness as well as its likeness to all human friendship.

There is no denying the soundness of the instinct which finds obedience a safer term than love by which to denote the right relation of man to his Maker. From one man to another, there can never be an absolute duty of obedience ; when it is given, it always requires justification : we should never obey a man for no other reason than that he is what he is. Unconditional obedience is due to God alone. Yet the very fact that this obedience presents itself to ethical religion, not as submission to any externally imposed authority, but as resolute following of the voice of conscience, is enough to show that obedience depends upon love and not love upon obedience. For the still, small voice is never the infallible revelation of a divine command. It is simply the naked sincerity of spirit, the man completely honest with himself, articulating his own apprehension of that which seems to him good—in other words, telling himself what it is that he loves best. His vision of the good may be woefully inadequate ; his choice of action may fall far short of the wisdom of God. Yet we are sure that it is right for him to act according to his lights, just because we believe that God's claim for obedience is always for an obedience that springs from love and therefore is wholly free.

The same considerations will hold in regard to that other term which has seemed and seems to many the only fitting description of the Christian attitude to God—faith. If by faith is meant something more than resignation, if it is the self-surrender of perfect confidence, then it is difficult to see how such an attitude can be conceived without love as its pre-supposition. That it could not, was clear even to Luther. ' If we rightly consider it ', he once said, ' love comes first, or at the same moment with faith. For I could not trust God if I did not think He desired to be favourable and gracious towards me, whereby I may become gracious towards Him, and may be moved to trust Him heartily and to expect from Him every good thing.' [1] A man may resign himself to a power that is indifferent or hostile : he can only trust a person of whose goodness he is altogether convinced, and to be convinced of goodness is—once more—to love. When St. Paul struck out his great phrase *faith working through love*, he was not thinking of a love whose object is other than faith's, but defining Christian faith's character and foundation in contradistinction to such belief as devils may hold, and tremble. The Christian can commend his spirit into no other hands but those of a Father.

We must hold, then, to St. Thomas's ideal of friendship with God, safeguarding it as he did by the acknowledgment that only God's grace makes it possible to our creaturely condition, only ' in Christ ' can we have boldness to enter the holy place. Friend-

---

[1] Quoted by W. Herrmann, *Communion with God* (E.T.), p. 212. So Calvin : ' Il n'ya nul vrayement fidéle, sinon celui qui étant assuré de certain persuasion qui Dieu lui est Père propice et bien vueillant, attend toutes choses de sa benignité ; sinon celui qui estant appuyé sur les promesses de la bonne volonté de Dieu, conceoit une attente indubitable de son salut.'

ship with God will rest upon the explicit recognition of His presence in the world. *For without Him not one thing came into being, and what has been given being in Him is life.* The friend of God will see Him everywhere—His face in nature's beauty and wonder, the working of His Spirit and the appeal of His love in men, in the many who take no account of His Fatherhood, in the few who in sincerity of heart confess it or deny it. Without this sense of the environing God, His infinite Otherness, the love of Him cannot keep its humility nor escape out of self-centredness to the service of His Kingdom. But it is no less needful to be aware of His presence within, to know that we ourselves are His temples, and that our own life is a part of His self-disclosure. In prayer there must always be a ' turning inward '. The ' invocation ' of God, as Augustine used to say, cannot be a calling upon Him to enter where He was not : it must be a going to meet Him where He is. Spatial metaphors must fail us, though they cannot be avoided : to Augustine it seemed better to think of ourselves as *in* God. But our chief need is to know that (as Plotinus put it) there is ' nothing between ', that what is impossible with men, the complete penetration of spirit by spirit, is possible with God.

It is a conspicuous merit in Nygren's treatment of Augustine to have decisively rejected the superficial criticism which alleges that the Catholic doctrine of grace—as distinct from perversions of practice—is ' magical ' or ' mechanical '.[1] What St. Thomas calls the ' infusion ' of charity is that same working of the Holy Spirit for which Augustine found his *locus classicus* in the Epistle to the Romans. It is no ' thing-like ' substance introduced from without, but the purely spiritual influence of the divine Person whose dwelling is within the believer's heart. The testimony of the mystics is that the life of prayer *can* be lifted by God's grace into a perception of His loving presence that has an immediacy comparable to that of our own consciousness of self. It does not befit those of us who know how little and how poorly we pray to disparage the value of this testimony. Nor is it wise

[1] *Eros und Agape, II.* (G.T.), pp. 336 f. Cf. pp. 444 f.

to pretend to such a knowledge of the ways of God as could enable us to pronounce upon the conditions, moral and spiritual, which must be fulfilled before any experience of the kind could be valid. Judgement upon the ' truth ' or ' falsehood ' of any mysticism can only be an inference from those facts of the mystic's life and faith which are actually observable ; and the lives of the saints afford examples enough in which the force of this pragmatic verification does appear overwhelming.

All Christians will agree that the aim of religion is union with God, and that there can be no union with God which is not surrender of the will to His purpose of love. No Christian should hesitate to admit that God's Spirit, His loving purpose, is active in many who are not at all ' religious ', who never ' refer ' their own activity to God. Righteousness is always the service of God, even if the service is rendered without thought of Him who inspires it. But we cannot believe that God's purpose is fulfilled so long as He is served unconsciously by men who neglect or deny His real sovereignty. It *is* possible to love what God loves, to set forward His Kingdom of righteousness, without loving God. It is not possible to love God without the faith that God is love. There is no such thing as personal relationship without consciousness of the relationship,[1] no such thing as love that is not aware of its object ; and therefore religion must not only reconcile men to God, but also make them know that they are reconciled.

The Christian Gospel offers this reconciliation, the message of forgiveness which is assurance of God's love, to Faith. It says, Believe that you have received, that God is gracious to you, that there is ' nothing between '—and you will abide in His love. To those who ask for proof, it points to the Cross, and the Cross can prove nothing except to faith. It promises no satisfying experience of certitude, no irresistible demonstration : it demands the daily renewal of faith's venture. The Church's

[1] See R. N. Flew, *The Idea of Perfection in Christian Theology*, pp. 24, 64, etc.

supreme act of worship is at the same time the supremely urgent call for faith. The real presence of God is given to those who can believe that the Broken Body of Christ is the food of their souls, that God is with them in the act of sacrifice, and they with Him when their faltering devotion is taken up and made fast in the self-offering of the Redeemer. The Eucharist is the Christian *Memento mori,* the unceasing echo of Christ's *If any man will come after me.* . . . We can never be nearer to Him than when we are concrescent into the likeness of His Death. The dying must needs be felt ; the life is hid with Christ in God, and it must be believed. The risen Christ says : *I am with you all the days;* He does not promise that all will see the empty tomb or put their finger into the print of the nails. The Resurrection and the Life is ' in us ', but our life ' in the flesh ' is still a life of faith —faith in the Son of God who loved us and gave Himself for us, whom therefore not having seen we love.

Theology at the present time shows no inclination to give too small a place to the ' Life Eternal Here and Now '.[1] There is probably no living authority on the New Testament who has not been carried in reaction from Schweitzer at least so far as to disallow *his* whole conception of *Interimsethik.* Preference goes to the Matthean form of the Beatitudes over the Lucan, largely because Luke's underlining of the tenses, his contrast between present and future, is a stumbling-block for the expositor who wants a blessedness that is not eschatological, or at least one that belongs to a ' realised' eschatology. The poor in spirit, the merciful, the pure in heart are to be held blessed, not as Augustine would say ' in hope ', but in fact ; for theirs is already the timeless present of the Kingdom of God, the Kingdom that cometh not by observation. *He that heareth my word and believeth on Him that sent me hath eternal life, and cometh not into judgment, but is passed from death into life.* The Fourth Gospel begins to win acceptance as the truest interpretation of the historical Jesus and his message.

But in the Fourth Gospel Judgement no less than Eternal Life

[1] The title of a little book by Prof. A. Nairne.

315

is a present reality. Light and Darkness, the Kingdom of God and the Kingdom of the Evil One, are arrayed against one another as vividly and implacably as Augustine's Two Cities. Augustine began with a misconceived ideal of the life eternal here and now, a fruition of God attainable by the individual in solitary contemplation. In the transitoriness of the mystical experience he found proof that in this life we can have no more than foreshadowings of beatitude. He never doubted that eternal life is love as well as vision, nor that the only reason why we cannot possess the vision is that we do not love enough. His Two Cities are spiritual entities, 'principalities and powers', not two divisions of humanity. The Church can be called the Kingdom of God only as God's instrument for recruiting its citizens.[1] But to the Church that task is given, and the power of the Earthly City is the measure of her failure to accomplish it. Here and now, my lack of love keeps outside the City of God, not myself only, but this and this brother of mine for whom Christ died. If there were a believer who felt no need for such self-reproach, it would mean only that his faith was in himself more than in Christ.

And therefore the presence promised to faith has a term— *all the days up to the fulfilment of the age.* The Christian is to look forward as well as inward. He is not only to believe that he has received, but to look for something more : *to him that hath, shall be given.* That which is to be given can be nothing *less* than what has already been received by faith ; it cannot bring a cancelling of the sacrifice, the dying to self, which faith has made absolute, once for all. Yet the traditional account of Hope as a Christian virtue has in fact implied some such cancellation.

St. Thomas rightly noted that hope gets its distinctive character from the difficulty, the arduousness of the good to be attained.[2] Hope is the courageous acceptance of a position in which the odds may be against us, and the refusal to let any odds deter us from the wager of our life. But St. Thomas wrongly defined the 'arduous good' which is hope's object as our own happiness ;

---

[1] See esp. *De Sancta Virgin.* 24.
[2] *S.T.* I^a II^ae. q. 40, a. 1 ; II^a II^ae. q. 17, a. 1.

and so he could only see in hope an ' imperfect love ', ' whereby we love something not for its own sake (as a friend), but in order to obtain possession of something for ourselves '.[1] In the ' Pure Love ' controversy, hope so egocentrised was not easy to reconcile with charity. The best that could be done was to say that the pure love of God commands us to hope for our own salvation because it is God's will and for His glory. But we may suspect that such submissive acts of formal egoism played a very small part in the religion of Fénélon.

There is indeed a hope which every Christian needs in his personal contest with evil. Not to despair, never to lack courage for a fresh start after the repeated fall, is necessary if the pilgrim is to continue his journeying. But this is not the hope that inspires the pilgrimage. The banner of the Church militant bears the one device—*Christus Victor*—and every soldier in her army fights not for his own survival but for the Kingdom of God. Faith is the *sacramentum,* the oath of enlistment in which the individual accepts allegiance to God's sovereignty ; but if His Kingdom were already come in the fullness of its power, there would be no warfare to wage. The soldier of Christ goes into battle not only with eyes open to his own danger but knowing that his Leader's cause is really at stake ; and just because the fight is real, and no bloodless, predetermined manoeuvre, he must quit himself like a man, hoping not to save his soul but to do his part in winning the victory.

The Christian hope is degraded if its object is anything less than the complete and final victory of love. The only hope that love can command is the hope that God will be ' all in all ', and it can never be satisfied with a division between elect and re-probate. It has been urged often enough that no man can desire a heaven that would separate him from anyone that he has loved on earth. The truth is that no man could be in heaven while any-one that he might have loved, and did not, were in hell. Until and unless Heaven has altogether conquered Hell, it is not Heaven.

The real objection to a universalism which declares that love

[2] *S. T.* II^a II^ae. q. 17, a. 3, 8.

must triumph is not that it cuts the nerve of moral activity, nor that it burks the fact of sin's 'abiding consequences'. That determinism necessarily leads to quietism is manifestly untrue ; and though sin's consequences are abiding, to hold that they are untransformable is to make the Cross of Christ of none effect. But dogmatic universalism contradicts the very nature of love, by claiming for it the kind of omnipotence which it refuses. Love cannot, because it will not, compel the surrender of a single heart that holds out against it. Without the symbolism of warfare, of struggle and victory, our picture of the Christian life would be incomplete. But the comparison breaks down at the crucial point, for all the fighting of this world is with the weapon of force. Love never forces, and therefore there can be no certainty that it will overcome. But there may, and there must, be an unconquerable hope.

My soul is athirst for God, yea even for the living God : when shall I come to appear before the presence of God ? . . . O send out thy light and thy truth, let them lead me : let them bring me unto thy holy hill and to thy dwelling. 'Nothing short of the knowledge of the true God will save [men] from the impiety of making themselves God, and the cruelty of seeing their fellowmen as devils because they are involved in the same pretension.' That last sad sentence of Reinhold Niebuhr's *Interpretation of Christian Ethics* might have been written by Augustine ; but Augustine would have added that the knowledge of the true God is a knowledge that can be ours here only in part. And perhaps Niebuhr himself would find it hard to deny the truth of Augustine's saying, that the perfection of righteousness waits upon the perfection of the soul's health, and that upon the perfection of charity ; and charity will not be perfect until we see God as He is. God's promise to the pure in heart is of that knowledge of Himself through love which is eternal life ; and the heart will be pure when it is filled with the love of God 'in all things and above all things'. To be filled with such love is to have obtained the promises which exceed all that we can desire.

Appendix

APPENDIX

The following list of books is given as an acknowledgment of debt, not as a bibliography. The most useful bibliographies known to me are to be found in the three books marked with an asterisk.

K. Adam : *Die geistige Entwicklung des heiligen Augustinus.* Augsburg, 1931.

R. Arnou : *Le Désir de Dieu dans la philosophie de Plotin.* Paris, 1921.

J. Barion : *Plotin und Augustinus : Untersuchungen zum Gottesproblem.* Berlin, 1935.

C. Boyer : *Christianisme et Néo-Platonisme dans la formation de Saint Augustin.* Paris, 1922.

E. Bréhier : *Plotin, Ennéades I-V* (text and translation with prefatory notes to each Book). Collection Budé. Paris, 1924-31.

H. Brémond : *Histoire Littéraire du Sentiment Religieux en France* (vols. i, iii, vii, viii). Paris, 1916 and following years.

C. Butler : *Western Mysticism : The Teaching of SS. Augustine, Gregory, and Bernard on Contemplation and the Contemplative Life.* Constable, 1922.

F. Cayré : *La Contemplation Augustinienne : principes de la spiritualité de Saint Augustin.* Paris, 1927.

R. Egenter : *Gottesfreundschaft : die Lehre von der Gottesfreundschaft in der Scholastik und Mystik des 12. and 13. Jahrhunderts.* Augsburg, 1928.

A. Gardeil : *La Structure de l'Âme et l'Expérience Mystique* (2 vols.). Paris, 1927.

R. Garrigou-Lagrange : *L'Amour de Dieu et la Croix de Jésus : Étude de Théologie mystique* (2 vols.). Editions de Cerf. Juvisy, 1929.

*E. Gilson : *Introduction à l'étude de Saint Augustin.* Paris, 1929.
The Spirit of Mediaeval Philosophy ; Gifford Lectures, 1931-32. (E.T. by A. H. C. Downes.) Sheed & Ward, 1936.
Théologie Mystique de Saint Bernard. Paris, 1934.

A. Harnack : *Lehrbuch der Dogmengeschichte* (vol. iii.). 4th edit. Tübingen, 1909.

*E. Hendrikx : *Augustins Verhältnis zur Mystik.* Wurzburg, 1936.

W. R. Inge : *The Philosophy of Plotinus ;* Gifford Lectures, 1917-18. 3rd edit. Longmans, 1929.

K. E. Kirk : *The Vision of God ; The Christian Doctrine of the Summum Bonum ;* Bampton Lectures, 1928. Longmans, 1931.

J. Klein : *Die Caritaslehre des Johannes Duns Scotus.* 1926.

F. Loofs : *Leitfaden der Dogmengeschichte.* Halle, 1906.

S. Mackenna : *Enneads of Plotinus.* (Translated into English.) Medici Society, 1917-30.

J. Mausbach : *Die Ethik des heiligen Augustinus* (2 vols.). 2nd edit. Freiburg, 1929.

E. Mersch : *Le Corps Mystique du Christ ; études de theologie historique* (2 vols.). 2nd edit. Museum Lessianum, 1936.

Amor Dei

J. Nörregaard : *Augustins Bekehrung.* (G.T. by A. Spelmeyer.) Tübingen, 1923.

A. Nygren : *Agape and Eros ; a Study of the Christian Idea of Love : Part I.* (E.T. by A. G. Herbert.) S.P.C.K. 1932.

Eros und Agape ; Gestaltwandlungen der christlichen Liebe : Zweiter Teil. (G.T. by I. Nygren.) Gütersloh, 1937.

E. Portalié : *Saint Augustin* (article in *Dictionnaire de Théologie Catholique*). 1902.

H. Reuter : *Augustinische Studien.* Gotha, 1887.

P. Rousselot : *Pour l'histoire du problème de l'amour au moyen âge.* Münster, 1908.

*M. Schmaus : *Die psychologische Trinitätslehre des hl. Augustinus.* Münster, 1927.

H. Scholz : *Eros und Caritas ; die platonische Liebe und die Liebe im Sinne des Christentums.* Halle, 1929.

Glaube und Unglaube in der Weltgeschichte : ein Kommentar zu Augustins ' De Civitate Dei '. Leipzig, 1911.

E. Troeltsch : *Augustin, die christliche Antike und das Mittelalter : im Anschluss an die Schrift ' De Civitate Dei '.* München und Berlin, 1915.

Fr. von Hügel : *The Mystical Element of Religion* (2 vols.). Dent, 1909.

H. Weinand : *Die Gottesidee : der Grundzug der Weltanschauung des hl. Augustinus.* Paderborn, 1910.

A Monument to Saint Augustine (various writers). Sheed & Ward, 1934.

I. *Index of Quotations from St. Augustine*

(The figures in brackets give the date of each work, ascertained or approximate. The most recent chronological study is that of Fr. Hugh Pope in *Saint Augustine of Hippo*. A study of the chronology of the *Sermons* has lately been made by A. Kunzelmann in *Miscellanea Agostiniana*. He believes that 'about two-thirds of Augustine's Sermons can be dated with more or less accuracy'; and it seemed worth while to give his datings of individual Sermons, though many are hardly more than conjectural. We still wait for a similar study of the *Enarrationes in Psalmos*.)

Amor Dei

Index of Quotations from St. Augustine

Index of Quotations from St. Augustine

Amor Dei

Index of Quotations from St. Augustine

Amor Dei

Index of Quotations from St. Augustine

Amor Dei

Index of Quotations from St. Augustine

Amor Dei

II. General Index